The Outbreak of the First World War

The First World War had profound consequences both for the evolution of the international system and for domestic political systems. How and why did the war start? Offering a unique interdisciplinary perspective, this volume brings together a distinguished group of diplomatic historians and international relations scholars to debate the causes of the war. Organized around several theoretically based questions, it shows how power, alliances, historical rivalries, militarism, nationalism, public opinion, internal politics, and powerful personalities shaped decision-making in each of the major countries in the lead up to war. The emphasis on the interplay of theory and history is a significant contribution to the dialogue between historians and political scientists, and will contribute to a better understanding of the war in both disciplines.

Jack S. Levy is Board of Governors' Professor in the Department of Political Science at Rutgers University.

John A. Vasquez is Mackie Scholar in International Relations in the Department of Political Science at the University of Illinois at Urbana-Champaign.

The Outbreak of the First World War

Structure, Politics, and Decision-Making

Edited by

Jack S. Levy

and

John A. Vasquez

CAMBRIDGE
UNIVERSITY PRESS

CAMBRIDGE
UNIVERSITY PRESS

University Printing House, Cambridge CB2 8BS, United Kingdom

Published in the United States of America by Cambridge University Press, New York

Cambridge University Press is part of the University of Cambridge.

It furthers the University's mission by disseminating knowledge in the pursuit of
education, learning and research at the highest international levels of excellence.

www.cambridge.org
Information on this title: www.cambridge.org/9781107616028

© Cambridge University Press 2014

First published 2014

Printed in the United Kingdom by Clays, St Ives plc

A catalogue record for this publication is available from the British Library

ISBN 978-1-107-04245-2 Hardback
ISBN 978-1-107-61602-8 Paperback

To my sister, Caroline Jonas, the artist – JSL
and
To my nephews and niece, Rick, Brian, Michael, Scott, and Cristina – JAV

Contents

List of figures   *page* ix
List of tables   x
List of contributors   xi
Preface   xv

Part I Overview of debates about the causes of the First World War

1   Introduction: historians, political scientists,
    and the causes of the First World War   3
    JACK S. LEVY AND JOHN A. VASQUEZ

2   July 1914 revisited and revised: the erosion
    of the German paradigm   30
    SAMUEL R. WILLIAMSON, JR.

Part II Structure and agency

3   Strategic rivalries and complex causality in 1914   65
    KAREN RASLER AND WILLIAM R. THOMPSON

4   A "formidable factor in European politics": views
    of Russia in 1914   87
    T. G. OTTE

Part III The question of preventive war

5   Restraints on preventive war before 1914   115
    WILLIAM MULLIGAN

6   The sources of preventive logic in German
    decision-making in 1914   139
    JACK S. LEVY

7 International relations theory and the three great
   puzzles of the First World War   167
   DALE C. COPELAND

8 Was the First World War a preventive war? Concepts,
   criteria, and evidence   199
   JOHN A. VASQUEZ

Part IV   The role of the other powers

9 War accepted but unsought: Russia's growing
   militancy and the July Crisis, 1914   227
   RONALD P. BOBROFF

10 France's unreadiness for war in 1914 and its
   implications for French decision-making in the July
   Crisis   252
   J. F. V. KEIGER

   References   273
   Index   294

Figures

3.1 Bivariate correlations across varying time periods,
starting with 1813–1913 and ending with 1900–1913. *page* 70

3.2 Average bivariate correlations across varying time
periods (for correlations in graphs B–F in Figure 3.1). 72

3.3 Four rivalry streams. 75

Tables

3.1 Indicators for nonlinear rivalry ripeness model.   *page* 69
3.2 Rivalries begun and ended, 1864–1913.   73
8.1 Dyadic participants in the First World War,
    July 1914–May 1915.   219

Contributors

RONALD P. BOBROFF is Associate Professor of History at Oglethorpe University and Visiting Associate Professor at Wake Forest University. He has also taught at Duke University. Bobroff's research interests focus on topics related to the international history of Europe, and especially imperial Russia in the latter part of the long nineteenth century. He is author of *Roads to Glory: Late Imperial Russia and the Turkish Straits* (2006), and is currently working on a book on the Franco-Russian Alliance.

DALE C. COPELAND is Associate Professor of Politics at the University of Virginia. His first book is *The Origins of Major War*, a study of the link between the rise and decline of great powers and the outbreak of system-wide wars. He is currently finishing a second book on economic interdependence and international conflict, which examines the conditions under which interstate trade will lead to either war or peace.

J. F. V. KEIGER is Professor of International History in the Department of Politics and International Studies at Cambridge University. A specialist of war, foreign, and defense policy, he is the author of *France and the Origins of the First World War* (1983), *Raymond Poincaré* (Cambridge University Press, 1997), *France and the World since 1870* (2001); and editor of nineteen volumes of *British Documents on Foreign Affairs: Reports and Papers from the Foreign Office Confidential Print* (1989–1991), as well as two co-edited volumes on the Algerian War.

JACK S. LEVY is Board of Governors' Professor of Political Science at Rutgers University, and an affiliate of the Saltzman Institute of War and Peace Studies at Columbia University. He is a former President of the International Studies Association (2007–2008) and of the Peace Science Society (2005–2006). He is author of *War in the Modern Great Power System, 1495–1975* (1983); co-author (with William R. Thompson) of *Causes of War* (2010), and *The Arc of War: Origins, Escalation, and Transformation* (2011); and co-editor (with Leonie Huddy and David O. Sears) of the *Oxford Handbook of Political Psychology*, 2nd edition (2013).

WILLIAM MULLIGAN lectures in Modern European History at University College Dublin. He is the author of *The Origins of the First World War* (Cambridge University Press, 2010) and *The Creation of the Modern German Army: General Walther Reinhardt and the Weimar Republic* (2005). He has taught at the University of Glasgow and has held a fellowship at the Institute of Advanced Study in Princeton.

T. G. OTTE is Professor of Diplomatic History at the University of East Anglia. He has written or edited thirteen books. Among the more recent are *The Foreign Office Mind: The Making of British Foreign Policy, 1865–1914* (Cambridge University Press, 2011), *Diplomacy and Power: Studies in Modern Diplomatic Practice* (2012), and *July 1914: Europe's Descent into World War* (Cambridge University Press, 2014).

KAREN RASLER is Professor of Political Science at Indiana University. Her research interests are in general theories of international conflict and cooperation; relative decline of world powers; war and state-building processes; societal consequences of war; modeling long cycles of war; distribution of power and technological innovations; political violence and internal wars. She co-authored (with William R. Thompson) *War and Statemaking: The Shaping of the Global Powers* (1989), *The Great Powers and Global Struggle, 1490–1990* (1994), and *Puzzles of the Democratic Peace: Theory, Geopolitics and the Transformation of World Politics* (2005).

WILLIAM R. THOMPSON is Distinguished Professor and Donald A. Rogers Professor of Political Science at Indiana University. He was the Managing Editor of *International Studies Quarterly* through 2013. Recent books include *The Arc of War* (with Jack Levy), *The Handbook of International Rivalry, 1494–2010* (with David Dreyer), *How Rivalries End* (with Karen Rasler and Sumit Ganguly), and *Transition Scenarios: China and the United States in the Twenty-first Century* (with David Rapkin).

JOHN A. VASQUEZ is the Thomas B. Mackie Scholar in International Relations at the University of Illinois at Urbana-Champaign. His most recent books are *The Steps to War* (with Paul D. Senese, 2008); *The War Puzzle Revisited* (2009); and *Territory, War, and Peace* (with Marie T. Henehan, 2011). He is senior editor of a special issue of *Foreign Policy Analysis* (2011) on 'The Spread of War, 1914–1917.' He has been President of the Peace Science Society (International) and the International Studies Association.

SAMUEL R. WILLIAMSON, JR. has taught at West Point, Harvard, UNC-Chapel Hill, and the University of the South. He has written frequently about the origins of the First World War, including *The Politics of Grand Strategy: Britain and France Prepare for War*, and *Austria-Hungary and the Origins of the First World War*. In articles and reviews he has often argued that Russian actions in 1914 require reevaluation, and that German actions should be judged from a comparative, rather than a unilateralist, perspective.

Preface

Like many international relations scholars, we have always been fascinated by the First World War. Our own theoretical training in political science and our focus on interstate conflict initially led us each to think primarily about the implications of the war for theories of the causes of war. In the process, however, we have each come to take an increasing interest in the question of the causes of the First World War as a singular historical episode. Our respective interests were motivated by the fact that the war was probably the most consequential interstate conflict in modern history, and that it has had an enormous impact on the development of international relations theories. The continuing proliferation of interpretations about the origins of the war and the lack of consensus among historians after nearly a century has created a puzzle that is hard to ignore. Our interest, like that of other scholars, has grown as the centennial of the war approaches.

At the same time, during the last decade or so we have each been interacting more and more with historians at annual meetings of the International Studies Association, and at other, more specialized, conferences. We were aware that historians were planning numerous things to commemorate the 100th anniversary of the war, and began to think that we might do something as well, but in a way that provided a different perspective. We concluded that the most distinctive thing we might do would be to organize a conference and follow-up volume that brought together historians and political scientists. The aim was to reconsider some of the leading arguments about the causes of war within each discipline, expose political scientists to new archival research by historians, expose historians to new conceptual approaches in international relations theory, and to promote the ongoing collaboration between scholars in the two disciplines. Plans for a conference expanded into plans to set up additional panels at conventions.

We each thought that one of the selfish pleasures we would get out of the process was that for at least two years we would read nothing except works on the First World War. As we should have expected, of course, we each had too many commitments for that to be possible, but we were able to devote a fair amount of time to reading the expanding literature on the origins of the war. In this way, the coming of the 100th anniversary has led each of us, as it has many others, to rethink our earlier beliefs about the causes of the war and about how to approach the study of those causes. We hope that this book will lead our readers to do the same.

Our own respective interests in the First World War go back many years. Jack Levy's interest in the theoretical question of the impact of rigid organizational routines on the causes of war led him to write an article on the subject in 1986 that included a case study of the First World War (*International Studies Quarterly*, June 1986). He was then asked to write an essay on the question of whether the First World War was driven more by tangible conflicts of interests between states or by the mismanagement of the crisis by political leaders, culminating in an article, "Preferences, Constraints, and Choices in July 1914," in *International Security* in 1990/1.

Initially, John Vasquez had been applying his theoretical models to the Second World War, but he soon found that the intellectual intricacies of the First World War proved too interesting to resist. When Samuel Williamson, Jr. and Russel Van Wyk released their documentary history *July 1914: Soldiers, Statesmen, and the Coming of the Great War* in 2003, it became a staple of Vasquez's course on Crisis Diplomacy that compares crises that resulted in war with those that did not from 1815 to 1948. Williamson's fresh approach played a large role in Vasquez's decision to begin working on the First World War. In 2010, he put together a conference among historians and political scientists (including Levy) on the spread of the war from 1914 to 1917. The stimulation and success of that conference, and of the symposium in *Foreign Policy Analysis* (April 2011) that followed, helped to motivate us to do more on the causes of the First World War. Our thinking about the war was further stimulated by a conference we attended in Syracuse, New York, in April 2012. Organized by Colin Elman, the "First World War Data Workshop" gave us the opportunity to engage in debates about the war by political scientists familiar with the war, while also discussing efforts to increase the transparency of qualitative research in political science.

Meanwhile, we had invited several historians to join us on a panel on the First World War at the joint meeting of the British International Studies Association (ISA) and International Studies Association in Edinburgh, Scotland, in June 2012. We also organized a panel for the 2012 annual meeting of the American Political Science Association (APSA) a couple of months later. Papers from each of these conferences (including the APSA conference, which had to be canceled due to a hurricane) were revised and then presented, along with other papers, at our major conference on the war, a day-long workshop in San Francisco just prior to the International Studies Association meeting of April 2013. We also organized an additional panel on the war for the same ISA conference. The papers from the ISA workshop, with two others, form the core of this volume.

In selecting scholars currently working on the causes of the First World War to join us in this interdisciplinary effort, we found no dearth of candidates. We had three main criteria in selecting our contributors in addition to the excellence of their scholarly work, and their fit with some of the analytic and historiographical themes we wanted represented. First, we wanted a mix of historians and political scientists, and among these we wanted some who had worked in an interdisciplinary fashion before so as to facilitate communication across disciplinary boundaries. Second, we wanted a mix of North Americans and Europeans, because we believed that these differences in geography reflect deeper influences, different historical memories, and a diversity of perspectives. Third, we wanted as many contributors as possible to be familiar with non-English sources. Lastly, we wanted a mix of senior scholars, who have long worked in this field and have had a lasting impact on it, and of rising younger scholars, who were mining new sources and exploring new analytic perspectives.

Several people have helped us enormously at various stages in our efforts to put this volume together. Early on, we benefited from the advice of Peter Jackson and David Stevenson about European historians whom we might approach with regard to contributing to the volume. The final drafts of most of the chapters in the volume benefited from feedback at our 2013 ISA workshop. We thank the International Studies Association and the ISA Workshop Committee, chaired by Cameron Thies, for financial support. We give special thanks to Marc Trachtenberg and David Rowe for their role as formal discussants at the workshop. We thank Paul Schroeder and Mira Rapp-Hooper for presenting papers at the workshop, and a number of other scholars who attended the workshop and contributed significantly to the discussion. We all benefited enormously from their contributions.

We received some assistance in the process of putting together the footnotes and references, and for their help we thank Delinda Swanson and Gillian Gryz. For research support, Jack Levy thanks the Executive Dean of Arts and Sciences at Rutgers University and John Vasquez thanks the Mackie Research Fund at the University of Illinois.

We are particularly grateful to the people at Cambridge University Press for their work on the publication of this volume. We especially want to thank John Haslam, our editor, who offered much encouragement for the project, and who provided exceptional guidance throughout the process. We are grateful to Carrie Parkinson for providing excellent assistance and for ensuring that the project moved forward in a timely fashion. We also want to thank Joanna Breeze, our production editor; Phyllis van Reenen, who prepared the index; Lyn Flight, who did a superb job of copy-editing; and the rest of the team at Cambridge.

Lastly, Jack Levy dedicates the volume to his sister, Caroline Jonas, and John Vasquez dedicates the volume to his nephews and niece, Rick, Brian, Michael, Scott, and Cristina.

Part I

Overview of debates about the causes
of the First World War

1 Introduction

Historians, political scientists, and the causes of the First World War

Jack S. Levy and John A. Vasquez

Overview

It has been 100 years since the Great War, as it was called at the time, scorched the earth and psyches of the West, transforming our lives and world forever. As George Kennan remarked, the First World War was "*the* great seminal catastrophe" of the twentieth century.[1] The war destroyed empires and it led to political and social upheavals across Europe, the emergence of new national states, and a redrawing of the map of the Continent. It set the stage for the rise of Hitler and the Second World War and, indirectly, for the Cold War. It also triggered a significant shift in attitudes toward war, from one in which war was seen as acceptable and natural to one in which war was seen as abhorrent, if not irrational, and to be avoided. In military terms, the First World War also marked a shift away from the limited wars of the mid-nineteenth century to total war with extensive social mobilization. The experiences of the war also produced a substantial body of work in literature and film that continues to shape images of war generations later. The impact of the war was all the greater because it became a political and emotional issue after the inclusion of the war guilt clause in the Versailles Treaty.

Historians have now debated the origins of the First World War for a century. These debates have been motivated in part by the complexity of the processes leading to the war, and by the fact that the war provides some evidence to support a large number of different interpretations. As Paul Kennedy remarked, "the First World War offers so much data that conclusions can be drawn from it to suit any *a priori* hypothesis which contemporary strategists wish to advance."[2] Those clinging to a version of the

---

[1] George F. Kennan, *The Decline of Bismarck's European Order: Franco-Russian Relations, 1875–1890* (Princeton University Press, 1979), p. 3.
[2] Paul M. Kennedy, "The First World War and the International Power System," *International Security*, 9(1) (1984): 7–40, at 37.

"slide to war" hypothesis have been further motivated by the gap between what they regard as the relatively limited aims of most of the participants, and the enormity of the destruction of the war and of its political and social consequences. Many others have been motivated by the politicized nature of interpretations of the war, affecting conceptions of national identity and having implications for government policies years later.[3]

The First World War has also captured the imagination of international relations (IR) scholars. The war has had a disproportionate impact on the development of numerous theories of international conflict, from theories of balance of power, power transitions, alliances, economic interdependence, and offense–defense, to theories of scapegoating, rigid organizational routines, and misperceptions. It is also a commonly used case to illustrate and test a wide range of theories of international conflict.[4] The First World War remains *the* case to which nearly every IR conflict theorist is drawn.

This should not be surprising. Historiographical debates about the origins of the First World War parallel many theoretical debates that are central to the international relations field: structure and agency; the relative importance of international and domestic sources of causation; the causal role of individual personalities and belief systems; the rationality and coherence of the decision-making process; the dynamics of the security dilemma; the role of international norms and institutions; and the impact of strategic and societal culture, to name a few. The war is also intriguing because it started with a crisis that most observers at the time thought would be managed successfully. Within a few days it spiraled out of control and diffused rapidly from a local war to a continental war, and then to a world war that eventually engulfed all the major states in every region of the globe. Seemingly rational decisions led to irrational outcomes. The processes leading to war were characterized by extraordinary causal complexity involving an intricate interplay of variables from all levels of analysis: structural pressures, dyadic rivalries, social upheaval, insecure regimes, bureaucratic intrigue, long-standing strategic cultures, idiosyncratic leaders, and decision-making under enormous uncertainty.

In addition, the First World War has left an extensive documentary record. After the new Bolshevik government attempted to discredit the tsarist regime by publishing its secret treaties, other governments, determined to demonstrate that they were not to blame for the war and had

---

[3] The politicization of historiographical debates is emphasized by Annika Mombauer, *The Origins of the First World War: Controversies and Consensus* (New York: Longman, 2002).

[4] This raises a potentially serious problem, of course, if a historical case that is influential in the formulation of a theory is then used to test the same theory.

little to hide, published volumes of documents from their own archives. This has generated a vast literature reflecting different perspectives on a variety of events for all the countries involved, making this by far the most studied interstate war in history. The selective nature of the publication of these documents further politicized early debates about the origins of the war.

After nearly a hundred years, extensive research and debate about the outbreak of the Great War have resolved many questions. New questions have emerged, however, as historians have uncovered new documents and as political scientists have invoked new theories in an attempt to explain the war. Research in each discipline has also broadened its scope in recent years, from a primary focus on the outbreak of the war to heightened interest in the conduct of the war and the processes leading to its termination. The centennial of the war is generating a wave of new research, with new books, articles, and anthologies. What is distinctive about this volume is that it is the only one we know of that attempts to bring historians and international relations theorists together on a topic that has long been a central question in each discipline.

This volume focuses on the causes and immediate expansion of the First World War. It touches upon a number of the analytic themes mentioned above, including structure and agency, international and domestic sources of causation, and the impact of shifting power and preventive logic. It also addresses the questions of whether the primary causes of the war were located in Berlin, or in Vienna and the Balkans, or elsewhere, and the critical, but long-neglected, question of why the war broke out in 1914 but not before. In the process, our contributors highlight the complex nature of causation in the outbreak and spread of war. The volume links historiographical debates about the causes of the First World War to debates in the theoretical literature on international conflict.

We see our niche and contribution to the literature as providing analytic perspectives on a set of critical questions on the war from an interdisciplinary perspective of political scientists and diplomatic historians. Our overarching focus, as reflected in the subtitle of the volume, is on the relationship among, and interplay between, structure, politics, and decision-making. The structure of the system – global, European, and local – embodies long-term causes of the war and creates the incentives and constraints shaping the choices open to decision-makers. That structure evolves over time, and is itself influenced by the strategic interactions of states. The domestic politics of each state help to shape the preferences of the state, the resources available to it, the range of feasible options within international constraints, the internal distributional consequences of various options for both society and bureaucratic organizations, and policy-makers' choices among these options. All of this is filtered through the mindsets, perceptions, judgments, and decision-making of key individuals and their closest advisors, which shape the final decisions that determine state policy. Equally important is how these different variables from various levels of analysis interact. How one makes sense of the highly complex interactions of these various factors is a function not only of the sequences of events, but also of the analytic perspectives one brings to the table.

Diplomatic historians and IR scholars have each struggled with the problem of understanding the complexity of the processes leading to the First World War, but each in their own way. The different perspectives, approaches, and methodologies adopted by each discipline only enhance the extent to which they can learn from each other. By facilitating a dialogue among diplomatic historians and political scientists, and building on their different, but complementary, approaches to the study of international relations, we expect to gain new insights about the First World War – both in terms of providing novel answers to some perennial questions, as well as raising fresh questions and perspectives that shed new light on the underlying causes of the war. We also expect that this dialogue will help to sharpen the analytic perspectives that scholars bring to the study of the First World War and of war in general.

Our volume is not intended to summarize well-known events or to provide new narratives of the war as a whole. Our audience is scholars and advanced students, and our aim is to present new scholarly contributions that enhance understanding of the outbreak of the war. The centennial has already produced new narratives that provide new interpretations of the war and new perspectives on old historiographical debates, and much more is on the way.[5] We see no need to duplicate that material. Our volume follows more in the footsteps of Holger Afflerbach and David Stevenson, who collected a group of scholars in a conference to focus on a set of specific questions, in their case a group of historians to debate the question of whether the war was improbable.[6] Here, we have brought together both historians and political scientists to focus on a limited number of theoretically based questions relating to the causes of the war. At the broadest level, these questions concern causal factors relating to structure, politics, and decision-making. It is possible, however, to identify a more specific set of questions that serve as central themes running throughout the volume.

---

[5] See, among others, Christopher Clark, *The Sleepwalkers: How Europe Went to War in 1914* (New York: HarperCollins, 2013); Sean McMeekin, *July 1914: Countdown to War* (New York: Basic Books, 2013).

[6] Holger Afflerbach and David Stevenson (eds.), *An Improbable War? The Outbreak of World War I and European Political Culture before 1914* (New York: Berghahn, 2007).

One central question, addressed explicitly by some of our contributors and more indirectly by others, is the accuracy of the view that Germany was the key actor in bringing about the war. This view goes back to the Treaty of Versailles, of course, but it has really dominated historiographical debates in the half century since Fritz Fischer published *Griff nach der Weltmacht*.[7] This "German paradigm," as Samuel Williamson calls it, has been increasingly challenged.[8] Both sides of this debate are represented in this volume. The question of the validity and utility of the German paradigm naturally leads to the question of preventive war, which is a central theme of the German paradigm.[9] This is the argument that Germany's primary motivation for war was its fear of the rising power of Russia and the consequences of shifting power for Germany's position in Europe.

The question of preventive war in response to shifting power is directly related to the broader theme of the impact of structural change in the international system, which is central to all realist theories of international relations.[10] Because many conceptualizations of preventive war define the concept in terms of perceptions or anticipations of decline in relative power, the question of perceptions of power and of changes in power is another key theme in the volume. This is the focus of T. G. Otte's chapter on perceptions of Russia by the other Great Powers, but it is addressed by most other contributors as well. Preventive war is just one of many alternative responses to perceptions of relative decline, of course, and which of those policy alternatives is selected is significantly shaped by the political decision-making process within the state in question.

The questions of preventive war, perceptions of power, and the deeply political nature of a state's strategic response to anticipated decline raises another important question that has received insufficient attention by neither historians nor political scientists. Germany had faced the rising power of France after the latter's defeat in the Franco-Prussian War of

---

[7] Fritz Fischer, *Griff nach der Weltmacht* (Düsseldorf: Droste, 1961). English translation, *Germany's Aims in the First World War* (New York: W. W. Norton, 1967). For recent perspectives on the Fischer controversy, see Annika Mombauer, "Special Issue: The Fischer Controversy after 50 Years," *Journal of Contemporary History* 48(2) (2013): 231–417.

[8] Williamson, Chapter 2, this volume.

[9] The German paradigm also includes arguments about the domestic sources of German foreign policy leading to the war. This was a central theme in Fritz Fischer's second major book, *Krieg der Illusionen: Die deutsche Politik von 1911 bis 1914* (Düsseldorf: Droste, 1969); translated as *War of Illusions: German Policies from 1911 to 1914*, trans. Marian Jackson (New York: W. W. Norton, 1975). See also Volker R. Berghahn, *Germany and the Approach of War in 1914* (New York: St. Martin's Press, 1973, 2nd edn. London: Macmillan, 1993); Wolfgang J. Mommsen, "Domestic Factors in German Foreign Policy before 1914," *Central European History*, 6(1) (1973): 3–43.

[10] The key text in realist theory is Kenneth N. Waltz, *Theory of International Politics* (New York: McGraw-Hill, 1979).

1870–1871, and the rising power of Russia since Japan's humiliating defeat of Russia in the Russo-Japanese War of 1904–1905. The German military had been pressing their political leaders for a preventive war for years in response to these challenges.[11] If preventive logic was as important in bringing about war in 1914 as some scholars argue, why did it not bring about war before then, when crises provided the opportunity for war and when German leaders could have been even more confident of a military victory? Both William Mulligan and Dale Copeland directly address this question in their chapters, but several other scholars engage it as well.

This question of "why 1914 but not before" can be generalized to the many other causal factors invoked to account for the outbreak and immediate spread of the First World War. Many of those hypothesized causal factors have been in place for several years. The polarization of the alliance system, intense strategic rivalries, and aristocratic societal cultures are a few such factors that come to mind. If it is true that many (though perhaps not all) of the same military, diplomatic, political, and cultural conditions hypothesized to cause the First World War were also present in the years leading up to the war, one is forced to ask why those same factors did not lead to war before, especially during the several crises that broke out in 1905, 1908–1909, 1911, and 1912–1913. What was different? Differences in the outcome variable in two or more cases can be explained only by identifying differences in causal variables or their interaction effects. A good explanation for the First World War should explain not only why war occurred in 1914, but why it did not occur before.[12] Such explanations need to be tested historically through comparative case studies.[13]

---

[11] Similarly, fears of the relative decline of the Austro-Hungarian Empire had led to calls from within the Austrian military for preventive war while the opportunity was still available.

[12] The same question can be raised in response to the occasional argument that the First World War was over-determined. This argument is often driven by the belief that an extraordinarily large number of causal factors played a role in the processes leading to the war. Technically, however, what causal over-determination means is that there are multiple sets of sufficient conditions for a particular outcome, in this case the outbreak of the First World War. The removal of a critical factor from a set of sufficient conditions – which we might think of as one causal path to war – would not undercut the integrity of another causal path, and war would still have occurred. One problem with the over-determination argument is that the factors hypothesized to over-determine war in 1914 had been in place for a number of years. This is an empirical question, of course, but if that was the case the same factors over-determining war in 1914 should have over-determined war during an earlier crisis. On the role of necessary and sufficient conditions in causal explanation, see Gary Goertz and Jack S. Levy, "Causal Explanation, Necessary Conditions, and Case Studies," in Gary Goertz and Jack S. Levy (eds.), *Explaining War and Peace: Case Studies and Necessary Condition Counterfactuals* (London: Routledge, 2007), pp. 9–45.

[13] On the methodology of comparative case studies, see Alexander L. George and Andrew Bennett, *Case Studies and Theory Development in the Social Sciences* (Cambridge,

If one challenges the German paradigm, then one must address what role the other states played. What were the causal factors driving the decision-making of other states: their goals, motivations, external and internal constraints, leadership, key domestic actors and their respective preferences, and the nature of their political decision-making processes. Indeed, one reaction to the Fischer controversy was the belief that the historiography on the war had become too preoccupied with Germany and that a more balanced comparative perspective was needed. The same kind of intensive analysis that Fischer applied to Germany ought to be applied to the other European Great Powers. More attention also needs to be given not only to state foreign policies, but also to strategic interactions between them, and to signaling and bargaining between states. For these purposes, some international relations models might be useful.

It is these and related questions that guide the contributions to this volume: the role and interplay of structure and agency; the continued viability of the German paradigm as a primary explanatory model; the role of other states; the role of fears of decline, shifts in power, and preventive logic in Germany and elsewhere; and the question of why 1914 and not before or later. Although the studies will address other questions, the substantive contribution of the volume centers on these interrelated questions. Each of these tells us something about the relationship between structure, politics, and decision-making in the processes leading to war in 1914, and in international relations more generally.

An interdisciplinary approach

The most distinctive thing about this collection of essays on the outbreak of the First World War is its interdisciplinary orientation. The volume brings together diplomatic historians and international relations scholars with a common interest in the origins of the war.[14] Historically oriented political scientists have been reading the work of diplomatic historians on the war for years, and historians are increasingly reading political science research on the war, but more direct engagements are relatively rare. One early example of such interdisciplinary engagement on the First World War goes back to the 1970s, with the "1914 project" of Robert

MA: MIT Press, 2005). For a good example of the application of the methodology, see Alexander L. George and Richard Smoke, *Deterrence in American Foreign Policy: Theory and Practice* (New York: Columbia University Press, 1974).

[14] In their discussions of the outbreak of the First World War and of other wars, historians usually use the language of the "origins" of the war. This is reflected in the titles of countless books. Political scientists usually speak in terms of the "causes" of war. Anthropologists use the term origins to refer to the advent of war at the dawn of human civilization.

North and his colleagues. That project analyzed both the impact of changing international structures in the processes leading to the war, and the role of decision-making factors such as misperceptions.[15] North's 1914 project and the related work of Ole Holsti attracted the attention of diplomatic historians, who were often quite critical, especially of the attempt at quantification.[16]

An interdisciplinary approach is valuable because each party brings different theoretical and methodological perspectives to the table. In the case of diplomatic history and international relations theory, the conventional wisdom is that diplomatic historians are primarily interested in explaining fairly well-defined events or historical episodes, while international relations scholars are primarily interested in refining concepts and developing and testing theoretical generalizations.[17] This does not imply that historians are atheoretical, only that they use theory in different ways. Among other things, historians are often less explicit than are political scientists about the theoretical preconceptions underlying their historical analysis and the meanings of some of the concepts they use. Political scientists are trained to lay out their analytic assumptions, and develop and justify their theoretical propositions before they even think about applying their theory to a particular historical case.

These differences in the research objectives of historians and political scientists lead to other important differences. Given their generalizing objectives, political scientists often aim for parsimonious explanations that can be applied to other cases. The goal of providing complete explanations of individual historical cases leads historians to more complex explanations involving a larger number of variables. Political scientists argue that the more complex an explanation for a war, the less likely it is that all its nuances will be applicable to other cases, making it more difficult to generalize. Their emphasis on parsimony, however, means that they are less likely to provide complete explanations of individual cases.

---

[15] Nazli Choucri and Robert North, *Nations in Conflict: National Growth and International Violence* (San Francisco, CA: W. H. Freeman, 1975); Ole R. Holsti, *Crisis, Escalation, War* (Montreal: McGill-Queens University Press, 1972).

[16] See, for instance, Arthur N. Gilbert and Paul Gordon Lauren, "Crisis Management: An Assessment and a Critique," *Journal of Conflict Resolution* 24(4) (1980): 641–644, and the reply by Ole R. Holsti, "Historians, Social Scientists, and Crisis Management: An Alternative View," *Journal of Conflict Resolution* 24(4) (1980), 665–682.

[17] Colin Elman and Miriam Fendius Elman, "Introduction: Negotiating International History and Politics," in Colin Elman and Miriam Fendius Elman (eds.), *Bridges and Boundaries: Historians, Political Scientists and the Study of International Relations* (Cambridge, MA: MIT Press, 2001), pp. 1–36; see also Jack S. Levy, "Explaining Events and Developing Theories: History, Political Science, and the Analysis of International Relations," in Colin Elman and Miriam Fendius Elman (eds.), *Bridges and Boundaries: Historians, Political Scientists and the Study of International Relations* (Cambridge, MA: MIT Press, 2001), pp. 39–84.

Different explanatory objectives also lead to methodological differences. Historians are trained to rely heavily on the archives and on other primary sources. Political scientists' aims of testing general theories of conflict or other phenomena often lead them to examine several historical cases through a comparative case study methodology, based on the belief that such comparisons are the best way to maximize theoretical leverage and to rule out alternative explanations. This focus on multiple cases is one reason why international relations scholars, by training, tend to shy away from detailed and data-intensive archival research, and rely more on the secondary sources produced by historians. In their coverage of multiple cases, however, political scientists are often insensitive to the historiographical debates underlying particular secondary sources, and are often too willing to treat such sources as theoretically neutral accounts.[18] They also lack historians' training and skill in using and interpreting archival evidence.

One of the many benefits of interdisciplinary collaboration between diplomatic historians and international relations scholars is that interdisciplinary dialogue will help to bridge the gap between those who actively engage the archival evidential base and those who reflect on that evidence from the lens of concepts and models. We should emphasize, however, that historians have always used theories to explain. In fact, what we see today is more cross-fertilization, with an increasing number of historians explicitly using social science theories to analyze the diplomatic record, and international relations scholars trying to understand historical cases in their own right and not just as tests of their hypotheses. In addition, an increasing number of political scientists deal directly with the documentary base. Nonetheless, there is a difference between those who by their training spend so much of their time dealing with archives, and those who spend so much of their time dealing with concepts and theories.

Although identifying the differences between historians and political scientists in their study of international relations has attracted a fair amount of attention in recent years, one should not make too much of those differences. The two disciplines share much in common.[19] Indeed, in many respects the differences within each discipline are often greater than the differences between the two disciplines.[20] One advantage that diplomatic historians and international relations scholars have over other

---

[18] Ian Lustick, "History, Historiography, and Political Science: Multiple Historical Records and the Problem of Selection Bias," *American Political Science Review* 90(3) (1996): 605–618.

[19] This point is nicely developed by Elman and Elman (eds.), "Introduction," *Bridges and Boundaries*, pp. 28–35.

[20] Levy, "Explaining Events and Developing Theories."

interdisciplinary efforts is that they often study the same event. This is particularly the case with the First World War, although the Cold War and the Second World War are two other subjects of common interest. In addition, the two disciplines approach the subject with the same goals of explanation and an analysis of causes, dynamics, and consequences. This provides an opportunity to learn from each other in terms of overcoming the same pitfalls and sharing lessons regarding fruitful avenues of inquiry as well as new information and concepts.

Both disciplines also share a positivist stance, broadly defined, in that both maintain that an objective knowledge of the subject is possible – philosophically and practicably – and that certain protocols permit knowledge claims to be established through a rigorous analysis of evidence.[21] This shared "positivism" has come more to the fore as postmodernist perspectives have swept both disciplines, although the impact of postmodernism, coupled with the "democratization of history," has been much greater in diplomatic history than international relations.[22] As Annika Mombauer argues, however, in an important respect postmodernism has not significantly influenced debates on the First World War. The Fischer school and its critics have each believed that a positivist focus on documents would eventually reveal the "truth" about the origins of the war.[23] These commonalities make interdisciplinary work easier and less arduous than in situations where the purpose, case studies, and underlying philosophy of inquiry may differ.

As noted, recent years have witnessed a tendency toward greater interaction among historians and political scientists. Almost fifteen years ago Colin Elman and Miriam Fendius Elman brought together diplomatic historians and international relations scholars in a conference to discuss the bridges that could be built across the two disciplines, and the boundaries that separated the two. They discussed not only philosophical and disciplinary questions, but also shared work on specific cases. This was a landmark event, and later gave rise to organized sections in the American Political Science Association and then the International Studies Association to institutionalize such efforts. Likewise journals such as the

---

[21] This theme is emphasized by Stephen Haber, David M. Kennedy, and Stephen D. Krasner, "Brothers Under the Skin: Diplomatic History and International Relations," *International Security* 22(1) (1997): 34–43; and Elman and Elman (eds.), "Introduction," *Bridges and Boundaries*, pp. 2–5.

[22] On postmodernism and diplomatic history, see John Lynn, "The Embattled Future of Academic Military History," *Journal of Military History* 61(4) (1997): 777–789, cited in Elman and Elman (eds.), "Introduction," *Bridges and Boundaries*, pp. 3–4.

[23] Annika Mombauer, "The Fischer Controversy, Documents, and the 'Truth' about the Origins of the First World War," *Journal of Contemporary History*, 48(2) (2013): 290–314.

International History Review, *International Security*, and *Security Studies* have provided outlets read by scholars from each discipline. The advent of H-Diplo and more recently H-Diplo/ISSF (International Security Studies Forum) has done much to make for more routine interactions.[24]

Conferences with sustained face-to-face conversation play an important role in the promotion of interdisciplinary engagement. More and more diplomatic historians have been attending the annual meetings of the International Studies Association, and we have begun to see more and more panels and roundtables involving a mixture of historians and political scientists. We have each participated on a number of such panels – on intelligence, grand strategy, the Second World War, and, more recently, on the First World War, as detailed in the Preface to this volume. It is our hope that the latest in a continuing dialogue between diplomatic historians and international relations scholars will provide new insights, new answers to old questions, and new questions that help to advance the debate. To have any hope of doing that we felt it necessary to focus on a few questions in depth rather than deal with all the questions that could be addressed regarding the First World War, although we will mention some of these in the section on future research.

Sources of bias

From the very beginning, debates on the origins of the First World War have been framed from the perspective of blame and guilt. This was a prime motivation in the initial release of documents by governments. It was also the motivation behind the writing of some memoirs and release of diaries.[25] Such motivations are also evident in the release or compilation of documents by domestic critics or opponents of the war regimes, such as in the collection by Kautsky in Germany and the Soviet release of documents.[26] Contenders have been concerned primarily with questions of justice, which, in our view, have distorted the more important task of understanding and causal explanation. Conflicting interpretations of the war often became embroiled in domestic political contention, in terms of

---

[24] See www.h-net.org/~diplo and www.h-net.org/~diplo/ISSF.

[25] Some diaries, such as those of Kurt Riezler, appeared to have been partially rewritten after the fact, see Sean McMeekin, *The Russian Origins of the First World War* (Cambridge, CA: Belknap Press of Harvard University Press, 2011), p. 256, n. 5. See also Clark, *Sleepwalkers*, p. 643, n. 52; Mombauer, *Origins of the First World War*, pp. 158–159. Our thanks to Mira Rapp-Hooper for detailing how different sections of the diaries have been classified by historians in terms of their authenticity.

[26] Max Montgelas and Walter Schücking (eds.), *The Outbreak of the World War*, 4 vols., collected by Karl Kautsky (New York: Oxford University Press, [1919] 1924).

their implications for national identity, foreign policy, and party support. This was particularly the case in Germany. Annika Mombauer has outlined this process and how it shaped historiography both inside and outside Germany.[27] The Fischer thesis, the most recent controversy, was certainly conducted in this vein.[28] As a result, many scholars have entered debates about the origins of the war with preconceived answers or are looking for answers that support a normative case. In this sense a number of previous efforts, including the early compilation of the major collections of documents, were conducted by scholars who were behaving more like lawyers than neutral scholars.

A general problem with the emphasis on responsibility is that it rests on a number of assumptions that are not always made explicit, but that shape the analysis in a number of ways. For one thing, the focus on responsibility tends to bias the analysis toward agent-centered explanations and away from structural explanations, by giving more attention to the choices made by political leaders than to the international structural forces that shape those choices. Both sets of variables are important, but scholars need to be more explicit about the criteria they use to evaluate the causal weights of these very different sets of factors. Closely related, the focus on responsibility biases the analysis toward the actions of single states, while underestimating the role of strategic interactions between states in the form of the dynamics of international rivalries, crisis bargaining, and other multilateral processes. In addition, the focus on blame tends to assume that behavior is intentional, minimizing the effects of inadvertent consequences. As Christopher Clark notes, "the quest for blame predisposes the investigator to construe the actions of decision-makers as planned and driven by a coherent intention. You have to show that someone willed war as well as caused it."[29]

Clark highlights additional problems with what he calls the "blame-centered account." It presumes, he argues, that "in conflictual interactions one protagonist must ultimately be right and the other wrong," or at least that we can apportion blame proportionately. In the case of the First World War, based on Clark's own narrative, he argues that "the question is meaningless." Clark concludes that the outbreak of the war was "a tragedy, not a crime," for which it is nearly impossible to apportion responsibility.[30]

---

[27] Mombauer, *Origins of the First World War*.
[28] Fischer, *Germany's Aims*; Fischer, *War of Illusions*; Mombauer, "The Fischer Controversy after 50 Years."
[29] Clark, *Sleepwalkers*, pp. 560–561.   [30] *Ibid.*

The search for "blame" is not the only kind of bias that hinders understanding. Some critics of the generalizing enterprise argue that some political scientists, in "testing" their theories in specific historical cases, are more interested in interpreting the facts to fit their theories than in letting the facts fall where they may.[31] This is an equally damaging but slightly different kind of bias. Instead of analysts seeing what they *want* to see based on their political interests or emotional needs, they see what they *expect* to see based on their prior theoretical expectations. The former is a kind of "motivated reasoning." The latter is often described as an unmotivated cognitive bias.[32] Analysts often invoke these biases to explain the judgments and actions of political leaders, but analysts themselves are vulnerable to the same kind of biases. The more they can be made aware of these biases, the greater the chances of minimizing them.

Having expressed our views about two sources of bias, we will now summarize some of the substantive questions guiding the organization of this volume, explaining in the process how the various chapters in the volume fit into these broader themes.

Substantive questions

This volume is organized around a number of analytic issues and related substantive questions, each related to our overarching themes of structure, politics, and decision-making. The first major substantive question we focus on is the German paradigm and challenges to it. Samuel Williamson raises this question in Chapter 2. As we noted in the last section, much of the intellectual history of scholarship and commentary on the causes of the First World War has been focused on Germany, and the debate over its responsibility and war guilt. Williamson reviews the historical work on the war and shows how the German paradigm has gradually been eroded as the question of war guilt has taken more of a back seat. His analysis makes clear how more normative questions dominated the empirical questions in early studies of the origins of the war. Nonetheless, the empirical questions were still analyzed and even the questions of responsibility provide evidence for addressing the empirical question of who and what brought about the war. Generally, much of the

---

[31] Political scientists reply that this danger is countered to a certain extent by the disciplinary norm for analysts doing case study research to test their preferred theory against the leading alternative theoretical explanations, and to use the same standards of rigor and evidence in analyzing alternative theories as they do their own.

[32] See Robert Jervis, *Perception and Misperception in International Politics* (Princeton University Press, 1976); Leonie Huddy, David O. Sears, and Jack S. Levy (eds.), *Oxford Handbook of Political Psychology*, 2nd edn. (Oxford University Press, 2013).

historical literature sees Germany as central, with other states playing a lesser or ancillary role.

One of the exceptions to this is the work of Sidney Fay, which is an early revisionist interpretation of the war published in the late 1920s. Adopting what is in many respects a more objective and neutral stance, Fay argued that no single power bore primary responsibility for the war. He traced the causes of the war to the nature of the state system, the nature of secret alliances, and economic imperialism, along with militarism, nationalism, and the role of newspapers in nearly all the Great Powers.[33] Fay's work became the "slide into war" thesis, which relates to theories of conflict spirals and inadvertent war.[34] This was captured by the widely cited comment of Lloyd George, a former British prime minister and leader of a wartime coalition government from 1916 to 1922. In his *War Memoirs*, Lloyd George wrote that: "The nations slithered over the brink into the boiling cauldron of war without any trace of apprehension or dismay . . . The nations backed their machines over the precipice . . . not one of them wanted war; certainly not on this scale."[35] The "slide into war" thesis was itself political, however, because Lloyd George had been an early critic of British policy.

Many political scientists have also seen Germany as primary, although they have given less attention to the question of responsibility. Early power transition theorists like Organski and Kugler focused on Germany as a rising challenger to Britain as the dominant power in the system.[36] Long-cycle theory also saw the Germany–Britain dyad as key, with the two in a struggle for global leadership.[37] The focus on Britain as the dominant power was based on power transition theory's emphasis on gross national product as the key element of power, and on long-cycle theory's emphasis on naval power and position in leading sector technologies. Germany was a challenger on each dimension. Although many historians emphasize the

---

[33] Sidney B. Fay, *The Origins of the World War*, 2 vols. (New York: Macmillan, [1928] 1966). Fay's first two factors reflect a neorealist theoretical perspective that emphasizes the role of the anarchic structure of the system and uncertainty about the intentions of others.

[34] On models of conflict spirals, see Jervis, *Perception and Misperception*, ch. 3.

[35] David Lloyd George, *War Memoirs*, 2 vols. (London: Odhams Press, 1938), vol. 1, p. 49.

[36] A. F. K. Organski and Jacek Kugler, *The War Ledger* (University of Chicago Press, 1980); see also Robert Gilpin, *War and Change in World Politics* (New York: Cambridge University Press, 1981).

[37] William R. Thompson, *On Global War: Historical-Structural Approaches to World Politics* (Columbia, SC: University of South Carolina Press, 1988). For critiques of both the power transition and long-cycle positions, see John A. Vasquez, *The War Puzzle* (Cambridge University Press, 1993), pp. 93–111; Jonathan M. DiCicco and Jack S. Levy, "Power Shifts and Problem Shifts: The Evolution of the Power Transition Research Program," *Journal of Conflict Resolution* 43(6) (1999): 675–704.

importance of the Anglo-German naval race, few argue that this was the primary rivalry leading to the outbreak of war, especially after 1912 when Germany basically unilaterally conceded victory in the naval arms race to Britain. In 1914, Britain was more committed to peace than was any other power. On the German side, avoiding a war with Britain was a central policy goal of both the kaiser and Chancellor Bethmann-Hollweg.[38]

International relations research in the 1980s on the cult of the offensive also took Germany to be the key actor in bringing about the war, based largely on the consequences of the Schlieffen Plan and the assumptions upon which it was based. This was the case with Jack Snyder (who also looks at Russia and France) and with Stephen Van Evera.[39] More recently, Keir Lieber summarized for international relations theorists recent debates about Terence Zuber's work, which questioned the nature of the Schlieffen Plan and, in fact, its very existence as an operational war plan. That led to debates among IR scholars concerning the implications of the debates about war plans for theories of offensive and defensive realism.[40] Again, Germany has been seen as the key actor in bringing about the war. This has been typical in political science even though other actors have received attention.[41]

Samuel Williamson has challenged this German focus, and identifies factors and interpretations leading to the gradual erosion of the German paradigm. Williamson's earlier work on Austria-Hungary places the Dual Monarchy and its struggle with Serbia as central to the war.[42] His more recent work, including his study in this volume (Chapter 2), has made that

---

[38] See Clark, *Sleepwalkers*, p. 524; John A. Vasquez, Chapter 8, this volume; Jack S. Levy, Chapter 6, this volume; also Jack S. Levy "Preferences, Constraints, and Choices in July 1914," *International Security* 15(3) (1990/1): 151–186.

[39] Jack Snyder, *The Ideology of the Offensive: Military Decision Making and the Disasters of 1914* (Ithaca, NY: Cornell University Press, 1984); Jack Snyder, "Perceptions of the Security Dilemma in 1914," in Robert Jervis, Richard Ned Lebow, and Janice Gross (eds.), *Psychology and Deterrence* (Baltimore, MD: Johns Hopkins University Press, 1985), pp. 153–179, esp. pp. 168–172; Stephen Van Evera, "The Cult of the Offensive and the Origins of the First World War," *International Security* 9(1) (1984): 58–107.

[40] Keir A. Lieber, "The New History of World War I and What it Means for International Relations Theory," *International Security* 32(2) (2007): 155–191; Terence Zuber, "The Schlieffen Plan Reconsidered," *War in History* 6(3) (1999): 262–305; Jack Snyder and Keir Lieber, "Correspondence: Defensive Realism and the 'New' History of World War I," *International Security* 33(1) (2008): 174–194.

[41] Levy, "Preferences, Constraints, and Choices"; on Russia, see Marc Trachtenberg, "The Meaning of Mobilization in 1914," *International Security* 15(3) (1990/1): 120–150. See also Jack S. Levy, Thomas J. Christenson, and Marc Trachtenberg, "Correspondence: Mobilization and Inadvertence in the July Crisis," *International Security* 16(1) (1991): 189–203.

[42] Samuel R. Williamson, Jr., *Austria-Hungary and the Origins of the First World War* (New York: Macmillan, 1991).

more explicit.[43] The role of Austria-Hungary and Serbia's nationalist and territorial claims on the Empire are a major reason for both why the assassination of Archduke Franz Ferdinand occurred and why Austria-Hungary reacted in the way that it did. It was not simply the assassination, but Serbia's long-simmering irredentist struggle with both Austria-Hungary and the Ottoman Empire – two multinational empires.[44] The challenge to the German paradigm raises questions about the role of other states.

With a change in perspective away from Germany, Russia's role looms larger. It has long been argued that the Russian mobilization was the last act that precipitated the war and was a decisive event. Thinking in counterfactual terms, if one thing could have prevented the war from breaking out when it did and given more time for the Halt in Belgrade proposal to be considered, it would have been for the tsar to adhere to his decision to cancel his initial mobilization order late on July 29. In this sense, Russia was the last actor in a position to avoid the collision. Williamson maintains that Russian premobilization actions were also important. He notes more recent research on hardening attitudes within Russia, and Russian leaders' growing interest in the Turkish Straits. Any reconsideration of Russia leads to a reevaluation of the role of France, including the extension of the French commitment to Russia to issues that might arise in the Balkans. Emphasizing the nearly unconditional commitments made by several of the Great Powers, Williamson states in his chapter (p. 50) that "Germany gave Vienna a 'blank check,' Paris gave Russia a 'blank check,' and France and Russia gave Belgrade a 'blank check.'"

As we noted earlier, most applications of the German paradigm emphasize the response of German political and military elites to their perception that Germany was in a position of relative decline in the international system, particularly with respect to Russia. This raises issues relating to the changing structure of the international system, and changing distributions of power in particular. This links directly to a second central theme in this volume, which concerns debates between the role of structure and agency in the outbreak of the First World War. Structural accounts are often linked to arguments about inevitability, whereas agency-based accounts are more closely linked to arguments about contingency.

---

[43] Samuel R. Williamson, Jr., "Aggressive and Defensive Aims of Political Elites? Austro-Hungarian Policy in 1914," in Holger Afflerback and David Stevenson (eds.), *An Improbable War? The Outbreak of World War I and European Political Culture before 1914* (New York: Berghahn, 2007), pp. 61–74.

[44] Clark, *Sleepwalkers*, ch. 1.

Debates over agency and structure, the relative importance of each, and the nature of their interrelationship have become standard in the social sciences, and in the study of history as well. They are central to the study of the causes of war in general, and of the First World War in particular. Christopher Clark provides a particularly interesting reflection on the agent–structure debate through his distinction between *why* the war occurred and *how* it was brought about.[45] Clark argues that although these questions are logically inseparable, they lead the analyst in different directions: "The question of *how* invites us to look closely at the sequences of interactions that produced certain outcomes. By contrast, the question of *why* invites us to go in search of remote and categorical causes: imperialism, nationalism, armaments, alliances, high finance, ideas of national honour, the mechanics of mobilization." Clark self-consciously focuses on the *how* question, and notes that the story he tells in *The Sleepwalkers* is "saturated with agency."[46]

Debates about structure and agency include questions about the interrelationship between the two. One useful metaphor is reflected in "powder-keg" models, which combine both structure and agency by incorporating both windows of opportunity and catalysts.[47] Windows of opportunity are created by changing international structures and serve as necessary conditions for catalysts (usually the result of actions by agents) to have their maximum causal effect. For interpretations of the First World War, the structure provides the powder keg and the assassination and the resulting July 1914 crisis provide the spark.[48]

Many scholars, of course, give much greater emphasis to either the powder keg or the spark. Those who emphasize the powder keg see the war as the product of long-term forces that produced an environment or set of conditions that made it highly likely that some crisis at some point would come along that would escalate into war even if the July 1914 crisis could have been successfully managed for a time. This is another way of saying that the repeated crises worked within a structure and helped to refine the existing structure to make it increasingly difficult for the decision-makers to avoid war. For some, like William Thompson, it

---

[45] See Clark, *Sleepwalkers*, p. xxix.   [46] *Ibid.*

[47] Goertz and Levy, "Causal Explanation, Necessary Conditions, and Case Studies," pp. 36–39.

[48] An interesting example of a powder-keg model (but one that does not use that term) is Richard N. Lebow, "Contingency, Catalysts, and Nonlinear Change: The Origins of World War I," in Gary Goertz and Jack S. Levy (eds.), *Explaining War and Peace: Case Studies and Necessary Condition Counterfactuals* (London: Routledge, 2007), pp. 85–112. Lebow emphasizes three underlying causal chains – centered in Germany, Austria-Hungary, and Russia, respectively – and the spark or catalyst of the assassination, which he regards as a necessary condition for the First World War.

is because rivalries were becoming more intense. For others, like Paul Schroeder, it is because the existing peace system – the Concert of Europe – was no longer following the norms that it had effectively created, and was breaking down so that individual states were now following their particular interests unilaterally rather than taking care of their collective interests.[49]

The debate between structure and agency is reflected in the two chapters in Part II of this volume. The chapter by Karen Rasler and William Thompson examines four systemic elements: the decline of the global leader, namely, Britain; the rise of a regional leadership challenge by Germany; the bipolarization of the major states into two blocs, and non-linear rivalry dynamics. The latter provides a new way of conceptualizing the role of rivalries and interstate interactions in bringing about the war. It maintains that it was not just the individual rivalries that helped to bring about the war – for example, the Franco-German, Anglo-German, or Austro-Hungarian–Russian rivalries – but the interaction of these rivalries. Rasler and Thompson see the war as coming out of four streams of rivalries (see Figure 3.3). They also add an element of contingency by their "pinball model," which is a step toward resolving the debate between structure and decision-making. They state explicitly that: "It is not a case of the system making them do it." They argue, however, that rivalry dynamics signifi-cantly increased the probability of war.

T. G. Otte takes a more agency-oriented approach, one that emphasizes the role of perception, interpretation, judgment, and decision-making in international relations. He begins by challenging the "quasi-teleological" approach that sees the war as an outcome of successive crises. He argues that history is less deterministic and more open than that. In particular, he sees that perceptions of two factors – the changing nature of Russian power and the possibility of détente – made things far from inevitable. For Otte, the attitudes and perceptions toward Russia made the situation just prior to 1914 quite fluid. The rise of Russian power, as a result of its economic recovery from the 1904–5 debacle and the prospect of the completion of its railroad system, made for a fluid situation that produced concerns. The British were concerned about the future of the

---

[49] See William R. Thompson, "Powder Kegs, Sparks and World War I," in Gary Goertz and Jack S. Levy (eds.), *Explaining War and Peace: Case Studies and Necessary Condition Counterfactuals* (London: Routledge, 2007), pp. 147–193, and his chapter with Karen Rasler in this volume (Chapter 3); Paul W. Schroeder, "Necessary Conditions and World War I as an Unavoidable War," in Gary Goertz and Jack S. Levy (eds.), *Explaining War and Peace: Case Studies and Necessary Condition Counterfactuals* (London: Routledge, 2007), pp. 113–145; Paul W. Schroeder, "World War I as Galloping Gertie: A Reply to Joachim Remak," *Journal of Modern History* 44(2) (1972): 319–344.

1907 Anglo-Russian convention. The French were worried that increased Russian power would make Russia less dependent on them. They also worried about a possible German–Russian alliance.

Détente with Russia and the hopes for a German–Russian alliance pushed Germany in one direction, while Russia's growth in power gave support to hard-liners who sought a preventive war.[50] Austria-Hungary focused on the short term, and there it saw Russia as militarily unprepared for war. This pushed Austria in two directions: either use this as an opportunity for a grand compromise or exploit the weaknesses to gain an advantage through firm action. Otte points out that these contradictory tendencies made war far from inevitable as crises repeated, and that many decisions and outcomes were contingent. This, he argues, places decision-making at the heart of any satisfactory analysis of the causes of the war.

Part III of the volume examines the extent to which the First World War grew out of a German strategy of preventive war. These chapters nicely follow those in Part II on rivalries and on perceptions of power. Many, but not all, proponents of the German paradigm argue that Germany was driven by preventive logic (or the preventive motivation) in bringing about the war. Our contributors offer several different perspectives on this question. If preventive war thinking was so important, William Mulligan asks, why did it not lead to war earlier when circumstances seemed to be ripe.[51] Defining preventive war more broadly than either Levy or Vasquez in their perspective chapters, Mulligan examines the nature and influence of preventive war thinking in the decades prior to 1914. Focusing on the question of why Germany and Austria did not adopt a strategy of preventive war in earlier crises, Mulligan examines the 1875 "War in Sight" crisis; pressure from the German and Austrian militaries for war against France and Russia between 1886 and 1888; the First Moroccan Crisis in 1905–1906; and Chief of the Austrian General Staff Conrad's pressure for a preventive war against Italy in 1911. Mulligan emphasizes the fear of triggering a hostile coalition; the inherent risks of war; concerns about domestic reactions; the civilian control of the military; and ethical constraints on the idea of preventive war limiting preventive wars.

Though Mulligan does not examine the 1914 case in detail, it is clear that each of these constraints had eroded by that time. Mulligan highlights the role of restraints in the system, including the restraints imposed by norms. This emphasis on the importance of ethical constraints is particularly notable because that factor has received relatively little attention

---

[50] Otte does not see Bethmann-Hollweg among the latter, but as one who thought that some *modus vivendi* was possible with Russia.

[51] Dale Copeland also engages this question in Chapter 7 in this volume.

in the theoretical literature on the conditions under which states are most likely to adopt preventive war strategies.[52] Mulligan's discussion of Bismarck and Franz Joseph shows how these norms affected specific decisions about war in general and preventive war specifically.

In the second study in this section, Jack Levy begins with a clarification of the meaning of the preventive war concept, and in the process distinguishes between prevention and preemption, and between "status quo" and "revisionist" preventive war strategies. He also calls for theoretically differentiating among military, economic, and demographic elements of shifting power on the grounds that they generate different perceptions of threats over different time horizons and for different types of states, and elicit different responses. Levy then examines the military, economic, and financial factors that led to perceptions of relative decline by German political and military leaders in the years leading up to 1914, along with the political constraints that complicated German efforts to keep up with Russia in the arms race. He argues that preventive logic had an important influence on German decision-makers – on some more than others – but that there is insufficient evidence to support the argument that Germany had a sustained strategy of preventive war from the end of 1912.

Dale Copeland argues that preventive war thinking was the primary influence on German security policy, and the primary cause of the First World War as a whole. In this sense his chapter provides an exemplary example of the German paradigm. For Copeland, the Russian mobilization is not the real cause of Germany's involvement, but simply a move that Bethmann-Hollweg welcomed and even encouraged because it created the diplomatic and political conditions facilitating the war that he and Moltke had sought all along. Copeland compares his preventive war explanation with three leading competitors: a spiral model, a domestic model, and a structural realist model emphasizing multipolarity and alliances. He argues that the preventive war model outperforms the others not only in explaining the outbreak of war in 1914, but also in explaining other puzzles associated with the First World War.

John Vasquez disagrees with the preventive war explanation. In Chapter 8, he outlines a set of criteria that need to be satisfied in order for any war to be seen as a preventive war. He then applies these to individual decision-makers in Germany and finds the case for preventive

---

[52] Two recent exceptions are Scott A. Silverstone, *Preventive War and American Democracy* (New York: Routledge, 2007); Paul W. Schroeder, "Preventive Wars to Restore and Stabilize the International System," *International Interactions* 37(1) (2011): 96–107. For a general list of preventive war propositions, see Jack S. Levy, "Preventive War: Concept and Propositions," *International Interactions* 37(1) (2011): 87–96.

war deficient. He argues that among the major decision-makers only Molkte held a consistent preventive motivation as a reason for going to war against Russia. He argues that the First World War was not a preventive war because the two decision-makers in charge of foreign policy, namely, the kaiser and Chancellor Bethmann-Hollweg, were not pursuing a policy of preventive war in July 1914, and that their position was clearly distinguishable from that of Moltke. In fact, both the kaiser and Bethmann-Hollweg were trying to avoid a world war once it was clear that Britain would intervene. As with Williamson, Vasquez finds a shift away from the German paradigm as helpful in understanding the war. He argues that the war emerged from the local Austro-Hungarian–Serbian local war through a series of diffusion processes.

These different perspectives of Levy, Copeland, and Vasquez on preventive war in 1914 make it clear that the question of the role and impact of the preventive motivation and its sources is critical to determining how central Germany was in bringing about the war. The final part of the book returns to the question with which the book began – the viability of the German paradigm – by looking at the role of Germany's two primary adversaries, Russia and France, and their role in bringing about the war. Ronald Bobroff raises new questions about the role of Russia. He sees Russia as having grievances that led to an aggressive foreign policy. Russia was not just reacting to events, but attempting to shape them. The mobilization plays a key part in bringing about the war for Bobroff as well as for many other scholars, and he tries to explain why Russian leaders took the actions they did. Unlike McMeekin, Bobroff does not see Russia as having certain preordained goals (like greater influence over the Turkish Straits) for which it wanted a war.[53] Rather, the war emerged out of a process that made for crisis escalation. Williamson is also willing to see a greater role for Russia, though he believes that Russia is ancillary to Austria-Hungary.

For Bobroff, the main reason Russia was brought into the war was that Russian leaders were trying to deter Germany and Austria through a demonstration of its resolve and ultimately a mobilization. They resorted to this policy because they felt that Russia had no choice given the way that it had been treated, especially by Germany. Russian leaders had, in Bobroff's words, grown to distrust Germany because many of the events of the previous decade had challenged both Russia's political and economic vital interests. Any further backing down would be at great cost to its prestige among the Great Powers and with its Serbian ally, and could

[53] McMeekin, *Russian Origins*.

even jeopardize Russia's status as a Great Power. Bobroff does not think Russia wanted a war, but got into one because the other side would not back down. The rise of some hawks within Russia prevented its own backing down.

One cannot speak of Russia without speaking of France. To place J. F. V. Keiger's chapter (Chapter 10) in context, it would be useful to remember Williamson's argument in Chapter 2, Part I, of this volume. Williamson sees France as playing an important role in bringing about the war. Poincaré, in particular, had foreign policy goals that could be facilitated by going to war, and in some cases, like Alsace and Lorraine, could be attained only by war. Waiting for the right diplomatic opportunity is a key strategy. Williamson points out some of the recent research that supports the view that both Russia and France were more aggressive than they have been seen in the past.[54] In addition, France played a key role as Russia's banker, helping it to stage a remarkable economic recovery after its military defeat in 1905, and then helping it to finance strategic railroads that were perceived by German leaders as such a threat.

Keiger, however, reaffirms the more traditional view that France did not play a key causal role in bringing about the war. He begins by raising general theoretical questions about the extent to which political leaders engage in rational cost–benefit calculations in international crises, and whether they carefully identify, assess, and prioritize various risks to the national interest that might result from different strategies. Invoking Clausewitz, Keiger gives particular attention to the question of how sensitive leaders are to questions of military readiness when they find themselves in escalating crises. Keiger's main argument is that France was not ready for war in 1914, and that that lack of readiness served as a significant constraint on French behavior. He concludes, however, that rational models give insufficient attention to the human dimension, including the vagaries of leaders' personalities, their risk orientations, their responses to highly stressful environments, and distortions in their processing of information. Keiger emphasizes that French President Poincaré was risk averse, and that this basic personality trait, combined with French lack of readiness, was a powerful constraining factor on French behavior.

Future research

The analyses in the book answer many questions about the First World War, but in the process they raise new questions that historians and political

---

[54] Otte, in Chapter 4, also sees France as playing a significant role in bringing about the war.

scientists will need to address, and they suggest new approaches that should be considered. We will mention two questions and approaches that seem particularly promising – one methodological and one substantive – using counterfactuals and examining the diffusion of the war.

Of the two, counterfactuals are the better known, though they are often used loosely. Historians and political scientists have long speculated about key turning points in the processes leading to war, have asked whether political leaders might have made different decisions at those critical junctures, and argued about what the consequences might have been. One particularly important form of counterfactual is the necessary condition counterfactual.[55] If condition or action x is hypothesized as a necessary condition for outcome y, the necessary condition counterfactual posits that if decision or action x had not been taken or did not occur, y would not have occurred.

The classic counterfactual question with respect to the First World War, of course, is what would have happened in the absence of the assassination of the archduke. The argument that without the assassination the war would not have occurred, at least not in summer 1914, is a necessary condition counterfactual. Counterfactuals like this are important for assessing causality. The best way of validating a necessary condition counterfactual is to provide a compelling argument that in the absence of the posited necessary condition (the assassination), the observed outcome (the First World War) would not have occurred. Many scholars have made this argument, with Lebow providing one of the most rigorous analyses.[56]

Scholars have identified a number of other conditions, actions, and events generating counterfactual implications. Clark argues that the bipolarization of the European alliance system was a "crucial precondition" for the war of 1914.[57] Levy and others argue that Germany's "blank check" to Austria-Hungary on July 6–7 was a necessary condition for an Austrian war against Serbia, which was a necessary condition for a general war.[58] Some scholars argue that the German assumption of British neutrality was a necessary condition for German support for Austria-Hungary, which was a necessary condition for war. Others argue that if Austria-Hungary had accepted the Halt in Belgrade plan, war might have been avoided. Niall Ferguson raises the question of what might have happened

[55] Gary Goertz and Jack S. Levy, *Explaining War and Peace: Case Studies and Necessary Condition Counterfactuals* (London: Routledge, 2007).
[56] Lebow, "Contingency, Catalysts, and Nonlinear Change." See also his chapter, "Franz Ferdinand Found Alive: World War I Unnecessary," in *Forbidden Fruit: Counterfactuals and International Relations* (Princeton University Press, 2010), ch. 3.
[57] Clark, *Sleepwalkers*, p. 123.   [58] Levy, Chapter 6, this volume, p. 147.

if Britain had stood aside rather than entering the war.[59] One can identify numerous other counterfactuals worth investigating. We still do not have clear markers in the process of the onset of war of whether certain decisions, if made differently, could have put the collectivities on a path that could have avoided the catastrophe. It would be useful to have a more systematic list of possible turning points. Different analytic perspectives and different historical narratives, of course, will generate different turning points.

Some counterfactual arguments are more persuasive than others, especially for the purposes of shedding light on causation. In this regard, it is important to note that there is a growing literature on the methodology of counterfactual analysis in historical case studies.[60] Scholars have attempted to specify criteria by which the rigor and plausibility of a counterfactual analysis ought to be evaluated. The use of counterfactual analysis in the study of the First World War would benefit from closer attention to these criteria. This is not the place for a complete survey of criteria for useful counterfactuals, but it would be useful to mention two to give a flavor to the argument we are making.

One is the "minimal rewrite criterion," which concerns the plausibility of the antecedent in the alternative world (for example, the absence of an assassination). The fewer things that change in moving from the real world to the counterfactual world, the easier it is to argue that the differences in outcomes in the real and counterfactual worlds are due to a single causal factor. That is why highly contingent events like the hypothesized failure of the assassination attempt against the archduke make such useful counterfactuals. It would be necessary to change very little for the assassination not to have happened. In fact, the *a priori* probability of the assassination attempt failing was considerably higher than of it succeeding. If one can make a compelling argument that a European war would not have erupted in a parallel world without an assassination, one can confidently claim that the assassination was a necessary condition for the war.

Compare that to the counterfactual that if Bismarck had been German chancellor in 1914, the probability of war would have been much lower.

---

[59] Niall Ferguson, "Virtual History: Toward a 'Chaotic' Theory of the Past," in Niall Ferguson (ed.), *Virtual History: Alternatives and Counterfactuals* (New York: Basic Books, 1999), pp. 1–90.

[60] Philip Tetlock and Aaron Belkin (eds.), *Counterfactual Thought Experiments in International Relations: Logical, Methodological, and Psychological Perspectives* (Princeton University Press, 1996); Levy, "Preferences, Constraints, and Choices," p. 156; Jack S. Levy, "Counterfactuals and Case Studies," in Janet Box-Steffensmeier, Henry Brady, and David Collier (eds.), *Oxford Handbook of Political Methodology* (Oxford University Press, 2008), pp. 627–644; Lebow, *Forbidden Fruit*.

Even if that were true, what inferences could we draw from that about causation? It would be tempting to say that it suggests the causal importance of individual political leaders. So many things would have needed to change for Bismarck (or someone like him) to be chancellor, however, that we would have a tough time arguing that it was the leader, his belief systems, and personality that caused the lower probability of war, as opposed to the range of other changes that would have been necessary to create that counterfactual world. Counterfactuals involving short causal chains are generally seen as more plausible than counterfactuals involving longer causal chains.

A second, and related, criterion concerns the question of the likelihood that political leaders might have made different decisions. The more leaders seriously considered making a different decision, the greater the explanatory utility of the counterfactual. If the structure of the situation truly gave them little choice, or if they had a strong interest (national or domestic) in not making a different decision, it is less useful to pose the alternative as a useful antecedent in a counterfactual scenario. To take an example, a general war might have been avoided if Austria-Hungary had accepted the Halt in Belgrade plan. But that would have been contrary to Austro-Hungarian interests as defined by their leaders. It would have required going back on a declaration of war and halting military operations already begun, which would have been very difficult politically. In addition, the Halt in Belgrade plan was contrary to German interests as defined by Bethmann-Hollweg. Bethmann-Hollweg preferred an Austro-Serbian war over a negotiated peace, and, at least until the evening of July 29–30, believed that such a war could be localized.[61] More interesting than the counterfactual question of the consequences of accepting the Halt in Belgrade plan are the questions of why Austrian and German leaders defined their interests in a way that made them hostile to the plan. Similarly, the utility of the counterfactual of whether an earlier unambiguous statement by British Foreign Secretary Sir Edward Grey might have deterred Germany from an aggressive stance is undercut by the fact that such a statement would have been politically unacceptable and consequently would not have been made. Churchill claimed that the Cabinet would have broken up.[62]

---

[61] The kaiser had proposed a Halt in Belgrade on July 28, but Bethmann-Hollweg diluted the message sent to Vienna and helped to marginalize the kaiser's influence at this time. Levy, "Preferences, Constraints, and Choices," pp. 175–177.

[62] Luigi Albertini, *The Origins of the War of 1914*, 3 vols., trans. and ed. Isabella M. Massey (London: Oxford University Press, 1952–1957), vol. 2, p. 515.

Qualitative methodologists offer other criteria as well for the evaluation of the utility of different kinds of counterfactual arguments. We cannot summarize them all here. Our point is that more attention to these criteria by scholars of the First World War would increase the value of counterfactual argumentation for the purposes of making causal claims about the conditions, events, and processes leading to the war.

A second set of ideas for future research that deserves greater scrutiny than it has received is the question of why the war spread. Most analyses, like those in this volume, focus on the onset of the war. Yet after 1914 many more states entered the war. Why did they? Why did so many have a difficult time remaining neutral? These are questions that are very relevant to the study of the First World War. In his chapter in this volume Vasquez even goes as far as to frame the entry of Germany, Russia, France, and Britain as a question of diffusion. He argues that explaining the diffusion or spread of war requires a different explanatory structure than that required to explain the outbreak of war.

A recent special issue of *Foreign Policy Analysis* examined the question of the spread of the war using both quantitative analysis and historical analysis involving both political scientists and historians.[63] They lay out both some initial findings and an agenda for further research. The question of why the war spread raises some of the same issues as does the initial outbreak of the war, in particular the relationship between structure and agency. Were political leaders' decisions on whether or not to enter an ongoing war shaped more by structural pressures or by the nature of their political decision-making systems and processes? This interrelationship raises the additional question of how structures affect decisions in general, and how previous decisions themselves produce a structure, or at least an environment, that constrains decision-makers from adopting certain policies while encouraging them to take others. Vasquez *et al.* analyze the role of the system and also lay out at the theoretical level how they think system structures and actor decisions feed off each other.[64] Stevenson, in the same special issue, identifies the factors that affected each individual country's decision to intervene, including how over time the cumulative impact of intervention became a force in its own right.

[63] See John A. Vasquez, Paul F. Diehl, Colin Flint, and Jürgen Scheffran, "Forum on the Spread of War, 1914–1917: A Dialogue between Political Scientists and Historians," *Foreign Policy Analysis* 7(2) (2011): 139–141; John A. Vasquez, Paul F. Diehl, Colin Flint, Jürgen Scheffran, Sang-Hyun Chi, and Toby J. Rider, "The ConflictSpace of Cataclysm: The International System and the Spread of War, 1914–1917," *Foreign Policy Analysis* 7(2) (2011): 143–168; David Stevenson, "From Balkan Conflict to Global Conflict: The Spread of the First World War, 1914–1917," *Foreign Policy Analysis* 7(2) (2011): 169–182.

[64] Vasquez *et al.*, "Forum"; Vasquez *et al.*, "ConflictSpace."

The main theoretical difference between analyzing the outbreak of the war and its spread, is that the latter seeks to investigate the extent to which a contagion or diffusion process is causally shaping the process. What the nature of such a process would be, how and why it produces a clustering, and how it is related to other diffusion processes like city riots, democratization, or even fashion trends or fads are theoretical questions not relevant to two-party wars. The latter raises the issue of whether the initial outbreak of the First World War after the Austro-Hungarian declaration of war through the end of August should be seen as a multiparty war with an overarching set of causes or as a two-party war that spread quickly by some sort of diffusion process. Vasquez argues the latter, while Levy the former in the *Foreign Policy Analysis* special issue.[65]

Nonetheless, everyone agrees that by 1915 the factors that produced the initial outbreak were different from those that made the war spread. Diffusion or contagion is a causal factor when as one state intervenes it affects, positively, the probability that another state will intervene. A question that deserves further study is whether there are certain diffusion mechanisms or processes that operate. Vasquez *et al.* examine four: contiguity, alliances, rivalry, and shared territorial disputes. Others have also been posited, such as the breakdown of the political order, economic dependence, and bandwagon effects themselves.[66] How the various diffusion processes interacted and how they operated in each pair of states that joined the war are two subjects that have rarely been investigated by either historians or social scientists. These questions deserve more attention. On the whole, if there is one question on the First World War that has been understudied, it is diffusion. And this is somewhat ironic, since the impact of the war had so much to do with its spreading across Europe and across the globe.

The last one hundred years of scholarship and writing on the First World War have produced much – more than anyone can read – and given us important theoretical and policy insights. The case is so complex, however, that there is still much to learn. While the work is difficult, it is also fascinating. We have enjoyed studying the First World War and engaging scholars from another discipline. We have learned an enormous amount in the process. We hope our readers will feel the same way.

---

[65] *Ibid.*; and Jack S. Levy, "The Initiation and Spread of the First World War: Interdependent Decisions," *Foreign Policy Analysis* 7(2) (2011): 183–188.
[66] Vasquez, *The War Puzzle*, ch. 7.

2   July 1914 revisited and revised
The erosion of the German paradigm*

Samuel R. Williamson, Jr.

"Austrian Fear of Serb Empire is Real War Cause," wrote Harvard histor-ian Albert Bushnell Hart in the Sunday *New York Times* on August 2, 1914. Two days later Germany launched its invasion of Belgium. Within weeks Hart's view would be eclipsed by the emergence, in Britain, France, Russia, and the United States, of the paradigm of full German responsibility for the Great War. Only now, close to a century later, is that paradigm in the process of erosion, though some historians in the 1920s sought to challenge its prominence. Recent research shows a more culpable Serbia, a more aggressive Franco-Russian alliance, a more desperate Austria-Hungary, a more assertive Russian foreign policy, a more ineffective Britain in its efforts to contain the crisis, and internal tensions among all the powers on the eve of Sarajevo. Germany remains central to any explanation of the origins of the war, but it is now joined by other powers and other consid-erations. The paradigm no longer dominates the discussion; indeed, Hart's assessment of August 2, 1914, now possesses new credibility. This chapter will track the emergence of the German paradigm and the numerous recent challenges to it. It will then suggest further areas for research on the continuing question: why did war come to Europe in the summer of 1914?

The German paradigm

The unprovoked German attack on Belgium, quickly followed by murder-ous reprisals against civilians and the destruction of the famed University of Louvain, soon caused the Triple Entente powers and the United States to see Germany as the prime mover behind the war. They believed the Germans had deliberately launched the war. That view gained rein-forcement with the sinking by a German submarine of the RMS *Lusitania* on May 7, 1915, and the loss of 128 American lives. Months of tension

---

* An earlier version of this chapter was given at the National History Center in Washington; the author is appreciative of the comments made then about the argument and to Wm. Roger Louis for the invitation to speak.

between Washington and Berlin, the resumption of unrestricted submarine warfare in January 1917, and the maladroit Zimmermann telegram seeking to entice Mexico to attack its neighbor further hardened American views. Once the United States entered the war, many American historians actively joined the cause of blaming the Germans for the war, with an occasional nod to Austria-Hungary. Not surprisingly, American diplomats played a key role in the insertion of the "War Guilt" clause, Article 231, into the Treaty of Versailles, as a justification for war reparations that would help to repay French and British loans to America. A legal paradigm of German responsibility had been established.[1]

At the end of the war, some American historians, called "revisionists" because they thought the peace treaty misrepresented the origins of the war, began to reassess the diplomatic and military moves behind what came to be called the July Crisis. The most polemical, Harry Elmer Barnes, charged that France and Russia had started the war. Harvard historian Sidney Fay said all the European governments shared some responsibility, with Austria-Hungary the principal culprit, followed by Germany and Russia. Nor did he ignore Serbia's role. By contrast, the Versailles verdict had defenders, including Fay's rival, Bernadotte E. Schmitt, who blamed Berlin for the war, and whose role as editor of the new *Journal of Modern History* ensured that that view was well represented in the pages of the periodical during the 1930s and 1940s.[2]

The Germans, of course, kept the issue in play as they sought to refute the "War Guilt" clause. Their efforts included the publication of German diplomatic documents, a step that soon prompted all the powers, except Italy and Serbia, to publish their documents. The new Soviet government helped by releasing Russian documents that indicted the tsarist regime. But in the 1930s the rise of Hitler to power in Germany saw a diminution of interest in the "war guilt" question, except for a solitary effort under way in Italy.

There Luigi Albertini, after being ousted from the editorship of *Corriere della Sera* by Mussolini in the mid-1920s, devoted the rest of his life to studying the July Crisis. Albertini had been a prominent editor and political figure in 1914, so he easily managed to interview many of the

---

[1] Annika Mombauer, *The Origins of the First World War: Controversies and Consensus* (New York: Longman, 2002), pp. 21–98; John W. Langdon, *July 1914: The Long Debate, 1918–1990* (New York: Berg, 1991); Samuel R. Williamson, Jr. and Ernest R. May, "An Identity of Opinions: Historians and July 1914," *Journal of Modern History* 79(2) (2007): 335–387.

[2] Harry Elmer Barnes, *The Genesis of the World War*, 2nd edn. (New York: Alfred A. Knopf, 1927); Sidney B. Fay, *The Origins of the World War*, 2 vols., rev. 2nd edn. (New York: Macmillan, 1930); Bernadotte E. Schmitt, *The Coming of the War*, 2 vols. (New York: Charles Scribner, 1930).

surviving decision-makers, used all the printed documents, and apparently saw some of the unpublished Italian ones. From these he prepared a three-volume work, published in Italy after his death during the Second World War. It would be translated into English, but never into German. His work initially received modest attention from historians, though Schmitt reviewed the Italian edition in the *Journal of Modern History*, mostly giving it praise. Albertini cast his net of responsibility wide, with the Germans and Austrians leading the way, though he had few kind words for Sir Edward Grey and almost none for the Russian leadership. Nor was he easy on his own Italian compatriots or the Serbian government. Because Albertini's volumes are so detailed, and include so many document extracts, they have been influential among political scientists.[3]

In the 1950s, in the United States and Britain the German paradigm still held strong. On the Continent, French and German historians worked to mute the impact of the War Guilt clause. While David Lloyd George had talked of Europe "slithering" into war, still the standard works in Britain and the United States took the more conventional view of the German paradigm. A. J. P. Taylor's major work cast Germany as the chief culprit. In America, the popular history textbook by R. R. Palmer, *A History of the Modern World*, explained the war in terms that remain almost as valid today as they were in 1951. Palmer wrote: "The Germans, issuing their famous 'blank check,' encouraged the Austrians to be firm ... The German decisions were posited on the reckless hope that Great Britain might not enter the war at all." And in 1962, Barbara Tuchman published the best-selling *The Guns of August*, which reflected the German paradigm even as she completely ignored Eastern Europe and the Balkans in her account, limiting her discussion of the origins of the war to a single page. The German paradigm held.[4]

Then, in 1961, Fritz Fischer published *Griff nach der Weltmacht*, becoming the first prominent German historian to affirm Germany's role in starting the war. His second book, *Krieg der Illusionen* in 1969, suggested that Germany had indeed plotted the war.[5] Fischer and his students stressed (and continue to stress) Germany's principal role in the

---

[3] Luigi Albertini, *The Origins of the War of 1914*, 3 vols., trans. and ed. Isabella M. Massey (London: Oxford University Press, 1952–1957). Bernadotte E. Schmitt's review of the original edition of Albertini, *Le origini della guerra del 1914*, 3 vols. (Milan: Fratelli Bocca, 1942–1943) is in the *Journal of Modern History* 24(1) (1952): 69–74.

[4] A. J. P. Taylor, *The Struggle for Mastery in Europe, 1848–1918* (Oxford University Press, 1954), pp. 522–523; Robert R. Palmer, *A History of the Modern World* (New York: Alfred A. Knopf, 1951), p. 666; Barbara Tuchman, *The Guns of August* (New York: Macmillan, 1962), pp. 71–72, but only one full page of print.

[5] Fritz Fischer, *Griff nach der Weltmacht* (Düsseldorf: Droste, 1961); translated as *Germany's Aims in the First World War* (New York: W. W. Norton, 1967); Fritz Fischer, *Krieg der*

origins of the First World War, and many political scientists have followed those arguments.

Now, as the centennial of the July Crisis nears, the paramount position of the German paradigm has been modified. But the erosion should not obscure the valuable work done by historians and political scientists, who still espouse the view that Germany started the war, perhaps deliberately or with a certain recklessness. Their contributions are valuable. John Röhl has provided a masterful account of the part played by German Kaiser Wilhelm II, while Dieter Hoffmann has pressed the case for Berlin's desire for a preventive war. Mark Hewitson, in a neo-Fischer approach, sees Germany's action in 1914 as born of confidence, not by concern or anxiety over its (and Austria-Hungary's) sagging international position: thus, the will to war. And Dale Copeland argued in 2000 that Germany launched a preventive war, though his rather benign view of Russian and French actions now stands challenged by more recent works.[6]

Historians benefited from the fall of the Soviet government with the discovery of German army documents thought to have been destroyed by bombing at the end of the Second World War, and later returned to Germany.[7] The Soviet collapse also allowed historians, if only erratically, into the Russian archives, with the result that new historical works about Russia are slowly emerging. These studies develop more fully, and sometimes with more damage, the role of Russia in the crisis of 1914.[8]

In the search for explanations of the origins of the Forst World War, the works of political scientists have been very important. They have explored

---

Illusionen: Die deutsche Politik von 1911 bis 1914 (Düsseldorf: Droste, 1969); translated as *War of Illusions: German Policies from 1911 to 1914*, trans. Marian Jackson (New York: W. W. Norton, 1975).

[6] John C. G. Röhl, *Wilhelm II: Der Weg in den Abgrund 1900–1941* (Munich: C. H. Beck, 2008); Dieter Hoffmann, *Der Sprung ins Dunkle: Oder wie der 1. Weltkrieg entfesselt wurde* (Leipzig: Militzke, 2010); Mark Hewitson, *Germany and the Causes of the First World War* (Oxford: Berg, 2004); Dale A. Copeland, *The Origins of Major War* (Ithaca, NY: Cornell University Press, 2000). See also Lüder Meyer-Arndt, *Die Julikrise 1914: Wie Deutschland in den Ersten Weltkrieg stolperte* (Cologne: Böhlau, 2006); Annika Mombauer, "The Fischer Controversy, Documents, and the 'Truth' about the Origins of the First World War," *Journal of Contemporary History* 48(2) (2013): 290–314. For a popular work, see David Fromkin, *Europe's Last Summer: Who Started the Great War?* (New York: Alfred A. Knopf, 2004).

[7] Among the more controversial books from this access is Terence Zuber, *Inventing the Schlieffen Plan: German War Planning 1871–1914* (Oxford University Press, 2002).

[8] Two excellent examples that made use of either the new German or Russian documents are: Annika Mombauer, *Helmuth von Moltke and the Origins of the First World War* (Cambridge University Press, 2001); Bruce W. Menning, "War Plans and Initial Operations in the Russian Context," in Richard F. Hamilton and Holger H. Herwig (eds.), *War Planning 1914* (Cambridge University Press, 2010), pp. 80–142. Mombauer has just edited a collection of documents on the July Crisis, *The Origins of the First World War: Diplomatic and Military Documents* (Manchester University Press, 2013).

the question from almost every conceivable theoretical approach, usually using the standard printed works in English with their stress on Germany: war plans, militarism, issues of mobilization, deterrence theory, alliance politics, arms races, offensive–defensive modes, realism and neorealism, domestic upheaval.[9] Thoughtful studies from peace research have usefully asked why the earlier crises, some of which we will consider, ended peacefully, but not that of July 1914.[10]

Clearly Germany played a key role in July 1914. But now new research and comparative analysis suggest that France, Russia, and especially Austria-Hungary also bore responsibility for the emerging crisis. Nor are the roles of Serbia and Britain in the unfolding tragedy ignored.[11] Few doubt that Germany was important, but to say that it plotted the war, that other governments were more or less blameless, and that unilateral explanations suffice, are no longer the dominant themes. Rather, there is a comparative focus on other countries, on a clearer understanding of the operation of intelligence functions, and on exploiting the new information available in the Russian documents. All these efforts also reexamine the older document collections, as well as using newly discovered private archive collections. Some historians are also using new methodological frameworks and are displaying a willingness to ask once more the questions posed three generations ago by historians, but this time employing a more multifaceted approach. All in all, what is emerging is a more nuanced and complex assessment of the origins of the First World War.

---

[9] For recent works that address the July Crisis from theoretical perspectives, see Jack S. Levy and William R. Thompson, *Causes of War* (Chichester: Wiley-Blackwell, 2010); Frank C. Zagare, *The Games of July: Explaining the Great War* (Ann Arbor, MI: University of Michigan Press, 2011); Keir A. Lieber, "The New History of World War I and What it Means for International Relations Theory," *International Security* 32(2) (2007): 155–191; Keir A. Lieber, *War and the Engineers: The Primacy of Politics over Technology* (Ithaca, NY: Cornell University Press, 2005), pp. 59–62, 88–98; Patricia A. Weitsman, *Dangerous Alliances: Proponents of Peace, Weapons of War* (Stanford University Press, 2004); Richard N. Lebow, *A Cultural Theory of International Relations* (Cambridge University Press, 2008); Stephen Van Evera, *Causes of War: Power and the Roots of Conflict* (Ithaca, NY: Cornell University Press, 1999); the essays in *Foreign Policy Analysis* 7(4) (2011): 139–216, which reflect different approaches from eleven different authors. For a critical view of other theoretical efforts, see Samuel R. Williamson, Jr., "Austria-Hungary and the Coming of the First World War," in Ernest R. May, Richard Rosecrance, and Zara Steiner (eds.), *History and Neorealism* (Cambridge University Press, 2010), pp. 103–128.

[10] A key new work is Friedrich Kießling, *Gegen den "Großen Krieg"? Entspannung in den internationalen Beziehungen 1911–1914* (Munich: Oldenbourg, 2002).

[11] An early effort at a comparative approach was Keith Wilson (ed.), *Decisions for War, 1914* (New York: St. Martin's Press, 1995); also see Richard F. Hamilton and Holger H. Herwig (eds.), *The Origins of the First World War* (Cambridge University Press, 2003) and their more recent *War Planning 1914*; Holger Afflerbach and David Stevenson (eds.), *An Improbable War? The Outbreak of World War I and European Political Culture* (New York: Berghahn, 2007).

Germany still holds a major place in the understanding of the catastrophe, but there were other actors and factors that, if altered or absent, might have seen the response to the murders at Sarajevo end with a peaceful resolution.[12]

The results of this new work can be quickly summarized. In July 1914, after the murders at Sarajevo that implicated some Serbian contacts, Vienna resolved to go to war against Serbia, who it believed had plotted the attack. Berlin, anxious to support its ally, thought that Russia would accept a short, quick punitive war, and thus backed Vienna. Then came delays and actions that did not accord with Austro-German expectations. The French and Russian leadership learned, through code intercepts, of the planned Habsburg action and resolved to block it, taking preemptive military steps that accelerated the momentum of European mobilization. Under no circumstances were Paris and St. Petersburg prepared to allow any chastisement of Belgrade. Britain, caught up in the Irish question, came to realize the danger of war late, not just to its strategic position but also to its economic leadership. It decided to join the emerging fray as much for economic as for strategic reasons. These brief comments in effect capture much of the current thinking about the origins of the First World War.

The international system under challenge: 1911–1914

A central part of the new approach to understanding the July Crisis begins with an appreciation of the profound changes that challenged the international system from the start of 1911 to the eve of Sarajevo. The Moroccan Crisis of 1911, the Italo-Turkish War of 1911, and the two Balkan Wars of 1912–1913 decisively altered the European situation and revealed the real possibility of both an Austro-Russian and/or an Austro-Serbian war in 1912–1913. These near misses deeply influenced the attitudes and perceptions of the European leaders, almost all of whom were still in power in

---

[12] For some of the most recent works, see the magisterial study by Christopher Clark, *The Sleepwalkers: How Europe Went to War in 1914* (London: Allen Lane, 2012); Konrad Canis, *Der Weg in den Abgrund: Deutsche Außenpolitik 1902–1914* (Paderborn: Ferdinand Schöningh, 2011); William Mulligan, *The Origins of the First World War* (Cambridge University Press, 2010); Jürgen Angelow, *Der Weg in die Urkatastrophe: Der Zerfall des Alten Europa 1900–1914* (Berlin: be.bra verlag, 2010); Eric Dorn Brose, *A History of the Great War: World War One and the International Crisis of the Early Twentieth Century* (Oxford University Press, 2010); the popular study, Miranda Carter, *George, Nicholas and Wilhelm: Three Royal Cousins and the Road to World War I* (New York: Random House, 2009). See also the review article by Annika Mombauer, "The First World War, Avoidable, Improbable or Desirable? Recent Interpretations on War Guilt and the War's Origins," *Germany History* 25(1) (2007): 78–95.

July 1914, including many (especially Sir Edward Grey in London) who seemed to have assumed that the 1914 situation was simply another iteration of the earlier crises.[13]

The wars of 1911 and after brought major strategic changes. Italy gained tenuous control of Libya; Serbia doubled its population and geographical size at the expense of Turkey; Bulgaria was humbled during the Second Balkan War; while Romania slowly moved away from its secret ties with the Triple Alliance and into the Russian orbit. And two allies, Italy and Austria-Hungary, openly struggled for control of the newly created Albanian state that served to block Serbian access to the Adriatic. More dangerously, before and during the First Balkan Wars the Russians had conducted a "trial mobilization exercise" along the Habsburg frontier, keeping an additional 400,000 troops that were scheduled for release on active duty across Russia – a move seen in Vienna as sheer intimidation. Eventually, the Habsburg leadership would increase troop strength in units along the Russian border and even more on the Serbian border, an increase of perhaps 224,000. Thanks to the spying of Colonel Alfred Redl of the Habsburg army and others, the Russians were well informed of Vienna's actions. Three times the Vienna leadership considered the question of war and opted instead for peace, almost certainly because Berlin offered no assured support and Emperor Franz Joseph and Archduke Franz Ferdinand blocked military calls for a showdown. But the risks of war remained real.[14]

While the Anglo-German naval race eased after 1913 when Berlin accepted a 16:10 ratio of British supremacy, a tidal wave of manpower increases took place among all the European armies, including the Habsburg forces, which had not been increased since 1889.[15] The total

---

[13] Clark, *Sleepwalkers*, p. 90.

[14] Samuel R. Williamson, Jr., "Military Dimensions of Habsburg–Romanov Relations during the Era of the Balkan Wars," in Béla K. Király and Dimitrije Djordjevic (eds.), *East Central European Society and the Balkan Wars* (New York: Columbia University Press, 1987), pp. 317–337; and for more detail, based on intelligence reports in the Russian archives, see the article by Bruce W. Menning, "The Mobilization Crises of 1912 and 1914 in Russian Perspective: Neglected and Overlooked Linkages," forthcoming. The two authors disagree on the number of Austro-Hungarian troops mobilized; the present writer believes Russian operatives grossly overestimated the actual number of Habsburg troops on duty, which seems on all fronts at the height of the crisis to have been about 625,000 men, an increase of 224,000 over normal troop strength. On the Balkan Wars, the study by E. C. Helmreich, *The Diplomacy of the Balkan Wars, 1912–1913* (Cambridge, MA: Harvard University Press, 1938) remains valuable.

[15] On the Anglo-German antagonism and the part played by the naval race, see Jan Rüger, "Review Article: Revisiting the Anglo-German Antagonism," *Journal of Modern History* 83(3) (2011): 579–617.

number of men on active duty in Europe, on the eve of war, stood at roughly 4 million.[16]

The crises during these years (1911–1914) also gave new impetus to enhancing the coherence of the Triple Alliance of Germany, Austria-Hungary, and Italy, as well as to the Triple Entente of Russia, France, and Britain, with the latter far more successful. Berlin and Vienna worked out military and naval plans with Rome, but correctly doubted how the Italians would perform. Moreover, the severity of the setbacks suffered by Vienna in the wake of Serbia's success and increased size and population, not to mention the obviously closer ties that Belgrade had formed with St. Petersburg, was troublesome. In both Berlin and Vienna worry about Austria-Hungary's future became more prevalent, and the prospect of a new emperor, Franz Ferdinand, at some point did not inspire confidence, especially in Budapest. By late spring 1914, German and Habsburg officials assessed the status of the alliance pessimistically.[17]

By contrast, although not an alliance, Britain and France drew closer, with more detailed naval and military agreements. Raymond Poincaré, first as premier and then president of France, worked tirelessly to tighten the alliance with Russia, providing huge financial subsidies so the Russians could increase their railroad network and accelerate their mobilization. These steps alarmed the senior German military leaders, including generals Helmuth von Moltke and Georg von Waldersee, prompting frequent talk of preventive war before the full extent of Russian rearmament could be reached in 1917. Increasingly, the two allies, who still hoped to edge Britain into an alliance, coordinated their Balkan policies. At the same time, Paris fretted over the continuing frictions that troubled Anglo-Russian relations, especially over Persia and Central Asia. But by

---

[16] David Stevenson, *Armaments and the Coming of War: Europe, 1900–1914* (Oxford University Press, 1996), chs. 5, 6, Conclusion; David Stevenson, *Cataclysm: The First World War as Political Tragedy* (New York: Basic Books, 2004), pp. 3–21; David G. Herrmann, *The Arming of Europe and the Making of the First World War* (Princeton University Press, 1996); Hew Strachan, *The First World War*, vol. 1: *To Arms* (New York: Oxford University Press, 2001); the opening chapter, with other material, has also appeared as *The Outbreak of the First World War* (Oxford University Press, 2004).

[17] On the alliance, Holger Afflerbach, *Der Dreibund: Europäische Großmacht- und Allianzpolitik vor dem Ersten Weltkrieg* (Vienna: Bohlau, 2002), pp. 721–812; Jürgen Angelow, *Kalkül und Prestige: Der Zweibund am Vorabend des Ersten Weltkrieges* (Cologne: Böhlau, 2000), pp. 374–465; Canis, *Der Weg*, pp. 557–585; Clark, *Sleepwalkers*, pp. 321–364. See the analysis of the Austro-German relationship from a "systems' perspective" in Robert Jervis, *System Effects: Complexity in Political and Social Life* (Princeton University Press, 1997), pp. 243–250.

the eve of Sarajevo the Triple Entente was essentially a virtual alliance, regardless of official disclaimers in London.[18]

To complicate things, the winter of 1913/14 saw a Russo-German squabble over the assignment of German General Liman von Sanders to Constantinople to train Turkish troops. This issue brought new tensions, and in the spring there was a veritable Russo-German press war among the military publications of the two countries. However calculated, Russo-German relations in June 1914 were tensile.[19] Tsar Nicholas II visited Romania in early June, and the Russian foreign minister, Sergei Sazonov, who accompanied him dared to step into Transylvania, territory held by Hungary but the home of 3 million Romanians. All these events sent warning signals to Vienna and Berlin that Romania might be lost to the Triple Alliance. And, although Anglo-German relations appeared more relaxed publicly, Grey and the British Cabinet had agreed to hold secret naval talks with Russia, a move that German intelligence soon discovered and which Grey promptly denied, thereby undercutting his credibility in Berlin.[20]

Furthermore, in June 1914 each of the European governments experienced significant internal political crises. In Germany, conservative Chancellor Theobald von Bethmann-Hollweg no longer had a reliable majority in the Reichstag, with the Social Democrats now the largest party. Nor had the ripples from the Zabern incident and its civil–military ramifications ended. In France, the May elections saw the socialists make significant gains, bringing a moderate socialist René Viviani to power

---

[18] On Moltke and Waldersee, see Holger H. Herwig, *The First World War: Germany and Austria-Hungary, 1914–1918* (London: Arnold, 1997), pp. 20–21; also Mombauer, *Helmuth von Moltke*, pp. 183–191; Clark, *Sleepwalkers*, pp. 308–325; Canis, *Der Weg*, pp. 611–655; John F. V. Keiger, *Raymond Poincaré* (Cambridge University Press, 1997), pp. 130–201; cf. Stefan Schmidt, *Frankreichs Außenpolitik in der Julikrise 1914: Ein Beitrag zur Geschichte des Ausbruchs des Ersten Weltkrieges* (Munich: Oldenbourg, 2009), pp. 246–288; M. B. Hayne, *The French Foreign Office and the Origins of the First World War, 1898–1914* (Oxford: Clarendon Press, 1993), pp. 229–266.

[19] Clark, *Sleepwalkers*, pp. 338–343; Canis, *Der Weg*, pp. 586–610.

[20] Canis, *Der Weg*, pp. 627–633; Clark, *Sleepwalkers*, pp. 421–423. On the German intelligence coup, often overlooked in explaining Berlin's skepticism toward Grey, see Manfred Rauh, "Die britisch–russiche Marinekonvention von 1914 und der Ausbruch des Ersten Weltkrieges," *Militärgeschichtliche Mitteilungen* 41(10) (1987): 37–62; also Heinz Höhne, *Der Krieg im Dunkeln: Macht und Einfluß der deutschen und russischen Geheimdienstes* (Munich: C. Bertelsmann, 1985), pp. 113–121. Strangely, the new study on Ambassador Benckendorff by Marina Soroka, *Britain, Russia and the Road to the First World War: The Fateful Embassy of Count Aleksandr Benckendorff (1903–1916)* (Farnham: Ashgate, 2011), makes no mention of the espionage and indeed adds little of interest on the July 1914 crisis. See also Jean Stengers, "1914: The Safety of Ciphers and the Outbreak of the First World War," in Christopher Andrew and Jeremy Noakes (eds.), *Intelligence and International Relations, 1900–1945* (Exeter University Press, 1987), pp. 29–48.

as premier and putting the future of the three-year enlistment law in jeopardy. In Italy, political strife in June during "Red Week" saw cities momentarily proclaiming their independence from the central government, causing almost total chaos in the kingdom. In Austria, the parliament had been prorogued in March. Concerns about Transylvania and the preservation of Magyar power dominated the agenda in Hungary, along with fears of what would happen when Franz Ferdinand came to the Habsburg throne. In Russia, domestic strikes had flared anew and some German diplomats thought Russia could not possibly think of war, even after Sarajevo. Across the Channel, there loomed the prospect of possible civil war if Ireland gained Home Rule. Almost certainly, for some of the political leadership in these countries, even Britain, war must have seemed a way to avert a domestic Armageddon.[21]

New approaches: Serbia, Austria-Hungary, and Germany

Serbia and the "Black Hand"

None of the European states faced as much domestic turmoil as Serbia. Clark's recent study, *The Sleepwalkers*, once again, as Fay and Albertini did two generations ago, reminds scholars that Serbia bore significant responsibility for the outbreak of the First World War. Those attached to the German paradigm or those who choose to tread lightly in the volatile Balkans in discussing July 1914 often ignore this perspective. After describing the struggle for Serbian independence against Ottoman rule, Clark explores the vicious rivalry between the Karadjordjević and Obrenović clans, leading eventually in 1903 to the murder of King Alexander and his mistress turned wife, Draga. For Vienna, nothing but trouble came from those murders. The once placid Belgrade–Vienna relationship soon soured, highlighted by the "Pig War" and Russia's increasingly aggressive support of the new dynasty. The annexation crisis over Bosnia-Herzegovina in 1908–1909 permanently estranged the two countries.

More dangerously, in 1911 some of the 1903 regicides, led by Dragutin Dimitrijević (nicknamed "Apis") a colonel in the Serbian army intelligence,

---

[21] Clark, *Sleepwalkers*, p. 490; Canis, *Der Weg*, pp. 637–654. Fischer made the domestic turmoil a central theme of why Germany wanted war. See also a pungent British comment in the context of the Irish crisis in July 1914 in Samuel R. Williamson, Jr., "General Henry Wilson, Ireland, and the Great War," in Wm. Roger Louis (ed.), *Resurgent Adventures with Britannia: Personalities, Politics and Culture in Britain* (London: I. B. Tauris, 2011), p. 98.

created the *Ujedinjenje ili smrt!* (Union or Death or, more casually, the Black Hand), which was devoted to the unification of all south Slavs by any means. Soon the conspiratorial organization had its tentacles throughout Serbian civil and military society, with thousands of members planted in every conceivable organization. The Black Hand had become a government within the government. This relentless penetration made the group difficult to control, as the government of Nikolai Pašić discovered in 1913 and 1914 as it struggled to rule the newly conquered lands in Macedonia and the Sanjak of Novi Pazar. The military leadership wanted control over the area, and ruled it harshly and aggressively against non-Serbs. In May 1914, the clash between civilians and the army led to a major government crisis over who had procedural priority in the new areas, military or civilian officials. Eventually this led to the collapse of the Pašić government. Only the intervention of the Russian minister to Belgrade, Nikolai Hartwig, put Pašić back in power, but the upheaval forced a call for elections. This Russian intervention, it should be noted, suggests just how closely Pašić and Hartwig collaborated.[22]

Meanwhile, the Black Hand had created cells and plotted terror attacks against Habsburg officials. In late spring 1914, Rade Malobabić, a Black Hand operative and confidant of Apis, who now headed Serbian intelligence, suggested that Bosnian Serb students (or former students) be sent to assassinate Archduke Franz Ferdinand when he came to Bosnia in late June. Apis agreed, but in the best sense of modern terror cells used two cutouts, Voja Tankosić and Milan Ciganović, to do the work so nothing could be linked directly to him. They recruited the three nineteen-year-old students who fervently supported the Black Hand. They trained the conspirators on how to use their weapons (Gavrilo Princip proved to be an apt pupil) and then smuggled the three men across the border into Bosnia. Everything was done by word of mouth. Furnished with bombs from the Belgrade arsenal as well as guns and poison, since they were also supposed to kill themselves, the men reached Sarajevo and joined others committed to the plot. The Black Hand had launched its transnational terror plot. The reasons for Apis' decision for the plot remain uncertain. Clearly he

---

[22] Clark, *Sleepwalkers*, pp. 3–42; Vladimir Dedijer, *The Road to Sarajevo* (New York: Simon & Schuster, 1966), pp. 373–400; David MacKenzie, *Apis, the Congenial Conspirator: The Life of Colonel Dragutin Dimitrijević* (Boulder, CO: East European Monographs, 1989), pp. 123–138; David MacKenzie, *The "Black Hand" on Trial: Salonika, 1917* (New York: East European Monographs, 1995); Mark Cornwall, "Serbia," in Keith Wilson (ed.), *Decisions for War, 1914* (New York: St. Martin's Press, 1995), pp. 55–96; Samuel R. Williamson, Jr. and Russell Van Wyk (eds.), *July 1914: Soldiers, Statesmen, and the Coming of the Great War: A Brief Documentary History* (Boston, MA: Bedford/St. Martin's Press, 2003), pp. 15–42.

hoped to damage Habsburg rule and thwart any possible realignment of Habsburg policy toward south Slavs, by which he really meant Serbs, under Franz Ferdinand as ruler. It also remains unclear whether any of the Russian staff assigned to Belgrade knew of the plot. The writer, for one, agrees with Albertini that Victor Artamonov, the Russian military attaché, probably knew of it.[23]

What Clark makes clear, as earlier writers had, including Fay and Albertini, is that Serbia's official government learned of the plot in early June. The minister of the interior, Stojan Protić, warned Pašić of dire consequences if the plot went forward. The Serbian Cabinet may have discussed the problem, because some members of the Cabinet knew of it. Belatedly, Pašić did three things: he sought to close the border, far too tardily, and thus of no use; he confronted Apis and the army leadership about it, only to have them dissemble; and he had the Serbian minister in Vienna, Jovan Jovanović, offer a warning to Leon Biliński, the Habsburg minister in charge of Bosnia. Alas, Jovanović was himself a member of the Black Hand, and his warning to Biliński was so obscure that the Habsburg official did not grasp the full import of the communication.

Pašić, knowing the power of the Black Hand and the murderous reputation of men like Apis, had done what he could to thwart the plot. But the stark fact remains that the Serbian government, just as Vienna suspected on June 29, had knowledge of the plot. Further, this knowledge meant that Pašić, after the success of the plot, could never acknowledge his attempts to foil the plot and had to block any effort to investigate further. With his analysis of the Serbian role, from the very first chapter in *The Sleepwalkers*, Clark has reminded contemporaries of the nature of terrorism, and of the unprecedented nature of a transnational assassination in European politics in 1914. In sum, he has helped to reshape the debate on the origins.[24]

Into this uneasy international and political milieu on Sunday, June 28, at the corner of Franz Josef Street, came the assassinations of Franz Ferdinand and his wife Sophie. If only the driver of the car had received the correct orders, he would never have paused and Princip would not have had his chance.

Exactly one month later, on July 28, Austria-Hungary declared war on Serbia. Princip's two shots brought the "perfect storm."[25]

---

[23] Clark, *Sleepwalkers*, pp. 411–412, is not sure, but argues that it makes no difference. Albertini, *Origins of the War of 1914*, vol. 2, pp. 82–86, is sure, as is Sean McMeekin, *The Russian Origins of the First World War* (Cambridge, MA: Belknap Press of Harvard University Press, 2011), pp. 47–50.

[24] Clark, *Sleepwalkers*, pp. 3–64.

[25] After the first abortive attack on the archduke that resulted in the wounding of an officer in the official party, General Oskar Potiorek, Governor-General of Bosnia-Herzegovina and

Austria-Hungary and the "hangman's noose"

An important reason for the erosion of the German paradigm has been the renewed interest in the role of Vienna and its initial decisions for war, even before there was any alleged German pressure on Vienna. The points can be quickly cited.[26]

Archduke Franz Ferdinand had, in life, been a force for peace; now, ironically, his death became the galvanizing event for Vienna's decision to attack Serbia. It did not take long for Austro-Hungarian investigators to link some of the assassins to contacts and training in Belgrade. On June 30, two days after the murders, Count Leopold Berchtold, the Habsburg foreign minister, had already resolved for war; indeed, he was very likely the only person in July 1914 who could have prevented the war had he changed his mind, for his advice deeply swayed Emperor Franz Joseph. Had he resolved for peace, the emperor would have accepted that approach. But he did not; he opted for war and told that to Franz Joseph. On July 3, Berchtold and Emperor Franz Joseph talked of war. The aging emperor had two conditions: (1) a pledge of unequivocal German support; and (2) the consent of Hungarian Prime Minister István Tisza.[27]

the archduke's host, decided to alter the planned trip into the middle of Sarajevo. But he forgot to tell his driver of the change in plans, thus the driver turned as originally scheduled at the fateful corner, only to be ordered to back up. Princip then stepped forward and fired. On this incident, see Rudolf Jeřábek, *Potiorek: General im Schatten von Sarajevo* (Graz: Verlag Styria, 1991), pp. 84–87.

[26] Manfried Rauchensteiner, *Der Tod des Doppeladlers: Österreich-Ungarn und der Erste Weltkrieg* (Graz: Verlag Styria, 1993), pp. 68–136; Günther Kronenbitter, *"Krieg im Frieden": Die Führung der k.u.k. Armee und die Großmachtpolitik Österreich-Ungarns 1906–1914* (Munich: Oldenbourg, 2003), pp. 455–486; Samuel R. Williamson, Jr., *Austria-Hungary and the Origins of the First World War* (New York: Macmillan, 1991), pp. 190–216; Herwig, *The First World War*, pp. 6–42; Lawrence Sondhaus, *Franz Conrad von Hötzendorf: Architect of the Apocalypse* (Boston, MA: Humanities Press, 2000), pp. 139–148; Fritz Fellner, "Die 'Mission Hoyos'" [1976], and "Zwischen Kriegsbegeisterung und Resignation – ein Memorandum des Sektionschefs Forgách von Jänner 1915" [1975], in Heidrun Maschl and Brigitte Mazohl-Wallnig (eds.), *Vom Dreibund zum Völkerbund: Studien zur Geschichte der internationalen Beziehungen, 1882–1919* (Vienna: Verlag für Geschichte & Politik, 1994), pp. 112–154. See also F. R. Bridge, *The Habsburg Monarchy among the Great Powers, 1815–1918* (New York: Berg, 1990), pp. 335–344; John Leslie, "The Antecedents of Austria-Hungary's War Aims: Policies and Policy-Makers in Vienna and Budapest Before and During 1914," in Elisabeth Springer and Leopold Kammerhold (eds.), *Archiv und Forschung: Das Haus-, Hof- und Staatsarchiv in seiner Bedeutung für die Geschichte Österreichs und Europas* (Vienna: Verlag für Geschichte & Politik, 1993), pp. 307–394; John Leslie, "Österreich-Ungarn vor dem Kriegsausbruch: Der Ballhausplatz in Wien im Juli 1914 aus der Sicht eines Österreichisch-Ungarischen Diplomaten," in Ralph Melville, Claus Scharf, Martin Vogt, and Ulrich Wengenroth (eds.), *Deutschland und Europa in der Neuzeit* (Stuttgart: Franz Steiner, 1988), pp. 661–684.

[27] Samuel R. Williamson, Jr., "Leopold Count Berchtold: The Man Who Could Have Prevented the Great War," in Günter Bischof, Fritz Plasser, and Peter Berger (eds.), *From Empire to Republic: Post-World War I Austria* (University of New Orleans Press,

Kaiser Wilhelm II did not come to Vienna for the funeral of his friend Franz Ferdinand for fear of another attack. So, on the night of July 4, Berchtold sent one of his senior assistants, Alexander Hoyos, to Berlin with a letter from the emperor and a memorandum proposal for action. In a series of meetings on July 5 and 6, the German leadership, including Kaiser Wilhelm II and Bethmann-Hollweg, agreed to support Vienna.[28] The "blank check" had been given. The German rulers considered the question of Russian intervention, but put a low probability on it. The kaiser wanted a quick, short punitive war; he wanted Vienna to start at once, a view that Hoyos apparently suggested would happen. In their hope for prompt action, the Germans would be thoroughly frustrated.[29]

Clark has reexamined the German decision in detail. His analysis is set in the context of alliance considerations and Germany's belief that their chief ally had to be supported. The Berlin leadership recognized that Russia might intervene, but concluded that the chances for victory were far greater in 1914 than they would be after Russia's scheduled rearmament was completed in 1917. In that sense, the German decision was a calculated risk in response to the Habsburg request. It was not a deliberate attempt to start a war because of Sarajevo. The German and Austrian expectations of the Russian reaction were both wildly inaccurate, and will be discussed below.[30]

Almost immediately the Austrians managed to upend one of the principal assumptions behind German support: quick action. First, Berchtold could not convince Tisza to agree to a military solution until July 14. Second, the foreign minister sought a "smoking gun" that linked Princip directly with the Serbian government; this effort failed, even though

---

2010), pp. 24–51; Kronenbitter, *"Krieg im Frieden"*, pp. 455–519. Also see the provocative articles by Paul W. Schroeder, "World War I as Galloping Gertie: A Reply to Joachim Remak," *Journal of Modern History* 44(3) (1972): 319–345; Paul W. Schroeder, "Stealing Horses to Great Applause: Austria-Hungary's Decision in 1914 in System Perspective," in Holger Afflerbach and David Stevenson (eds.), *An Improbable War? The Outbreak of World War I and European Political Culture* (New York: Berghahn, 2007), pp. 17–42.

[28] Röhl, *Wilhelm II*, pp. 1066–1089; Stig Förster, "Im Reich des Absurden: Die Ursachen des Ersten Weltkrieges," in Bernd Wegner, Ernst Willi Hansen, Kerstin Rehwinkel, and Matthias Reiss (eds.), *Wie Kriege enstehen: Zum Historischen Hintergrund von Staatenpolitik* (Paderborn: Ferdinand Schöningh, 2000), pp. 211–252.

[29] Clark, *Sleepwalkers*, pp. 404–422; Christopher Clark, *Kaiser Wilhelm II: Profiles in Power* (London: Longman, 2000), pp. 197–211; for a recent restatement of German pressure, see Röhl, *Wilhelm II*, pp. 1067–1089; also Fischer, *War of Illusions*, pp. 461–492.

[30] Clark, *Sleepwalkers*, pp. 412–423.

Vienna knew a great deal about the Black Hand and the recent political turmoil in Belgrade.[31]

A final reason for the delay stemmed from actions taken previously by the greatest of the "hawks" in 1914. General Franz Conrad von Hötzendorf, Chief of the Habsburg General Staff, had earlier instituted a policy of "harvest leaves," allowing troops to return to their homes to help with the harvest. By July 6, after the German commitment, Conrad learned that thousands of troops were actually scattered across the monarchy. To recall them now would reveal the attack plans, so he simply canceled further leaves while allowing the others to end as scheduled around July 22. Organizational routines had thwarted Berchtold's efforts for action, though it must also be noted that Conrad's definition of quick action – sixteen days – did not match that of the Germans. Nor does it explain why the general failed to have an operational plan for the seizure of Belgrade, which lay just across from Habsburg territory.[32]

Berchtold was thus trapped in a situation that he could not easily accelerate. The delay would mean that the long-planned state visit by Poincaré and Viviani to Russia would be taking place when he wanted the ultimatum, clearly intended to be unacceptable, to be delivered in Belgrade. So Vienna delayed, to the dismay of Berlin, setting the delivery date on July 23 with a deadline of forty-eight hours.

The long delay had two other consequences. First, Vienna lulled Europe, engaging in deliberate deceptions that did little to foster good will. Second, indiscretions in Berlin and Vienna, along with code intercepts, meant that St. Petersburg was not surprised by the ultimatum, despite pretending otherwise.[33]

The rest of the sad story is familiar. Vienna sent the ultimatum and refused pleas to extend the deadline. It also rejected the Serbian reply, which met most of the demands. But, in a point often overlooked, Serbia did balk at the *one* essential demand: an investigation of the plot by

[31] On Vienna's knowledge of the Black Hand, see Barbara Jelavich, "What the Habsburg Government Knew about the Black Hand," *Austrian History Yearbook* 22(10) (1991): 131–150. See also Friedrich Würthle, *Die Spur führt nach Belgrad: Die Hintergründe des Dramas von Sarajevo 1914* (Vienna: Fritz Molden, 1975); Friedrich Würthle, "Dokumente zum Sarajevoprozess," *Mitteilungen des Österreichischen Staatsarchivs*, Erganzungsband 9 (Vienna, 1978).

[32] Samuel R. Williamson, Jr., "Confrontation with Serbia: The Consequences of Vienna's Failure to Achieve Surprise in July 1914," *Mitteilungen des Österreichischen Staatsarchivs* (1993): 167–177; see also Kronenbitter, *"Krieg im Frieden"*, pp. 487–519. Lebow, *A Cultural Theory*, pp. 348–352, provides an interesting approach to the decision process in Vienna.

[33] Williamson and Van Wyk (eds.), *July 1914: Soldiers*, pp. 160–167; Albertini, *Origins of the War of 1914*, vol. 2, pp. 220–241; Schmidt, *Frankreichs*, pp. 70–81.

Habsburg officials inside Serbia. That was a point that Pašić could not concede, since it would reveal the warnings that he and others had received about the plot.[34]

On July 25, as soon as the rejection took place, Emperor Franz Joseph authorized some military measures across the monarchy, with the first troop mobilizations to take place on July 28. Naturally Russian intelligence noticed. Simultaneously, an alarmed Berlin now realized that Russia might not stay out of any local Austro-Serbian war, and began a series of efforts, not well coordinated, to slow the momentum to war, even suggesting that Vienna be content with simply occupying Belgrade.

But Berchtold wanted his war, as did Conrad, who hoped martial successes might make possible marital success with his beloved Gina von Reininghaus. To thwart any foreign intrusion, Berchtold now convinced the emperor to declare war on Serbia on July 28. That night, shots were fired along the riverfront near Belgrade, resulting in a few casualties. News of the attack quickly reached St. Petersburg, and general Russian mobilization came on July 30. This step, of course, threatened the very basis of German war planning. The Russian decision meant that there was now no chance of stopping a wider European war.[35]

Austria wanted, and got, its war with Serbia. The Austrian desire for military action is the essential difference from the earlier crises, whether in 1908–1909 or during the Balkan Wars. Why this desire? Fear, the restoration of prestige, possible territorial gain from the collapse of Serbia, the need to assert its Great Power status, a conviction that earlier failures to act had only made the international situation worse, and misplaced confidence in the judgment of General Conrad: all of these factors influenced the decision. With the hope that German support would deter Russia, the Habsburgs gambled everything. The somber judgment of Wilhelm II, made at the height of the crisis and quoted by Fay, remains valid: the Austrians had "made a hangman's noose for us."[36]

Germany confronts the new reality

The German reaction to the dilatory moves by Vienna brought concern that the Austrians were losing the opportunity to achieve a quick victory over Serbia. This led to efforts to encourage action, pressure often seen as

[34] Williamson and Van Wyk (eds.), *July 1914: Soldiers*, pp. 31–42; Cornwall, "Serbia," pp. 71–84.
[35] Rauchensteiner, *Der Tod des Doppeladlers*, pp. 87–127; Kronenbitter, "*Krieg im Frieden*", pp. 503–519. On Conrad's love affair with Gina von Reininghaus and eventual marriage, see Sondhaus, *Conrad*, pp. 108–116, 151–153, 180–200.
[36] Fay, *Origins of the World War*, vol. 2, p. 223.

inciting the Austrians to war, rather than as a more understandable desire to see the policy decisions implemented. Initially, the German kaiser continued on his annual North Sea cruise, albeit rather closer to home than usual. General Helmuth von Moltke, Chief of the Prussian General Staff, remained away from Berlin, and Bethmann-Hollweg made occasional trips to Berlin from his estate in the weeks before the ultimatum reached Belgrade. On July 7, the German naval staff reviewed plans, as did the army staff, but no overt preparations were made and there was no mobilization of the German fleet.[37] Even after the ultimatum was delivered, senior officials in Berlin still did not visualize a war, or at most they expected a localized, punitive Austrian move against Serbia.

But the situation changed rapidly after July 25. First, Moltke returned to Berlin. Then, reports began to arrive on July 25–26 of activity in Russia that suggested a move to mobilization. These were the first overt signs that Russia was taking measures "preparatory to mobilization," steps that rapidly created concern in Berlin. Still, Germany took no military countermeasures. Bethmann-Hollweg, fearing that such actions might trigger a further Russian reaction, was still convinced that the crisis could be contained. With the return of the kaiser on July 27, things got more complicated and Bethmann-Hollweg sought to keep control of the situation, a point that those who support the German paradigm rightly note. Wilhelm wanted the chancellor to pressure Vienna, a step that he accepted and then hesitated to implement. This allowed Berchtold to proceed with a declaration of war on July 28 for fear of further German hesitancy. Nor did the Austrian minister give more attention later to the quite sensible "Halt in Belgrade" proposal that came from Berlin.[38]

By July 28 the Prussian General Staff had concluded that Russia was on the verge of partial mobilization. Meanwhile, War Minister Erich von Falkenhayn pressured Moltke to move more assertively. This prompted Moltke's long analysis to Bethmann-Hollweg on the need for action. But the chancellor resisted, hoping that the Russians might waver or desist. At the same time he was assessing the need to make any war appear to be defensive, with Russia seen as the aggressor. To do so would help to dampen resistance to a war from the German socialists. This consideration led in part to the famous "Willy–Nicky" letters in a belated attempt

---

[37] For details of the naval review, see entry for July 7, 1914, from the diary of Vice-Admiral Albert Hopman, *Das ereignisreiche Leben eines "Wilhelminers": Tagebücher, Briefe, Aufzeichnungen 1901 bis 1920*, ed. Michael Epkenhans (Munich: Oldenbourg, 2004), pp. 382–386; cf. Copeland, *Origins of Major War*, p. 87.

[38] Röhl, *Wilhelm II*, pp. 1109–1126; Clark, *Sleepwalkers*, pp. 515–523; Canis, *Der Weg*, pp. 663–668.

to contain the crisis, but to no avail. On July 30, the Russians declared general mobilization.[39]

Even then the Germans did not immediately respond militarily. Moltke insisted on seeing documents proclaiming the Russian mobilization, which did not reach him until noon on July 31. With this evidence in hand, he and Bethmann-Hollweg realized that the chances for peace had vanished. Berlin demanded that St. Petersburg and Paris cease their military measures or else face war; neither did. On Saturday, August 1, Germany declared war on Russia. But this action was less a preventive measure that assured war, than a measured step that reflected a realistic assessment of Russia's deliberate decision to confront Austria-Hungary over Serbia. The July 5–6 decisions in Berlin to support Vienna had assumed a quick, punitive war, and that Russia would stay out. There had been no quick, punitive war, and intelligence indicated that Russia had decided from the start to take a militant stance rather than negotiate further.[40]

In the late afternoon, on Saturday, August 1, one last glimmer of hope emerged. A message from London suggested that the British might stay out, a step that the kaiser had always hoped would be the case (Bethmann-Hollweg was far less sanguine, because of his spy in the Russian embassy in London). This message led Wilhelm II to summon Moltke and demand that he think about an invasion just of Russia, apparently unaware that the war plans had abandoned that option in 1913. The general said it was not possible. The kaiser then ordered the general to issue orders delaying any attack in the west against Luxembourg; this Moltke did, but quite reluctantly. Then hours later came word from London that hopes for British neutrality were nonexistent. The kaiser, near midnight, rescinded his opposition and the war plans rolled ahead. The invasion of Belgium was only hours away.[41]

New approaches: the Franco-Russian alliance and the Balkans

The Franco-Russian alliance, Barnes charged in the 1920s, had started the Great War; no other revisionist made the case so stridently. Indeed, usually the more that historians blame Berlin (and sometimes Vienna) for

---

[39] Mombauer, *Helmuth von Moltke*, pp. 208–211; Clark, *Sleepwalkers*, pp. 512–513, 523–524. Also, Röhl, *Wilhelm II*, pp. 1004–1010, for discussions in late 1913 and on the July 1914 letters, pp. 1129–1135.

[40] Copeland, *Origins of Major War*, p. 109; Clark, *Sleepwalkers*, pp. 524–530.

[41] Clark, *Sleepwalkers*, pp. 527–533; Mombauer, *Helmuth von Moltke*, pp. 202–226.

the war, the more they see Russia and France as simply reacting to events, not initiating them. The current writer has certainly taken that position toward France. A wholly new conceptual approach and new archival research in both France and Russia suggest a far more aggressive Russian and French foreign policy after 1911.[42]

Poincaré's arrival in power, first as premier and then as president of France, had seen a single-minded focus on strengthening the Triple Entente and the alliance with Russia, and he was successful on both counts. But the new studies take the position much further, arguing convincingly that the Franco-Russian alliance had, by the summer of 1914, become Balkanized. The dramatic power shifts in the Balkans saw the French offer financial support to Serbia, and agree to follow Russia's lead in its policies toward Romania and Bulgaria as well as Serbia. Implicit in the Franco-Russian support for Serbia was the assumption that eventually the Serbs might gain further territory, such as Bosnia-Herzegovina, from a possible collapse of Austria-Hungary. For pan-Slavs in Russia, this prospect assumed the significance of something akin to a holy grail; and the Russian Cabinet shuffles in early 1914 accelerated this process. In the new Russian government, the aging Ivan Goremykin served as premier, but his minister of agriculture, Alexander Krivoshein, became the strong personality in the government, and he was an ardent pan-Slavist. An assertive Russian policy in the Balkans and at the Straits had gained new support.[43]

Three additional points that buttress the strength of these new assessments about Franco-Russian policy must be made. First, Sazonov, though he looked like a banker rather than a skilled diplomat, played an aggressive hand during the Balkan Wars and in his efforts to woo Romania away from its secret connection to the Triple Alliance. He had his detractors, but his Balkan successes protected him. Second, Sazonov gave free rein to Hartwig, the Russian minister in Belgrade, who had helped to

---

[42] Barnes, *Genesis*, esp. chs. 6 and 7; Schmidt, *Frankreichs*, pp. 246–312; Clark, *Sleepwalkers*, pp. 349–364, 433–450; Keiger, *Poincaré*, pp. 190–192. See also David MacLaren McDonald, *United Government and Foreign Policy in Russia, 1900–1914* (Cambridge, MA: Harvard University Press, 1992), pp. 199–207; Dietrich Geyer, *Der russische Imperialismus: Studien über den Zusammenhang von innerer und auswärtiger Politik, 1860–1914* (Göttingen: Vandenhoeck & Ruprecht, 1977), pp. 189–258; translated as *Russian Imperialism: The Interaction of Domestic and Foreign Policy, 1860–1914*, trans. Bruce Little (New Haven, CT: Yale University Press, 1987), pp. 249–346.

[43] Clark, *Sleepwalkers*, pp. 314–361; McMeekin, *Russian Origins*, pp. 30–40. A new multi-faceted study by Sean McMeekin, *July 1914: Countdown to War* (New York: Basic Books, 2013), assigns principal responsibility to Russia for the general war, while casting blame on all the states involved in July 1914. Well argued, if erratically documented, McMeekin's new work is a recent example of the erosion of the German paradigm.

create the Balkan League. The minister had then adroitly assisted Serbia during the Balkan Wars, and had carefully schemed for the day when the Habsburg monarchy might be ripe for the picking. Hartwig inspired no confidence in Vienna, where there were careful calibrations of his influence on Serbian politics. Ironically, on July 10, Hartwig visited the Austrian legation in Belgrade, and while there he died of a heart attack. Though there were rumors of foul play, his heart problems were readily accepted as the reason for his death. His importance to Serbia was clearly described by the French minister in Belgrade, who wrote to Paris that Hartwig had died "at the very moment when his 'indomitable will' had triumphed by 'imposing on Serbism his absolute authority, and on Europe the Serbian question in the violent form dear to his heart.' "[44]

Third, Sazonov and his tsarist colleagues never lost sight of the Russian desire for control of the Straits if the Ottoman Empire tottered to an end. One does not have to agree with McMeekin's often-caustic analysis of Russian policy to recognize that Russia had its own imperial goals in 1914, just as did Germany and the other powers. While Clark notes Russian interest in the Straits, his stress rests chiefly with the Balkans. On the other hand, Canis explores at some length the Russian ambitions at Constantinople, and reminds readers of the tensions that existed between Russia and Britain over this issue.[45]

A key part of the new arguments about the July Crisis focuses on the Franco-Russian actions during the visit of Poincaré and Viviani to Russia and the initial decisions taken by the Russian government upon learning of the ultimatum. In early July the German ambassador to Italy, Hans von Flotow, informed the Italian Foreign Minister Antonino San Giuliano of Berlin's expectation that Vienna would take strong action against Belgrade. The foreign minister then sent two sets of telegrams to his envoys abroad with this information, including to St. Petersburg and at least one to Vienna. In both instances the local decryption operations quickly broke the coded telegrams. This information also appears to have been communicated to Belgrade, because on July 19 Pašić sent telegrams to his diplomats stating that Belgrade would not be cowed by Vienna. The intelligence about Austrian plans, as well as indiscretions in Vienna and the request for information on the departure time of the French delegation on July 23, leaves no doubt that the Russians were well informed of

---

[44] Quoted in Clark, *Sleepwalkers*, pp. 432 and 430–432.
[45] McMeekin, *Russian Origins*, pp. 1–75; Schmidt, *Frankreichs*, pp. 55–104; Ronald Bobroff, *Roads to Glory: Late Imperial Russia and the Turkish Straits* (London: I. B. Tauris, 2006), pp. 20–95; Clark, *Sleepwalkers*, pp. 341–355; Canis, *Der Weg*, pp. 599–610.

Vienna's intentions.[46] Thus, as Schmitt and Clark explain, the leaders of the French and Russian governments had plenty of opportunity to discuss their response to Vienna. Indeed, immediately upon his arrival in St. Petersburg, Poincaré warned Habsburg ambassador Friedrich Szápáry that "any Austrian action would produce 'a situation dangerous for peace.'"[47]

Clark explores in detail the visit and the increasingly inconsequential part played by Viviani, who seems to have become ill over the thought of possible action, and the consequential part played by French ambassador Maurice Paléologue, who had become as zealous as the Russians in their support of Serbia. The net result of the Franco-Russian discussions seems clear: the two governments would support Serbia in all circumstances, would allow no chastisement of Serbia, and were prepared to go to war if necessary. At a diplomatic reception, Poincaré expressed the view that war was likely, a position that French ambassador Paléologue supported. Schmidt further argues that Poincaré gave strong assurances of French support to Tsar Nicholas, just at the moment of the French president's departure for home on the afternoon of July 23. He believes that the French were, in fact, worried that the Russians might not be strong enough in their response to the Serbian plight.[48]

The net result of this new conceptual approach to the Franco-Russian alliance is to give it far more importance during the crisis. Germany gave Vienna a "blank check," Paris gave Russia a "blank check," and France and Russia gave Belgrade a "blank check." A more benign assessment of the alliance on the road to war now seems less assured than nearly a century ago. In the contemporary age, when acts of terrorism bring some form of response, the Franco-Russian determination to allow Serbia to flaunt its support of terrorism offers a new perspective on the summer of 1914 even as the situation was perhaps novel in 1914.

The French delegation had hardly left St. Petersburg on July 23 when the ultimatum with its forty-eight-hour deadline arrived at the Serbian Foreign Ministry. When word of the document reached Sazonov the next morning, he is famously reported to have said: "this is a European war." By late morning he was exploring the possibility of a partial mobilization

---

[46] D. C. B. Lieven, *Russia and the Origins of the First World War* (New York: Macmillan, 1983), p. 140, asserts that the Russians were completely surprised by the ultimatum. That view is simply not correct. See Albertini, *Origins of the War of 1914*, vol. 2, pp. 183–187. From the middle of July, thanks to code intercepts, Sazonov knew that Vienna planned some dramatic action; Schmidt, *Frankreichs*, pp. 74–78.

[47] Clark, *Sleepwalkers*, p. 445; Williamson and Van Wyk (eds.), *July 1914: Soldiers*, pp. 33–35, 128–147, 159–162.

[48] Schmidt, *Frankreichs*, pp. 75–82; Clark, *Sleepwalkers*, pp. 443–450.

with the Russian military, in effect seeking to duplicate the pressure brought against Vienna in the fall of 1912. Later that day, a ministerial council agreed to start certain military measures at once in four Russian districts. Those actions were to be part of what was euphemistically called the "period preparatory to mobilization." The measures went into effect on July 25 and, though designed to intimidate Vienna, were immediately detected by German intelligence operatives. Historians differ about these early Russian military moves, some seeing them merely as precautions, others as actual mobilization steps.[49]

But two points should be made about these measures. First, the "preparatory measures" initiated on July 24 and 25 were sharply different from the *ad hoc* measures that Russia used during the First Balkan War to intimidate Austria-Hungary. In that instance troops had simply been retained on active duty across Russia at the end of their enlistments, and as part of a "trial mobilization" exercise and other measures were limited in geographical scope, focused chiefly against Austria. The measures taken in 1914 were part of a new program, "Period Preparatory to Mobilization," that went into effect in 1913 and were deliberately designed to accelerate later mobilization. None of the Austrian actions after July 23, it should be noted, came as a surprise to Sazonov. We now know, thanks to the work of Bruce Menning, that the Russians were reading in the fashion of Enigma, the coded Austrian telegrams to its embassy in St. Petersburg.[50] Russian military intelligence concluded early, based apparently on erroneous reports, that Austria's plans were aimed, not at Serbia, but at Russia, because the Habsburgs were believed to be mobilizing eleven corps rather than the eight needed for an attack on Serbia.[51]

More escalatory, even if Sazonov may not have realized it (and his grasp of military matters appears to have been limited), was the fact that such preparatory measures would take place along the entire Russian frontier, not just the Habsburg border. This meant that the German "tension travellers" sent out on July 26 soon picked up indications of Russian

[49] Clark, *Sleepwalkers*, pp. 471–487; McMeekin, *Russian Origins*, pp. 53–64; Menning, "The Mobilization Crises." See also Alex Marshall, "Russian Military Intelligence, 1905–1917: The Untold Story behind Tsarist Russia in the First World War," *War in History* 11(4) (2004): 393–423. For earlier views, see L. C. F. Turner, "The Russian Mobilization in 1914," *Journal of Contemporary History* 3(1) (1968): 65–88; Stevenson, *Armaments and the Coming of War*, pp. 379–384. On German intelligence reports about the Russian preparatory steps, see Ulrich Trumpener, "War Premeditated? German Intelligence Operations in July 1914," *Central European History* 9(1) (1976): 58–85.
[50] Turner, "Russian Mobilization," p. 67; Copeland, *Origins of Major War*, pp. 89, 96. Private communication from Menning to the author.
[51] Menning, "The Mobilization Crises"; Kronenbitter, *"Krieg im Frieden"*, pp. 473–486.

military activity along the German border. Thus, the measures, which were meant to be kept secret and designed to prepare Russia for mobilization, were quickly discovered, and fatefully by German intelligence.[52]

There is general agreement that Russia did not have an actual plan for partial mobilization. The military measures taken in the fall of 1912 were more *ad hoc* than part of any design, and there were no plans for a partial mobilization in 1914. In any event, by July 25, 1914, even before Germany had taken any steps toward its own mobilization, the Russian leadership had agreed upon a course of action that would assist its later mobilization.

From July 25 to July 29 Sazonov continued to talk as if partial mobilization was an option, even as the Russian military pressed for general mobilization. Certainly by July 29 the Russian General Staff wanted to plunge ahead, and were held back only by Tsar Nicholas II and his exchange of letters with Kaiser Wilhelm. But when news reached St. Petersburg of the attack on Belgrade, all doubts eased about the path to mobilization.[53]

What drove the Russian policymakers to make almost spontaneous decisions on the afternoon of July 24, before the Serbians had barely started to frame their reply to Vienna? To be sure, the Austrians appeared ready to strike Serbia, yet Russian intelligence knew that any actual military operation was at least two weeks away unless the Habsburg response was limited to the taking of Belgrade. Why not let the Austrians become embroiled with the Serbs, then mobilize and attack? Or did they fear that a delay might see international pressure for a conference that St. Petersburg could not resist? Or was it because they might have anticipated the imminent collapse of the Ottoman Empire? Or was Sazonov anxious to protect Russian interests in the Balkans and Serbia in particular? Or, as suggested above, did French pressure make St. Petersburg anxious not to appear hesitant? Then, there is another possibility, linking domestic with foreign policies, as David Stevenson and Hew Strachan have suggested: Russian fears of domestic unrest if St. Petersburg failed to protect its Slavic brothers, retreating once more as they had done in 1909. The fear of revolution and military unpreparedness had stymied action in 1909; this time the fear

[52] Trumpener, "War Premeditated?" pp. 66–72; Jack S. Levy, "Preferences, Constraints, and Choices in July 1914," *International Security* 15(3) (1990/1): 151–186, at 178–180; Van Evera, *Causes of War*, pp. 62, 139–143, 209, fn. 70; Marc Trachtenberg, *History and Strategy* (Princeton University Press, 1991), pp. 80–96; cf. Copeland, *Origins of Major War*, pp. 87–117.

[53] Clark gives a succinct account in *Sleepwalkers*, pp. 506–515; see also pp. 480–487.

of revolution may have spurred action. Those mobilization steps, taken for whatever set of reasons, guaranteed Sazonov's European war.[54]

New approaches: France, Great Britain, and Italy

France

Traditionally, historians have seen the French as the victim of their alliance with Russia and the nature of German war plans. The fact that Poincaré and Viviani were traveling by ship from July 23 until their return to Paris on July 29 has long been used to explain France's failure to restrain Russia or to prevent the Russian general mobilization on July 30. Now a far more cynical appraisal seems appropriate, starting with the obvious question: why did the two statesmen not leave the ship and take the overnight train back to Paris? And while we know that their ship had wireless radio contact with Paris, could the same have been true for St. Petersburg? What is clearly established is the inflammatory role played by Ambassador Paléologue, who gave Sazonov full support at every point and was later accused, mistakenly as it turns out, of deliberately delaying news of Russian mobilization from Paris. On the other hand, Clark has found evidence that by the time Poincaré returned to France he was convinced, "though there were still no signs of military counter-measures from Germany – that a European war could no longer be avoided."[55] Nor did the French make any effort to curb Russia, since French war plans were dependent on quick Russian assistance. Poincaré would do nothing to jeopardize that possibility. Still, because he wanted to assure London that he was doing something to restrain his Russian ally, Poincaré sent a carefully worded telegram to Sazonov at 4 am on July 30 that appeared to urge caution. The true purpose sounds entirely plausible; Poincaré wanted to do everything he could to ensure that the British would not bolt from his new Balkanization policy. To ensure this further, he ordered General Joseph Joffre to keep French troops 10 km back from the German border, to avoid the suggestion that France had started a war. Then his chief worries turned to ensuring that Britain would enter the war; and that decision would not come easily.[56]

[54] Stevenson, *Armaments and the Coming of War*, p. 387; Strachan, *The First World War*, vol. 1, p. 83; Menning, "The Mobilization Crises."
[55] Clark, *Sleepwalkers*, pp. 503, 503–506; Hayne, *French Foreign Office*, pp. 267–295; Keiger, *Poincaré*, pp. 170–183.
[56] Clark, *Sleepwalkers*, pp. 503–506; Robert A. Doughty, *Pyrrhic Victory: French Strategy and Operations in the Great War* (Cambridge, MA: Harvard University Press, 2005), pp. 4–56; Williamson and Van Wyk (eds.), *July 1914: Soldiers*, pp. 202–217.

Great Britain

France now looked to London. For days that decision did not come. For decades Sir Edward Grey, the British foreign secretary, enjoyed a good press from historians. That esteem has slowly faded, started first by Albertini and then by the work of Zara Steiner, and continued by other historians. Grey, despite the frank statements from Lichnowsky on July 6, was not unduly alarmed about a European crisis, though on July 9 he did again tell the German ambassador that there was no secret, binding agreement with France or Russia. This statement verged on duplicity as a small number in Berlin knew. Then, while the Irish question engulfed British politics for more than two weeks, Grey remained on the sidelines.

At the Foreign Office various senior officials followed events on the Continent, but none was too alarmed. Ambassador Sir Rennell Rodd in Rome and others in the Foreign Office in Whitehall saw the need for Russia to restrain Serbia. But Permanent Under-Secretary Sir Arthur Nicolson, one of the most pro-Russian members of the Foreign Office, thought the Germans were calling all the shots. British diplomats had, for many reasons, limited faith in the survival of the Habsburg monarchy, so direct negotiations or contact with Vienna did not rank high on their agenda.[57]

Not until news of the Vienna ultimatum did Grey become more involved, seeking belatedly to convene some of the Great Powers in order to mediate the situation. Throughout July he operated as if the situation was similar to 1912: that war would not come even if the Russians mobilized; that he had time to check the slide to actual hostilities; and that Britain would be the pivotal arbiter. Nor could he ignore the possibility of strong opposition in the British Cabinet to the prospect of any involvement in a Continental war. Ireland, not Europe, was the vital problem of the moment.[58]

By Sunday, August 2, Grey had almost decided to resign, a step that would break up the Liberal government and bring a coalition government, with Tory participation, to power. Indeed, that is just what the conspiratorially minded General Henry Wilson, Director of Military Operations, sought as he worked tirelessly to rally the Unionists to war. The deciding

---

[57] T. G. Otte, *The Foreign Office Mind: The Making of British Foreign Policy, 1865–1914* (Cambridge University Press, 2011), pp. 374–392.

[58] Clark, *Sleepwalkers*, pp. 488–498; Zara S. Steiner and Keith Neilson, *Britain and the Origins of the First World War*, 2nd edn. (Basingstoke: Palgrave Macmillan, 2003), pp. 229–257; Keith Robbins, *Sir Edward Grey* (London: Cassell, 1971), pp. 264–297; Samuel R. Williamson, Jr., *The Politics of Grand Strategy, Britain and France Prepare for War, 1904–1914* (Cambridge, MA: Harvard University Press, 1969), pp. 344–361; Williamson and Van Wyk (eds.), *July 1914: Soldiers*, pp. 218–256.

action came from a letter sent to the Cabinet on Sunday, August 2, by Andrew Bonar Law, leader of the Tories, supporting intervention. That intrusion, a thorough mixing of domestic politics with international considerations, deeply affected many of the hesitant Liberal ministers. Then the Germans made it easier with their demands on Belgium. This summary represents a general agreement about British actions for two or more decades among historians.[59]

Nicholas Lambert, in his book *Planning Armageddon: British Economic Warfare and the First World War* (2012), has recently put the Cabinet's decisions in a much broader economic context, with a description of British grand strategy that significantly modifies the accepted wisdom. He argues that by the end of 1912 the Committee of Imperial Defence and the Admiralty had agreed upon a policy of economic warfare. This policy would seek to inflict maximum damage on the German economy the moment the war started. While there might be a great naval showdown, the strategy dealt with less heroic actions: blockading the entire North Sea; government control of all British shipping; stopping trade through neutral ports; direction of the financial markets; and the severance of German communication links with the rest of the world. Future problems with the United States were noted, but accepted. It was this strategy, Lambert argues, that formed the subtext of Grey's famous August 3 speech to Parliament about the relatively light damage that British participation in the war would involve. Only later would the Cabinet consent to accept army intervention on the Continent, and even then with the condition that two divisions remain at home for the preservation of order.[60]

But Lambert has gone further; he has put the Cabinet considerations in the context of the near-collapse of the world economy in the last week of July 1914. The entire week offers echoes the chaos of American financial markets in September 2008. The data are staggering: on July 27, the Vienna stock market closed because of the flurry of transactions; on July 28–29,

---

[59] Clark, *Sleepwalkers*, pp. 541–551; Williamson, "General Henry Wilson," pp. 91–105; Steiner and Neilson, *Britain*, pp. 249–254. For a contrarian view about British entry, see Niall Ferguson, *The Pity of War: Explaining World War I* (New York: Basic Books, 1999), pp. 143–173.

[60] Nicholas A. Lambert, *Planning Armageddon: British Economic Warfare and the First World War* (Cambridge, MA: Harvard University Press, 2012). Matthew S. Seligmann, *The Royal Navy and the German Threat, 1901–1914: Admiralty Plans to Protect British Trade in a War Against Germany* (Oxford University Press, 2012), approaches the topic from a bilateral dimension that offers useful insights without the overall approach of Lambert. Also see Keith Wilson, "Britain," in Wilson (ed.), *Decisions for War*, pp. 175–208. Strachan provides an extensive, overall assessment of the economic crisis at the start of the war, but does not relate it to the British decision for war, *The First World War*, vol. 1, pp. 815–827; the entire chapter is a superb analysis of war finance for the war as a whole.

firms on Wall Street dealt only with sell orders from Europe; and by July 31 exchanges around the world were closed. Simultaneously, a liquidity crisis occurred as investors sought gold. The discount rate quickly rose to 10 percent. The credit markets were paralyzed. Nowhere was the panic more acute than in London, the center of the world's financial system. Cabinet ministers were aghast; the forthcoming bank holiday was extended for the entire first week of August. There were genuine fears of a collapse of the entire British economy and of massive labor unrest.[61]

The suddenness of this economic challenge put Grey in an awkward position. On July 31 he thought Britain might have to stand aside just to preserve its economic standing. As Lambert shows in his analysis of the Cabinet discussions, the impact of economics criss-crossed that of grand strategy. Britain's world position was under attack in a manner few had anticipated; the pressures upon the Cabinet were multiple. Not surprisingly, the Cabinet also saw intervention in the war as a way to calm the markets, a point to which Grey alluded in several different forms in his parliamentary remarks. In that sense, the question of Belgium not only brought Britain into the war, it also helped to calm the British economic situation.[62]

Indeed, the policy of economic warfare might just work. Its early success, as Lambert describes it, so terrified the London financial community that they soon forced the government to ease some of the policies. Money became more important than casualties. Then came the trenches, and the war did, indeed, become very costly.

Italy

For one power, Italy, the soldiers were mobilized in July 1914, but did not immediately go to war; that would come only in April 1915. The story of Italy's role in the origins of the war can be summarized quickly. Albertini remains a useful guide to tracking Rome's policy during July. He had mostly caustic comments to make about Foreign Minister San Giuliano's decision to try to barter for Italy's intervention by the surrender of

---

[61] Lambert, *Planning Armageddon*, pp. 185–231. Both German and Russian financiers started to move funds on the instructions of their governments even before the large mobilizations had occurred. See also David Rowe, "The Tragedy of Liberalism: How Globalization Caused the First World War," *Security Studies* 14(3) (2005): 407–447.

[62] See Lambert, *Planning Armageddon*, for more details of, first, the implementation and, then, the steady reduction of measures, due to pressures from the financial community. For Grey's speech to Parliament on Monday, August 3, 1914, see Great Britain, *Parliamentary Debates*, House of Commons, 5th series, vol. LXV, 1914, cols. 1809–1834, and many other places.

Habsburg territory occupied by Italians, a moral choice that meant Italy was prepared to sacrifice Serbia for its own ends.[63]

From the beginning of the crisis Vienna resolved to ignore Italy, a decision that the Germans accepted in early July and then sought to reverse thereafter. On July 11, Germany did inform its ambassador, Flotow, that Vienna might take strong measures against Serbia, and the ambassador conveyed this to the Italians, whether indiscreetly or deliberately is unclear. In any event, by July 14, Foreign Minister San Giuliano was informing his emissaries of possible Habsburg moves, and did so again on July 16. While San Giuliano remonstrated with Berlin, Vienna kept its counsel, after breaking the Italian codes and learning of the German leak. Rome did not receive an advance copy of the ultimatum. Upon receiving it on July 24, San Giuliano declared that the proposed action violated section 7 of the secret Triple Alliance and started to negotiate for territorial concessions. During this period he made no effort to inform the Italian military leadership of his thinking. Indeed, not until July 29 did the Italian army have a new chief of staff, General Luigi Cardona, to replace General Alberto Pollio who had died unexpectedly on July 1. While the diplomats strove to gain advantage for Italy, Cardona, working from Pollio's previously agreed upon war plans with General Conrad, set about honoring Italy's military obligations to the Triple Alliance. Not until August 2 did he discover that the Italian government had decided on a policy of neutrality, which it proclaimed the next day. Of this confusion within the Italian government, Albertini has only scorching comments to make.[64]

Observations and the future research agenda

The erosion of the German paradigm ends a unilateral approach to the July Crisis, focused mainly on Berlin, and with Berlin the chief aggressor in the crisis. As Hart wrote in the *New York Times* on August 2, 1914, Vienna's fear of Serbia led to the fateful decisions that brought war. Now a far more complicated picture of Serbian terrorism as seen by Vienna emerges, triggering a decision for war that brought support from its German ally. Those decisions were based upon a set of assumptions – a

[63] Afflerbach, *Der Dreibund*, pp. 826–833; Angelow, *Kalkül*, pp. 442–465; Albertini, *Origins of the War of 1914*, vol. 2, pp. 217–254, vol. 3, pp. 254–363; R. J. B. Bosworth, *Italy, the Least of the Great Powers: Italian Foreign Policy before the First World War* (Cambridge University Press, 1979), pp. 377–397.

[64] Afflerbach, *Der Dreibund*, pp. 834–846; Albertini, *Origins of the War of 1914*, vol. 3, pp. 307–308; Williamson and Van Wyk (eds.), *July 1914: Soldiers*, pp. 167–179.

short war and no Russian intervention – which turned out to be incorrect. Austria-Hungary did not launch a quick war, and the determination of France and Russia to protect Serbia from any adverse consequences of the Sarajevo murders injected a new dimension that neither Berlin nor Vienna anticipated. Vienna continued to think in terms of a local war against Serbia, and Conrad pressed that attack even when there were indications that Russia would not stand aside. The Russians were prepared to respond militarily from the first news of the ultimatum. If there were second thoughts about this course of action in St. Petersburg, Vienna's declaration of war and then the attack on Belgrade checked any caution on the Russian side.

As the slide to war accelerated in late July, Bethmann-Hollweg sought, too late and in confusing fashion, to suggest to Vienna a modest effort while still hoping the Russians would not take the final step toward mobilization. In neither case did this happen. And Berlin's final hope, that Britain might stand aside, fell apart on August 3 over the pending invasion of Belgium. Austria-Hungary and Germany drove the crisis toward local war; the French and the Russians in their support of Serbia pushed the crisis to a world war. The terrorist act had succeeded in ways that Princip and Apis could never have imagined.

Nearly a century after Sarajevo historians know a great deal about what happened, when it happened, and who made it happen. We still, however, know far less of *why* things happened, and what prompted some of the decisions. Very likely new details, possibly new chronologies, new comparative analyses of intelligence reports, and new archival and private paper caches will surface to alter our understanding of events.[65] Furthermore, long and extensive biographical study of some of the major decision-makers has provided insights into the motivations and fears lying behind some of the actions.

Perhaps the most sensational revelation thus far has been the degree to which Conrad saw war as a way to marry Gina von Reininghaus, as indeed he did in 1915 after his venerable mother died. Röhl's detailed study of Wilhelm II has revealed a more complex, nuanced leader, who mixed brilliant intuitive insights with biases and mental preconceptions that reality did little to alter. And Annika Mombauer has shown a conflicted Moltke who veered between great self-confidence and agonizing self-doubt. But most of the other key decision-makers remain almost opaque to us. Even Grey, who has had substantial analysis,

---

[65] Clark and Schmidt have shown how new material from the Serbian, French, and Russian archives can reshape assumptions and thus conclusions.

remains almost as obtuse now as ever, while the Russian leadership remains mostly unknown to historians. In the biographical realm alone there is much work to be done, and possibly some of the "whys" will be answered.[66]

Then there is the question of societal and cultural norms and their impact on the key decision-makers, those hundred or so men who made the crucial choices in 1914. How did conceptions of "honor," "prestige," "security," "revanche," and "intuitive thinking" impact on their decision processes, and were these categories rational or non-rational? Did these concepts shape the policymakers' cognitive and intellectual approaches to the crisis? Some work on these topics has been done, but far more awaits historians.[67] And what was the relationship between the impact of organizational routines, required for the operation of military and naval forces, upon the options available to the senior decision-makers at the moment of choice? We know a great deal about the plans, but little about how the political leadership understood the details.[68] Certainly, the civilian leaders in each of the powers grasped only the barest essentials of the military plans and of the requirements for success, despite the fact that some of the generals warned, and warned repeatedly, of the illusions of a short war and of the dangers of a full European war.[69]

Then there remains the puzzling question: why did the Germans abandon the defensive caution of the elder Moltke for the far more dangerous offensive risks of Schlieffen and the younger Moltke? The talk of offensive strategies and their impact on the decisions in 1914 has long dominated

[66] Sondhaus, *Conrad*; Mombauer, *Helmuth von Moltke*; Röhl, *Wilhelm II*; Keiger, *Poincaré*, are some examples. Also see John Maurer, "Field Marshal Conrad von Hötzendorf and the Outbreak of the First World War," in T. G. Otte and Constantine A. Pagedas (eds.), *Personalities, War, and Diplomacy: Essays in International History* (London: Frank Cass, 1997), pp. 38–65. Lothar Höbelt's brief study, *Franz Joseph I: Der Kaiser und sein Reich: Eine politische Geschichte* (Vienna: Böhlau, 2009). is suggestive. Stig Förster, at the 2011 Fischer conference in London, argued for a new study of Bethmann-Hollweg, "Staatskunst und Kriegshandwerk: Bethmann-Hollweg and the Coming of the First World War," unpublished note; also see some of the insights in Leslie, "The Antecedents".

[67] Avner Offer, "Going to War in 1914: A Matter of Honor?" *Politics & Society* 23(2) (1995): 213–241; Lebow, *A Cultural Theory*, pp. 361–363. In his speech to Parliament on August 3, 1914, Grey used the word "honour" at least six times in different contexts, while using other words that essentially had the same meaning.

[68] Samuel R. Williamson, Jr., "Theories of Organizational Process and Foreign Policy Outcomes," in P. G. Lauren (ed.), *Diplomatic History: New Approaches* (New York: Free Press, 1979), pp. 137–161.

[69] See Stig Förster, "Der deutsche Generalstab und die Illusion des kurzen Krieges, 1871–1914. Metakritik eines Mythos," *Militärgeschichtliche Mitteilungen* 54(10) (1995): 61–95.

one field of study by political scientists, but does not really explain this tectonic shift by German policymakers.[70]

An intriguing topic for future researchers: what role did intuitive thinking play in the decisions of 1914? Was this a case of "fast thinking" by the decision-makers, in the words of Daniel Kahneman, when slower thinking, a more careful analysis, might have brought a different result?[71] Or put still another way, did the experiences of the key leaders, all of whom had lived through war–peace crises in the last forty-eight months, shape their psychological responses to this crisis? Perhaps they viewed the crisis as simply a continuation of the previous Balkan crises, one that once more would unfold in deliberate fashion, as had those in 1912–1913. Why were the Germans and Austrians so confident that Russia would accept once again, as it had in October 1913, an ultimatum to Belgrade? Why did Sazonov and the Russian military assume that some version of the 1912 measures could be instituted without sparking a militant German response? Why did Grey and other civilian leaders so misunderstand the nature of mobilization, in Grey's case thinking that even with Russian mobilization he still had time to intervene? Why was there so little understanding of the organizational routines of modern warfare, despite the four wars since 1900? Were there "lessons learned" or the "lessons of history" that shaped the mental maps of the policymakers, intuitively or otherwise? Why did they, as veteran statesmen, fail to understand the systemic connections between their actions upon each other and upon the opposing alliance/entente? And then, of course, the entire question of their perceptions and misperceptions, first posed by Robert Jervis and generally ignored by historians, would complement this approach.[72]

Or to use another Kahneman argument, was this an instance when the strong, strident voices put the more cautious voices, the more prudent ones, on the defensive – "hawks versus wimps," so to speak? This dichotomy certainly has some application to the British Cabinet's final

---

[70] Two of the best works on this approach are Jack Snyder, "Civil–Military Relations and the Cult of the Offensive, 1914 and 1984," *International Security* 9(1) (1984): 20–58; and Stephen Van Evera, "The Cult of the Offensive and the Origins of the First World War," *International Security* 9(1) (1984): 58–107. See also Jack Snyder, *The Ideology of the Offensive: Military Decision Making and the Disasters of 1914* (Ithaca, NY: Cornell University Press, 1984).

[71] Daniel Kahneman, *Thinking, Fast and Slow* (New York: Farrar, Straus & Giroux, 2011); Daniel Kahneman, "The Surety of Fools," *New York Times Magazine*, October 23, 2011, pp. 30–33, 62; Daniel Kahneman and Jonathan Renshon, "Why Hawks Win," *Foreign Policy* 158 (2007): 34–38.

[72] Robert Jervis, *Perception and Misperception in International Politics* (Princeton University Press, 1976); Jervis, *System Effects*, pp. 243–245. See also John Maurer, *The Outbreak of the First World War: Strategic Planning, Crisis Decision-Making and Deterrence Failure* (Westport, CT: Praeger, 1995).

decisions. Moreover, decision analysis and the work of political scientists offers, as Ernest May and I suggested in 2007, useful approaches that far too few historians have utilized.[73]

Then there is the need to examine the intersection between culture, society, domestic politics, and the overall "mentality" of the leadership cliques in each of the countries. A great deal of research has been done on many of these topics, but to this point no overall work has integrated all this material into a study of the origins of the war, though Strachan and Stevenson have made major contributions, and Clark's new work seeks to integrate an analysis of governmental structures and their impact on decision-making. The role of bureaucracies and their part in shaping the choices and the information that reached the decision-makers remains an area of great potential for study, as does a vast array of financial issues for all the countries. Certainly, the assessment of intelligence operations and their products beg for a comparative analysis that focuses upon how those who made the decisions used intelligence for whatever purpose. The array of issues that deserve attention can keep many future scholars busy with important questions for years to come.

"The perfect storm": that metaphor for 1914 is easily given. But does it really apply to the origins of the First World War? On some days the writer would argue yes, on others no. This chapter opts for "yes." The dress rehearsals of 1912–1913 had programmed the Austrian–Russian–German decision-makers to act intuitively and instinctively, blissfully ignoring contrary evidence and simply hoping for the best. For London and Paris, their relationship with Russia had become the keystone of their foreign policy, against Germany in the first instance, and, for London, against Russian pretensions elsewhere. Bravado, not caution; honor, not conciliation; we can win, the other country will lose; if we lose, we will have done our best; act now, the war plans demand it: all of these clichés were at work and certainly criss-crossed the minds of the key participants.

Unlike 1912–1913, this time events moved quickly, decisively; there was no point when the momentum slowed. From the start Vienna forced the process, confidently hoping that Berlin would deter St. Petersburg. Then Russia and Germany, for their own reasons, accelerated the pace and the Germans discovered that they could not control their Habsburg ally. For their part, the French and British exacerbated the situation and gave their own "blank check" to Serbia. Allies and

---

[73] Williamson and May, "Identity of Opinions," pp. 385–387.

friends could be as dangerous as enemies, as London, Berlin, Paris, and even St. Petersburg would discover. Meanwhile, the Italians simply waited, hoping for the best deal possible, and they got it in 1915. For Serbian nationalists, they too won; the kingdom of Serbs, Croats, and Slovenes (it was not called Yugoslavia until 1929) was their monument after 1918.

As for the cost of this success, 10 million military lives were lost. Sarajevo was the most successful terrorist act of all time. The effects of July 1914 continue to reverberate across our contemporary world and nowhere more than in the Middle East.[74]

---

[74] For a somber assessment of the war's impact on the international system, see Zara S. Steiner, *The Lights That Failed: European International History, 1919–1933* (Oxford University Press, 2005).

Part II

Structure and agency

3 Strategic rivalries and complex causality in 1914

Karen Rasler and William R. Thompson*

It sometimes seems as if explaining the outbreak of war in 1914 is a holy grail for international relations specialists in war etiology. The First World War, of course, was not a minor event in the annals of international history and that helps to explain some of its allure. Its reputation as the war no one wanted also makes it something of a magnet for scholarly entrepreneurs. Explaining the inexplicable is always a worthy challenge. Moreover, the developments that transpired prior to the outbreak of war are sufficiently complicated that almost every model ever created in international relations seems to fit. Yet underlying the whole explanatory edifice is the early and continuing search for blame, its evasion, and its former implications for postwar reparations and war guilt. Which country was most responsible for bringing about the onset of the First World War?[1] In addition, a disproportional number of the central research foci in international relations – security dilemmas, spiral dynamics, offensive–defensive arguments, crisis dynamics, alliances, arms races – stem to varying extents from interpretations of the onset of the First World War.[2] If we get the outbreak of this "wrong" or have overlooked significant factors, we may be heading in the wrong direction in our search for general explanations of war causes.

We do not propose to introduce a novel approach to explaining the First World War. To the contrary, we choose to elaborate a model that was introduced in 2003. The model encompasses several elements: relative

---

* This chapter was originally prepared for delivery at the canceled annual meeting of the American Political Science Association, New Orleans, Louisiana, September 2012, and the annual meeting of the International Studies Association, San Francisco, California, April 2013.

[1] Certainly, earlier analyses should have laid this hoary question to rest. See, for instance, Sidney B. Fay, *The Origins of the World War*, rev. 2nd edn. (New York: Macmillan, 1930); Luigi Albertini, *The Origins of the War of 1914*, 3 vols., trans. and ed. Isabella M. Massey (London: Oxford University Press, 1952–1957). But as Samuel R. Williamson, Jr. notes, the German blame paradigm has been with us for nearly a century. See his "July 1914 Revisited and Revised: The Erosion of the German Paradigm," Chapter 2, this volume.

[2] See, for example, Keir A. Lieber, "The New History of World War I and What it Means for International Relations Theory," *International Security* 32(2): (2007): 155–191.

decline of the global leader; regional leadership challenge; bipolarization among major powers; and nonlinear rivalry dynamics. The first three factors are fairly well known. The fourth factor, nonlinear rivalry dynamics, needs to be elucidated. In an earlier journal article, Thompson advanced an argument about the importance of nonlinear dynamics prior to the First World War.[3] However, an explanation about how precisely these dynamics actually played out was not spelled out. In this chapter, we propose to resolve this omission. In doing so, we will advance an argument that implicitly absolves any single country from blame for the onset of war in 1914. Although a general war might well have been avoided in 1914, a complicated sequence of interactions within a favorable structural context made it more probable. At the same time, an emphasis on rivalry dynamics is not exactly novel either. Scholars have noted the importance of rivalry in the onset of the First World War, but they tend to focus on a single rivalry, represent it as dyadic conflict, or in some cases single out a couple of rivalries for special attention.[4] Alternatively, they leave the rivalry

---

[3] William R. Thompson, "A Streetcar Named Sarajevo: Catalysts, Multiple Causation Chains, and Rivalry Structures," *International Studies Quarterly* 47(3) (2003): 453–474. More general exposure to the explicit analysis of rivalries may be found in William R. Thompson (ed.), *Great Power Rivalries* (Columbia, SC: University of South Carolina Press, 1999); William R. Thompson, "Identifying Rivals and Rivalries in World Politics," *International Studies Quarterly* 45(4) 557–586; Michael P. Colaresi, Karen Rasler, and William R. Thompson, *Strategic Rivalry: Space, Position and Conflict Escalation in World Politics* (Cambridge University Press, 2007); William R. Thompson and David R. Dreyer, *Handbook of International Rivalries, 1494–2010* (Washington, DC: Congressional Quarterly Press, 2011). Rivalries are deemed to be important to an understanding of interstate conflict because they have been responsible for generating roughly 75 percent of conflict between states in the past two centuries. Yet their numbers are relatively small when one stops to think about how many possible pairs of states there are in the world. Despite being relatively rare phenomena, rivalries take up a wholly disproportionate amount of space in diplomatic histories. For political science, the argument is that we should spend more time studying recidivism in conflict patterns as opposed to assuming that all states have an equal probability of engaging in conflict with one another. It could be quite beneficial if historians could be persuaded to view rivalries in a more self-conscious way as well.

[4] The point is not that First World War specialists are unfamiliar with rivalry dynamics in a general sense. They are, but they tend to focus on one or two rivalries as most critical and neglect the rest. For instance, G. P. Gooch long ago advanced France–Germany, Austro-Hungary–Russia, and Britain–Germany as the key to understanding the First World War; Dale C. Copeland stresses the Russian–German rivalry; Paul W. Schoeder focuses on the Austrian–German–Russian triangle, which encompasses three rivalries; Ned Lebow prefers to privilege France–Germany, Russia–Germany, and Britain–Germany; long-cycle analyses have long emphasized the significance of the Anglo-German rivalry, as does N. Ferguson; and both J. Vasquez and S. Williamson urge us not to forget the Austro-Hungarian–Serbian rivalry that initiated the formal onset of war. See G. P. Gooch, *Franco-German Relations, 1871–1914* (London: Longman, Green, 1923); Dale C. Copeland, *The Origins of Major War* (Ithaca, NY: Cornell University Press, 2000); Dale C. Copeland, "International Relations Theory and the Three Great Puzzles of the Great War," Chapter 7, this volume; Paul W. Schroeder, "The Life and Death of a Long Peace, 1763–1914," in Raimo Vayrynen (ed.), *The Waning of Major War: Contrary Views* (London: Routledge, 2005); Richard N. Lebow, "Contingency Catalysts and International System Change," *Political Science*

dimension of the dyadic relationships implicit. It is, for instance, the Russo-German or Anglo-German dyads that are thought to be critical. Instead, we believe that we can gain greater explanatory leverage if we explicitly link the interactive effects of rivalry dynamics as a key causal mechanism to the onset of the First World War. Some dyads are more important than others, but it is the way in which the field of rivalries interacts in larger structural contexts that we think is most critical.

The nonlinear rivalry ripeness model

The nonlinear rivalry ripeness (NRR) model is inspired in part by massive freeway auto accidents.[5] For instance, one driver falls asleep and hits another car. That car bounces into two or three others, one of which turns sideways and is hit by a fast moving truck. The car immediately behind the truck slams into the now-flaming truck, as do three other vehicles. Still more collisions occur, especially in the presence of heavy traffic, constrained space, and the disruption of normal traffic. Without a great deal of intent, a single actor can trigger a series of cascading events that can produce tremendous damage. We believe that rivalry fields – multiple rivalries that overlap to varying degrees – can function similarly. A change in one rivalry can impact how several other intersecting rivalries function. Changes in a second rivalry can then reverberate through the field of other rivalries. In a complex rivalry field, it may not be possible for any decision-maker to foresee or even track the implications of a change in one part of a tightly connected network of interstate hostilities.

Quarterly 115(4) (2000): 591–616; William R. Thompson, *On Global War: Historical-Structural Approaches to World Politics* (Columbia, SC: University of South Carolina Press, 1988); Niall Ferguson, *The Pity of War: Explaining World War I* (New York: Basic Books, 1999); John A. Vasquez, "Was the First World War a Preventive War? Concepts, Criteria and Evidence," Chapter 8, this volume; Samuel R. Williamson, Jr., "July 1914 Revisited and Revised, Chapter 2, this volume. Even so, these analyses tend to treat rivalries as foreign policy dyads of particular interest, as opposed to rivalries explicitly. Our emphasis is on the field of explicit rivalries and its impact on conflict probabilities. That said, we found Mulligan particularly helpful in providing a comprehensive overview of the dynamics of feuding dyads in the developments leading to the First World War. See William Mulligan, *The Origins of the First World War* (Cambridge University Press, 2010).

[5] More intellectually, it was inspired by Perrow's analysis of the complexity of technological accidents. See Charles Perrow, *Normal Accidents: Living with High Risk Technologies* (New York: Basic Books, 1984). Bruce Russett suggested something similar; see his "Cause, Surprise and No Escape," *Journal of Politics* 24(1) (1962): 3–22. What Russett suggested, however, is very different from what we have in mind. He applies an accident report template to each of the major actors that differentiates between remote causes with later consequences, points of surprise as decision-makers abruptly realize that the danger of war has escalated, and points of no escape when decision-makers believe that war cannot be avoided. Thus, his approach is monadic and assumes that no drivers intended to have an accident, but that a variety of factors made one involving multiple "automobiles" more probable. Our approach is neither monadic nor does it assume the absence of premeditation. Where we overlap is the emphasis on unforeseen developments that have later consequences for making war more probable.

Our quantifiable model has three components. The first, *rivalry intensity*, exploits the generalization that serial clashes within a rivalry improve the probability of escalation to war. After two or three clashes, a rivalry is more likely to go to war than it is after its first clash.[6] If the disputants are constrained in their choice of allies and are obliged to come to their aid, the spread of conflict, once it starts, is more likely to occur than situations in which the actors had no alliance obligations. The second component, *major power bipolarization*, looks at the extent to which the field is bipolarized into two competing communities. The third element of our model, *global leader decline* and *regional leader ascent*, is based on the assumption that all rivalries are not equally important. Those rivalries that involve structural transitions, either at the global or regional level, tend to be more dangerous than rivalries in nonstructural transitions.[7] Therefore, the presence of regional and global transitions that involve competitions over leadership positions should make conflict and its diffusion more likely than in nontransitional situations.

Is this all that we can say about nonlinear rivalry ripeness? The answer is no, and in a later section of this chapter we will make an attempt at isolating the specific "pinball" dynamics of the 1914 case. Unfortunately, rivalry pinball dynamics do not yet lend themselves readily to quantitative analysis. Until we can devise a way to capture them directly and systematically, we opt for a different strategy that involves operationalizing those factors that will increase the probability that a complex rivalry field will produce conflict and conflict diffusion. We expect to find that the operationalized components will come together just before 1914 in such a way that conflict throughout the rivalry field becomes highly probable.

In an earlier test of the NRR model in the First World War, Thompson measured *rivalry intensity* as the number of militarized disputes within the European or major power rivalries – some of which were given increasing weight as more clashes occurred within each rivalry.[8] *Bipolarization* was calculated with the use of Wayman's bipolarization index.[9] *Global*

---

[6] Of course, this argument ignores other considerations. For instance, von Strandmann notes that the two Moroccan crises, although not that far apart in timing, involved different international constellations of actors and concerned North African territory about which most European decision-makers found it difficult to become too excited. He also notes that the 1908–1909 Bosnian crisis did involve many of the same actors as in 1914, but in the earlier confrontation Russia, France, and Britain were all unwilling to take a strong stand – unlike 1914. See Hartmut P. von Strandmann, "Germany and the Coming of the War," in R. J. W. Evans and Hartmut P. Strandmann (eds.), *The Coming of the First World War* (Oxford: Clarendon Press, 1988), pp. 140–159.

[7] See, for instance, Karen Rasler and William R. Thompson, *The Great Powers and Global Struggle, 1490–1990* (Lexington, KY: University Press of Kentucky, 1994).

[8] To be given more weight, a second or third clash had to occur within ten years of the preceding one. Otherwise, it was assumed that the clashes were not really serial in nature. See Thompson, "A Streetcar Named Sarajevo."

[9] Wayman first counts the number of major powers that form blocs by possessing defense pacts with each other. He then counts the number of poles (the number of blocs plus the number of nonbloc major powers) and computes the ratio of actual poles to potential

Table 3.1 *Indicators for nonlinear rivalry ripeness model*

Years	Rivalry intensity	Bipolarization	Global leader decline	Regional leader ascent	Average score
1815–19	0.011	0.60	0.451	0.050	0.278
1820–24	0.011	0.80	0.451	0.230	0.373
1825–29	0.114	0.20	0.451	0.188	0.238
1830–34	0.125	0.20	0.357	0.192	0.219
1835–39	0.015	0.40	0.357	0.213	0.246
1840–44	0.162	0.60	0.417	0.150	0.332
1845–49	0.140	0.40	0.417	0.191	0.287
1850–54	0.324	0.20	0.454	0.204	0.296
1855–59	0.430	0.20	0.454	0.245	0.332
1860–64	0.051	0.17	0.500	0.187	0.227
1865–69	0.143	0.17	0.500	0.159	0.243
1870–74	0.162	0.00	0.481	0.156	0.200
1875–79	0.254	0.17	0.481	0.176	0.270
1880–84	0.081	0.17	0.570	0.178	0.250
1885–89	0.283	0.33	0.570	0.192	0.344
1890–94	0.007	0.33	0.667	0.182	0.297
1895–99	0.577	0.44	0.667	0.167	0.463
1900–4	0.463	0.38	0.755	0.159	0.439
1905–9	0.452	0.50	0.755	0.172	0.470
1910–13	1.000	0.50	0.854	0.304	0.665

Source: Based on William R. Thompson, "A Streetcar Named Sarajevo: Catalysts, Multiple Causation Chains, and Rivalry Structures," *International Studies Quarterly* 47(3) (2003): 469.

leader decline – as a proxy for global transition – was computed by examining the size of the gap in the shares of major power leading sector production of Britain and its German challenger. *Regional leader ascent,* as a proxy for regional transition, was gauged by examining the size of the gap in French and German shares of European major army sizes.[10] Table 3.1 displays the values of these variables by five-year increments, starting in 1815 and ending in 1913. As Table 3.1 shows, the average of the scores across these four variables for each five-year increment represents a

poles (the total number of major powers). An index score that approaches 1.0 suggests a high degree of multipolarization, while a score approaching 0 is taken to signify a tendency toward bipolarization. However, for the 2003 analysis, the scale was reversed by subtracting the outcome from 1.0 so that a high score suggests bipolarization and a low score indicates multipolarization. See Frank W. Wayman, "Bipolarity, Multipolarity, and the Threat of War," in Alan N. Sabrosky (ed.), *Polarity and War: The Changing Structure of International Conflict* (Boulder, CO.: Westview Press, 1985), pp. 115–144.

[10] The global transition scores are subtracted from 1 so that higher scores indicate approaching transition. In the case of the regional transition scores, France is designated as the regional leader up to 1871, and Germany is the leader afterwards. However, the army share gaps in the nineteenth century were normally not great, and those involving France and Germany, in particular, were often not large. So, in this case, we are looking for major shifts in relative position gap as an indicator of trouble.

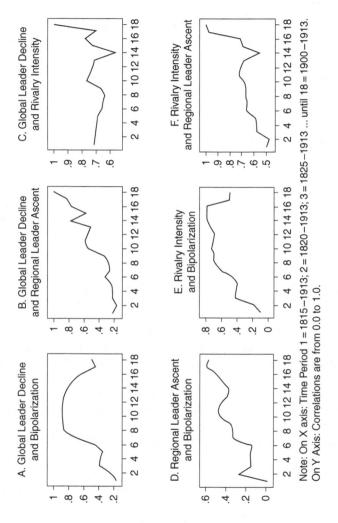

Figure 3.1 Bivariate correlations across varying time periods, starting with 1815–1913 and ending with 1900–1913

composite indicator (see Table 3.1, column 6) that does not change until the 1890s. At this point, the composite indicator values shift upward rapidly in the last three time increments. Meanwhile, the values of three of the four variables (that is, *rivalry intensity, global leader decline,* and *regional leader ascent*) have higher scores in the 1910–1913 time period than at any previous time increment.

We can extend this examination a bit further. Figure 3.1 displays the bivariate correlations among the four indicators of *global leader decline, bipolarization, regional leader ascent,* and *rivalry intensity* at five-year increments, starting in 1815. The plots are not standard time series plots with each time period reflecting a single year. Instead, each time period reflects the bivariate correlation between two variables for a systematically varying slice of time. For instance, in subplot A in Figure 3.1, the first observation on the *x* axis reflects the bivariate correlation between global leader decline and bipolarization for the full time period, 1816–1913. The second observation reflects the bivariate correlation between these variables for 1820–1913; the third observations reflects the bivariate correlation for 1825–1913, and so on until the eighteenth observation, which reflects the 1900–1913 period. Hence, each observation on the *x* axis reflects a different slice or cross-section of time. What we expect to observe is that the correlations between the variables will become higher as the cross-section of time gets smaller and closer to 1914. If so, then the increasing correlations over these periods support our argument that the key ripeness variables, and the rivalry field in general, become more tightly connected in the years immediately prior to 1914.

In four of the six plots in Figure 3.1 (B, C, D, and F), the bivariate correlations demonstrate a clear positive trend across the long nineteenth century. In two cases – (a) global leader decline–bipolarization and (e) rivalry intensity–bipolarization – the trend is also positive, but the size of the correlations drops off in the later portion of the nineteenth century. This deviation suggests that all four indicators were not as closely intertwined over time as they might have been. However, there may be some measurement issues that are influencing the results. A glance at Table 3.1 (column 2), shows that the *bipolarization* index is the partial "culprit" due perhaps to its ambiguous climb in the second half of the century. In First World War annals, the split between Austria-Hungary and Germany on one side and France and Russia on the other is given prime attention. But, even so, it was an incomplete bipolarization. Another anomaly is the early peak (1895–1899) in the *rivalry intensity* scores, which then decrease in the early twentieth century while the *bipolarization* values increase. These outcomes say more about the crude operational measures we are relying on than the events that

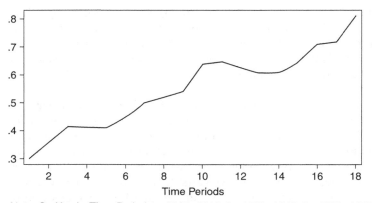

Note: On X axis: Time Period 1 = 1815–1913; 2 = 1820–1913; 3 = 1825–1913 ...
until 18 = 1900–1913. On Y Axis: Correlations are from 0.0 to 1.0.

Figure 3.2 Average bivariate correlations across varying time periods.
(for correlations in graphs B–F in Figure 3.1)

actually took place. We will explore this facet of rivalry ripeness more
closely in the qualitative analysis section below.

Nonetheless, overall the indicators seem to point in the right direction.
Figure 3.2, which plots the average bivariate correlations between the
values that appear in subgraphs B–F, also reinforces this view. Figure 3.2,
in fact, suggests a clear march toward the probability of conflict escalation
throughout the 1816–1913 period, albeit with some leveling off in the
mid-century. This image contrasts sharply with the notion that the First
World War was the war no one wanted or expected. Conceivably, it remains
possible that no one wanted or expected a world war, but the pertinent
indicators suggest that the context was becoming increasingly ripe for some
kind of trouble. Yet Figure 3.2 seems more linear than nonlinear. It would
appear that we need to examine the specifics of rivalry interconnections
and dynamics more closely.

The complexity of rivalry fields is certainly influenced by the number
of rivalries underway.[11] In the fifty years preceding 1914, a less complex
rivalry field with eight rivalries between major powers and four involving
non-major powers in 1864 expanded to eleven rivalries between major
powers and eleven involving non-major powers (see Table 3.2). In other
words, a field with twelve rivalries almost doubled into a twenty-two rivalry

---

[11] See, for instance, John A. Vasquez, Paul F. Diehl, Colin Flint, Jürgen Scheffran, Sang-
Hyun Chi, and Toby J. Rider, "The ConflictSpace of Cataclysm: The International
System and the Spread of War, 1914–1917," *Foreign Policy Analysis* 7(2) (2011): 143–168.

Table 3.2 *Rivalries begun and ended, 1864–1913*

Year	Rivalries begun	Rivalries ended
1864	*Rivalries already underway by 1864*	
	Austria–France, Austria–Italy, Austria–Ottoman Empire, Austria–Prussia, Austria–Russia, Britain–France, Britain–Russia, France–Prussia, France–Russia, Greece–Ottoman Empire, Ottoman Empire–Russia, Britain–United States	
1870		Austria–Prussia
1874	Japan–Russia	
1878	Bulgaria–Greece, Bulgaria–Ottoman Empire, Bulgaria–Serbia, Ottoman Empire–Serbia	
1879	Greece–Serbia	
1881	France–Italy	
1884	Italy–Ottoman Empire	
1889	Germany–United States	
1890	Germany–Russia	
1894		France–Russia
1896	Britain-Germany	
1898	Japan–United States	
1903	Austria–Serbia	
1904		Britain–France, Britain–United States
1908		Austria–Ottoman Empire
1913	Albania–Greece	

Note: Austria refers to Austria-Hungary during most of this interval. The rivalry onset and termination information is based on William R. Thompson and D. R. Dreyer, *Handbook of International Rivalries, 1494–2010* (Washington, DC: Congressional Quarterly Press, 2011).

field. That accounting also ignores the four major power rivalries (Austria–Prussia, France–Russia, Britain–France, and Britain–United States) that were terminated during this era. Yet the termination of these four rivalries probably made war more, rather than less, likely because they contributed to determining, or at least reflected, who eventually aligned with whom in the 1914–1918 combat. This quirk is one reason why it does not suffice to merely count the number of rivalries. The number of rivalries can provide useful information, but it can also be misleading if terminated rivalries can be just as significant as ones that are still underway. Another reason is that a simple count of rivalries does not tell us which rivalries are operating hot or cold. Hot rivalries, presumably, are more dangerous than ones that are relatively inactive. Finally, counting rivalries does not capture how changes in one rivalry influence the operation of other rivalries. These "pinball" dynamics" lie at the very heart of why a rivalry field can exert nonlinear effects on the outbreak of war.

A qualitative analysis of "pinball" dynamics in the pre-First World War rivalry field

The most evident nonlinear component, and the least easy to operationalize, is the "pinball" process linking the functioning of multiple rivalries. It can be called a pinball process because an initial stimulus, not unlike launching a ball in a pinball game, affects (or can affect) a number of rivalry relationships existing in a field or network. The effect of a stimulus on one rivalry impacts other rivalries, which, in turn, have effects on still other rivalries. The initial stimulus (or stimuli) thus alters the way in which the rivalries in the field interact in direct and indirect ways that are often difficult to predict at the time of occurrence. We have the advantage of hindsight, however, and can at least make a case for a sequence of direct and indirect impacts.

Figure 3.3 portrays the multiple streams of interrivalry "pinball" dynamics in the First World War case. One stream begins in 1905 with Russia's defeat in the Russo-Japanese War. A second stream is initiated by Italy's attack on Turkey in partial response to French gains in North Africa. A third input is the bipolarization of European major powers, which was the outcome of eight rivalries. Meanwhile, the second stream of rivalry relationships intersects the French–German and British–German structural rivalries. How these last two rivalries functioned in 1914 was influenced by what had transpired earlier in the other rivalries. We highlight the "pinball" dynamics that occurred primarily in the last decade prior to the onset of the 1914 war. Although we acknowledge that rivalry behaviors interacted much earlier, we believe that the war outcome can be traced most directly to the rivalry interactions of the decade prior to the First World War.

This approach does not mean that the rivalry dynamics that preceded 1905 are insignificant. For us, it is primarily a matter of emphasis. We do believe that the rapprochements of 1904 (Britain with the United States and France) and the emergence of the Austro-Serbian rivalry in 1903 were critical. Before 1903, Serbia had more or less accepted its subordination to Austro-Hungarian preferences. Without a trouble-making Serbia, the lead up to the First World War might have worked out differently. We also acknowledge that the global and regional contests for leadership that are very much part of our model certainly preceded 1905. The ending of the Franco-Russian rivalry and the beginning of a German–Russian rivalry in the early 1890s were equally and perhaps even more crucial. If Austria had

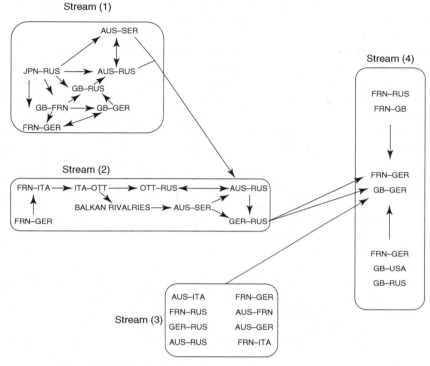

Figure 3.3 Four rivalry streams

not acquiesced to German superiority in 1870, would there have been a blank check in 1914? Rivalry field dynamics are a bit like pulling on loose strings in a ball of twine. It is difficult to know where to start. We think, however, that the nonlinear aspects of pre-First World War dynamics can be best demonstrated by the beginning of 1905 – ten years before the outbreak of war in 1914.

Mulligan suggests that 1871, 1879, 1890, 1894, 1905, 1908, and 1911 are the usual suspects for turning points in the movement toward the First World War.[12] Certainly, plausible cases can be advanced for pushing the starting point back in time. Our choice of 1905 (Mulligan credits 1904–1907 as "a great turning point") reflects only a feeling that developments became increasingly nonlinear after this point. For instance, Mulligan also argues that Europe was closer to war in 1885–1887 than

[12] Mulligan, *Origins of the First World War*, p. 91.

at any other time between 1871 and 1914. He notes the following about prominent pairs of states – what we would call increasing rivalry intensities: France and Italy were clashing over colonial territory in North Africa; French revanchism over Alsace-Lorraine was briefly in the ascendance; Britain and France were engaged in friction over Egypt; Britain was greatly concerned about the Russian advance toward India; Britain and Austria-Hungary were opposing Russian and Bulgarian attempts to expand their influence in the Balkans; and in Germany some voices were calling for a preventive war on Russia. With the advantage of hindsight, however, one could point to how these frictions checked one another. It is unlikely that all major powers would fight one another in an unstructured melee encompassing multiple warring dyads. Britain and Austria-Hungary were cooperating; Britain, France, and Russia were not.

Various developments took place after 1885–1887 to change the context of conflict within the rivalry field and to make a general European war more probable. These considerations do not justify directly an emphasis on post-1905 dynamics, but they do suggest that we need not survey the entire century prior to 1914. If we had to pick one development, our choice is the Russian defeat in the 1904–1905 Russo-Japanese War, and Russia's renewed interest in the Balkans and the Straits which set up a respectable proportion of the dynamics on which we focus. As long as Russia remained preoccupied in the Far East, its rivalry with Austria-Hungary was less likely to escalate into war. On the contrary, the two powers were able to cooperate in attempting to contain tensions in southeastern Europe prior to Russia's defeat, as Mulligan and others have noted. We hasten to add that such a choice does not mean that Russia (or Japan) should be blamed for starting the First World War.

Stream 1: Russian foreign policy, according to LeDonne, can be viewed as a series of alternating initiatives to the east, south, and west.[13] When an initiative in one direction faced too much resistance, the Russians shifted their foreign policy to a new one. In 1904–1905, Russia performed poorly in the Russo-Japanese War, signaling a major foreign policy defeat in terms of its Manchurian/Korean ambitions. In the decade or so prior to the war, Russia had cooperated with Austria on Balkan issues. After the war, Russia renewed its competitive interests in the Balkans and the Black Sea Straits, thereby switching its foreign policy priorities from the west to the south. In the absence of its war defeat, there is no guarantee that Russia would have continued cooperating with Austria in southeastern Europe, but the probability of increased Austro-Russian conflict was

---

[13] John P. LeDonne, *The Russian Empire and the World, 1700–1917: The Geopolitics of Expansion and Contraction* (Oxford University Press, 1997).

certainly enhanced. The Russians' shift in focus to the south was further encouraged by the de-escalation of the long-running Anglo-Russian rivalry in 1907, which was, in turn, made more probable by their defeat in 1905 and subsequent revolutionary turmoil in that year.[14] Russian decision-makers were encouraged to reconsider their foreign policy objectives at a time when British decision-makers were searching for ways to reduce the number of perceived threats to their global empire. Far from being over, the downturn in Anglo-Russian rivalry relations reflected a temporary truce in Central Asia/Persia in order for both sides to focus more narrowly on a mutual German threat. The British initiatives on this front were designed to simplify the threat environment, in conjunction with the de-escalation of rivalries with France and the United States in 1904. Even the Russo-Japanese rivalry helped to diminish the threat environment with a temporary de-escalation in 1907, and a secret treaty between the parties acknowledging their respective spheres of influence in Manchuria and Mongolia. Consequently, Russian foreign policy objectives in the south were less likely to be menaced by developments in the Far East. In sum, events and several interactive rivalry dynamics "conspired" to encourage a Russian refocus on the Balkans in the half-decade or so leading up to 1914.[15]

But this first stream is further complicated by other considerations. One inter-rivalry connection is asserted by Mombauer, who argues that the Schlieffen Plan predicating a German attack on France first was influenced by the German appreciation that a Russia defeated by the Japanese was not likely to represent much of a threat in the east, at least very quickly.[16] Thus, one had time to knock France out before turning on the Russians. Another consideration is that Britain had allied with Japan in part to discourage Russian expansion in east Asia. With Russia and France and Britain and Japan allied in separate pacts, the threat of Britain and France being drawn into a war between Russia and Japan had become

---

[14] Hew Strachan, *The First World War, vol. 1: To Arms* (New York: Oxford University Press, 2001), p. 20.

[15] Zeman argues that Austria-Hungary sought to encourage conflict between Bulgaria and Serbia after 1905, with the primary and unintentional outcome of driving Serbia closer to Russia. See Zbyněk Anthony Bohuslav Zeman, "The Balkans and the Coming of War," in R. J. W. Evans and Hartmut P. von Strandmann (eds.), *The Coming of the First World War* (Oxford: Clarendon Press, 1988), pp. 19–32. The most recent examination of the Russian entry into the First World War is Sean McMeekin, *The Russian Origins of the First World War* (Cambridge, MA: Belknap Press of Harvard University Press, 2011).

[16] Annika Mombauer, *The Origins of the First World War: Controversies and Consensus* (London: Longman, 2002), pp. 7–8

greater. Both Williamson and Mombauer credit the British interest in improving relations with France to this factor.[17] France had on its own problems in Morocco and therefore had reasons to seek cooperation with the British, who initially preferred no European power to occupy the African shore across from Gibraltar. After the Russian defeat in 1904–1905, France had all the more incentive to keep Britain on its side because it could not rely on Russian support in Great Power machinations. To complicate things further, Mombauer describes Germany as willing to challenge France in Morocco (1905) because (a) it knew Russian support for France would not be forthcoming and (b) it hoped to break up the fledgling Anglo-French entente.[18] That it had the opposite effect – reinforcing Anglo-French cooperation – in turn had implications for Anglo-German relations. In brief, it meant that an Anglo-German understanding was less likely to come about. Nearly a decade later, the combination of the early German decision to attack France first (most likely through Belgium, given the best route of attack) and the improvement in Anglo-French relations increased the probability of British intervention on behalf of the French. As it turned out, these early developments were not enough to ensure British intervention, but it made British intervention and the side on which the British chose to intervene more probable.

Stream 2: Italy and France competed for territorial control in North Africa, a competition that France was consistently winning after 1881 and its gains in Tunisia at Italy's expense. In the early 1900s, however, France and Italy had secretly agreed to acknowledge their respective claims in Morocco and Libya. Yet French advances in Morocco and the outcome of the second Franco-German crisis over Morocco encouraged Italy to make its claims on Libya, then controlled by Turkey, more overt. Bosworth relates how the Italian prime minister had resisted a Libyan adventure prior to the Second Moroccan Crisis.[19] Rather presciently, he had argued that:

The integrity of what is left of the Ottoman Empire is one of the principles on which is founded the equilibrium and peace of Europe . . . What if, after we attack Turkey, the Balkans move? And what if a Balkan war provokes a clash between the two groups of Powers and a European war?

[17] Samuel R. Williamson, Jr., *The Politics of Grand Strategy: Britain and France Prepare for War, 1904–1914* (Cambridge, MA: Harvard University Press, 1969), pp. 4–14; Mombauer, *Origins of the First World War*, pp. 7–8.
[18] Mombauer, *Origins of the First World War*, pp. 7–8.
[19] R. J. B. Bosworth, "Italy and the End of the Ottoman Empire," in Marion Kent (ed.), *The Great Powers and the End of the Ottoman Empire* (London: Allen & Unwin, 1984), pp. 51–72, at 60.

Nonetheless, faced with the prospect of being left out of North Africa, the Italian prime minister was able to suppress his own objections. Italy began a war with Turkey in 1911 to resolve the question.

As Giolitti had predicted, the weak Turkish response highlighted the recurring question of the disintegration of the Ottoman Empire. Much of the nineteenth century had been devoted to attempts to preserve the empire against various threats to dismember it. By the first decade of the twentieth century, dismemberment was perceived as increasingly likely even by former defenders of the imperial status quo. Two more direct effects of the Turkish defeat in the 1911 war involved Russian concerns over controlling the Black Sea Straits and Balkan interests in expelling the Turks from southeastern Europe.

The Russian interest in controlling Constantinople and the Dardanelles was a long-standing one. In many respects, it was the primary focus of its push to the south which began as early as the seventeenth century. The Russian motivation went beyond the matter of traditional imperial expansion. The Turkish ability to close the Straits affected Russia's ability to export a considerable proportion of its grain to the west by sea. Russian decision-makers felt highly vulnerable to this economic threat, and not without reason.[20] The Turks tended to close the Straits in times of conflict in the general area, as they did during the Balkan Wars much to the alarm of the Russians. In addition, the Russians had a long-standing interest in removing restrictions on the movement of Russian naval vessels from the Black Sea to the Mediterranean, which they could eliminate with their control of the Straits. In this respect, the Italo-Turkish War encouraged greater tensions in the Russo-Turkish rivalry. Yet Russia also worried about Austrian gains in the area immediately north of the Straits.

German gains in Turkey also exacerbated tensions in the area. The Liman von Sanders crisis in late 1913–early 1914 exposed Russia's increased concerns about Germany's role in Turkey. Liman von Sanders was a German general sent to Turkey to assist in reforming the Turkish army in the aftermath of its poor performance in the wars of 1911–1913. The assistance in retraining troops was one matter; still another was the fact that von Sanders was to be given direct control of Turkish troops in the vicinity of the Straits. The Russians demanded that the appointment be reversed. It was reversed in a formal sense, but the German general continued to be in charge of the Turkish army's training. The Russians were alarmed by the German gains in position in the area, and this issue has been

[20] Some 37 percent of Russian exports and 75 percent of its grain shipments transited through the Straits from the Black Sea area according to Dominic C. Lieven, *Russia and the Origins of the First World War* (London: Macmillan, 1983), pp. 45–46.

isolated as a critical event that changed the nature of the Russo-German rivalry. Up until this point, Russo-German tensions had been largely indirect and influenced by Austro-Russian tensions. Now, Russia and Germany had direct reasons for conflict.[21]

The other arena affected by the Turkish defeat in 1911 was the Balkans, a hotbed of rivalries among states with varying degrees of official independence. Greece, Serbia, and Bulgaria sought to take Macedonian territory at Turkey's (and each others') expense. The Young Turk revolt in 1908 was motivated by a desire to defend the Ottoman position in Europe. However, Turkey's war with Italy and its subsequent defeat in 1911 exposed its vulnerabilities. In the aftermath, Serbia and Bulgaria recognized the opportunity to exploit the local weakness of their Turkish rival. The first Balkan War in 1912 focused on finally expelling the Ottoman Empire from Europe. Successes in the first war led to a falling out among the victors, which was less than surprising since most had been rivals with one another prior to the outbreak of war. The second Balkan War in 1913 primarily focused on the reduction of Bulgarian gains and the re-division of Macedonian territory. The defeat of Bulgarian ambitions had at least three indirect consequences. Turkish weaknesses were further highlighted. Serbia was a major winner in the two Balkan wars, roughly doubling its territorial and population size, which made it a more formidable foe of Austria-Hungary. Further Serbian expansion heightened threat perceptions by Austria-Hungary and increased Austro-Serbian conflict over control of Albania. Finally, the Bulgarian defeat in the second Balkans War meant that Russia was encouraged to give more attention to supporting Serbia, as opposed to dividing its diplomatic support among Slavic states in the area.

Stream 3: The European region became increasingly bipolarized in the late nineteenth and early twentieth centuries. This process encompassed eight rivalries most directly. At one point, the conservative major powers had been united in their opposition to France and the threat of its reemergence as a hegemonic aspirant. But that point of view had collapsed around the mid-nineteenth century. A strong rivalry between Prussia and Austria-Hungary terminated after Prussia defeated Austria-Hungary and then went on to defeat France in 1870–1871. Italy, although aided by France initially, drifted toward the more formidable support that Germany could provide. France and Russia, former rivals, became allies in the early 1890s. Germany and Russia, former allies, became rivals at

---

[21] Schroeder argues that the key to the First World War lies in the changing relationships among Austria, Germany, and Russia. See Schroeder, "The Life and Death of a Long Peace."

roughly the same time. Thus, by the end of the nineteenth century, a French–Russian bloc confronted the triple alliance of Germany, Austria-Hungary, and Italy. Neither side was so strongly connected to its allies that anyone could predict without qualification who would side with whom if it came to a showdown. Italy eventually defected and joined the opposite side. The Austro-German relationship became more closely connected, but the German blank check for Austrian aggression in the Balkans only emerged quite late in the game. At times, French decision-makers seemed to fear a Russo-German rapprochement as much as they regarded Germany as a threat. Britain's position seemed ambiguous for some of the period leading up to 1914, but it eventually sided with two of its former rivals, France and Russia, against states with which it had once been allied in opposition to France in earlier times.

Nonetheless, the bipolarization tendencies reduced freedom of maneuver in times of crisis. It also encouraged German war plans that were predicated on removing France as a threat quickly in order to deal with a presumably slowly mobilizing Russia. If it came to war in Europe, the Germans not only felt it necessary to attack France quickly, it also meant that an attack through Belgium was quite likely. Both considerations increased the likelihood that a war between Austria-Hungary and Russia would quickly draw Germany, France, and, because of the Belgian attack, Britain into the fray.

Stream 4: One of the structural ironies of the lead up to the First World War is that neither the global leader–challenger confrontation between Britain and Germany nor the regional leadership contest between France and Germany seems to have loomed large in the dynamics that led to the immediate outbreak of war in 1914.[22] We are certainly not suggesting that these rivalries played no role whatsoever. However, we do understand that the Anglo-German rivalry had de-escalated somewhat by 1912, with Germany conceding its global naval inferiority so that it could direct its attention more on developing its army for continental purposes. Of course, that meant that its rivalries within Europe became more salient as its rivalry with Britain, a state separated from the continent by the English Channel, receded in priority. Nonetheless, Britain had de-escalated three of its rivalries (with France, the United States, and Russia) in order to concentrate on the German threat. This fact ultimately meant that if Britain intervened, it was less likely to do so on behalf of the Germans. As it turned out, Britain was not at all eager to come to the aid of France,

---

[22] Arguments for deemphasizing the Anglo-German rivalry's role are reviewed in Jan Rüger, "Review Article: Revisiting the Anglo-German Antagonism," *Journal of Modern History* 83(3) (2011): 579–617.

but was drawn in by the full German assault on Belgium and the implications of German control of opposing shores.[23] That Britain could intervene on the French–Russian side, in turn, had been made more probable by the earlier de-escalation of the Anglo-French and Anglo-Russian rivalries.

The related issue is whether Germany expected British intervention or hoped that Britain would sit out the continental war. The conventional view has been that German decision-makers had hoped unrealistically that Britain could be made into an ally or, at best, would remain aloof. If British behavior encouraged the Germans to think that the forces arrayed against them might be less than more, British vacillation could be blamed for encouraging pro-war forces in Germany. However, Lieber argues quite strongly that this view is simply wrong and that most of the main decision-makers in Germany anticipated British entry into the war against them.[24] If so, the potential British entry had little deterrent effect.

Does that imply that a theoretical emphasis on system leader–challenger relations as critical to understanding the outbreak of major power warfare is also wrong? The answer lies in the affirmative if the argument is that the system leader–challenger rivalry is the key rivalry and that others count for much less. But this perspective seems more applicable to a power transition approach in which the catch-up of an ascending challenger provokes war with a declining dominant power.[25] In the leadership long-cycle program, system leader decline and rising regional challengers are important, but not only for their specific rivalry dynamics. The movement toward leadership decline and aggressive challengers tells us more about "system time" than anything else. It is a larger context in which rivalry fields are apt to become less predictable. Power is/has deconcentrated. Actors are scrambling for allies as old alignments are seen to be less reliable than they once were. Revisionist powers see new and enticing opportunities to advance their expansionist and irredentist programs. In the absence of a declining system leader and rising challenger(s), these behaviors are less likely to emerge. In this respect, the system leader–challenger rivalry is

---

[23] Michael Brock, "Britain Enters the War," in R. J. W. Evans and Hartmut P. von Strandmann (eds.), *The Coming of the First World War* (Oxford: Clarendon Press, 1988), pp. 145–178, but, for a different interpretation, see J. Joll, *The Origins of the First World War* (New York: Longman, 1984). Lambert's new focus on economic warfare puts still a different spin on this question. See Nicholas A. Lambert, *Planning Armageddon: British Economic Warfare and the First World War* (Cambridge, MA: Harvard University Press, 2012).

[24] Lieber, "The New History of World War I," p. 187.

[25] See, for instance, Ronald L. Tammen, Jacek Kugler, Douglas Lemke, Carole Asharabati, Brian Efird, and A. F. K. Organski, *Power Transitions: Strategies for the 21st Century* (New York: Chatham House, 2000).

critical, but not always because of its specific dynamics. Rather, it should be viewed as an important manifestation of larger forces afoot.

In the build-up to 1914, the Franco-German rivalry, paradoxically, appears to be one of the least significant sources of increasing tension.[26] France and Germany had clashed verbally in Morocco, but there was no discernible movement on the part of France to get even over the earlier loss of Alsace-Lorraine before the war started. French decision-makers were certainly aware of the German military threat, but its activation was linked to war with France's ally (but former rival), Russia, as opposed to rising Franco-German tensions. Nevertheless, it is rather difficult to disentangle the Franco-German rivalry from the German strategic problem of fighting a two-front war. Whether or not there was a Schlieffen Plan, a war between Austria-Hungary and Russia over Serbia could not be limited to the Balkans. To defeat France and Russia, Germany needed to do significant damage to one before the other mobilized. A slower mobilizing Russia, therefore, meant that Germany needed to attack quickly and hard in the west so that it could deal with its eastern foe later. While this interpretation seemingly places emphasis on the Franco-Russian alliance, the less direct question is why there was a Franco-Russian alliance in the first place. In this respect, the Franco-German rivalry is an easy explanation for at least the French side of the motivation question.

The two structural rivalries, Britain–Germany and France–Germany, therefore, were contributory to the general setting of the rivalry field. In particular, they increased tensions in the period prior to the last few years of the lead up to world war. The antagonists made choices that led to some alignments becoming more probable and feasible by terminating or de-escalating major power rivalries (France–Russia, Britain–France, and Britain–Russia) so that they could deal with a rising Germany. Yet their direct contribution to the overall conflagration should not be exaggerated. The First World War was not brought about by one or two rivalries; it took a village of rivalries to bring it about.

---

[26] See Michael S. Neiberg, *Dance of the Furies: Europe and the Outbreak of World War I* (Cambridge, MA: Harvard University Press, 2011), pp. 58–60, for instance, on how the French population seemed to be largely indifferent or not inclined to resort to violence over the status of Alsace-Lorraine in the years leading up to 1914. Keiger also argues that French decision-makers knew that they were unprepared for war and acted accordingly. See Keiger, Chapter 10, this volume. Schroeder, in contrast, makes a strong case for the Austro-French rivalry as the least significant major power antagonism leading up to 1914. The case is made in Paul W. Schroeder, "A Pointless Enduring Rivalry: France and the Habsburg Monarchy, 1715–1918," in William R. Thompson (ed.), *Great Power Rivalries* (Columbia, SC: University of South Carolina Press, 1999), pp. 60–85.

The stream metaphor envisions the confluence of four channels converging and energizing a turbulent gyre from which the First World War emerged. Presumably, the more contributing streams and the stronger the converging flows, the greater the potential for something like a world war spreading rapidly. Another apt metaphor, this one borrowed from meteorological phenomena, is the perfect storm. Different types of storms converging from multiple vectors create monster storms on rare occasion. Of course, these metaphors (freeway pile-ups, pinball dynamics, converging streams, perfect storms) – while they can provide quick mental images of complicated processes – do not substitute for well-defined theory.[27] Our argument is that within a larger field of rivalries, changes in one rivalry reverberate through a chained sequence of a string of rivalries. For instance, the Italian problem of competing with France in Tunisia led to Italian–Ottoman problems in Libya and contributed to increased activity in the Balkan nest of rivalries, both of which had implications for Russo-Ottoman relations (see Stream 2). One of these sequences can be sufficiently complicated in its own right. If there are several ongoing simultaneously, international politics become incredibly complicated and less predictable. The potential for escalation in conflict and warfare are accentuated in a nonlinear fashion. The First World War was the product, at least in part, of interactions among an unusual number of intensifying rivalries.

When viewed from this perspective, alternative interpretations need not be dismissed out of hand. Some interpretative emphases are complementary. Alliances and arms races, for instance, add various types of fuel to the intensifying rivalry "flames." Alliances can help to cluster rivalries and thereby make sequential reverberations more probable within the clusters. Arms races between rivals can contribute to their intensification. Structural rivalries, as in the case of regional leadership competitions or a declining system leader–ascending challengers situation, can create their own streams of rivalry escalation, just as they also contribute to a larger context of heightened tensions. Crisis dynamics, if not treated as a stand-alone explanation, but instead linked to rivalry interactions, can certainly contribute more explanatory power. Of course, the emphasis on rivalry streams brings into question the comparative explanatory value of cumulative rivalry antagonisms versus the July Crisis *per se*.[28] At the same time, once one starts with rivalry considerations, other types of explanations,

---

[27] An endorsement of the "perfect storm" imagery is found in Williamson, "July 1914 Revisited and Revised: The Erosion of the German Paradigm," Chapter 2, this volume.

[28] We do not see this as an "either–or" question. Analytically, it is a matter of how much additional variance is explained by adding the crisis pathologies to the rivalry antagonisms.

such as security dilemmas or the cult of the offensive, pale in attractiveness because they seem either out of place (security dilemmas) or more than a bit esoteric (offense–defense arguments).

Conclusions

When we say that a field of rivalry dynamics was responsible for the outbreak of war in 1914, we do not mean to imply that the field alone was responsible. First, the nonlinear rivalry ripeness model incorporates both bipolarization and structural transition tensions. Second, we are fully aware that other authors have made strong cases for the contribution of processes that we have ignored in this chapter. Arms races have already been mentioned, but even they are also a reflection of rivalry dynamics.[29] Similarly, much of the interest in alliances as a causal factor in explaining conflict dates back to the First World War. We have not given much explicit attention to alliances other than through the bipolarization component. Ideally, we might model the relationships that we have been talking about as a network linking both rivalries and alignments, and then show how both types of relationship have negative and positive effects.[30] We are not quite there, though. It serves our immediate purpose to focus primarily on rivalries.

Nonetheless, we have no interest in promoting a single-factor causal argument. Our only claim is that the field of rivalry dynamics appears to have contributed significantly to the outbreak of war. Just how much significance should be attributed to rivalry dynamics and how much credit/blame to bestow on other phenomena would require a different kind of investigation. Our intent in this chapter was to elaborate a claim made in 2003 that had yet to be substantiated. The evidence in Figures 3.1 and 3.2 provides further substantiation to claims made earlier about the interaction among the NRR model's components. The diagram of rivalry

---

[29] The presumption is that arms races between nonrivals are not as dangerous as those between rivals. More generally, see Toby J. Rider, "Understanding Arms Races Onset: Rivalry, Threat, and Territorial Competition," *Journal of Politics* 71(2) (2009): 693–703; Toby J. Rider, Michael Findley, and Paul F. Diehl, "Just Part of the Game? Arms Races, Rivalry and War," *Journal of Peace Research* 48(1) (2011): 85–100. First World War-specific work can be found in David Stevenson, *Armaments and the Coming of War: Europe, 1904–1914* (Oxford University Press, 1996); David G. Herrmann, *The Arming of Europe and the Making of the First World War* (Princeton University Press, 1997).

[30] See Zeev Maoz, Lesley C. Terris, Ranan D. Kuperman, and Ilan Talmud, "What is the Enemy of My Enemy? Causes and Consequences of Imbalanced International Relations," *Journal of Politics* 69(1) (2007): 100–115; John A. Vasquez *et al.*, "The ConflictSpace of Cataclysm," for network analyses that do combine rivalry and other types of information.

dynamics in Figure 3.3 sketches what we have in mind about the pinball nature of dynamics in the immediate pre-1914 rivalry field. Regrettably, to take the argument any further would require events data for a number of states in the decades leading up to 1914. It might then be possible to test how behavior in one rivalry impacted other rivalries. Yet even if we had these data, it might remain a serious methodological challenge to try to capture the dynamics sketched in Figure 3.3.

Our inability to measure rivalry dynamics with any precision, nevertheless, is no reason to ignore the phenomena. They seem important – perhaps vitally so. It cannot be said that the events that we are highlighting have been entirely ignored by First World War historians.[31] How else would we know about them if they had not been described and, quite often, singled out as important behaviors? Our modest contribution is to propose that the outbreak of the First World War be attributed in some degree to the ripeness of a complex field of rivalries that were subject to pinball dynamics in the years immediately leading up to 1914. If our case is plausible, it means that we need to pay more attention explicitly to rivalry behavior and to interactions between and among rivalries. In 1914, Austrian intransigence, Serbian-assisted terrorism, German ambitions, Russian desires to get even for backing down earlier or just to get control of the Dardanelles, French revanchism, British waffling, Italian opportunism in the Mediterranean, or Japanese opportunism in Asia and the South Pacific were not singularly responsible for the outbreak of war. They all were. It is not a case of the system making them do it. It was a case of their complex interactions via rivalries and alliances that contributed to the increased probability of a general war breaking out in ways that few observers at the time foresaw – or perhaps could have seen.

---

[31] In some respects, our approach parallels Paul W. Schroeder's tone in "World War I as Galloping Gertie: A Reply to Joachim Remak," *Journal of Modern History* 44(3) (1972): 319–345. The difference is that Schroeder's argument is almost entirely focused on individual countries, as opposed to our emphasis on rivalries.

4   A "formidable factor in European politics"
Views of Russia in 1914

T. G. Otte

All too often accounts of pre-1914 Great Power politics still tend to view their subject through the prism of a succession of crises. These then appear as preludes to the grand finale in July 1914. In consequence, an implicit quasi-teleology, with world war as Europe's inevitable destiny, remains endemic in much of the literature. In their efforts to discern patterns of accelerating crises historians (and political scientists in their wake) have missed other elements that were as characteristic, if not more so, of the international politics of this period. Not infrequently, these elements point in different directions to those mapped out in the extant literature. This is not to argue that generations of scholars were "wrong." Rather, it is a plea for a more nuanced look at the events of the period before 1914, one that is aware of the openness of historical situations and the complexities of decision-making.[1]

Two developments in the years 1911–1914 remain underdeveloped in the scholarly debate: (1) the degree to which the notion of détente had entered into the calculations of the Great Powers; and (2) the revival of Russian power. There were tensions between these two developments, tensions that cannot be resolved easily by historians, any more than they could be resolved by the decision-makers at the time. Indeed, the coexistence, in those years, of hope and pessimism, of détente and fear of war was linked together by perceptions of a revitalized Russia as the central factor in Great Power politics. As the following analysis will argue, these perceptions shaped decision-making in London, Paris, Berlin, and Vienna in July 1914.

At one level, emphasizing the significance of Russia in international politics before 1914 is nothing new.[2] The debate surrounding the meaning

---

[1] The tide has begun to turn now, Christopher Clark, *The Sleepwalkers: How Europe Went to War in 1914* (London: Allen Lane, 2012); Holger Afflerbach, "The Improbable War in Europe before 1914," in Holger Afflerbach and David Stevenson (eds.), *An Improbable War? The Outbreak of World War I and European Political Culture before 1914* (Oxford: Berghahn, 2007), pp. 161–182.

[2] Michael Ekstein, "Great Britain and the Triple Entente on the Eve of the Sarajevo Crisis," in F. H. Hinsley (ed.), *British Foreign Policy under Sir Edward Grey* (Cambridge University Press, 1977), pp. 342–348.

of Russia's mobilization in 1914 springs to mind.[3] The importance of Russia for Britain has also been stressed by scholars of quite different stripes. Keith Wilson deserves credit for having been the first to have recognized the Russian factor in British foreign policy.[4] Keith Neilson has offered an infinitely more sustained and sophisticated analysis; and this has been followed more recently by Jennifer Siegel, albeit within a chronologically and geographically more limited frame.[5] In their wake, a number of studies of Russian foreign policy appeared, most notably the works of Ronald P. Bobroff, Marina E. Soroka, and Michael A. Reynolds, as well as Sean McMeekin's attempt at iconoclasm.[6]

By contrast, Russia's revival in the two years before 1914 as a factor in European diplomacy has been largely ignored.[7] What follows here is not so much concerned with one might call the "objective reality" of Russia's power.[8] Rather, it is concerned with foreign perceptions and assessments of Russia. These offer crucial insights into foreign policy decision-making in the chancelleries of Europe on the eve of the First World War. This is not the place to discuss the concept of perception in the abstract. Suffice it to say that, for all their professional training to observe and report objectively, diplomats were not immune to flawed or wishful thinking, and their political masters possibly even less so. Nor were they immune to the dangers of "group think." Their perceptions and misperceptions

---

[3] Günther Frantz, *Russlands Eintritt in den Weltkrieg: Der Ausbau der Russischen Wehrmacht und ihr Einsatz bei Kriegsausbruch* (Berlin: Deutsche Verlagsgesellschaft für Politik & Geschichte, 1924); C. F. Turner, "The Russian Mobilization in 1914," *Journal of Contemporary History* 3(1) (1968): 65–88; Marc Trachtenberg, "The Meaning of Mobilization," in Steven E. Miller, Sean M. Lynn-Jones, and Stephen Van Evera (eds.), *Military Strategy and the Origins of the First World War* (Princeton University Press, 1991), pp. 195–225.

[4] Keith M. Wilson, *The Policy of the Ententes: Essays in the Determinants of British Foreign Policy* (Cambridge University Press, 1985).

[5] Keith Neilson, *Britain and the Last Tsar: British Policy towards Russia, 1894–1917* (Oxford: Clarendon, 1995); Jennifer Siegel, *Endgame: Britain, Russia and the Final Struggle for Central Asia* (London: I. B. Tauris, 2002).

[6] Ronald P. Bobroff, *Roads to Glory: Late Imperial Russia and the Turkish Straits* (London: I. B. Tauris, 2006); Marina E. Soroka, *Britain, Russia and the Road to the First World War: The Fateful Embassy of Count Aleksandr Benckendorff (1903–1916)* (Farnham: Ashgate, 2011); Michael A. Reynolds, *Shattering Empires: The Clash and Collapse of the Ottoman and Russian Empires, 1908–1918* (Cambridge University Press, 2011); Sean McMeekin, *The Russian Origins of the First World War* (Cambridge, MA: Belknap Press of Harvard University Press, 2011).

[7] One notable exception is Risto Ropponen, *Die Kraft Russlands* (Helsinki: Turku, 1968).

[8] The statistics contained in A. P. Korelin (ed.) (for Rossiskaya Akademiya Nauk/Institut Rossiiskoi Istorii), *Rossiya 1913 God: Statistiko-dokumental'nyi Spravochnik* (St. Petersburg: Blits, 1995), provide some insights into this; see also Peter Gatrell, *Government, Industry and Rearmament in Russia, 1900–1914: The Last Argument of Tsarism* (Cambridge University Press, 1994), pp. 161–196.

nevertheless shaped policy debates and decisions; and, to that extent, they are no less real than the "objective reality" of Russian power.[9]

"The present uncertainty": Britain and Russia

The 1907 Anglo-Russian convention remained the point of reference for British assessments of Russia between 1911 and 1914. That agreement itself served principally imperial purposes rather than considerations of the European equilibrium. British diplomacy had exploited the diminution of Russian power in the aftermath of the Russo-Japanese War to place Britain's strategic interests in Central Asia on a more secure footing, thereby easing Britain's imperial defense burden: "That is our fundamental argument for the Convention, for we have not got the men to spare, and that's the plain truth of it."[10]

The nadir of Russian power was a strategic opportunity for Britain. It was not, however, without risks. For there was an element of tension between Russia's reduced international stature, her rekindled ambitions in the Near East and southeastern Europe, and Britain's aim of securing continued Anglo-Russian cooperation around India's security glacis. That tension had the potential to erode the internal coherence of British policy toward Russia. And that tension grew as Russia recovered from the setback of 1905.

Debates within Britain's foreign policy elite underlined the extent to which its members appreciated the difficulties ahead. Some, like Sir Arthur Nicolson, the Permanent Under-Secretary, and the senior clerk in the Eastern Department, G. R. Clerk, were driven by a deepening fear that the 1907 arrangement might unravel. Others took a more relaxed view of that same scenario, among them Sir William Tyrrell, Sir Edward Grey's influential private secretary, and the Assistant Under-Secretary, Sir Eyre Crowe.

The resurgence of Russian military power as a result of the "Great Programme" and various military reforms affiliated to it, was carefully monitored in British diplomatic reporting. Improvements in Russia's railroad network meant speedier mobilization in a European war, an eventuality now discussed more regularly in Russian military circles,

---

[9] Plato's cave offers the pertinent insight here; otherwise Robert Jervis, *Perceptions and Misperceptions in International Politics* (Princeton University Press, 1976), remains the *locus classicus*; see also T. G. Otte, *The Foreign Office Mind: The Making of British Foreign Policy, 1865–1914* (Cambridge University Press, 2011).

[10] Morley to Minto (private), September 19, 1907, Minto MSS, MS 12737; for a full discussion see Neilson, *Britain and the Last Tsar*, pp. 267–288.

observed the military attaché at St. Petersburg, Lieutenant-Colonel Alfred Knox. But crucially, he suggested that the necessary improvements would require another five years to be completed.[11] In general, it was accepted in London that "Russia [was] naturally anxious to re-establish her much damaged prestige in the Balkans."[12] Yet there were also fears of Russia's lack of restraint. During the Liman von Sanders crisis, for instance, Sir Francis Bertie, the ambassador at Paris, "pointed out the danger of leaving Russia tête à tête with Germany."[13]

Nicolson repeatedly pressed for closer ties with St. Petersburg. No doubt, as ambassador to Russia before 1910, he "had succumbed ... to that attractive form of charlatanism known as 'le charme slav' [sic]."[14] And yet this was not merely a matter of sentiment. Nicolson's growing apprehensions about the state of Anglo-Russian relations were rooted in strategic calculations. Russia's recent economic progress and her revived military prowess made her "a formidable factor in European politics, and it is of the highest, and indeed essential importance that we should remain on the best terms with her."[15] Like others, Nicolson accepted that the 1907 arrangement was no longer functioning smoothly; unlike some of his colleagues, however, he was anxious to avoid discussions about a "radical revision" as this might lead to the collapse of any such talks.[16] Nicolson was haunted by the "present uncertainty" in relations with Russia; and Crowe, too, acknowledged that the fall of Prime Minister Vladimir N. Kokovtsov in February 1914, and his replacement with the aged Ivan L. Goremykin was "likely to react unfavourably on our relations with Russia."[17] Both Nicolson and Clerk, in fact, feared that the recent strengthening of the reactionary faction at St. Petersburg might over time lead to a Russo-German combination. Further, "if and when Austria breaks up, Germany & Russia will be brought very close together, for

[11] Knox to Buchanan (No. XLVI), January 22, 1914, FO 371/2090/3595. G. R. Clerk came to a similar view, see minute Clerk, March 1, 1914, on Bunsen to Grey (No. 37), February 27, 1914, FO 371/2091/9851.

[12] Minute Vansittart, February 17, 1914, on Bunsen to Grey (No. 32), February 13, 1914, FO 371/1899/6901.

[13] Memo Bertie, December 2, 1913, Bertie MSS, Add. MSS. 63032; Buchanan to Crowe, January 8, 1914, FO 371/2090/3140.

[14] Harold Nicolson, *Lord Carnock: A Study in the Old Diplomacy* (London: Constable, 1937), p. 246; the best assessment is Keith Neilson, "'My Beloved Russians': Sir Arthur Nicolson and Russia, 1906–1914," *International History Review* 9(4) (1987): 521–554.

[15] Nicolson to Goschen (private), March 11, 1913, Nicolson MSS, FO 800/364.

[16] Nicolson to Bunsen, January 13, 1914, Nicolson MSS, FO 800/372.

[17] Quotes from Nicolson to Hardinge (private), February 25, 1914, Nicolson MSS, FO 800/372; minute Crowe, February 12, 1914, FO 371/2091/6329.

both will prefer a peaceable division of the heritage to fighting over it, and the result may easily be a Russo-German alliance."[18]

Privately, Nicolson favored the conversion of the existing agreements with France and Russia into "definite alliances," but accepted that the hostility of the radical section of the ruling Liberal Party made this impossible. Still, he feared that unless "our relations with Russia ... [are] given a more definite and precise form" as regards Europe, St. Petersburg "may become weary of us and throw us overboard." It would "seriously shake our political position in India and the adjoining countries."[19] George Clerk struck a similarly alarmist tone in a lengthy memorandum on the "growing catalogue of our grievances against Russia" in Persia in July 1914. In it, he stipulated "that the first principle of our foreign policy must be genuinely good relations with Russia." To that end, sacrifices had to be made in Persia in order to safeguard Britain's position in the Persian Gulf.[20]

The views of Nicolson and Clerk mattered, but they were not decisive. The former was increasingly isolated at the Foreign Office, and the middle-ranking Clerk carried no real weight. There were, in fact, profound divisions among senior diplomats. Crowe and Tyrrell argued for a firmer line against Russia. For Crowe, there was "real danger ... [in] our continuing to remain closely associated in one and the same region with the absolutely dishonest policy of the Russian authorities."[21] The post-1907 policy, he argued, "of relying on Russia to carry out the spirit of the Anglo-Russian agreement concerning Persia is bankrupt."[22] He accepted the need for Anglo-Russian relations to be placed "on a satisfactory and so far as possible lasting foundation," but insisted on avoiding "responsibilities more onerous than would be the menace of the Russification of the whole of Persia."[23]

Tyrrell's stance was even more robust. Already in the spring of 1913, in light of recent shifts in the international landscape, Grey's secretive private secretary "paint[ed] our own position as absolutely *couleur de rose*.

---

[18] Minute, Clerk, April 6, 1914, on Buchanan to Grey (No. 93), March 31, 1914, FO 371/2092/15087.

[19] Nicolson to Bunsen, April 27, 1914, De Bunsen MSS, box 15; for radical opposition, see Harold Weinroth, "British Radicals and the Balance of Power, 1902–1914," *Historical Journal* 13(4) (1970): 653–682.

[20] Memo. Clerk, "Anglo-Russian Relations in Persia" (confidential), July 23, 1914, FO 371/2076/33484.

[21] Minute Crowe, May 1914, on Townley to Crowe (No. 123), April 28, 1914, FO 371/2073/22510; for some of this, see also Otte, *Foreign Office Mind*, pp. 365–388.

[22] Minute Crowe, June 2, 1914, on Townley to Grey (No. 143, confidential), May 13, 1914, FO 371/2059/24443.

[23] Minute Crowe, July 23, 1914, FO 371/2076/33484.

He seems to think that we can now snap our fingers both at the Triple Alliance and at France and Russia."[24] Tyrrell argued that the "cynical selfishness" of Russian policy posed a threat to the policy of the ententes: "he holds that Russia must be brought to her bearings."[25] Indeed, he favored some form of "a two-camp policy," a benign, neo-Bismarckian policy of acting as a bridge between the two European alliance groupings.[26]

The views expressed by Crowe and Tyrrell underlined the extent to which Foreign Office officials differed in their assessments of the Russian factor. The ambassador at St. Petersburg, Sir George Buchanan, took a mediating position. In the aftermath of the first Balkan conflict, he had still emphasized the latent fragility of the post-Stolypin "régime of 'exceptional laws.'" This also affected the conduct of Russian foreign policy: "There can be little doubt that the possibility of internal disturbances in case of a war [with Austria-Hungary] is one of the considerations which have contributed to induce the Russian Government to take up a resolutely pacific attitude."[27]

One year on, his views had changed. Russia's finances had been further consolidated, her army augmented, and her domestic politics bore a more favorable aspect. Russia, he prognosticated, would pursue a more vigorous policy in future, and warned against assumptions that she remained "committed to a policy of peace at any price." This had implications for Anglo-Russian relations: "it is useless to blind our eyes to the fact that, if we are to remain friends, with Russia, we must be prepared to give her our material as well as moral support in any conflict in which she becomes involved in Europe."[28] As for Central Asia, Buchanan acknowledged that the balance had shifted in Russia's favor, but he insisted that the best means of containing the further spread of Russian influence there would be to renegotiate the 1907 convention, even though it would raise "awkward questions."[29]

If there was divided counsel on how to deal with Russia, there was nevertheless a tacit acknowledgment that relations with her had reached

---

[24] Chirol to Hardinge (private), April 10, 1913, Hardinge MSS, vol. 93.

[25] Chirol to Hardinge, April 18, 1913, Hardinge MSS, vol. 93; see also T. G. Otte, "Détente 1914: Sir William Tyrrell's Secret Mission to Germany," *Historical Journal* 56(4) (2013): 175–204.

[26] Spring-Rice to Tyrrell, April 2, 1912, Spring-Rice MSS, FO 800/241.

[27] Buchanan to Grey (No. 15), January 17, 1913, FO 881/10175. There was a general consensus in Britain that "Russia cannot do much [in the Balkans] if Austria is backed by Germany," Paget to Barclay, August 6, 1912, Barclay MSS, 4/1.

[28] Buchanan to Grey (No. 60), March 4, 1914, FO 371/2092/10333; see also Knox to Buchanan (No. 52), April 14, 1914, FO 371/2092/17124 (on Russo-Romanian rapprochement).

[29] Buchanan to Nicolson, January 21, 1914, Nicolson MSS, FO 800/372.

a crucial juncture. This was also the view of the foreign secretary. Grey shared Tyrrell's assessment of the relative weakening of the two Germanic powers, and welcomed the recent improvement in relations with Berlin. He conceded that following Russia's effective relegation from the top flight of Great Power politics in 1905, Germany had harbored "aggressive intentions under the impression that Russia was not prepared ... to come to the aid of France." Faced with a revitalized Russia, Berlin was "now genuinely alarmed at the military preparations in Russia, the prospective increase in her military forces and particularly at the intended construction ... of strategic railways to converge on the German frontier." With the balance of power now largely restored, the foreign secretary hoped to act as the "connecting link between Germany and the Triple Entente and a restraint on the hastiness of Austria and Italy."[30]

Already his diplomacy during the last Balkan war was suggestive of his wider ambition for Britain to act as the "honest broker" in Europe. One of the architects of the 1907 convention, he was by no means a Russophile. Indeed, he shared many of the Liberal suspicions of tsarist Russia, and later, in 1917, rejoiced when Russia struck "out for freedom."[31] This did not mean that he wished to terminate the 1907 arrangement, but he was pessimistic about its chances of renewal in 1915. Given these uncertainties, he wished at least to create new options. For that reason, a joint Franco-Russian initiative, in April 1914, for closer Anglo-Russian ties was unwelcome: "It is a very delicate matter."[32] During his conversations with Doumergue and Poincaré in Paris, he threw cold water on any notion of far-reaching arrangements with Russia. A military agreement was outside the realm of practical politics; and naval talks, on the same basis as the Cambon–Grey notes of November 1912, "could not amount to very much." Though he did not admit to this in his Paris conversations, there could be no question of the Royal Navy operating in the Baltic, let alone jointly with the Russian fleet.[33]

This was also the Cabinet's view. On May 13, ministers decided that any naval talks with the Russians had to be on the basis of "Grey's letter to Cambon in Nov. [19]12 explaining that conversations between staffs commits us to nothing."[34] Grey was under no illusions that whatever

[30] Memo. Bertie (on conversation with Grey), June 25, 1914, Bertie MSS, Add. MSS 63033.
[31] Grey to Haldane, March 25, 1917, Haldane MSS, MS 5913.
[32] Minute Grey, n.d., on minute Nicolson (secret), April 17, 1914, FO 371/2092/17370.
[33] Grey to Bertie (No. 249, secret), May 1, 1914, FO 371/2092/19288; see also Raymond Poincaré, *Au service de la France, vol. IV: L'union sacrée 1914* (Paris: Plon, 1928), vol. 4, pp. 96–97, 112–115.
[34] Harcourt diary, May 13, 1914, Harcourt MSS, no accession number; Grey to Bertie (No. 343, secret), May 21, 1914, FO 371/2092/22807.

Britain's relations with Russia might be, they had the potential to affect Anglo-French relations as well: "I found that everyone conversant with politics ... were [sic] immensely impressed by the growing strength of Russia, and her tremendous resources and potential power and wealth."[35] Loosening the ties with Russia, then, was likely to strain those with France.

"Prodigious manifestations of vitality": France and Russia

Grey's comment on the prevailing attitude in Paris was perceptive. French policy, indeed, was more significant in the period under examination here than much of the extant literature would suggest – the effect, perhaps, of Renouvin's closing down of the debate about France and July 1914.[36] The Russian factor was the key to French policy, which revolved around the Russian alliance as its central axis. Given its significance for the stability of Great Power politics, this had implications for international relations. Indeed, for Raymond Poincaré, premier and foreign minister until 1913 and then president, it was *"la garantie suprême de l'ordre européen."*[37]

The revival of their ally's power could not but impress French officials and policymakers. Kokovtsov's fiscal consolidation schemes had produced a *"situation financière et économique tout à fait extraordinaire,"* a senior French financier observed at the end of 1913.[38] The state of Russia's public finances, combined with her military rearmament program, had a dual impact on French diplomatic calculations. At one level it reinforced the significance of Russia. Georges Louis, until 1913 French ambassador at St. Petersburg, reflected in early 1914 on Russia's recent progress: *"la Russie a un avenir immense. Sa force est en plein developpement."*[39] His Russophile successor but one, Maurice Paléologue, never ceased to impress upon the Quai d'Orsay that the financial and military efforts by the Russian government were *"prodigieuse manifestations de vitalité"* of this vast empire. They were likely to herald a more active foreign policy.[40]

---

[35] Grey to Bertie (No. 249, secret), May 1, 1914, FO 371/2092/19288.

[36] Pierre Renouvin, *Les origines immédiates de la guerre, 28 Juin–4 Août 1914* (Paris: Costes, 1924).

[37] As quoted in Pierre Miquel, *Poincaré* (Paris: Fayard, 1984), p. 333.

[38] Verneuil [Paris bourse] to Pichon, November 10, 1913, *Documents diplomatiques français* (henceforth *DDF*) (3), vol. 8, No. 469; for the background see René Girault, *Emprunts russes et investissements français en Russie, 1887–1914* (Paris: Colin, 1973).

[39] Louis journal, January 12, 1914; Georges Louis, *Les carnets de Georges Louis, 1908–1917*, 2 vols. (Paris: F. Rieder, 1926); vol. 2, p. 94.

[40] Paléologue to Doumergue, March 21, 1914, *DDF* (3), vol. 10, No. 52. This resonated with contemporary preoccupations with an *élan vital*, reflected also in French military doctrine, Stephen Van Evera, "The Cult of the Offensive and the Origins of the First

But therein lay a problem. A strengthened Russia was likely to be less dependent on France, and with it the relative balance of influence within the Franco-Russian alliance would be altered, irrespective of France's own rearmament efforts under the contentious Three Years law.[41] To appreciate this it is necessary to consider also French assessments of the two Germanic powers, for the likely future more especially of Russo-German relations was the reverse of the Franco-Russian coin. Britain's ambassador at Paris had grasped this, and warned that "there are many Frenchmen who think that war is inevitable within the next two years and that it might be better for France to have it soon. The arguments in favour of an early war are the improbability of Austria on account of Slavs being able to give much assistance to Germany and the hostile feeling against Austria in the Balkans."[42] General Édouard de Castelnau, of the French General Staff, made similar observations to his British counterpart, Lieutenant-General Sir Henry Wilson: "It was curious to find that Castelnau is in favour of a war now as being a good opportunity, France Russia being ready, Austria in a state of confusion. Germany unwilling."[43] This is not to suggest that the French government or elements in the French military sought to bring about an early conflict, let alone a preventive war. Nevertheless, the statements by Castelnau and others are suggestive of the importance French officials accorded to Austria-Hungary's entanglement in the Balkans and its effect on Germany and Russia.

The strains in Franco-German relations after Agadir were profound. Nevertheless, there was a widely shared assumption that the German chancellor, Theobald von Bethmann-Hollweg, was earnest in his desire for peace.[44] Even the two German army laws of 1912 and 1913 were not necessarily seen as active preparation for a war. Lieutenant-Colonel Marcel Serret, the military attaché at Berlin, judged that *"sans avoir d'intentions belligieuses, elle* [that is, Germany] *est decidée à se constituer une force militaire d'une supériorité impressante. Elle veut que dans les conflits . . . le poids de son epée*

World War," Steven E. Miller, Sean M. Lynn-Jones, and Stephen Van Evera (eds.), *Military Strategy and the Origins of the First World War* (Princeton University Press, 1991), pp. 59–108.

[41] D. R. Ralston, *The Army of the Republic: The Place of the Military in the Political Evolution of France, 1871–1914* (Cambridge, MA: MIT Press, 1967), pp. 343–371; Gerd Krumeich, *Armaments and Politics in France on the Eve of the First World War* (Oxford: Berg, 1984), pp. 118–125.

[42] Bertie to Grey (private), March 3, 1913, Bertie MSS, FO 800/166. Grey reacted swiftly, impressing upon Bertie that "if France is aggressive to Germany there will be no support from Great Britain," vice versa (private), March 4, 1913, Bertie MSS, FO 800/166.

[43] Wilson diary, February 13, 1913, Wilson MSS, DS/MISC/80 (not in C. E. Caldwell, *Field-Marshal Sir Henry Wilson: His Life and Diaries*, 2 vols. (London: Cassell, 1927), vol. 1, p. 122); see also Clark, *Sleepwalkers*, p. 302.

[44] J. Cambon to Poincaré, September 19, 1912, *DDF* (3), vol. 3, No. 432.

fasse immédiatement pencher la balance sans même qu'il soit nécessaire de sortir la lame du fourreau."[45]

Serret's comments underline the extent to which deterrence was accepted as an element of contemporary international relations. Such calculations were balanced, however, by fears that the "war party" in Berlin might gain the upper hand by exploiting any future crisis in the Balkans to foment nationalist hysteria in favor of a European war. It was, as Jules Cambon observed to his Italian colleague Alberto Pansa, *"que tout serait facile s'il n'existait ni presse, ni opinion."*[46] Austria-Hungary's mounting problems in the Balkans might bring about such an eventuality. Cambon had a shrewd appreciation of the Wilhelmstrasse's concerns about the possible demise of the Habsburg monarchy: *"Ils considèrent l'Autriche, toute leur alliés, qu'elle soit comme à la veille de tomber en pièces."*[47]

The prospect of that ancient edifice, the Habsburg monarchy, "going to pieces" mattered all the more in light of Austro-Russian tensions in the Balkans and their likely impact on Germany's relations with Russia. This was not something any French government could safely ignore. Historians have tended to conclude that Poincaré pursued a consistent policy of restraining Russia.[48] And yet there is clear evidence that he, a native of Lorraine and by no means averse to *revanchisme*, revised the terms of France's engagement toward Russia. At the height of the 1912 Austro-Serb crisis after the First Balkan War, Russian diplomacy appeared disinclined to support Belgrade over the issue of Serbian access to the Adriatic. For his part, Poincaré sought to stiffen Russia's position. He made it clear to Aleksandr P. Izvolsky, the Russian ambassador at Paris, that insofar as France was concerned, *"il n'a rien dit, ni rien laissé supposer qui puisse impliquer de sa part une défaillance de concours."*[49] Advanced with the lawyerly rigidity so characteristic of Poincaré, Izvolsky

---

[45] Serret to Etienne, March 1, 1913, *DDF* (3), vol. 5, No. 494.

[46] J. Cambon to Pansa, January 4, 1914, in Enrico Serra, "Lettres de Jules Cambon à Alberto Pansa," *Revue d'histoire diplomatique* 116(1) (2002): 88.

[47] J. Cambon to Doumergue (No. 187, *absolument secret*), April 13, 1914, *DDF* (3), vol. 10, No. 101.

[48] For this argument, see J. F. V. Keiger, *France and the Origins of the First World War* (London: Macmillan, 1983), p. 96; M. B. Hayne, *The French Foreign Office and the Origins of the First World War* (Oxford: Clarendon Press, 1993), pp. 244–246.

[49] Poincaré to Izvolsky, November 16, 1912, *DDF* (3), vol. 4, No. 468. Further evidence of Poincaré's harder line can be found in his proposal for a preemptive intervention *à trois* in the Balkans to thwart Austria, which so startled the Russians; Izvolsky to Sazonov, October 25/November 7, 1912; Friedrich Stieve (ed.), *Der diplomatische Schriftwechsel Iswolskis, 1911–1914*, 4 vols. (Berlin: Deutsche Verlagsgesellschaft für Politik & Geschichte, 1925), vol. 4, No. 554.

rendered his words in more emphatic terms: "If Russia wages war, France also will wage war."[50]

Whether or not the exchanges at the close of 1912 constituted a "Balkanization of the Franco-Russian alliance," let alone a "blank check" *avant la lettre*,[51] they undoubtedly narrowed the French definition of the *casus foederis*.[52] The specific circumstances of any putative conflict were no longer decisive. What mattered was whether or not Germany intervened and how Russia reacted.[53] From now on, French diplomacy was less inclined to restrain Russia in the east, much to the annoyance of British officials.[54] During the Liman von Sanders crisis, for instance, Théophile Delcassé, architect of the 1904 entente and ambassador during the brief interval between Louis and Paléologue, vehemently agreed with the tsar that the crisis "*a rendu manifeste la menace allemande aux intérêts essentiels de la Russie,*" and that the Russian government should not allow the Germans "*marcher sur les pieds.*"[55]

The deterioration in Russo-German relations in early 1914 was carefully noted, but French diplomats cast their glances farther ahead. In contrast to Cambon at Berlin, Paléologue dismissed public opinion as negligible "*car jusqu'au dernier moment, il y'a possibilité d'un arrangement direct entre les monarques.*" Indeed, what is striking about the reports from this highly strung ambassador is the extent to which they focused on the activities of the "pro-German" clique at the St. Petersburg court. The activities of the former finance minister, Sergei Yulevich Witte, were the frequent topic of his comments: "*Le comte Witte poursuit sa campagne en faveur d'une alliance russo-franco-allemande.*"[56]

Paléologue's insistent warnings of pro-German intrigues did not fail to make an impression on Poincaré and the foreign minister, Gaston

---

[50] Izvolsky to Sazonov, November 17, 1912, *Die International Beziehungen im Zeitalter des Imperialismus* (henceforth *IBZI*), vol. 4(1), No. 258. *Caveat Lector*: Poincaré later suggested that Izvolsky "*suivant son habitude . . . a fait de notre entretien un récit pittoresque et un peu chargé de couleurs*", *ibid., Au service*, vol. 2, p. 199.

[51] Clark, *Sleepwalkers*, pp. 293–301; Wilhelm von Schoen, *Erlebtes: Beiträge zur politischen Geschichte der Neuesten Zeit* (Stuttgart: Deutsche Verlags-Anstalt, 1921), pp. 144–145.

[52] The French Cabinet had sanctioned Poincaré's choice of words, *ibid., Au service*, vol. 2, p. 338.

[53] Ribot's comment on Poincaré's strong sense of obligation to Russia, see Stefan Schmidt, *Frankreichs Außenpolitik in der Julikrise 1914: ein Beitrag zur Geschichte des Ausbruchs des Ersten Weltkrieges* (Munich: Oldenbourg, 2009), p. 257.

[54] Cartwright to Nicolson, April 11, 1913, Cartwright MSS, C(A)45; Otte, *Foreign Office Mind*, pp. 375–376.

[55] Delcassé to Doumergue, January 29, 1914, *DDF* (3), vol. 9, No. 189.

[56] Tel. Paléologue to Doumergue (Nos. 128–129, *très confidentiel*), March 24, 1914, *DDF* (3), vol. 10, No. 20; for the Russian background, see Dominic Lieven, "Pro-Germans and Russian Foreign Policy, 1890–1914," *International History Review* 2(1) (1980): 34–54.

Doumergue. During Edward Grey's visit to Paris, Doumergue impressed upon the visitor "that Germany would make great efforts to detach Russia from the French Alliance, and might possibly succeed."[57] Indeed, the perceived growth in Russian power since 1912 had created exaggerated fears in France of a *renversement des alliances*. A continued Russo-German antagonism was not considered to be inevitable; nor were the current tensions thought to be insuperable obstacles to re-establishing closer ties between the two eastern monarchies. If Paléologue is to be believed, even René Viviani, the highly strung Socialist prime minister and a neophyte in all matters diplomatic, was exercised by the specter of a reconstituted Romanov–Hohenzollern alliance: "*nous y perdrions notre indépendance nationale! . . . Ce ne serait pas seulement la fin de la République, ce serait la fin de la France.*"[58]

The revival of Russian power before 1914 had a profound impact on France. It encouraged both French arrogance and anxiety, the two mutually reinforcing elements of French policy during the second half of the long nineteenth century.

"Good personal dispositions"?: Germany and Russia

In so far as Germany was concerned, since the late 1880s relations with Russia had oscillated between periods of rapprochement and acute tensions.[59] In recent years, since the Potsdam *entrevue* in November 1910, German diplomacy had been steadily working toward a rapprochement. The subsequent agreement of August 1911 on the Baghdad railroad and Persia was significant on two counts. In terms of relations between Berlin and St. Petersburg, the agreement can be interpreted as part of a peripheral diplomatic strategy that sought to improve relations by resolving disputes outside core European affairs. It also helped further to calm Great Power relations in the aftermath of the Agadir crisis.[60]

One year later, following the meeting between the kaiser and the tsar at Baltic Port in early 1912, Bethmann-Hollweg viewed the state of relations

---

[57] Grey to Bertie (No. 249, secret), May 1, 1914, FO 371/2092/19288; for Doumergue, see Hayne, *French Foreign Office*, pp. 249–252.

[58] Maurice Paléoloque, *Au quai d'Orsay à la veille de la tourmente: Journal 1913–1914* (Paris: Plon, 1947), p. 318; for Viviani, see Hayne, *French Foreign Office*, pp. 274–275.

[59] I. I. Astafiev, *Russko–Germanskie Diplomaticheskie Otosheni'ia, 1905–1914: Ot Portsmutskogo Mira do Potsdamskogo Soglashenia* (Moscow, n.p., 1972); Barbara Vogel, *Deutsche Rußlandpolitik: Das Scheitern der deutschen Weltpolitik unter Bülow, 1900–1906* (Düsseldorf: Bertelsmann Universitätsverlag, 1973); Irmin Schneider, *Die deutsche Russlandpolitik, 1890– 1900* (Paderborn: F. Schöningh, 2003).

[60] The concept of a peripheral diplomatic strategy is well established in the literature on Anglo-German relations, see, for instance, Gregor Schöllgen, *Imperialismus und Gleichgewicht: Deutschland, England und die orientalische Frage* (Munich: Oldenbourg, 1992). There is,

with Russia with satisfaction. But he was under no illusion, as he explained to his cousin, Germany's ambassador at St. Petersburg, Count Friedrich von Pourtalès-Cronstern, that "Russia loves us no more than she loves any other Great Power. For that we are too strong, too much of a parvenu and just too disgusting." Nonetheless, Kokovtsov's policy of economic consolidation ruled out an aggressive foreign policy, for the moment at any rate. In east Asia, the rapprochement with Japan placed Russia in a much more secure position. Elsewhere, Britain, France, and Germany sought Russia's cooperation. Under these circumstances, there were no manifest advantages to be secured by Russia pursuing aggressive aims. But Bethmann-Hollweg was adamant "that we must use the situation to make our relations with Russia as friendly as possible, and that alone is the meaning of Potsdam and Baltic Port. We will thereby calm France, improve our relations with England and can calmly look forward to any future opening of the Balkan question."[61]

Remarkably, Bethmann-Hollweg's oft-reported pessimism is not borne out in the extant contemporaneous evidence. On his return from Russia, he poured scorn on the "super-clever, pan-German alarmist articles" about Russian perfidy. Such "blockheads", he concluded, were not cut out for serious politics.[62] If anything, the chancellor was "satisfied with Russia," as he confirmed to a leading German industrialist at the same time: "He trusts the Tsar, they want calm, but have no liking for Germany . . . Bethmann is hoping only for a *modus vivendi*."[63] He was not driven by visions of an ultimate racial struggle between Teutons and Slavs, as prognosticated by ultra-nationalist writers: "We must keep France in check through a cautious policy towards Russia and England. Naturally this does not please our chauvinists and is unpopular, but I see no alternative for Germany in the near future."[64]

---

however, sufficient evidence to suggest that German diplomacy pursued similar aims with regard to Russia, Friedrich Kießling, *Gegen den "Großen Krieg"? Entspannung in den internationalen Beziehungen, 1911–1914* (Munich: Oldenbourg, 2002), pp. 109–122.

[61] Bethmann-Hollweg to Pourtalès, July 30, 1912, Nachlass Pourtalès, GFM 25/3; Willibald Gutsche, *Aufstieg und Fall eines kaiserlichen Reichskanzlers: Theobald von Bethmann Hollweg, 1856–1921. Ein politisches Lebensbild* (East Berlin: Akademie Verlag, 1973), pp. 96–97, for a critical interpretation.

[62] Bethmann-Hollweg to Pourtalès, July 30, 1912, Nachlass Pourtalès, GFM 25/3. According to a later oral statement by the chancellor's son, Bethmann-Hollweg had decided against planting trees on his estate north of Berlin because the Russians would soon be there; see Eberhard von Vietsch, *Bethmann Hollweg: Staatsmann zwischen Macht und Ethos* (Boppard: Boldt, 1969), p. 143.

[63] Rathenau diary, July 25, 1912; Hartmut P. von Strandmann (ed.), *Walther Rathenau: Tagebuch, 1907–1922* (Düsseldorf: Droste, 1967), pp. 168–169.

[64] Bethmann-Hollweg to Eisendecher, March 23, 1912, Nachlass Eisendecher, GFM 25/10; Konrad H. Jarausch, "The Illusion of Limited War: Chancellor Bethmann-Hollweg's

Russia's desire for financial consolidation, internal development, and, in consequence, international calm were recurring themes in German discussions. The industrialist Felix Deutsch, well connected in Berlin and St. Petersburg, dismissed suggestions of Russian bellicosity: "Diplomacy and finance are thoroughly pacifically minded." In the aftermath of Turkey's collapse during the first Balkan conflict, he observed that "in Russia, they do not want war but they say they cannot abandon the Serbs, who are Slavs, because otherwise they would get nothing."[65] The conviction that domestic considerations constrained Russian foreign policy was well entrenched in Berlin. As the banker Robert von Mendelssohn impressed on Bethmann-Hollweg, "influential circles" in the Russian capital were against war: "they fear major internal complications as a consequence of a war; their interest in the Balkans was not so great that they would want to run such an immeasurable risk."[66] German consular reporting reinforced such views. The celebrations of the Borodino centenary, the consul-general at Moscow observed, had

brought about no rapprochement between the Tsar and the nation, but ... they show anew the broad and deep chasm that exists in Russia between Court, government, military and the clergy on the one hand and the economically and intellectually productive forces of the nation on the other, and which threaten to widen and deepen further under the pressure of the current reaction.[67]

Russia's latent instability, however, did not facilitate forward planning, as Ambassador Pourtalès observed during the St. Petersburg strikes in early 1914: "No-one here can have any doubts that, even if the current calm may last for years, one has to reckon with the possibility of a new revolution breaking out." There were further risks in that the tsar's ministers had come to view pan-Slavism as a "palliative against revolutionary propaganda."[68] The uncertain outlook in Russia also forced a more

Calculated Risk, July 1914," *Central European History* 2(1) (1969): 48–76, at 52–53; Konrad H. Jarausch, "Statesmen versus Structure: Germany's Role in the Outbreak of World War One Reconsidered," *Laurentian University Review* 5(3) (1973): 133–160.

[65] Quotes from Deutsch to Harden, March 31 and December 21, 1912, Nachlass Harden, No. 29, Heft 2; see also Ernst Schulin, "Walther Rathenaus Diotima: Lili Deutsch, ihre Familie und der Kreis um Gerhart Hauptmann," in Hans Wilderotter (ed.), *Die Extreme berühren sich: Walther Rathenau, 1867–1922* (Berlin: Argon Verlag, 1994), pp. 55–66.

[66] Mendelssohn to Bethmann-Hollweg (private), April 10, 1913, PAAA, Russland 61, Allgemeine Angelegenheiten, Bd. 121. His informant was Iakov Isaakovich Utin, director of the St. Petersburg Discount Bank.

[67] Kohlhaas to Bethmann-Hollweg (No. 6365), September 16, 1912, Kohlhaas to Bethmann-Hollweg, Bd. 120; the kaiser commented in the margins: "This will end badly."

[68] Quotes from Pourtalès to Bethmann-Hollweg (No. 34), January 31, 1914 and (No. 118), April 12, 1913; Pourtalès to Bethmann-Hollweg, Bd. 121.

passive attitude on Berlin, as the state secretary at the *Auswärtiges Amt*, Gottlieb von Jagow, reflected later during the war.[69] The chargé d'affaires at St. Petersburg, Baron Hellmuth Lucius von Stoedten, wove these different factors into an analysis of Russian policy. The fear of "internal tremors" as a result of external complications made Russian diplomacy pacific, he argued, just as the British ambassador did at the same time. He also laid particular stress on Sazonov's emphasis on the "traditionally friendly relations with Germany." Lucius also sensed growing Anglo-Russian tensions in Central Asia. In consequence, Russian policy was driven by "an honest desire" for a Balkan settlement with Austria-Hungary and a rapprochement with Germany.[70]

Jagow concurred with assessments of Russia's essentially pacific policy. If anything, he was "rather concerned about the conditions in Austria," where a "war party" threatened to gain the upper hand. Jagow's policy pursued the twin objectives of allaying Russian fears of Habsburg aggression lest pan-Slav militants drove the tsar's government into foreign complications, and of counteracting any military influence at Vienna. There "they seem to think that even during an Austro-Serb conflict Russia would look on quietly and would not interfere. They even imagine that, if Russia were indeed to move, France and England would sit still. I cannot share this belief."[71]

Pourtalès reinforced Jagow's concerns about Austro-Hungarian decision-making. At St. Petersburg, he averred, "the Emperor, Sazonow and Kokowzew 'pour tant et tant de raisons' ... do *not* want war and will do everything to avoid it." At the same time, in the event of an Austro-Hungarian invasion of Serbia, "nothing can be guaranteed." A Slavophile sentimental spasm ("*Gefühlspolitik*") would then sweep away all other calculations, and would even "affect those circles that only yesterday made fun of the exaggerated sympathies with the Slav brethren."[72] Indeed, there can be no doubt that German diplomacy put pressure on Vienna to moderate its behavior, even though Jagow sought to deflect some of Britain's pressure on the Ballhausplatz.[73]

---

[69] Gottlieb von Jagow, "Deutschland und Russland vor dem Krieg", n.d. unpublished TS (*c.* 1917/18), Nachlass Jagow, GFM 25/15.

[70] Lucius to Bethmann-Hollweg (No. 9), January 8, 1913, *Die Grosse Politik der Europäischen Kabinette, 1871–1914* (henceforth *GP*) 34/1, No. 12649; for Buchanan, see above, n. 27.

[71] Jagow to Pourtalès (*ganz geheim*), February 2, 1913, Nachlass Pourtalès, GFM 25/3. Such fears were widespread in Berlin, see Radziwill to Robilant, December 31, 1912: "Austria is in the grip of insanity and will eventually set Europe alight," Marie Radziwill, *Briefe vom deutschen Kaiserhof, 1889–1915* (Berlin: Ullstein, 1936), p. 359.

[72] Pourtalès to Jagow, February 6, 1913, Nachlass Pourtalès, GFM 25/3.

[73] Wilhelm II to Franz Ferdinand, February 24, 1913, *GP* 34/1, No. 12891, n. ***; also Kießling, *Gegen den "Großen Krieg"?*, p. 244. For Jagow, see Jagow to Tschirschky (No. 247), February 24, 1914, *GP* 34/1, No. 12888.

The importance that German officials placed on what Bethmann-Hollweg called good "personal dispositions" between leading members of the two governments in Berlin and St. Petersburg is striking, this at the time of the Brunswick nuptials, the last European monarchical reunion before 1914. Such dispositions, he hoped, would furnish a basis for further improvements in Russo-German relations, though he did not share the kaiser's enthusiasm for monarchical diplomacy:

His Majesty of course again sees the skies full of violins and I am already fearful of disappointments and set-backs. Here he has announced to all the world that together with his cousin [the tsar] he has solved the Balkan problem . . . and that everything went so speedily and smoothly because imbecile ministers had not been involved.[74]

The Wilhelmstrasse's efforts to avert Austro-Russian complications also affected Berlin's relations with Vienna and Paris. Indeed, these efforts were rooted in the fear that "the time is not so very far off when [Austria-Hungary] may go the way of the Ottoman Empire."[75] Linked to this was a profound mistrust in Habsburg reliability. Sazonov's statement that "in Balkan questions he was *au fond* in agreement with Austria" was all very well, Jagow commented in the summer of 1913. Vienna's inveterate sloppiness (*"K[aiserlich] u[nd] K[önigliche] Schlampigkeitskrämerei"*) might well wreck any negotiations.[76] As for France, for all the talk in recent years of a *réveil national*, "when the Balkan war conjured up the specter of serious European complications," Poincaré soon struck a peaceful tone, observed the ambassador at Paris, Wilhelm Baron von Schoen. Indeed, the French president had suggested that recent parallel efforts to resolve the Balkan crisis pointed to a broader settlement of Franco-German disputes. Other factors, such as France's disturbed domestic scene and temporary military weakness as a result of the transition to the three-year service period, made for peace.[77] For all its desire

---

[74] Bethmann-Hollweg to Pourtalès, June 2, 1913, Nachlass Pourtalès, GFM 25/3. Hence, also unflattering references to foreign diplomats who worked against such friendly dispositions, see Jagow's reference to Izvolsky as a "*Schwein*," Jagow to Pourtalès, January 16, 1914, Nachlass Pourtalès, GFM 25/3; Hintze's characterization of Nicolson as a "mischief-maker and diplomat without scruples" (*"Ränkeschmied und skrupelloser Diplomat"*), Hintze to Wilhelm II (No. 182), April 22, 1910 (copy), *ibid.*

[75] Rodd to Grey (private), January 6, 1913 (on conversation with Jagow), Rennell of Rodd MSS, Bodleian Library, vol. 15; also Nicolson to Bunsen, March 30, 1914, De Bunsen MSS, box 15.

[76] Jagow to Pourtalès, July 26, 1913, Nachlass Pourtalès, GFM 25/3.

[77] Schoen to Bethmann-Hollweg (No. 384), November 15, 1913, *GP* xxxix, No. 15657; Schoen, *Erlebtes*, pp. 148–149; for the background, see Jean-Marie Mayeur, *La vie politique sous la Troisième République* (Paris: Seuil, 1984), pp. 223–232.

for détente with France, however, Berlin did not favor a simultaneous Austro-French rapprochement.[78]

Not everything in Russo-German relations pointed to détente. There were countervailing tendencies. The German reaction to the two conflicts in the Balkans was a further round of army expansion. Expectations of a future war were real enough. Even Bethmann-Hollweg, though generally optimistic about the state of Russo-German relations, acknowledged that if "it were in Russia's interest to make war on us, they [the Russian government] would do so in cold blood."[79] Such fears never really ebbed away. The Balkan Wars lent greater weight to them, and the shifting military balance in Europe fueled them further still. Yet the 1913 *Wehrvorlage* was not driven by fears of an impending war, nor did it inaugurate active preparations for a major European conflict. At the time, the younger Moltke argued, Germany could "face a war with confidence, as Russia is not ready, while France is on the one hand heavily engaged in Morocco and on the other threatened by Italy's realignment with Austria and Germany." But the current situation could change, especially since Russia was likely to be in a much stronger position two or three years hence, while the latent Austro-Italian antagonism might be revived. "Then Germany must be strong enough to rely on her own power, and thus cannot commence the development of her military strength soon enough."[80] The need for an effective deterrence was thus the flipside of détente.

The Liman von Sanders crisis at the turn of 1913/14 might have been more a case of blunder rather than premeditation. But it certainly put a dampener on recent talk of a Russo-German rapprochement, so much so that Jagow moved swiftly to make a compromise possible.[81] In the aftermath of the crisis, in the spring of 1914, there was also a Russo-German press war which soured relations between Berlin and St. Petersburg. Indeed, at that moment, expectations of détente ran parallel to heightened fears of conflict. In January 1914, Moltke noted that "the war readiness of Russia has made tremendous progress since the Russo-Japanese War and has today reached a degree as never before."[82] Privately, Jagow operated with the argument of "the coming world war" during the pre-budget

---

[78] For the row over Austro-French railway cooperation in the Balkans, see Tschirschky to Jagow (No. 258), February 23, 1914, *GP* xxxvii/2, No. 15139.

[79] Bethmann-Hollweg to Pourtalès, July 30, 1912, Nachlass Pourtalès, GFM 25/3.

[80] Moltke to Heeringen, December 2, 1913, Reichsarchiv, *Der Weltkrieg, 1914–1918, vol. 1: Kriegsrüstung und Kriegswirtschaft* (Berlin: Mittler, 1930), App. No. 50, 150; Stig Förster, *Der Doppelte Militarismus: Die deutsche Rüstungspolitik zwischen Status-Quo-Sicherung und Aggression* (Wiesbaden: Steiner, 1985), pp. 208–296; David Stevenson, *Armaments and the Coming of War: Europe, 1904–1914* (Oxford University Press, 1996), pp. 285–298.

[81] Jagow to Pourtalès, January 16, 1914, Nachlass Pourtalès, GFM 25/3.

[82] Moltke to Jagow (No. 3035), February 24, 1914, *GP* 39, No. 15839.

negotiations with the parties in the *Reichstag*.[83] Both Jagow and Bethmann-Hollweg were anxious also on account of Russian attempts to persuade Grey to enter into naval talks, of which the Wilhelmstrasse knew through an intelligence source in the Russian embassy in London.[84]

Yet the deterioration in relations between Berlin and St. Petersburg in the first half of 1914 was but the latest turn of the Russo-German kaleidoscope. It created an element of uncertainty, but it did not presage war. Pourtalés remained unwavering in his conviction that the tsar and his government were animated by pacific designs.[85] And Jagow still affirmed the existence of a "general détente" in May 1914.[86] Indeed, in London, Nicolson thought he had discerned a "tendency" in Russia and Germany which would "become more and more marked towards a friendly understanding."[87]

"Weak and fickle": Austria-Hungary and Russia

Clearly, Berlin's pursuit of détente with Russia was a function of the state of relations between the two Central Powers. Conversely, Ballhausplatz assessments of Russia in this period reflected Vienna's concerns about the solidity of the Austro-German alliance.

Since 1908–1909, Habsburg foreign policy had become *Balkanpolitik*, and the one constant factor in all Vienna's diplomatic calculations was the antagonism with Russia.[88] There was no doubt as to the latent potential of the Habsburg monarchy's competitor for regional influence. The armaments program of 1912–1913 and the hike in military expenditure caused some unease among Austro-Hungarian diplomats.[89] At the same time, the opaque nature of Russia's national finances, the brittle basis of her economy, and her domestic, social, and political fragility featured

---

[83] See Fritz Fischer, *Griff nach der Weltmacht: Die Kriegsziele des Kaiserlichen Deutschland, 1914/18*, 3rd edn. (Düsseldorf: Droste, 1964), pp. 44–45.

[84] See Manfred Rauh, "Die britisch–russische Marinekonvention von 1914 und der Ausbruch des Ersten Weltkriegs," *Militärgeschichtliche Mitteilungen* 47(10) (1987): 37–62.

[85] Pourtalès to Bethmann-Hollweg (No. 85), March 11, 1914, *GP* 39, No. 15844. Even the kaiser did not anticipate conflict in the immediate future, see marginal notes by Wilhelm II, *ibid.*, pp. 553–554.

[86] J. Cambon to Doumergue (No. 332), June 8, 1914, *DDF* (3), vol. 10, No. 341.

[87] Nicolson to Bunsen, April 27, 1914, De Bunsen MSS, box 15.

[88] See the reflections by Alexander von Musulin, *Das Haus am Ballplatz: Erinnerungen eines österreich-ungarischen Diplomaten* (Munich: Verlag für Kulturpolitik, 1924), pp. 176–177. This was also reflected in Habsburg military preparations; for an authoritative account, see Günther Kronenbitter, *"Krieg im Frieden": Die Führung der k.u.k. Armee und die Großmachtpolitik Österreich-Ungarns, 1906–1914* (Munich: Oldenbourg, 2003), pp. 79–144.

[89] See, for example, Czernin to Berchtold (No. 40F, *vertraulich*), October 24/11, 1913, PA X/139.

prominently in the reports from the St. Petersburg embassy. Count Otto Czernin, the chargé d'affaires there, and the two last Habsburg ambassadors to Russia, Count Duglas Thurn and Count Friedrich Szápáry von Szápar stressed the weak financial underpinnings of Russia's military program, as well as her latent domestic instability. For all the forceful language deployed by Russian diplomacy during the Balkan Wars, in Thurn's analysis, it was not likely to use "energetic measures to make its positions prevail."[90] Like their German ally, senior Habsburg diplomats placed great emphasis on close personal relations between the leading personalities at the two courts as a means of managing Austro-Russian relations.[91]

Czernin repeatedly stressed the hairline fractures in the foundations of Russia's Great Power position. In the autumn of 1913, for instance, he argued that the current wave of industrial strikes and the confused state of Duma politics against a forceful foreign policy. Along with German diplomats, he contended that the alliance with France would have a corrosive effect on Russian society: "Friendship with the red republic ... must in time contribute to the spreading of revolutionary tendencies in Russia."[92]

Assumptions of "Russia's current weakness" undoubtedly contained an element of wishful thinking. Yet they were widespread in Austro-Hungarian circles. Russian policy during the recent Balkan crises had merely underlined Russia's impotence. St. Petersburg, Czernin reasoned, had pursued no "aggressive ideas of encircling ... the Monarchy." If anything, Russian diplomacy was "weak and fickle." It had

retreated in the question of Serbia's access to the sea, as in the frontier and evacuation questions and in the Scutari episode, [it] has allowed the Balkan alliance to self-destruct, has ruined Bulgaria for a long time, and has demonstrated anew to Serbia that, on Hartwig's [Russian minister at Belgrade] words there do not necessarily follow deeds by the Russian government.

The only danger to Austria-Hungary lay in her own internal situation. Complications here would, without fail, stimulate "the destructive tendencies of the Tsarist empire."[93]

---

[90] Tel. Thurn to Berchtold (No. 285), August 19, 1913, PA X/139.
[91] Mensdorff to Berchtold (private), November 21, 1913, PA VIII/149.
[92] Czernin to Berchtold (No. 42D), November 8/October 26, 1913, PA X/139; see also Czernin's comments on Durnovo's statement on the reciprocal effect of domestic and external politics, Czernin to Berchtold (No. 43D), 21, November 8, 1913, *ibid.*; for a German view, see Pourtalès to Bethmann-Hollweg (No. 295), October 13, 1913, PAAA, Russland 61, Bd. 121.
[93] Czernin to Berchtold (No. 46F), December 6/November 23, 1913, PA X/139. Ironically, Czernin's predecessor, Julius von Szilassy, had advocated a more accommodating policy, see memo. Szilassy, November 7/20, 1912; Julius von Szilassy, *Der Untergang der Donau-Monarchie: Diplomatische Erinnerungen* (Vienna: Neues Vaterland, 1921), pp. 218–219.

Szápáry argued that, for the foreseeable future, the Russian government still saw "the internal economic and national strengthening of the [Russian] empire as its most immediate task."[94] In a lengthy *tour d'horizon* in early 1914 for the benefit of the Habsburg foreign minister, Count Leopold Berchtold, himself a former ambassador at St. Petersburg, Szápáry emphasized the clear desire on the part of Goremykin – "otherwise not exactly our friend" – and his government "to turn over a new leaf." However, "with phrases alone we shall not be able to improve our relations [with Russia] permanently. If, however, we were in a position to make a beginning with any positive question, even a very insignificant one, we might perhaps progress from smaller [issues] to bigger ones."[95] Tensions with Germany in the aftermath of the Liman von Sanders crisis made Russia proceed with caution. Financial constraints and an unfavorable economic outlook in the spring of 1914 reinforced it.[96]

A further constraint on Russia was the uncertain state of relations with Britain, a frequently recurring topic of Austro-Hungarian reporting from St. Petersburg. In May 1913, Thurn observed that "the honeymoon of Anglo-Russian amity is now a little dimmed." Buchanan, his British colleague, he reported, had spoken "in a rather irritated tone about Russian proceedings in Persia."[97] Nearly a year later, Anglo-Russian animosities over Persia had not abated, and Sazonov's attempts to persuade Czernin that "Anglo-Russian relations left nothing to be desired as regards mutual confidence," convinced the chargé d'affaires only of the opposite.[98] If anything, his studies of Russian history had convinced Czernin that Russia's *Drang nach Süden* now aimed beyond the Transcaucasus and the Atrek basin, toward northern Persia with a poise against Britain.[99]

The notion of Russia's inherent expansionism had established a powerful hold on Austro-Hungarian thinking in 1914. Berthold Molden, the Vienna publicist with excellent contacts at the Ballhausplatz, reflected that Russia, "for she hungers after power and has the character of a half-Asiatic and theocratic state of the steppe, has the tendency to extend continuously." This made it all the more necessary to move against Serbia, he reasoned in July 1914, if only to demonstrate that Vienna would not be

[94] Szápáry to Berchtold (No. 10B), February 22/9, 1914, PA X/140. Berchtold marked this passage of the despatch.
[95] Szápáry to Berchtold (*streng vertraulich*), February 10/23, 1914, PA X/140, *varia*.
[96] Szápáry to Berchtold (Nos. 23B and 23G), both May 21/8, 1914, PA X/140; Reynolds, *Shattering Empires*, pp. 40–41.
[97] Thurn to Berchtold (No. 22A-K), May 17/4, 1913, PA X/139.
[98] Czernin to Berchtold (No. 14M), March 14/1, 1914, PA X/140.
[99] Czernin to Berchtold (No. 17G), March 28/15, 1914, PA X/140.

cowed by Russia.[100] This argument was also used in an attempt to soften up British opinion as the crisis reached its climax. Austria-Hungary was forced to act, Berchtold's *chef de cabinet*, Count Alexander Hoyos, impressed on the Lord Chancellor, not only to defend her own interests. If Russia "held the Balkans and Constantinople in undisputed sway and need fear no-one in her back and flanks ... she [will] follow ... the example of Alexander the Great and turn her eyes towards India."[101]

Hoyos' letter was dictated by the necessities of the July Crisis, but it also reflected a belief in Vienna that Anglo-Russian relations were steadily deteriorating. The tsar's musings on the decline of parliamentary institutions, "even in the classic parliamentary states," moreover, were suggestive of a growing disenchantment with Britain.[102]

There were reasons for concern, however. One of these was Russia's active wooing of Romania. The prospect of Bucharest's abandoning its traditional Habsburg alliance for either the tsar's warm embrace or for neutrality was viewed with unease at the Ballhausplatz.[103] Such a development foreshadowed the further deterioration of Austria-Hungary's position in the Balkans. By implication a more assertive policy in the region could force Bucharest back into the Habsburg orbit.

A more pressing consideration still was the state of the *Zweibund*, the alliance with Germany, and the *Dreibund*, the Triple Alliance with Italy. A month before the events at Sarajevo, Szápáry delivered a lengthy and scathing analysis of German policy toward Russia. Berlin had appeased St. Petersburg, readily sacrificing Austrian interests in the Balkans. Even the recent Liman von Sanders crisis had found an "inglorious end." It was a picture of "a sad diplomatic decline." German reluctance to stand up to Russia, the ambassador warned, would encourage Russia to be more assertive, and would weaken Italy's adherence to the triplice. At the same time, in light of the uncertain situation in the Balkans,

---

[100] Memo. Molden, "Memorandum des Herrn Molden über die Situation," July 6, 1914, PA I/811; see also F. R. Bridge, *Great Britain and Austria-Hungary, 1906–1914: A Diplomatic History* (London: Littlehampton Book Services, 1972), p. 213, on the wishful thinking at Vienna.

[101] Hoyos to Haldane, July 20, 1914, Haldane MSS, MS 5910; from late 1913, Hoyos had taken a gloomy view of Habsburg prospects, see Redlich diary, January 8, 1914; Fritz Fellner (ed.), *Schicksalsjahre Österreichs, 1908–1919: Das politische Tagebuch Josef Redlichs*, 2 vols. (Graz: Böhlau, 1953), vol. 2, p. 214.

[102] Tel. Thurn to Berchtold (No. 3), January 9, 1914, PA X/140.

[103] Czernin to Berchtold (No. 14G), March 14/1, 1914, PA X/140; see also Czernin to Berchtold (private), May 14, 1914, *Österreich-Ungarns Außenpolitik von der Bosnischen Krise bis zum Kriegsausbruch* (henceforth *ÖUA*), viii, No. 9668; Jean-Paul Bled, *François-Joseph* (Paris: Fayard, 1987), pp. 640–641.

Austria-Hungary was unable to loosen her own ties with Berlin.[104] By implication, a more assertive Austrian stance would galvanize Germany and bolster the Triple Alliance.

In contrast to the other Powers, the revival of Russian power posed potentially existential problems for Austria-Hungary. Yet, on the eve of the war, Habsburg diplomats were guided by assumptions of Russia's lack of preparedness for war in the immediate future. Indeed, if Berchtold's later reflections are to be believed, Szápáry was convinced until the very end that St. Petersburg would stay out of an Austro-Serb conflict.[105] At the same time, fears of the monarchy's longer-term decline and concerns about the reliability of the German ally pushed Vienna toward a policy of brinkmanship.

Conclusion: "A formidable factor"

This chapter has emphasized the coexistence of détente and anticipations of war in Great Power politics between 1911 and 1914. What linked these seemingly contrary elements together was the revival of Russian power. With the benefit of hindsight, the persistent exaggeration of Russia's power potential in the two years before 1914 may seem absurd.[106] From the perspective of 1912 or 1913 matters were far less obvious. Whatever the future might hold, it was clear that the post-1905 period in international politics was drawing to a close. The anticipated shift in the international landscape also suggested potential realignments of the Powers. This affected the Powers in different ways.

The "best case" scenario for Britain was a return to a situation roughly resembling that of the 1890s, with Britain holding the balance between the two alliance groupings, Tyrrell's and Bertie's proposition. In the worst case, Russia's revival threatened to rekindle the traditional antagonism between the two Asiatic empires, with the added complication, however, that St. Petersburg might in future lean toward Germany, Nicolson's latter-day *cauchemar des coalitions*.

---

[104] Szápáry to Berchtold (No. 21D), May 25/8, 1914, PA X/140; see also Holger Afflerbach, *Der Dreibund: Europäische Großmacht- und Allianzpolitik vor dem Ersten Weltkrieg* (Vienna: Böhlau, 2002), pp. 813–825; Jürgen Angelow, *Kalkül und Prestige: Der Zweibund am Vorabend des Ersten Weltkrieges* (Vienna: Böhlau, 2000), pp. 424–466.

[105] Berchtold diary, July 15, 1918, Nachlass Berchtold, Kt. 5, who recorded Szápáry as saying that "Russland werde sich nicht rühren!!!" ("Russia will not stir!!!"); Manfred Rauchensteiner, *Der Tod des Doppeladlers: Österreich-Ungarn und der Erste Weltkrieg* (Graz: Styria Verlag, 1993), pp. 84–85.

[106] See Paul M. Kennedy, "The First World War and the International Power System," *International Security* 9(1) (1984): 7–40, at 28.

For Germany, Russia's recovery from the nadir of 1905 posed a challenge of a different kind. Ever since the simultaneous rise of Prussia and Russia in the middle of the eighteenth century had created a new geopolitical logic in the affairs of eastern Central Europe, the two Powers had been forced to coexist.[107] Recurring tensions and frequent readjustments in their relations led both sides to develop bilateral mechanisms and diplomatic tools for managing Russo-German relations, ranging from the Polish partitions to alliances and more limited agreements. By 1913/14, Russo-German relations were once more on the cusp of another such readjustment. In consequence, German policy was characterized by a mixture of a very real sense of détente, on the one hand, and an equally real sense of peril, on the other.[108] Both sharpened German notions of a window of opportunity.[109] For the Wilhelmstrasse, the growth of Russian power also mattered in terms of managing Germany's existing alliances. In an odd sense, that contradictory combination of détente and anticipated future war made the risks of brinkmanship, if not calculable, then at least tolerable. It was a means of bolstering Germany's position in anticipation of the readjustment in Russo-German relations as much as of relinquishing responsibility if a conflict were to erupt after all.

Conversely, for Austria-Hungary a sense of German vacillation in recent international disputes and assumptions about Russia's lack of military preparedness opened up two quite different vistas. On the one hand, there was the prospect of a gradual improvement in Austro-Russian relations as a result of carefully negotiated compromises, as suggested by Szápáry. On the other hand, the seemingly weak underpinnings of Russia's military power suggested that firm and energetic action in the near future held out a realistic prospect of buttressing the monarchy's regional position.

The revival of their ally's power made French politicians even more reluctant to moderate Russian behavior. The fear of ultimately losing Russia thus limited France's freedom of maneuver, and abdicating any

[107] See Klaus Zernack, "Das preußische Königstum, und die polnische Republik im europäischen Mächtesystem des 18. Jahrhundert," Wolfram Fischer and Michael G. Müller (eds.), *Preußen–Deutschland–Polen: Aufsätze zur Geschichte der deutsch–polnischen Beziehungen* (Berlin: Duncker & Humblot, 1991), p. 253.

[108] For the Fischerite argument of German policy as driven by a fear of Russia, see Imanuel Geiss, "Kurt Riezler und der erste Weltkrieg", in Imanuel Geiss, Fritz Fischer, and Bernd-Jürgen Wendt (eds.), *Deutschland und die Weltpolitik des 19. und 20. Jahrhundert* (Düsseldorf: Bertelsmann Universitätsverlag, 1973), p. 401.

[109] See Richard N. Lebow, "Windows of Opportunity: Do States Jump Through Them?" *International Security* 9(2) (1984): 147–186; also David Stevenson, "Militarization and Diplomacy in Europe before 1914," *International Security* 22(1) (1997): 125–161, esp. 157–158.

restraining influence over Russia was preferable to risking the break-up of the alliance and thus French national security.

With Russia's imminent return to roughly the position she had occupied in 1904, Great Power relations were about to enter a new phase, though the precise shape of the new international politics was not yet discernible. Up to, and well into, the July Crisis the actions of the Powers reflected that parallelism of détente, as a proven method of crisis management, and the tensions and uncertainties engendered by the rise of Russia. And that should open up new avenues for further research. It should certainly once more focus scholarly attention on the constraints, options, and preferences in July 1914.[110] It is time to put decision-making back at the heart of the debate.

Appendix

The following archival materials were used in this chapter.

Archival sources

Official papers

Austria
Haus-, Hof- und Staatsarchiv, Vienna: PA VIII, England; PA X, Russland.

Germany
Politische Archiv Auswärtiges Amt, Berlin: Russland 61, Allgemeine Angelegenheiten

Great Britain
The National Archive (Public Records Office), Kew: FO 371 Foreign Office, general correspondence after 1906.

Private papers

Austria
Haus-, Hof- und Staatsarchiv Vienna: Nachlass Berchtold.

Germany
Bundesarchiv Koblenz: Nachlass Harden.

---

[110] See the important piece by Jack S. Levy, "Preferences, Constraints, and Choices in July 1914," *International Security* 15(3) (1990/1): 151–186.

The National Archive (Public Records Office), Kew: Nachlass Eisendecher; Nachlass Jagow; Nachlass Pourtalès.

Great Britain

Bodleian Library, Oxford: De Bunsen MSS; Harcourt MSS; Rennell of Rodd MSS.

Cambridge University Library: Hardinge MSS.

Imperial War Museum, London: Wilson MSS.

London School of Economics and Political Science Archive, London: Barclay MSS.

National Library of Scotland, Edinburgh: Haldane MSS; Minto MSS.

Northamptonshire Record Office, Northampton: Cartwright MSS.

The National Archive (Public Records Office), Kew: Bertie MSS; Nicolson MSS; Spring-Rice MSS.

Part III

The question of preventive war

William Mulligan

Preventive war seemed like a good idea at the time. Between 1871 and 1913 the Great Powers considered initiating a preventive war on several occasions, yet in each case civilian and military leaders rejected the strategy. This chapter considers four of these occasions: the War-in-Sight crisis in 1875; the demands of German and Austrian General Staff officers between 1886 and 1888 to attack France and Russia; the First Moroccan Crisis in 1905 and 1906; and the demands of the Austro-Hungarian Chief of the General Staff, Franz Conrad von Hötzendorf, to launch a war against Italy in 1911. In an article devoted to explaining the absence of preventive wars in the 1930s, Norrin Ripsman and Jack Levy noted that "explaining why theoretically unexpected events do not occur is just as important as explaining why theoretically unexpected events do occur."[1] The cases under consideration in this chapter demonstrate the specific restraints on preventive war in the late nineteenth and early twentieth centuries, while also illustrating how the employment of the concept of preventive war, rather than the actual initiation of a preventive war, functioned in international and domestic politics.

The absence of preventive war in this era of Great Power rivalry is surprising on three counts. First, the theoretical conditions for preventive war, that is, a war motivated by the expectation of a foreseeable deterioration in a state's relative military power and the fear of a future attack by a currently weaker rival, existed in Europe between the Franco-Prussian War and the First World War. The presence of six Great Powers, whose relative military power shifted on a periodic basis, created opportunities and incentives for preventive war. The shifts in military power were more predictable and more open than in previous eras of European history as states embarked on multi-year armaments programs, and set out their plans and budgets in parliaments and the press. This changed the dimension of time in international politics as each state could assess the trajectory

---

[1] Norrin M. Ripsman and Jack S. Levy, "The Preventive War that Never Happened: Britain, France, and the Rise of Germany in the 1930s," *Security Studies* 16(1) (2007): 32–67.

of another state's military force development. Of course, relative military power could also shift due to political events, such as war, revolution, and alliance formation. Recovery from war and revolution, and the long courtships that preceded the formation of an alliance were also calculated in terms of months and years, opening what has become known as "windows of opportunity."[2]

Second, contemporaries considered war as a legitimate instrument of a state's foreign policy, though they tended to distinguish between different motivations and types of war. The term preventive war was used widely in discussions of international politics before 1914, though often in a relatively loose sense. In other words, historians and political scientists are not imposing opportunities for preventive war in an anachronistic sense. Its meaning ranged from the initiation of a war to forestall the planned increases in the size of rival's army and navy, to the logic of starting a war to eliminate a future political constellation that would undermine the integrity of the state, such as the rise of a nationalist threat to Austria-Hungary. When Schlieffen discussed preventive war in an article in 1909, he defined it in terms of timing and relative military power: "Over the course of years there were moments when one or the other [state] believed he had reached his goal [in terms of achieving superior military force] and when it only needed the right moment to send a declaration of war to the other camp."[3] On the eve of the First World War an editorial in *The Times* denounced the prospect of a preventive war, but offered a wider conception than Schlieffen had, including the target state's future intention as well as capability to attack. It informed its readers that:

Such a war, it need hardly be explained, is a war undertaken by one State to forestall a possible attack by another. Its authors assume, amongst other things, that the rival State is permanently hostile; that for the moment it is the weaker of the two; that its military forces grow faster than theirs; and that, if left to develop them, it would strike when it was able.[4]

In the late 1880s a correspondent for the leading French paper, *Le Temps*, considered a preventive war to be synonymous with a war of aggression. Bismarck, the writer claimed, "is the man to favour the thought of a preventive, and as such an aggressive, war against us."[5]

---

[2] David Stevenson, *Armaments and the Coming of War: Europe, 1904–1914* (Oxford University Press, 1996).

[3] Alfred von Schlieffen, "War Today," in Robert Foley (ed.), *Alfred von Schlieffen's Military Writings* (London: Routledge, 2002), p. 1.

[4] "Preventive War," *The Times*, March 16, 1914, p. 9.

[5] "Lettres sur la politique étrangère," *Le Temps*, June 21, 1888, p. 1.

In many instances a leader's reasoning reflected the logic of preventive war, but the term was not used. Indeed, the term rarely, if at all, surfaced in Bismarck's speeches, memoranda, and letters, though the chancellor enjoyed the reputation of being the successful proponent of preventive war in nineteenth-century Europe. Nonetheless, he articulated the logic of preventive war clearly and in public. For example, he told the Reichstag in November 1871, just over one year after the battle of Sedan and the crushing of French military power:

I believe that defence through offence is in fact quite a common and in most cases the most effective strategy, and that it is very useful for a country that is in a central location in Europe and has three or four borders, across which it can be attacked, to follow the example of Frederick the Great at the start of the Seven Years War, who did not wait until the net, which had been closing in on him, was completed but rather tore it to pieces through a lightning offensive. In such cases it is the duty of the government, and the nation has the right to demand it from the government, if a war really cannot be avoided, to go to war at a point in time where it will have the least cost and the least risk for both country and nation.[6]

This was a response to reports of the first stirrings of French military recovery, and Bismarck legitimized preventive war on the ground of the primacy of the nation over the international order.

As the German decision to favor war in July 1914 can be seen in part as motivated by a preventive logic – either fear of growing Russian military power or fear of the imminent encirclement of Germany by the Triple Entente – the First World War can appear as the logical culmination of militarized, belligerent, and unrestrained international politics in the late nineteenth and early twentieth centuries. This fits with a broader historiographical interpretation of the international order between 1871 and 1914.[7] In the latter part of the nineteenth century the notion of a common European order had less purchase on statesmen's thinking; the Great Powers conducted foreign policy on the basis of a narrow reading of the national interest; security was reduced to a calculation of comparative military power; and statesmen had little or no faith in restraints inherent in the workings of any international system.[8] A key feature of the emerging

---

[6] Cited in James Stone, *The War Scare of 1875: Bismarck and Europe in the mid-1870s* (Stuttgart: Franz Steiner, 2010), p. 37. I have not been able to identify a single case where Bismarck used the term "*Präventivkrieg.*"

[7] Winfried Baumgart, *Europäisches Konzert und nationale Bewegung: Internationale Beziehungen 1830–1878* (Paderborn: Schöningh, 1999); C. J. Bartlett, *Peace, War and the European Powers, 1814–1914* (Basingstoke: Palgrave Macmillan, 1996).

[8] Peter Krüger, "Von Bismarck zu Hitler? Die Agonie des Europäischen Staatensystems 1938/1939", in Peter Krüger (ed.), *Kontinuität und Wandel in der Staatenordnung der Neuzeit* (Marburg: Hitzeroth, 1991), pp. 69–85; Baumgart, *Europäisches Konzert*, pp. 13–15.

system after 1870 was the militarization of relations between the Great Powers, due, in large part, to the successes of the Prussian and Piedmont states in using war to advance their interests. Eckart Conze argues that after 1870 a precarious balance of power and a militarization of international relations characterized European politics.[9]

In view of this characterization of the international order historians have argued that preventive wars became a "European norm."[10] "Preventive wars," argued Paul Schroeder, writing on the erosion of peace before 1914, "even risky preventive wars, are not extreme anomalies in politics, the bankruptcy of policy. They are a normal, even common tool, of statecraft, right down to our own day."[11] A. J. P. Taylor was particularly forthright, claiming that "Every war between Great Powers [between 1848 and 1914] with which this book deals started as a preventive war, not as a war of conquest." The Crimean Wars, the wars of Italian and German unification, and the First World War were waged by conservative powers on the defensive, baited into initiating a war by their more aggressive opponents.[12] In response to Fritz Fischer's argument that German military and civilian leaders had undertaken a planned war of conquest in 1914, Klaus Hildebrand and Andreas Hillgruber argue that the war resulted from Germany's increasingly precarious geopolitical position. On this reading the option for preventive war derived from the fundamentally defensive aims of German foreign policy.[13] More recently, Sönke Neitzel, Stephen Schroeder, and Annika Mombauer have noted the strategic pessimism that infused the thinking of German political and military elites on the eve of war.[14]

---

[9] Eckart Conze, "'Wer von Europa spricht, hat unrecht': Aufstieg und Verfall des vertraglichen multilateralismus im Europäischen Staatensystem des 19. Jahrhunderts," *Historisches Jahrbuch* 121 (2001): 240; see also Anselm Doering-Manteuffel, "Internationale Geschichte als Systemgeschichte des 19. und 20. Janhrhunderts," in Wilfried Loth and Jürgen Osterhammel (eds.), *Internationale Geschichte: Themen–Ergebnisse–Aussichten* (Munich: Oldenbourg, 2000), pp. 100–102.

[10] Hew Strachan, "Preemption and Prevention in Historical Perspective," in Henry Shue and David Rodin (eds.), *Preemption: Military Action and Moral Justification* (Oxford University Press, 2007), pp. 25–39.

[11] Paul W. Schroeder, *Systems, Stability, and Statecraft: Essays on the International History of Modern Europe*, eds. and Introduction David Wetzel, Robert Jervis, and Jack S. Levy (New York: Palgrave, 2004), p. 139.

[12] A. J. P. Taylor, *The Struggle for Mastery in Europe, 1848–1918* (Oxford University Press, 1954), p. 166.

[13] Klaus Hildebrand, *Das Vergangene Reich. Deutsche Außenpolitik zwischen Bismarck und Hitler* (Stuttgart: Deutsche Verlags-Anstalt, 1995); Andreas Hillgruber, *Deutsche Großmacht- und Weltpolitik im 19. und 20. Jahrhundert* (Düsseldorf: Droste, 1979), pp. 93–107.

[14] Annika Mombauer, *Helmuth von Moltke and the Origins of the First World War* (Cambridge University Press, 2001); Sönke Neitzel, *Kriegsausbruch: Deutschlands Weg in die*

Likewise, political scientists have drawn on international history before 1914 in their analysis of the concept of preventive wars, especially since declaration of the Bush doctrine in 2002.[15] Daniel Moran, for example, identifies the rise of a "strategic culture" and "calculus," especially in Germany, from the late nineteenth century, which considered war legitimate to "forestall some putatively foreseeable but still somewhat remote threat or disadvantage," by launching a preventive war.[16]

Yet the existence of optimal conditions for preventive war, the widespread contemporary discussion of it, and the broad historiographical consensus that the international system was militarized, aggressive, and anarchic render the absence of any preventive wars – indeed, any wars between the Great Powers – over four decades something of a puzzle. Analyzing the decision-making process demonstrates the significant restraints on preventive war as a policy option in the late nineteenth and early twentieth centuries. These included the reactions of the target state, which could rein in its more belligerent language and ambitions, denying the prospective aggressor the justification for initiating a preventive war. Equally, a targeted state could look for diplomatic support to deter an attack. However decision-makers also rejected preventive war for other reasons. They recognized that war was inherently risky, that even a victorious war might produce longer-term and more intractable challenges, such as isolation against a coalition of the remaining Great Powers. States normally had several options to preserve their security, such as diplomatic agreements leading toward détente and armament increases that enhanced future deterrence. Governments also needed a clear and immediate justification to initiate a war, given the necessity of securing popular consent and national cohesion in a Great Power war. A foreseeable deterioration in the relative military position of two powers did not qualify as a sufficient justification for war – it had to be bolstered by other justifications. Finally, there were moral and ethical restraints on preventive war. The sources of moral restraint were not always articulated clearly, but included religious sensibilities and a belief in underlying historical processes. These did not rule out war as such, but they did cast doubt on the legitimacy of preventive war. The ethical restraints included religious values, but also notions of sharing civilized, European values. The moral and ethical restraints on

Katastrophe 1900–1914 (Munich: Pendo, 2002); Stephen Schröder, *Die englisch–russische Marinekonvention: Das deustche Reich und die Flottenverhandlungen der Tripleentente am Vorabend des Ersten Weltkrieges* (Göttingen: Vandenhoeck & Ruprecht, 2006).

[15] Jack S. Levy, "Preventive War and Democratic Politics," *International Studies Quarterly* 52(1) (2008): 1–24; Thomas M. Nichols, "Anarchy and World Order in the New Age of Prevention," *World Policy Journal* 23(2) (2005): 1–23.

[16] Daniel Moran, *Strategic Insights: Preventive War and the Crisis of July 1914* (Monterey, CA: Center of Contemporary Conflict, 2002).

preventive war were part of a broader concern that an aggressive war, with which preventive war was associated, was not a legitimate instrument of state policy.

Although no European Great Power initiated a preventive war against another Great Power between 1871 and 1913, the concept clearly served a political function, or, rather, contemporaries believed that employing the prospect of preventive war could serve a purpose in domestic and international politics. In this sense preventive war became an instrument with which to influence the outcome of a particular political process, be it an international crisis, a conflict between civilian and military leaders, or negotiations for an increase in the size of the army and navy.

"War in Sight" crisis, 1875

On April 9, 1875, the Berlin newspaper, *Die Post*, asked "Is War in Sight?" Written by Konstantin Rößler, a journalist with close ties to the Foreign Office, the article claimed that France represented a growing threat to German security. European diplomats, accustomed to deciphering Bismarck's foreign policy in the runes of newspapers, took alarm. The title of the article gave its name to the first major war scare since the end of the Franco-Prussian War. Given the extent of France's defeat in 1870 and the annexation of Alsace and Lorraine, the newly formed German Reich enjoyed considerable security in the 1870s. Nonetheless, Bismarck, a pessimist by disposition and haunted by Prussia's historical experience, feared for German security. The *cauchemar des coalitions* – nightmare of coalitions – disturbed his serenity. In particular, he foresaw the emergence of a new Kaunitz coalition, an alliance between France, Austria-Hungary, and Russia, which would encircle and partition Germany.

This geopolitical exposure was a persistent structural problem for German policymakers, but, in addition, the speedy recovery of France from defeat caused concern. By 1873, the Third Republic had paid off the war indemnity and German occupation forces had left. The following year the reform of the armed forces began, while General MacMahon, on the right of the political spectrum, replaced Adolphe Thiers, the linchpin of the early Republic and Bismarck's preferred Frenchman. Bismarck feared that MacMahon's election marked a shift toward the reestablishment of a monarchy in France, which would centralize political authority and ensure greater national political cohesion.[17]

---

[17] Stone, *War Scare*, pp. 67–76.

The French threat, predicted to become more and more overbearing, posed difficulties for German policy. At this point, Germany and France had populations of similar size – the take-off of the German economy and its geopolitical implications could not then be foreseen. Moreover, German leaders were convinced that French politicians of all hues harbored ambitions to avenge the defeat of 1870–1871. Bismarck had various options, including the isolation of France and the diversion of France toward conquests in North Africa. After the crisis he would prioritize these options, but in early 1875 he considered the League of the Three Emperors, the alliance between Germany, Russia, and Austria-Hungary, to be fragile and he thought French colonial expansion might only whet their appetite for renewing the search for military glory in Europe. In these circumstances, preventive war became an increasingly attractive option.

Historians have debated whether Bismarck seriously considered preventive war or whether he issued an effective, but empty, threat.[18] The balance of evidence suggests that Bismarck never seriously considered initiating a preventive war in 1875, but, nonetheless, his willingness to issue the threat was significant for at least three reasons. First, others in the German leadership considered the option. Joseph Maria von Radowitz, a rising star of the diplomatic corps, offered a cogent defense of preventive war to the French ambassador, Gontaut-Biron. Radowitz argued that it would be more Christian to attack France at present than wait until later, when France had recovered and a Franco-German war would be a bloodier affair. Bismarck almost certainly authorized Radowitz's trenchant words. The Chief of the General Staff, Helmuth von Moltke, did not think that the French army constituted an immediate threat, but he also spoke of the temptations of waging preventive war. "How would the country react," he asked Johannes von Miquel, a prominent National Liberal politician in April 1875, "if we were to launch an offensive war against France this year?"[19]

Second, that Bismarck placed articles on preventive war and got diplomats to issue threats about preventive war indicates that at the very minimum he expected the threat to carry real weight. Preventive war had to be within the realm of plausible measures or otherwise the threats would have been ignored or Bismarck would have seemed ridiculous. He also allowed the threats carried in the press to fester. For example, on April 10,

---

[18] See the recent two studies, Stone, *War Scare*; Johannes Janorschke, *Bismarck, Europa und die "Krieg in Sicht"-Krise von 1875* (Paderborn: Schöningh, 2010).

[19] Stone, *War Scare*, pp. 205, 244–245; see also Ulrich Lappenküper, *Die Mission Radowitz. Untersuchungen zur Rußlandspolitik Otto von Bismarcks (1871–1875)* (Göttingen: Vandenhoeck & Ruprecht, 1990).

the day after the publication of the "Is War in Sight?" article, he wrote to the German ambassador in Paris, Chlodwig von Hohenlohe, to inform him that the notice in the officially inspired *Norddeutsche Allgemeine Zeitung* reflected the German government's view of European politics and the threat of war. This article dismissed fears about the alleged anti-German direction of Italian and Austro-Hungarian foreign policy, but claimed that French armaments policy was unsettling.[20] The influential *Preußische Jahrbücher*, a publication supportive of Bismarck, articulated the logic of preventive war: "If France wants to fight in two years, then in the interests of self-preservation we will be forced to bring about the conflict at an earlier point."[21] The appearance of these articles over a period weeks reinforced the impression around Europe, where diplomats assumed that Bismarck controlled the German press, that the chancellor was considering a preventive war.

Third, Bismarck viewed preventive war as a diplomatic instrument as well as a military action. His aim in the public discussions of war in the spring of 1875 was not to prepare the ground for an actual conflict, but to strike fear into the hearts of French leaders, to stymie the rise of the Catholic monarchist right in France, and to derail the revival of French military power. He had used the threat of preventive war on previous occasions in the 1860s to achieve a diplomatic advantage, but on this occasion his plan backfired.[22]

Why did German leaders decide not to adopt a preventive war strategy? The first and most significant reason lay in the denouement of the crisis. The French foreign minister, Duc de Décazes, prevailed upon Disraeli's Conservative government and, more importantly, on the Russian tsar, Alexander II and his foreign minister, Gorchakov, to warn Bismarck that a war against France would not be tolerated. The likely repercussions were vague, but that sufficed to end the drip of articles and warnings from the German Foreign Office about a preventive war against France. A preventive war in this instance would have been considered a violation of Europe's political order. The other powers simply dismissed German fears about the recovery of French power, which did not pose an immediate threat to the Reich. Reputation and security in this instance were closely intertwined. A preventive war, lacking the legitimizing justification of Prussia's previous wars, would have confirmed the suspicions that the

---

[20] "Bismarck to Hohenlohe, 10 April 1875," in Otto von Bismarck. *Gesammelte Werke, 1874–1876*, ed. Rainer Bendick (Paderborn: Schöningh, 2005), p. 340.

[21] Cited in Karl-Ernst Jeismann, *Das Problem des Präventivkrieges im europäischen Staatensystem mit besonderem Blick auf die Bismarckzeit* (Freiburg: Alber, 1957), p. 93.

[22] *Ibid.*, pp. 93–99.

new Reich would be a disruptive factor in European politics. Bismarck, who since the 1870–1871 war had enjoyed a reputation for disruptive belligerence, feared that a German attack on France would lead to the formation of an anti-German coalition in Europe in the longer term. In other words, preventive war would create the very conditions of a hostile coalition that he was seeking to avoid.

Second, Bismarck would have had to overcome the opposition of William I. Under the German constitution the emperor made war and peace. William I had no moral qualms about war qua war, but he did have moral qualms about the war discussed in the spring of 1875. William I did not view the wars of his regime as preventive, but as defensive wars for Prussian security and honor. In 1875, there was no immediate threat to the security of the Reich. The costs of war weighed heavily on his mind: "Every war, even the triumphant," he wrote, "is a misfortune for one's own people, because no territorial gains, no millions can replace the lives of people and ease the sadness of families."[23]

The War in Sight crisis was the first to test the post-1871 European system. In many ways this was a system under construction, one that Bismarck consolidated through patient diplomacy between 1875 and 1878. After the crisis Bismarck did not countenance war as an instrument of policy and even opposed discussion of preventive war in the press. The crisis and the subsequent discussion of it in the diplomatic corps and press established a limit on war as a policy choice. At the very minimum it is possible to conclude that preventive war had to meet more stringent conditions than Bismarck had advanced to be an acceptable strategy. The recovery of one state from defeat was not considered to be a threat that warranted preventive war, but a normal development that helped to restore equilibrium to the international order. Nor had there been significant declarations in France about a future war of revenge against Germany. The rise of monarchists, rather than revanchists, had troubled Bismarck. In the first major crisis after 1871, diplomatic and political considerations had triumphed over narrow military calculations, a step backward from the militarization of international politics. It demonstrated that there were limits to which war was considered a legitimate instrument of policy. In other words, the European system was developing in a very different way to the expectations of contemporaries, who claimed that Prussia's victories in the 1860s had enthroned force in the place of law.[24]

---

[23] Cited in Walter Kloster, *Der deutsche Generalstab und der Präventivkriegsgedanke* (Stuttgart: Kohlhammer, 1932), p. 17.

[24] For example, see Lord Acton, "The War of 1870," Lecture Delivered at Bridgnorth Literary and Scientific Institution, April 25, 1871; Reverend Jermyn Cooper, "Address on

Two war scares, 1886–1887

Between 1885 and 1888 international politics was beset by a series of interlocking crises. Anglo-Russian rivalry in Central Asia, Anglo-French rivalry in North Africa, Great Power competition in the Balkans, and tensions between Germany, on the one hand, and France and Russia, on the other, provided the context for a series of war scares and debates over preventive war. The rise of Boulangism in France, pan-Slavism in Russia, and a more assertive nationalist opinion in Germany created the context for press wars and popular tensions in international politics. In particular, leading figures in the German General Staff, notably Alfred von Waldersee, urged William I and Bismarck to initiate a preventive war against France in early 1887 and against Russia in the winter of 1887/8. The debate on preventive war was largely confined within the civilian and military elite of the Kaiserreich, though war scares and belligerent language characterized public discussion of international politics. The army bills passed by the Reichstag in 1887 and 1888 also signaled the onset of a continental arms race that lasted until the early 1890s.

From the perspective of German leaders, the French and Russian threats had increased significantly in the second half of the 1880s. The German military were confident of their momentary superiority, but they were concerned by long-term trends, such as the doubling in the size of the French army since 1870 and the increased speed of Russian mobilization due to improvements in railroad networks. In addition, the German advantage of speedy mobilization was being eroded by the decision of the Russian General Staff to station an increased number of military units in Poland. Moreover, in the late 1880s the potential alliances that would fight a future European war featured in assessments of relative military strength. Concerns about the relative weakness of Germany's ally, Austria-Hungary, figured prominently in the calculations of the General Staff. Although the alliance between France and Russia was not concluded until 1894, Waldersee and others assumed that France and Russia would effectively act as allies in the case of a war between either state and Germany. The anticipated configuration of alliances – Germany and Austria-Hungary versus Russia and France – significantly worsened the Reich's security.[25]

---

the War between France and Prussia and the Paramount Necessity for England to Arm Herself against Foreign Aggression," London, 1871, both available at the National Library of Scotland.

[25] Michael Schmid, *Der "Eiserne Kanzler" und die Generäle: Deutsche Rüstungspolitik in der Ära Bismarck (1871–1890)* (Paderborn: Schöningh, 2003), pp. 308–315.

The question of an intention to attack in the future also shaped assessments of international politics. German leaders feared that the Russian and French governments intended to attack Germany when the opportunity arose. Waldersee simply argued that once Russian forces achieved military superiority – which he feared would occur in 1888 – they would attack. He pointed to the disposition of Russian troops close to the borders with Germany and Austria-Hungary as evidence of preparations for war. He interpreted intention on the basis of capability. There were increasing concerns about nationalist movements in France and Russia. In 1886, General Georges Boulanger entered the French Cabinet and quickly developed a reputation for being the strong man of the Third Republic, committed to military reform and willing to stand firm against German threats. In the minds of German leaders Boulanger became associated with the revival of French revanchism, though this assessment was unjustified. There was little support for war in France in the late 1880s.[26] German diplomats confused French assertiveness and a revival of national confidence with the risk of war. Similarly, they viewed the rise of pan-Slavic societies in Russia as a threat to German security. As William I's reign neared its end the ties of conservative monarchists in Russia and Germany were challenged by the rise of popular nationalism, which pitted Slav against Teuton. An international order divided on ethnic lines compounded the geographical exposure of Germany in Central Europe.

In this context a coterie of officers, centered on Alfred von Waldersee, the Quartermaster General and heir apparent to Moltke as Chief of the General Staff, advocated a preventive war. The preventive war party included military attachés, such as Adolph von Weines in Vienna and Yorck von Wartenburg in St. Petersburg; senior commanders in the German army, such as General von Loë; and Friedrich von Holstein in the Foreign Office. In the winter of 1886/7 their target was France; the following year their attentions moved toward Russia.

The occasion for initiating a preventive war concentrated on the issue of timing and Germany's current, but slipping, advantage. The sole concern was Germany's future security, to which the stability of the international order, and the human and social consequences of war, had to be subordinated. "That I express frankly," Waldersee wrote in his diary on January 27, 1887, "that we must exploit the current favorable circumstances, to undertake a war against France, gives me the reputation of very bad person. That I am right, however, is clear, even recognized by many. The

[26] Bertrand Joly, "La France et la revanche, 1871–1914," *Revue d'histoire moderne et contemporaine* 46(2) (1999): 325–347.

War Minister [Bronsart von Schellendorff] agrees with me."[27] The competing claims of humanitarian sensibilities and a particular view of national security found expression in a letter from von Loë to Waldersee in December 1886:

> No person, who has five healthy senses and a trace of empathy [*Menschlichkeitsgefühl*] can wish a war on today's Europe, which would ruin the welfare of all people for the indefinite future ... From a military point of view I can only agree with you, that at the moment we can wage a double war in favourable circumstances, and that the chances will only become worse.[28]

In the view of the advocates of preventive war, security was defined solely by military factors.[29]

The war party also tended to dismiss the assurances given in public statements by the French and Russian governments and in private by their diplomatic representatives of their peaceful intentions. Waldersee believed that the "peace music" of the French government and the "friendly face" shown in St. Petersburg were a ruse to trick the German government into easing its armaments program. General Staff officers considered the visit of Alexander III to Berlin in November 1887 to be an attempt to deceive German leaders about the direction of Russo-German relations – or else meaningless as the tsar was not in a position to restrain belligerent pan-Slav opinion. In fact, the apparent change of tone in both states confirmed Waldersee's assessment of their future threat. The prospect of preventive war had frightened French and Russian opinion into adopting a more conciliatory stance toward Germany, but only as a way of postponing the reckoning until the relative shift in military power had been completed. There was nothing that French and Russian leaders could reasonably do that would reassure Waldersee, who fused capability and intention in his assessments of international politics. From Waldersee's point of view the deterrent value of the prospect of preventive war actually worsened German security by signaling to its putative enemies that they should seek to postpone a war.[30] Whereas in 1875 Bismarck had used the press to foment debate about preventive war, in a (ham-fisted) attempt to influence French domestic politics, in the late 1880s public discussion of the likelihood of war undermined Waldersee's aims.

As the Reichstag was dissolved and elections held in February 1887 in order to engineer a majority for an army bill, public discussion of future war was impossible to avoid. Whereas the reasoning behind the army bill

---

[27] Cited in Schmid, *Der "Eiserne Kanzler" und die Generäle*, p. 278.
[28] Cited in *ibid.*, p. 273.   [29] Strachan, "Preemption," pp. 27–36.
[30] Schmid, *Der "Eiserne Kanzler" und die Generäle*, pp. 293–299.

was to strengthen Germany in order to deter future attacks, the proponents of preventive war urged imminent military action. The two versions of military security ran in different directions. In contrast to 1875, Bismarck was unambiguously opposed to preventive war as he pursued a policy of peace through strength. In widely broadcast speeches to the Reichstag he did not shirk from what many perceived as aggressive language, yet the purpose remained one of deterrence. "The stronger we are, the more unlikely war is," he told the Reichstag in January 1887. In February 1888, he was mobbed by enthusiastic deputies after he declared that "we Germans fear God and nothing else."[31]

Bismarck restated his long-standing objections to preventive war. Mere mortals could not foresee the long-term direction of politics. Drawing on his religious convictions, preventive war represented, in his view, an intrusion of human agency into divine and historical order. Bismarck certainly did not attribute to God the power to shape particular events, but rather providence and history created overarching structures within which political leaders had to act. The role of the effective leader was to choose the right moment to act, rather than to bring about artificial constellations and political contexts.[32] Preventive war also created its own dangers, which Bismarck had recognized since 1875. War was costly and unpredictable, and even if victorious the consequences for the international reputation and security of the Reich were incalculable. To counter the possibility of a two-front war, Bismarck strengthened the army and patched up relations with Russia with the Reinsurance Treaty in June 1887. Dismissed by his critics as incompatible with German obligations to Austria-Hungary, the purpose of the Reinsurance Treaty was to avoid the emergence of rigid political blocs and to cultivate a degree of uncertainty in international relations, which moved away from the logic embedded in strict calculations of military power. Whereas Waldersee craved certainty, Bismarck's vision of security relied on ambiguities.

Bismarck's vision triumphed over the advocates of preventive war. Herbert von Bismarck, following a conversation with Yorck, the military attaché at St. Petersburg and supporter of Waldersee, wrote a revealing letter to his brother, Bill, in December 1887: "The issue is not that we should now attack, that would be frivolous in view of the unforeseeable consequences, which a world war, unleashed in this way, could have. The military are only so belligerent, because they do not have the final responsibility and decision."[33] In addition to the destructive consequence of war, Herbert von Bismarck noted that the final decision lay in the hands

---

[31] *Ibid.*, p. 271.   [32] Jeismann, *Problem des Präventivkrieges*, pp. 109–121.
[33] Schmid, *Der "Eiserne Kanzler" und die Generäle*, p. 373.

of the emperor and the chancellor. Although a secret war council, sum-
moned by William I and attended by Moltke, Waldersee, and Bronsart
von Schellendorff, met on December 17, 1887 to discuss the possibility
of war against Russia, the chancellor was absent. In any case, William
I opposed preventive war, while Moltke accepted the primacy of political
as opposed to purely military factors in determining foreign policy. "From
the military point of view," Moltke had told Herbert von Bismarck the
previous day, "one would have to say 'better today than tomorrow.' This
however cannot be decisive for the great political decisions."[34]

In this crisis there was one important exception in Bismarck's refusal
to countenance preventive war, but the exception illustrates Bismarck's
willingness to employ the concept of preventive war to achieve a political
goal. Fearing that Austria-Hungary might itself initiate a war against
Russia in the expectation that German forces would support their ally,
Bismarck warned that if Austria-Hungary and Russia found themselves at
war, then Germany would have to launch a preventive war against France
before turning its forces toward the eastern front against Russia. However,
Bismarck's purpose in sketching out this scenario of what amounted to a
"double preventive war" – Austria-Hungary against Russia and Germany
against France – was to warn Habsburg leaders that they could not expect
much German support in the opening stages of a conflict. As with his
willingness to publish the terms of the Dual Alliance, which showed that
Germany only had to fulfil the *casus foederis* in the case of an attack against
Austria-Hungary, Bismarck's instrumentalization of preventive war was
designed to restrain Vienna. In that sense Bismarck continued to use the
doctrine of preventive war as a diplomatic tactic, as he had in 1875, rather
than as a military strategy.

Missed opportunities, 1904–1906?

In July 1914, Bethmann-Hollweg remarked to a friend that 1905 had been
Germany's best opportunity to win a European war. The international
system was in the midst of revolutionary changes in 1905, triggered in
large part by Japan's victory over Russia in the Far East. The defeat and
subsequent revolution meant that Russia was no longer an effective alliance partner for France. At the same time, Germany and France had
clashed in Morocco, ending a period of relative calm between these two
states. The previous year France and Britain had struck a colonial bargain;
the Moroccan Crisis and the increasing concern of British politicians

---

[34] *Ibid.*, p. 407.

and admirals at Tirpitz's naval plans had led to a surge of Anglo-German antagonism that would remain the default setting in relations between the two countries until 1912. In 1905, the outlines of the Anglo-Russian entente of 1907, which would place the capstone on the Triple Entente and alliance system before the First World War, were visible. German leaders, therefore, recognized the risk of encirclement. "The situation begins to resemble that before the Seven Years War," remarked Wilhelm II in November 1904 in yet another nod to the Frederician tradition of preventive war.[35] At the same time the prospect of preventive war on the Continent was complicated by the possibility of a preventive strike by the Royal Navy against the German fleet. Between 1904 and 1906, different versions of preventive war interacted.

Between late 1904 and early 1906 German political and military leaders considered war as a means of breaking out of the as yet incomplete encirclement. Preventive war was countenanced as a possible scenario to enhance German security, rather than actively planned. In other words, civilian and especially military leaders recognized that an opportunity existed in the short term to alleviate a long-term deterioration of Germany's position in the international order.[36] Yet even among the military, support for a preventive war was tepid in comparison with Waldersee's efforts in the late 1880s. The Chief of the General Staff, Schlieffen, argued that Germany could win a decisive victory in a one-front war against France. France, bereft of its Russian ally and uncertain of British naval support, was momentarily vulnerable. "If the necessity of a war against France should present itself to us," Schlieffen told Prince Lichnowsky, ambassador to London between 1912 and 1914, "then the present moment is undoubtedly favourable for us."[37] According to his son-in-law, Wihlem von Hahnke, in a letter written in 1926, Schlieffen was more trenchant. At a state council meeting during the crisis Schlieffen offered the following analysis: "Russia is tied up in the East, England still weakened by the Boer War, France still behind with its armaments. Before long the German Reich has to prove its worth through a war. Now is the most convenient time. Therefore my solution: war with France."[38] A successful war against France would remove the French threat to German

---

[35] Barbara Vogel, *Deutsche Rußlandspolitik: Das Scheitern der Deustchen Weltpolitik unter Bülow 1900–1906* (Dusseldorf: Bertelsmann Universitätsverlag, 1973), p. 217.

[36] Albrecht Moritz, *Das Problem des Präventivkrieges in der deutschen Politik während der ersten Marokkokrise* (Bern: Peter Lang, 1974), argues that support for preventive war among German leaders in 1905 and 1906 was, at most, limited and ephemeral.

[37] Cited in Moritz, *Das Problem des Präventivkrieges*, p. 218.

[38] Cited in Annika Mombauer, "German War Plans," in Richard F. Hamilton and Holger H. Herwig (eds.), *War Planning 1914* (Cambridge University Press, 2010), p. 56.

security for another generation and, more importantly, it would replace the encirclement of Germany with German hegemony in Europe. Rising tensions between Germany and France over Morocco could provide the occasion for a declaration of war.

Diplomats also aired the possibility of preventive war with a view to unsettling the French government and, in particular, the position of Foreign Minister Théophile Delcassé. In April 1905, Count Monts, the German ambassador to Rome, tested the waters in a discussion with Luzzatti, a prominent Italian politician, and in this instance a conduit to Paris. Monts argued that Germany could no longer tolerate French hostility. "We recognise that the struggle would be terrible," Monts said, "that it would be different to 1870, that France might not be alone. But we are certain that we would defeat them in the long term."[39] The French government took the risk of war seriously. Prime Minister Maurice Rouvier removed Théophile Delcassé as foreign minister, fearing that Delcassé's unwillingness to compromise with German demands over Morocco would give Berlin the excuse to declare war.

However, there were significant restraints on German options in 1905, despite its overwhelming military superiority vis-à-vis France. For a start, there were significant differences within the German leadership on how best to defend and enhance national security. Where Schlieffen saw an opportunity to destroy France, Tirpitz feared that a German attack on France would prompt a British attack on the German High Seas Fleet. Germany would fall victim to a preventive war. Jonathan Steinberg has shown how the Copenhagen complex, referring to the Royal Navy's sudden attack on the neutral Danish fleet in Copenhagen in 1807, entered the lexicon of German politics in the late nineteenth century. Copenhagen stood for the British tradition of preventive war, just as Frederick II's offensive in 1756 symbolized the Prusso-German tradition. Commentators, even moderates such as Kurt Riezler and Friedrich Naumann, claimed that British foreign policy followed the single-minded pursuit of self-interest, ignoring dainty platitudes about international law and morality. By 1905, as Anglo-German relations deteriorated due to the emerging naval threat, German colonial ambitions, economic rivalry, and British suspicions of German diplomatic intrigues, Tirpitz was especially worried that the Royal Navy would descend on Kiel to destroy the fleet. The fear of British intentions reflected the assumptions that some German military and political leaders made about the workings of the international order, namely, that

---

[39] "Premier Entretien de M. Luzzatti avec le Comte Monts," May 1, 1905, *Documents diplomatiques français* (henceforth *DDF*) (2), vol. 6, pp. 447–451.

the stronger side should strike before the opponent developed its own capability to attack.[40]

German concerns about being the target of preventive war were epitomized by the reaction to a speech by Arthur Lee, the Civil Lord of the Admiralty, in February 1905. He justified the recent concentration of the Royal Navy in home waters by pointing to the threat to British security in the North Sea posed by Germany. In an amended version of the speech, Lee had referred to naval powers in general, rather than specifically to Germany. In the version sent by the German naval attaché, Lee told his audience that the "Royal Navy would get its blow in first before the other side had time to read in the papers that war had been declared."[41] Lee's speech had followed several months of Anglo-German tension, including training operations by the Royal Navy in which Germany figured as the enemy. The specter of Copenhagen stalked Tirpitz, Wilhelm II, and others throughout the winter of 1904/5.

A preventive strike against the German fleet was never contemplated as a serious option in the British Cabinet, though Sir John Fisher, appointed First Sea Lord in 1904, was prone to utter the occasional threat of an attack on the German fleet. A "creature of moods," as Reginald Esher, a leading figure in post-Boer war military reforms, called him, Fisher had developed a reputation as a radical and aggressive thinker. He told the naval historian, Julian Corbett, that the reason for concentrating the fleet in the North Sea was that "our drill ground should be our battle ground." After Lord Lansdowne, the foreign secretary, had smoothed some tensions with Germany over the Moroccan Crisis in April 1905, Fisher teased the foreign secretary that his note "will hold back the German emperor before going too far and we shall be cheated out of our trip to Kiel.'[42] The Admiralty began planning for war against Germany in the summer of 1905, but the basis of naval strategy was blockade, rather than an unannounced strike against a fleet resting at anchor in Kiel.[43] Fisher never sustained a campaign for a preventive strike against the German fleet in

---

[40] Jonathan Steinberg, "The Copenhagen Complex," *Journal of Contemporary History* 1(3) (1966): 23–46.

[41] *Ibid.*, p. 39; "Mr Lee's Speech at Eastleigh," *The Times*, February 7, 1905, p. 4. I am grateful to Andreas Rose for his advice on preventive war in British thinking during the First Moroccan Crisis.

[42] Fisher to Lansdowne, April 25, 1905, Fisher to Corbett, July 28, 1905, in Arthur Marder (ed.), *Fear God and Dread Nought: The Correspondence of Admiral of the Fleet Lord Fisher of Kilverstone* (London: Jonathan Cape, 1956), vol. 2, pp. 55–56, 63; Esher to MVB, January 14, 1906, in Maurice Brett (ed.), *Journals and Letters of Reginald Viscount Esher* (London, Nicholson & Watson, 1934), vol. 2, pp. 134–135.

[43] Nicholas A. Lambert, *Sir John Fisher's Naval Revolution* (Columbia, SC: University of South Carolina Press, 1999), pp. 177–180.

the same way that Waldersee had called for war against France and Russia between 1886 and 1888. Nor did British ministers consider a preventive war to be a legitimate instrument to defend national security. However, the invasion scare stories exchanged between the British and German press colored the mutual percpetions of decision-makers in both states.[44]

Although leaders in Berlin were mistaken in their assessments of British willingness to "Copenhagen" the German fleet, the prospect of falling victim to a preventive war restrained German policy in 1905. Moreover, initiating a preventive war had reputational consequences that could worsen German security in the long term, even in the event of a victorious war. When confronted with Monts' reasoning in favor of a preventive war, Luzzatti responded that the world would blame Germany for an act of aggression. "One does not seek war," Luzzatti said, "when all the sentiments and all the interests of the world are opposed to it. Or if one is ready for it, one undertakes a terrible responsibility. Because it is necessary to win at all costs and against everyone, or to perish."[45] In short, a preventive war would constitute such a breach of expectations that it risked diplomatic isolation and the formation of an anti-German coalition that, in the long term, would worsen German security. Paul Wolff Metternich, the German ambassador to London, echoed Bismarck's reasoning in his rejection of preventive war. He noted in November 1905 that:

There may be people with us who consider the moment favourable to us, to allow a breach between France and us, and who say that after the defeat of France we would have compensation in Europe for the loss of our overseas possessions to England. I consider it however wanton thoughtlessness to inflict violence on the course of history, and foolish to shake the fruit from the tree before it is ripe.[46]

There were alternatives to preventive war for Germany to improve its long-term position. Throughout 1905 Bülow pressed Wilhelm II to conclude an alliance treaty with Russia, which would prevent a British–French–Russian bloc and challenge British world power. Bülow sought a diplomatic solution to German security, concentrating on improving Berlin's relationship with Russia. He rejected preventive war, citing Bismarck's pithy analysis that it was like risking suicide for fear of death. War, Bülow argued, entailed incalculable risks, although he also warned that the option of war must remain on the agenda in order to bolster his negotiating position. Where military leaders weighed up figures and

---

[44] Andreas Rose, *Zwischen Empire und Kontinent: Britische Außenpolitik vor dem Ersten Weltkrieg* (Munich: Oldenbourg, 2011), pp. 83.1–2.

[45] "Premier Entretien de M. Luzzatti avec le Comte Monts," May 1, 1905, *DDF* (2), vol. 6, pp. 447–451.

[46] Moritz, *Präventivkrieg*, p. 198.

assessed their chances with mathematical precision – one thinks of Joffre's comment in 1911 that France had a 70 percent chance of victory in war against Germany[47] – Bülow preferred the less risky uncertainties of diplomacy. Finally, the ostensible German justification for war was the preservation of national honor due to its colonial dispute with France. Bülow and others recognized that this was a flimsy justification, unlikely to be accepted by large parts of the population beyond the radical nationalist associations. The absence of popular support, therefore, acted as a further restraint on preventive war.[48]

Bülow's diplomatic alternative failed. By the spring of 1906 the Anglo-French entente had spawned military conversations and smoothed the path for an Anglo-Russian entente, completed in early 1907. In retrospect German leaders appeared to have missed an opportunity to avoid encirclement and establish hegemony on the Continent. Yet there was little sustained support for preventive war, as opposed to sabre-rattling in 1905. Military, or rather naval, factors played an important role in the decision not to undertake a preventive war in 1905, while considerations of the long-term repercussions of preventive war also favored the counsels of restraint. The military advocates of preventive war never sought to undermine the civilian control of foreign policy, and even as its diplomatic position deteriorated in 1906 political alternatives to preventive war to improve Germany's position remained.

The Austro-Hungarian case, 1911

Franz Conrad von Hötzendorf was appointed chief of the Habsburg General Staff in 1906, and he remained in post until March 1917 when he was dismissed by the new emperor, Karl. However, there was one hiatus during this period when Franz Joseph dismissed him in November 1911, before welcoming him back in November 1912. His dismissal centered on his calls for war against Italy. Indeed, since coming to office, Conrad had repeatedly urged wars against Serbia and Italy, national states that he considered to be inherently hostile to the multinational Habsburg empire. Both states were becoming increasingly powerful not just in military terms, but also in terms of their diplomatic relations and their political projects. Viewing war as inevitable, Conrad wished to wage it at a moment favorable to Austria-Hungary. In 1907, he had identified 1909 as an ideal time to attack Italy. In 1909, in the midst of the Bosnian crisis, Conrad argued for

---

[47] Jean Claude Allain, *Joseph Caillaux: le défi victorieux* (Paris: Imprimerie nationale, 1978), pp. 380–381.
[48] Moritz, *Präventivkrieg*, pp. 124–144.

preventive war against Serbia.[49] Conrad's demands were as unsuccessful as they were shrill. Archduke Franz Ferdinand, the heir to the throne, noted that victory in a war against Serbia would not boost Habsburg prestige and would probably lead to an anti-Habsburg European coalition. In the autumn of 1911, yet another suitable opportunity to wage a preventive war against Italy presented itself. Following the Second Moroccan Crisis, the Italian government decided to invade the Ottoman territories of Tripolitania and Cyrenaica. Antonio di San Giuliano, the foreign minister, argued that this would preserve the balance of power in the Mediterranean, would shore up Italian prestige as a Great Power, and would satisfy the popular clamor for territorial expansion.

In November 1911, seeing Italian forces embroiled in North Africa, Conrad set out his arguments in favor of preventive war in a memorandum submitted to the emperor. This was the culmination of an ongoing debate with Foreign Minister Alois von Aehrenthal and the ambassador to Rome, von Merey. Since the beginning of the year, Conrad had sought more resources for the army and more control over the empire's foreign policy. His demand for a preventive war against Italy in the spring of 1912 was, in part, another tactical maneuver within the struggle between civilians and the military. His reasoning jumped from one justification to another. Hence, he began by arguing that a state must always pursue "positive," expansionist goals or it would decline. When opportunities arose, a great power must seize them, especially in the case of Austria-Hungary which had limited economic and financial resources. The Italian war against the Ottoman Empire provided such an opportunity. Moreover, if Austria-Hungary remained passive, Italy would consolidate its control in Tripolitania and Cyrenaica before turning to achieve its other territorial ambitions in the Habsburg lands of the Tyrol, Istria, Trieste, and Dalmatia. Spring 1912 offered the most opportune moment to strike, he concluded: "I am of the view that policy, in the decisive moments, must take account of the military balance."[50]

Conrad's argument had a compelling logic, if one shared his assumptions about the international system, the military balance, the inherent hostility of Austria-Hungary's neighbors, and the impossibility of achieving security through diplomatic relationships, including the Triple Alliance, to which Italy and Austria-Hungary were both party. Conrad

---

[49] Günther Kronenbitter, *"Krieg im Frieden": Die Führung der k.u.k. Armee und die Großmachtpolitik Österreich-Ungarns 1906–1914* (Munich: Oldenbourg, 2003), pp. 324–332, 349–354.

[50] Franz Conrad von Hötzendorf, *Aus meiner Dienstzeit, 1906–1918*, 5 vols. (Vienna: Rikola, 1922), vol. 2, pp. 436–452.

considered Italy to be inherently hostile to Austria-Hungary, and the war in North Africa as an opportunity to strike Italy before it completed its colonial conquest and turned its attentions northwards. However, these assumptions were not shared by Aehrenthal, Franz Joseph, and others. Security was neither absolute nor eternal; it was relative and contingent. Merey dismissed the concept of a "window of opportunity" by pointing out that nobody could precisely foresee whether the Italian military forces would have achieved readiness for war in a particular year. To decide on a preventive war in 1911 on the basis of a forecast about Italy's and Austria-Hungary's relative strength in the future was an affront to Merey's diplomatic sensibilities.[51] Aehrenthal argued that Italy's difficulties in North Africa made it opportune to renew the Triple Alliance with Italy and Germany. Italy's dependence on her allies had increased and, by implication, so too had the security of the Habsburg Empire. The most categorical rejection came from Franz Joseph, who told Conrad at a meeting on November 15: "My policy is one of peace. Everyone must adapt themselves to my policy. My Foreign Minister conducts my policy in this sense. It is possible that it will come to war, even likely. It will only be waged, however, when Italy attacks us." When Conrad interjected that the chances of victory would be diminished by awaiting an Italian attack, the emperor replied that "as long as Italy does not attack us, this war will not be waged. There is no war party here."[52] Two weeks later Conrad resigned.

The apparent end of Conrad's career in November 1911 owed much to his failed attempts to persuade Aehrenthal to adopt a preventive war strategy. While the logic of preventive war was popular in the officer corps, civilians retained control of foreign policymaking. They viewed the international system in different terms, dismissing the assumptions that underpinned preventive war arguments. Austrian security was dependent on the international system, the "nods and winks," as Churchill later called them, of alliances, détentes, and compensation. Diplomats were prepared to live with uncertainty. Any decisive measure that could be taken today was better postponed to an indefinite future. For Franz Joseph, preventive war would transgress the normative behavior of European politics. In 1907, he slapped down one of Conrad's demands by pointing to the Hague conference, the growth of pacifist movements, and economic interdependence as evidence that preventive war did not, or should not, belong within the realm of the twentieth-century's imagination. His argument in 1911 demonstrated that the politics of declaring war required

[51] *Ibid.*, pp. 222–225.   [52] *Ibid.*, p. 282.

Austria-Hungary to be the victim. A preventive war must be a war of aggression, and any war of aggression would place Austria-Hungary outside the European political community. Even if Franz Joseph had not internalized the moral restraints on preventive war, he recognized the clear political limitations, which often stemmed from moral arguments against aggressive wars between the European Great Powers.[53]

One year later Conrad was appointed Chief of the General Staff. During the Balkan Wars, Austrian diplomats lost faith in the security provided by the European state system. The arguments of Aehrenthal (who had died in February 1912) and Merey had less purchase in the Ballhausplatz. From December 1912, Foreign Minister Leopold von Berchtold considered war against Serbia to be inevitable. The decision to wage war against Serbia in early July 1914 can be construed as a decision for preventive war, but leaders in Vienna justified it as a punitive war against an outlaw state.

The July Crisis and preventive war in perspective

In July 1914, Bethmann-Hollweg seized upon the Russian mobilization orders as justification for the declaration of war. The Russian mobilization order has become one of the most controversial issues in the debate about the July Crisis. For the purpose of this argument, however, the significance of the Russian mobilization order was that it enabled the German government to claim that its declaration of war was a preemptive strike, rather than a preventive war. Later during the war, the distinction between preemptive and preventive war became blurred, as German publicists argued that the war was justified because of the Triple Entente's encirclement and slow strangulation of the Reich. Although the terms preemption and prevention were not used, they had an equivalent in official German military language. As soon as news of Russian mobilization reached Berlin on July 31, the government declared a "State of danger of imminent war" (*Zustand der drohenden Kriegsgefahr*). The following day Germany mobilized and declared war on Russia, but many papers printed the German declaration of war under the title "Russia opens the war." The Russian mobilization justified the preemptive declaration of war. In the July Crisis, however, preemption enjoyed a legitimacy that prevention did not. Crucially, Bethmann-Hollweg was able to convince Socialist leaders that Germany was waging a defensive war, even though Berlin had declared war on Russia and France. Bethmann-Hollweg had resisted full mobilization on July 29, despite the demands of Prussian Minister

---

[53] Kronenbitter, *"Krieg im Frieden"*, pp. 218–219.

of War Erich von Falkenhayn. Even if the logic of German strategy in 1914 was one of preventive war, that logic could not provide the public justification for war.[54]

Any preventive war involves an act of aggression, in that the state choosing a strategy of prevention must initiate the conflict. If preventive war was considered a legitimate and pervasive part of European strategic culture before 1914, then the denunciations of German aggression would have had a limited impact on international public opinion. British and French publicists routinely condemned the German declaration of war and invasion of Belgium and France as acts of barbarism, a word rarely used in relation to Germany before 1914. Civilized European states, according to this argument, recognized limitations and restraints on their political decisions.[55] By initiating a war or aggression, Germany had cast itself outside civilization and Europe. Granted these arguments were filled with cant, hypocrisy, and cynicism, but they cannot simply be dismissed as propaganda. As Franz Joseph had feared, an act of aggression, even if derived from the logic of preventive war, would be politically damaging. Far from being the logical culmination of the development of an international system that privileged militarized *Realpolitik* and accepted preventive war, Germany's declaration of war was condemned as a transgression and a violation of the norms of the European system.

There is a teleological temptation to view Great Power war in 1914 as the outcome of long-standing structures and ethos in the European Great Power system. One line of argument has been to stress the militarization of international politics and the seductive possibilities of preventive war. From a theoretical perspective, one would expect that several preventive wars would have been waged between the 1870s and 1914. And certainly the thought occurred to military and political leaders on several occasions. Yet the logic of preventive war was not pervasive in European strategic thinking. It was largely restricted to military leaders, whereas politicians and diplomats disputed the logic of preventive war. Even generals and admirals viewed preventive war as an ambiguous, dangerous, and possibly counterproductive instrument of security policy. War itself was inherently risky with no guarantee of a precise outcome. Moreover, even if victory was achieved the longer term political consequences could undermine

---

[54] Egmont Zechlin, *Krieg und Kriegsrisiko: zur deutschen Politik im Ersten Weltkrieg* (Düsseldorf: Droste, 1979), pp. 83–85; Ulrich Trumpener, "War Premeditated? German Intelligence Operations in July 1914," *Central European History* 9(1) (1976): 55–85; Strachan, "Preemption," p. 32.

[55] Sophie de Schaepdrijver, *La Belgique et la Première Guerre mondiale* (Frankfurt: Peter Lang, 2004), pp. 60–66; John Horne, *Labour at War: France and Britain, 1914–1918* (Oxford University Press, 1991), pp. 43–47, 60–61.

a state's security. A preventive war would be a war of aggression and liable to give rise to a hostile coalition. In the sphere of domestic politics, statesmen believed that internal unity was a pre-condition for military success. Unity required that any war be justified in the court of public opinion. So even if the politicians agreed with the logic of preventive war, they would have to scale one further obstacle and submit a just cause. Of course, a justification could be manufactured and popular opinion could be manipulated. Yet political leaders were not confident in their ability to present a publicly acceptable justification. It is difficult to go further than this and claim that politicians in general had internalized a moral repugnance toward preventive war, though some had. Without exception statesmen considered war a legitimate instrument of Great Power politics, but they also recognized the political restraints that severely limited the resort to war. Certainly, momentarily favorable military conditions – the core of the logic of preventive war – were insufficient. One significant feature of the July Crisis was that the assassination of Franz Ferdinand provided a just cause for war, at least in the eyes of Austro-Hungarian and German leaders, at a moment when conditions also favored a preventive war. But this coincidence was rare in European politics.

Indeed, between 1871 and 1914 the restraints on preventive war became tighter. Bismarck orchestrated a whole diplomatic campaign in 1875 on the terrors of preventive war; by the eve of the First World War, the doctrine was one that dare not speak its name – at least in public, without censure. The temper of the age inclined toward peace between the Great Powers, and statesmen were reluctant to wager political capital on preventive war. The widespread belief that there was a moral objection to preventive war, even if politicians were hard put to locate the source of this objection, was sufficient to create an ethical restraint on Great Power options in the numerous crises. There were more specific restraints, such as civilian control of the military, the fear of instigating the formation of a hostile coalition, the inherent risk in war, the preference for the uncertainty securities provided by the international system, and the fog surrounding popular reaction to and support for a preventive war.

6   The sources of preventive logic in German decision-making in 1914

*Jack S. Levy**

Preventive war is a familiar concept in the history and theory of international relations. It refers to the use of military force to forestall an adverse shift in relative power with respect to a rising adversary. Political leaders adopt "better-now-than-later" logic and calculate that it is better to try to defeat the adversary (or degrade its capabilities) while the opportunity is still available than to wait and risk the consequences of continued decline. Those consequences include diminishing bargaining leverage, the likelihood of escalating demands by an increasingly powerful adversary, the risk of war under worse circumstances later, and fear of the peace that one would have to accept to avoid a future war. In preventive logic, specific conflicts of issue at stake play a secondary role. The primary issue is power.

Historians and political scientists have described a number of historical cases as "preventive wars," with the First World War getting more than its share of attention. The German military had been advocating a strategy of preventive war against France since the 1870s and against Russia since 1905,[1] and Austrian Chief of Staff Conrad von Hötzendorf had been pushing for a preventive attack against Serbia and against other states as well.[2] I focus here on Germany in 1912–1914. Much of the literature addressing the role of preventive war thinking in German decision-making uses the term rather loosely, however, and fails to specify the full range of factors giving rise to the preventive motivation for war or the nature of the causal logic. My aim in this chapter is to identify the sources of preventive

* I thank Marc Trachtenberg and John Vasquez for their helpful comments on this chapter.
[1] See Mulligan, Chapter 5, this volume.
[2] Samuel R. Williamson, Jr., *Austria-Hungary and the Origins of the First World War* (New York: Macmillan, 1991); Christopher Clark, *The Sleepwalkers: How Europe Went to War in 1914* (London: HarperCollins, 2013), p. 104. The preventive motivation for war has also been attributed to Britain in the First Moroccan Crisis (see Mulligan, Chapter 5, this volume) and to France in 1914. Stefan Schmidt, *Frankreichs Außenpolitik in der Julikrise 1914: Ein Beitrag zur Geschichte des Ausbruchs des Ersten Weltkrieges* (Munich: Oldenbourg, 2009).

thinking in German decision-making leading to war in 1914, and to specify the underlying military, diplomatic, and domestic conditions that increased the influence of preventive logic.

I set aside the broader question of the causes of the First World War as a whole, which are extraordinarily complex. As Christopher Clark suggests, the First World War is "the most complex event of modern times."[3] This helps to explain why historians have been arguing about those causes since the war had barely begun.[4] Given that nearly all analysts agree that Germany played a central role in the outbreak of the war (with many arguing that it played *the* central role), German preventive logic is undoubtedly important in the overall structure of causality for the war. Exactly how important is a question I leave for another time.[5]

Before I engage the processes and events leading to the war, however, I briefly address some conceptual issues that have plagued the application of the preventive war concept to the First World War and to other historical cases.[6]

Conceptual issues

How broad a definition?

I define preventive war narrowly in terms of a military response to the anticipation of an adverse shift in relative power. Some scholars define preventive war more broadly to incorporate responses to a wider array of threats, including actions to forestall "a grave national security threat" such as the loss of prestige[7] or an anticipated breakdown in international order.[8] These are each important motivations for war, but to classify them under the single conceptual umbrella of preventive war stretches the concept too

---

[3] Clark, *Sleepwalkers*, p. 561.

[4] For overviews of the debate, see Annika Mombauer, *The Origins of the First World War: Controversies and Consensus* (London: Longman, 2002); Annika Mombauer (ed.), "Special Issue: The Fischer Controversy after 50 Years," *Journal of Contemporary History* 48(2) (2013): 231–417; Williamson, Chapter 2, this volume.

[5] For my interpretation of the causes of the war, see Jack S. Levy, "Preferences, Constraints, and Choices in July 1914," *International Security* 15(3) (1990/1): 151–186.

[6] This discussion builds on Jack S. Levy, "Declining Power and the Preventive Motivation of War," *World Politics* 40(1) (1987): 82–107; Jack S. Levy, "Preventive War and Democratic Politics," *International Studies Quarterly* 52(1) (2008): 1–24; Jack S. Levy, "Preventive War: Concept and Propositions," *International Interactions* 37(1) (2011): 87–96.

[7] Jonathan B. Renshon, *Why Leaders Choose War: The Psychology of Prevention* (Westport, CT: Praeger, 2006), ch. 1.

[8] Paul W. Schroeder, "Preventive Wars to Restore and Stabilize the International System," *International Interactions* 37(1) (2011): 96–107.

broadly and impedes a discriminating assessment of causation.[9] The aims of maintaining prestige or stabilizing a fragile international order are sufficiently different from the aim of defeating the adversary before it grows too strong that we need different concepts to describe them.

Preemption and prevention

Although it is common to use the concepts of preventive and preemptive attack interchangeably, and although both represent better-now-than-later thinking, they embody different causal logics and it is important to distinguish between them. Preemptive logic is driven by expectations of an imminent attack by the adversary and by the aim of securing first-mover advantages in a war perceived to be nearly certain. Preventive logic is driven by expectations of an adverse shift in power and the fear of a future in which one has relatively less military power and consequently less bargaining leverage.[10] Preventive strategies aim to forestall an adverse shift in power by defeating the adversary in war now (or, in the case of limited preventive strikes, degrading adversary capabilities). Preemptors do not want war, but feel that they have no choice. Preventers want war in the short term to avoid the risk of war under less favorable conditions in the long term. Although preventers usually initiate war, they do not always do so. They sometimes prefer to allow the adversary to strike first, to shift the blame for the war to their adversary, and to secure the diplomatic and/or domestic political benefits of doing so.

The underlying causal logics for preemption and prevention are different. The primary cause of wars begun by a preemptive attack is not preemption *per se*, but whatever it was that created the anticipation of an imminent attack and hence the decision to preempt.[11] Theoretically, preemption is central to theories of conflict spirals, offense–defense, defensive realism, crisis instability, and inadvertent war.[12] The underlying

---

[9] In the extreme, nearly all wars would be preventive, in the sense that nearly all wars are designed to prevent something worse from happening.

[10] Prevention and preemption are often confounded and used interchangeably in the historiography of the First World War. Scholars often talk about pressure from the German military for a "preemptive attack" against Russia going back to 1912, at a time when there was little fear of an imminent Russian attack and thus nothing to preempt.

[11] If the assumption that war is imminent is erroneous, the sources of that misperception are causally important.

[12] Robert Jervis, *Perception and Misperception in International Politics* (Princeton University Press, 1976), ch. 3; Stephen Van Evera, *Causes of War: Power and the Roots of Conflict* (Ithaca, NY: Cornell University Press, 1999); Jack Snyder and Keir A. Lieber, "Correspondence: Defensive Realism and the 'New' History of World War I," *International Security* 33(1) (2008): 174–194; Alexander L. George (ed.), *Avoiding Inadvertent War: Problems of Crisis Management* (Boulder, CO: Westview, 1991).

cause of wars associated with preventive strategies is shifting power (or at least the anticipation of such). Shifting power does not usually lead to war, however, and the conditions shaping whether it does or does not must be incorporated into the causal story.[13] Although preventive logic is primarily about power, not about issues, it is hard to find cases of "pure" preventive wars driven only by power considerations, and the interaction effects between declining power and other variables (including disputes over issues) usually need to be incorporated into the explanation. Theoretically, preventive war is central to theories of balance of power and power transitions.[14] It involves the "commitment problem" emphasized in the "bargaining model of war." Shifting power makes it difficult for adversaries to agree on a negotiated settlement that each side currently prefers to war and is confident will be honored in the future, after power has shifted.[15]

Some wars might be driven by a combination of preventive and preemptive logics. One side may fear both an adverse shift in power and its intermediate- to long-term consequences, and an imminent attack by the adversary and its short-term consequences. I will analyze the argument that this pattern applies to Germany in 1914.

Preventive war: type of war or state strategy?

In Chapter 8, John Vasquez makes an important contribution to the theoretical literature by positing a list of criteria that must be satisfied before a war can be classified as a preventive war. These are useful criteria, and I incorporate them into my analysis, but I prefer to frame the question in a slightly different way. Rather than ask "Was the First World War a

---

[13] On the conditions under which power shifts are most likely to lead to war, see Dale C. Copeland, *The Origins of Major War* (Ithaca, NY: Cornell University Press, 2000); Norrin M. Ripsman and Jack S. Levy, "The Preventive War that Never Happened: Britain, France, and the Rise of Germany in the 1930s," *Security Studies* 16(1) (2007): 32–67; Levy, "Preventive War: Concept and Propositions." An important part of the explanation is why the preventive use of force is preferred to other strategies for responding to decline.

[14] Hans J. Morgenthau, *Politics among Nations: The Struggle for Power and Peace*, 5th edn. (New York: Alfred A. Knopf, 1978), pp. 251–252; Robert Gilpin, *War and Change in World Politics* (New York: Cambridge University Press, 1981); Ronald L. Tammen, Jacek Kugler, Douglas Lemke, Carole Asharabati, Brian Efird, and A. F. K. Organski, *Power Transitions: Strategies for the 21st Century* (New York: Chatham House, 2000); Jonathan M. DiCicco and Jack S. Levy, "Power Shifts and Problem Shifts: The Evolution of the Power Transition Research Program," *Journal of Conflict Resolution* 42(4) (1999): 675–704.

[15] James D. Fearon, "Rationalist Explanations for War," *International Organization* 49(3) (1995): 379–414.

Preventive War?," I focus on the relative causal weight of preventive logic (or the preventive motivation) in the processes leading to war. Admittedly, Vasquez's usage of the preventive war concept is fairly standard, but I think it is necessary to highlight some analytic problems raised by this terminology. Most fundamentally, to ask whether a war is a preventive war implies that a preventive war is a kind of war. This confounds cause and effect in a single concept, in the sense that the cause of a preventive war becomes the preventive motivation for war. This complicates the task of assessing causation, in several ways.

For one thing, war – defined as sustained, coordinated violence between political organizations[16] – involves the intersection of the actions of two or more states (or other political entities). The preventive motivation for war, or preventive logic, describes the motivations of a single state (or a state-level strategy). Consequently, it cannot account for the strategic interaction that leads to war or to peace as a dyadic or systemic-level outcome. The perceptions, motivations, and constraints – internal as well as external – of both sides must be included in a complete explanation for war.[17]

Even if we put the issue of strategic interaction and bargaining aside and focus on explaining the decisions of a single state to resort to military force in response to an anticipated decline in relative power, the multi-causal nature of most decisions for war, including the First World War, raises the question of how important the preventive motivation has to be before we could call the resulting war a preventive war.[18] The preventive war label might be warranted if the preventive motivation is a sufficient condition for a particular war, but I can think of no empirical case that qualifies. More common are cases where the preventive motivation is a necessary condition for a particular war. Describing such a war as a preventive war, however, tends to suppress debate about the multiple causes of the war and how they interrelate. This is particularly troublesome for wars that

[16] Jack S. Levy and William R. Thompson, *Causes of War* (Chichester: Wiley-Blackwell, 2010), p. 5.

[17] Most of the theoretical literature on preventive war focuses on the preventer and says little about the perceptions, calculations, and strategies of their rising adversaries. Do leaders of rising states anticipate that they might be the target of a preventive military strike? How do they respond? Do they attempt to appease their adversary, adopting a strategy of "buying time" until the ongoing shift in power puts them in a stronger position? Do they consider preempting the preventer? This is an interesting question to ask of Russia in 1914. If trends in relative power gave Germany incentives to move sooner rather than later, why did those same trends not give Russia incentives to delay?

[18] Thus, I disagree with Copeland's comment (in *Origins of Major War*, p. 116, and Chapter 7, this volume) that the First World War was "one of the most mono-causally driven major wars in history."

have multiple necessary conditions.[19] To call the war a preventive war would inappropriately privilege one necessary cause over another.

For these reasons, it is better to refer to the preventive motivation for war or to preventive logic as a causal variable or mechanism, rather than to describe a war as a preventive war. We can also speak of preventive war as a state strategy, recognizing that it is the intersection of state strategies, not a single state's strategy, that determines war or peace. This line of argument in no way invalidates Vasquez's criteria in Chapter 8. It just reinterprets them as criteria for assessing the causal weight of preventive logic in a state's decision-making or, alternatively, for assessing whether a state has a strategy of preventive war.

To say that a state has a strategy of preventive war raises its own conceptual problems, of course. We observe state actions. Concluding that a state has a particular strategy involves a difficult inferential leap. It may be possible, in cases involving a dominant decision-maker or widespread consensus on policy in a collective decision-making body, to identify a well-defined state strategy. Often, however, there are multiple actors, in different organizational roles, each with different preferences, perceptions, and political power. Even if all major actors support a decision for war, they may do so for different reasons. Preventive logic may be more important for some actors than for others, and more important at some stages in the decision-making process than at other stages. It might be relatively easy to assess the relative causal weight of the preventive motivation for some individual actors (like Helmuth von Moltke, Chief of the German General Staff in 1914), but more difficult for others (like German Chancellor Bethmann-Hollweg). Aggregating these individual motivations over multiple individuals with different degrees of influence in a complex decision-making process compounds these analytic problems.

Status quo and revisionist preventive war strategies

It is generally assumed that preventive war strategies aim to maintain the status quo against an adverse shift in relative power. But there is another possibility, one that is neglected in the theoretical literature on preventive war. If a state has expansionist or hegemonic ambitions, and if it anticipates an adverse shift in power that would foreclose future opportunities to achieve its revisionist aims, the state may adopt a strategy of preventive

---

[19] One example is the 1956 Sinai War. See Jack S. Levy and Joseph R. Gochal, "Democracy and Preventive War: Israel and the 1956 Sinai Campaign," *Security Studies* 11(2) (2001/2): 1–49.

war to block the power shift and gain a position of hegemony, or at least remove the obstacles for doing so later.[20] "Revisionist" preventive war strategies are less common than "status quo" preventive war strategies, but we can find historical examples, or at least historiographical debates, about what type of strategy a particular state is pursuing.[21]

In fact, two conflicting interpretations of German strategy in 1914 reflect these different types of preventive war strategy. Some argue that German decision-makers were content with their position as the strongest European power, that they were driven primarily by the fear of decline, and that their primary aim was to maintain the status quo by blocking the rising power of Russia.[22] Others, most notably Fritz Fischer, suggest that Germany was driven more by hegemonic ambition than by fear. Fischer implicitly acknowledges the distinction between these two types of preventive war strategies when he argues that: "There is no doubt that the war which the German politicians started in July 1914 was not a preventive war fought out of 'fear and despair.' It was an attempt to defeat the enemy powers before they became too strong, and to realize Germany's political ambitions which may be summed up as German hegemony over Europe."[23] Similarly, in her attribution of preventive thinking to von Moltke, Annika Mombauer writes that: "'Preventive' war is here to be understood not in the sense of preempting an attack from one of Germany's possible future enemies, but of preventing a situation in which Germany would no longer herself be able to launch an attack successfully."[24]

A similar distinction is reflected in theoretical debates between "offensive realists," who argue that security in an anarchic and uncertain world requires offensive strategies and expansion, and "defensive realists," who argue that defensive strategies are generally sufficient for security. Each argument incorporates preventive war strategies, as illustrated by conflicting interpretations of the First World War offered by Keir Lieber

---

[20] My thinking about this issue has benefited from correspondence with Joshua Shifrinson.

[21] Explanations for revisionist preventive war strategies must include both shifting power and the sources of the state's revisionist objectives. It is probably less imperative that explanations for status quo preventive war strategies include an explanation for the goal of maintaining the status quo and avoiding decline. In this sense preventive logic plays a greater causal role in status quo preventive strategies than in revisionist preventive strategies.

[22] Copeland, *Origins of Major War*, and Chapter 7, this volume; Luigi Albertini, *The Origins of the War of 1914*, 3 vols., trans. and ed. Isabella M. Massey (London: Oxford University Press, 1952–1957); Gerhard Ritter, *The Sword and the Scepter*, 4 vols., trans. Heins Norden (Coral Gables, FL: University of Miami Press, 1970).

[23] Fritz Fischer, *War of Illusions: German Policies from 1911 to 1914*, trans. Marian Jackson (New York: W. W. Norton, 1975), p. 470.

[24] Annika Mombauer, *Helmuth von Moltke and the Origins of the First World War* (Cambridge University Press, 2001), p. 108.

and Jack Snyder.[25] This case demonstrates, however, that it is not always easy to separate the two motivations. If leading German decision-makers believed they faced a choice between "world power or decline," the distinction between status quo and revisionist strategies blurs considerably.[26]

Multiple dimensions of power

Nearly all the theoretical literature on preventive war treats power and power shifts in the aggregate, as unidimensional and undifferentiated concepts.[27] This might facilitate the task of constructing parsimonious theories, but it impedes a more detailed and nuanced analysis of the impact of shifting power among states. Certain states at certain times feel more threatened by some kinds of adverse power shifts than by others.[28] It is useful to differentiate among military, economic, and demographic power, and within these categories as well. In the 1930s, France most feared rapid increases in German land-based military power; Britain was consumed by the German air threat; and Hitler was concerned about Germany's long-term demographic and economic limitations. In 1941, Japan was most troubled by its shortages of resources and its inability to keep up with American economic power.[29] In 1981, Israel was concerned almost exclusively with Iraq's potential nuclear power. Often financial strength and the ability to tax and borrow are critical. States sometimes perceive increasing threats on multiple dimensions of power simultaneously.

Of course, fears of adverse changes in non-military elements of power are often driven by the anticipated consequences of those changes for military power and potential. It is still useful, however, to differentiate among the various components of declining power. States have different strategies for dealing with these different threats. The point in time at which each of these different threats will materialize is different, and thus differentially affects the trade-offs leaders make between current risks

---

[25] Keir A. Lieber, "The New History of World War I and What it Means for International Relations Theory," *International Security* 32(2) (2007): 155–191; Snyder and Lieber, "Correspondence."

[26] Snyder and Lieber, "Correspondence," pp. 177–178 (Snyder contribution).

[27] An exception is Copeland, *Origins of Major War*, who emphasizes the relationship between underlying economic power and military power.

[28] As Mulligan notes with respect to the First World War: "The window of opportunity was an economic phenomenon as well as a military one." William Mulligan, *The Origins of the First World War* (Cambridge University Press, 2010), p. 182. See also Steven E. Lobell, "Bringing Balancing Back In: Britain's Targeted Balancing, 1936–1939," *Journal of Strategic Studies* 35(6) (2012): 747–773.

[29] Dale C. Copeland, "A Tragic Choice: Japanese Preventive Motivations and the Origins of the Pacific War," *International Interactions* 37(1) (2011): 116–126.

and future risks. Leaders' time horizons are generally the shortest for military threats, intermediate for economic threats, and the longest for demographic threats.[30] Another advantage of separating components of power is that it makes it easier to analyze the effects of particular combinations of power shifts. One of the most dangerous situations is one in which a state holds a current advantage in military power (making war feasible now), but faces relative economic decline, undercutting its future military potential and power, and creating incentives for war now.[31]

With these theoretical considerations in place, let us turn to the role of preventive logic in German foreign policy on the eve of the First World War.

Germany and the First World War

The interdependence of decisions in Berlin and Vienna

My focus on Germany's decision calculus has no necessary implications for the ongoing debate over whether the overall causes of the First World War derive more from decisions in Berlin, Vienna, or elsewhere. I am not necessarily siding with what Williamson calls the "German paradigm."[32] The road to war went through both Vienna and Berlin, and their decisions were highly interdependent. Austria-Hungary would not have initiated a war against Serbia without unambiguous German support, given the perceived likelihood of Russian intervention in any Austro-Serbian war. Thus, the German "blank check" was a necessary condition for an Austro-Serbian war. Because an Austro-Serbian war approximated a necessary condition for a continental war pitting Germany against Russia and France,[33] the German blank check was a necessary condition for the First World War as a whole.[34]

At the same time, Germany could not have pushed Austria-Hungary into a war the latter did not want.[35] German leaders recognized this,

---

[30] These trade-offs between current and future risks often vary significantly across individual leaders. On time horizons, see Philip Streich and Jack S. Levy, "Time Horizons, Discounting, and Intertemporal Choice," *Journal of Conflict Resolution* 51(2) (2007): 199–226.

[31] Copeland, *Origins of Major War*, ch. 2.

[32] Williamson, Chapter 2, this volume. Also Hew Strachan, *The First World War, vol. 1: To Arms* (New York: Oxford University Press, 2001), ch. 1.

[33] Mombauer, *Helmuth von Moltke*, p. 107.

[34] Albertini, *Origins of the War of 1914*, vol. 2, p. 162; Levy, "Preferences, Constraints, and Choices," p. 156; David Stevenson, *Cataclysm: The First World War as Political Tragedy* (New York: Basic Books, 2004), p. 13; Mark Hewitson, *Germany and the Causes of the First World War* (Oxford: Berg, 2004), pp. 229–230.

[35] Williamson, *Austria-Hungary*; also Chapter 2, this volume.

which is why Moltke and other proponents of war in Germany insisted that "the *casus belli* had to result from circumstances that would definitely involve ... Austria-Hungary."[36] Consequently, the most favorable conditions for war for Germany involved a crisis in the Balkans. This would engage both Austro-Hungarian interests and the terms of the alliance between the two Central Powers.[37] This helps to explain why the assassination provided an ideal context for an aggressive German policy.[38] As Bethmann-Hollweg said ten days after the assassination: "If war comes from the east so that we have to fight for Austria-Hungary and not Austria-Hungary for us, we have a chance of winning."[39]

Thus, an Austro-Hungarian preference for war was a necessary condition for an Austro-Serbian war, and hence for a general war.[40] As I noted above, German support for Austria-Hungary was also a necessary condition for a local war and for a general war. Other scholars have talked about the responsibility of Serbia, Russia, and France.[41] With two or more necessary conditions for a continental war, causality (or responsibility) cannot be attributed exclusively to one capital over another.[42] Any complete analysis

---

[36] Mombauer, *Helmuth von Moltke*, p. 107.

[37] Another advantage of a crisis in the Balkans is that it held out some possibility that Germany might be able to split the entente. Fritz Fischer, *Germany's Aims in the First World War* (New York: W. W. Norton, [1961] 1967), p. 60; Konrad H. Jarausch, "The Illusion of Limited War: Chancellor Bethmann-Hollweg's Calculated Risk, July 1914," *Central European History* 2(1) (1969): 48–76, at 58; Niall Ferguson, "Public Finance and National Security: The Domestic Origins of the First World War Revisited," *Past and Present* 142(1) (1994): 141–168, at 144.

[38] Mulligan, *Origins of the First World War*. For an argument that the assassination was a necessary condition for war, see Richard N. Lebow, "Contingency, Catalysts, and Nonlinear Change: The Origins of World War I," in Gary Goertz and Jack S. Levy (eds.), *Explaining War and Peace: Case Studies and Necessary Condition Counterfactuals* (London: Routledge, 2007), pp. 85–111. For general criteria for assessing counterfactual hypotheses like this one, see Jack S. Levy, "Counterfactuals and Case Studies," in Janet Box-Steffensmeier, Henry Brady, and David Collier (eds.), *Oxford Handbook of Political Methodology* (New York: Oxford University Press, 2008), pp. 627–644.

[39] Riezler diary, July 8, 1914, cited in Jarausch, "Illusion of Limited War," p. 58. Ironically, French leaders also preferred a "Balkan inception scenario" because it ensured the maximum Russian military engagement against Germany. Clark, *Sleepwalkers*, pp. 293–301.

[40] I have argued that Austria-Hungarian leaders preferred a local war in the Balkans to a continental war, and both to a negotiated peace with Serbia. Levy, "Preferences, Constraints, and Choices," pp. 155–156; Albertini, *Origins of the War of 1914*, vol. 2, pp. 168–169, 286–289; Williamson, *Austria-Hungary*.

[41] Clark, *Sleepwalkers*; Williamson, Chapter 2, this volume; Otte, Chapter 4, this volume; Bobroff, Chapter 9, this volume; Sean McMeekin, *The Russian Origins of the First World War* (Cambridge, MA: Belknap Press of Harvard University Press, 2011), chs. 1–2; Schmidt, *Frankreichs*.

[42] On the difficult question of evaluating the weight of multiple necessary conditions, see Gary Goertz and Jack S. Levy, "Causal Explanation, Necessary Conditions, and Case Studies," in Gary Goertz and Jack S. Levy (eds.), *Explaining War and Peace: Case Studies and Necessary Condition Counterfactuals* (London: Routledge, 2007), pp. 9–45.

of the outbreak of the Austro-Serbian war and the general war that followed requires a careful assessment of decision-making in both Vienna and Berlin. I now turn to Berlin, and more specifically to the sources of the preventive motivation for war for German decision-makers.

The sources of German preventive logic

The First World War is a good example of the importance of the systemic context for a dyadic shift in relative power.[43] German leaders believed that the Franco-Russian alliance made it almost certain that any Great Power war in Europe would be a two-front war in which Germany would face enemies that were stronger in numbers and resources, which meant that Germany could not win a long war of attrition. This assumption was the basis for the Schlieffen Plan, developed in 1905 by Alfred Graf von Schlieffen, Chief of the German General Staff. The plan assumed that Russian mobilization would be slow, that a small German army in the east would provide a sufficient defense in the early stages of a war, and that the bulk of the German army, with an enveloping movement on the right flank moving through the Low Countries, could defeat France quickly in the west before turning to deal with the Russian "steamroller."[44]

One immediate problem with the Schlieffen Plan was that Germany did not have the army strength necessary to implement the plan or the transport system to move troops to the front as quickly as the plan required.[45] The plan might have been a bargaining ploy to argue for the enlargement of the army, but neither Schlieffen nor his successor Helmuth von Moltke (the Younger) made an effort to expand the army – at least not until after the 1911 Agadir crisis and the shift in Germany's attention from the naval race with Britain to the Continent.[46]

In addition, Schlieffen had not incorporated into his plan any allowance for a substantial increase in Russian military strength. This was critical. Russian military and economic power increased dramatically

---

[43] See the discussion of multiple rivalries in Rasler and Thompson, Chapter 3, this volume.

[44] Mombauer, *Helmuth von Moltke*, pp. 72–80. For debates about the Schlieffen Plan, see Annika Mombauer, "Of War Plans and War Guilt: The Debate Surrounding the Schlieffen Plan," *Journal of Strategic Studies* 28(5) (2005): 857–885. On the psychological and organizational biases that led Germany to adopt an offensive war plan and to eventually abandon its Eastern Deployment Plan by 1913, see Jack Snyder, *The Ideology of the Offensive: Military Decision Making and the Disasters of 1914* (Ithaca, NY: Cornell University Press, 1984), chs. 4–5.

[45] When fully mobilized, Germany and Austria could field 136 divisions, compared with 199 for France, Britain, Belgium, Russia, and Serbia. Snyder, *Ideology of the Offensive*, p. 107.

[46] Mombauer, *Helmuth von Moltke*, pp. 84–86, 106; Gerhard Ritter, *The Schlieffen Plan: Critique of a Myth* (New York: Praeger, 1958), pp. 66–67.

after its nadir in 1905 following Russia's defeat in the Russo-Japanese War. Whereas the combined peacetime strength of the French and Russian armies exceeded that of the German/Austro-Hungarian combination by 261,000 in 1904, that gap had grown to 1 million by 1914. In terms of full wartime strength in 1914, the German army could mobilize about 2.1 million men, plus another 1.4 million Austria troops. The combined wartime strength of Serbia, Russia, France, Belgium, and Britain was 5.4 million troops.[47] The growth in Russian power increasingly brought into question the assumption that Germany would be able to defeat France quickly in the west and still have time to defeat a more slowly mobilizing Russian army in the east. Indeed, as the Russian army was modernized, the time it would take to fully mobilize continued to shrink, putting more time pressure on the Schlieffen Plan.[48]

Subsequent military, diplomatic, economic, and political developments further eroded the effectiveness of the Schlieffen Plan. The Anglo-Russian entente of 1907 led German military planners to fear that any two-front war might become a three-front war with British intervention. By 1912, concerns about Russia's growing power and its shift in attention from the Far East to the Balkans, and the realization that Germany could not compete with Britain as a world power, had led German leaders to concede the naval race to Britain, redirect their defense spending away from the navy to the army,[49] and generally "retreat to the European continent."[50]

The Balkan Wars in 1912–1913, triggered in part by the Italo-Turkish War of 1911–1912, also had important implications for the distribution of power in the Balkans, the security threats facing Austria-Hungary, and consequently for the likely effectiveness of the Schlieffen Plan. Serbian territory doubled and its population grew by half, substantially increasing

[47] Figures are from Ferguson, "Public Finance," pp. 147–148. For more detailed data on army and navy sizes and military expenditures, see David G. Herrmann, *The Arming of Europe and the Making of the First World War* (Princeton University Press, 1996), appendices; and David Stevenson, *Armaments and the Coming of War: Europe, 1904–1914* (Oxford University Press, 1996), pp. 1–8. On the gaps between objective indicators and perceptions of power, see William C. Wohlforth, "The Perception of Power: Russia in the Pre-1914 Balance," *World Politics* 39(3) (1987): 353–381; also Otte, Chapter 4, this volume.

[48] These increases, along with the general recovery of the Russian economy from near-bankruptcy in 1905, were made possible by extensive loans from French banks, which were pressured by the French government. Patrick J. McDonald, *The Invisible Hand of Peace: Capitalism, the War Machine, and International Relations Theory* (Cambridge University Press, 2009), ch. 7.

[49] Strachan, *First World War*, p. 33; Paul M. Kennedy, *The Rise of the Anglo-German Naval Rivalry, 1860–1914* (London: Allen & Unwin, 1982).

[50] V. R. Berghahn, *Germany and the Approach of War in 1914* (New York: St. Martin's Press, 1973), ch. 7. The German military still regarded France as its main enemy and felt relatively secure. Hewitson, *Germany*, pp. 130–131.

the threat to an ever-more fragile Austro-Hungarian Empire. In addition, Bulgaria was lost as a possible counterweight, Romania proved to be an unreliable ally, and the likelihood of Italian support in any war diminished. As Clark argues, "the system of geopolitical balances" that had helped to contain local conflicts was "swept away," leaving Austria's Balkan policy "irreparably ruined."[51] German leaders worried that Austria-Hungary would focus its primary attention to the increased security threat from the Balkans, diverting additional troops away from the Russian front, and putting more pressure on the Schieffen Plan to secure a rapid defeat of France so that German armies could deal with the enhanced Russian threat.[52]

The altered security environment after the First Balkan War (along with Russia's partial mobilization in Poland during the war) led to the German army bill of July 1913, which called for an increase of 119,000 men. Though this was only 40 percent of what Moltke had requested in order to match increases in France, it was still substantial, the largest peacetime increase in German history.[53] The German army bill contributed to an increase in tensions and to an acceleration of the land arms race. It was a major factor leading France to introduce its three-year military service law (by undercutting political opposition to a lengthening of the term of service), which would eventually result in a significant increase in the size of the French army.[54]

More significantly, the German army bill led the Russian Duma to pass the "Great Programme" of rearmament in June 1914. The Great Programme called for a nearly 40 percent increase in the size of the army (by about 470,000 men) and a 29 percent increase in the officer corps by 1917, along with a substantial increase in artillery and other armaments.[55] The Great Programme built on other changes that St. Petersburg had initiated in the last five years. These included an army reorganization in 1910, which German leaders feared would substantially reduce mobilization times, along with a substantial expansion of the Russian railroads in western Russia, initiated in fall 1913.[56] As Holger Herwig argues, "the Great

---

[51] Clark, *Sleepwalkers*, pp. 242, 281.

[52] Mulligan, *Origins of the First World War*, p. 83; Mombauer, *Helmuth von Moltke*, pp. 144–145. The Balkan Wars also contributed to a significant hardening of Russian attitudes, a shift in Russia's internal balance of power, the increasing diplomatic isolation of Austria-Hungary, and its loss of confidence in the efficacy of diplomacy. Clark, *Sleepwalkers*, ch. 5.

[53] Herrmann, *Arming of Europe*, pp. 190–191; Mombauer, *Helmuth von Moltke*, p. 174.

[54] Stevenson, *Armaments and the Coming of War*, pp. 302–303; Gerd Krumeich, *Armaments and Politics in France on the Eve of the First World War* (Oxford: Berg, 1984).

[55] D. C. B. Lieven, *Russia and the Origins of the First World War* (New York: Macmillan, 1983), p. 111; Herrmann, *Arming of Europe*, p. 205; William C. Fuller, Jr., *Strategy and Power in Russia, 1600–1914* (New York: Free Press, 1992), p. 437.

[56] Fuller, *Strategy and Power in Russia*, pp. 423–433; Stevenson, *Armaments and the Coming of War*, pp. 159–163.

Programme soon became the 'key obsession' of German decision-makers."[57] Moltke feared (in Mombauer's words, perhaps with some exaggeration) that once Russia completed its army increases and once its railroad network was extended to the German border, "[Russian] troops would be in Berlin as quickly as the Germans hoped to be in Paris."[58]

The specific problems created by the Great Programme were compounded by German military and civilian leaders' growing fears that Germany would not be able to keep up with Russia and France in the arms race, leading to the continued erosion of the viability of the Schlieffen Plan and the prospects for a German military victory. These fears were enormously consequential. Niall Ferguson argues that "The decisive factor in 1914 which pushed the German Reich over the brink into war was the conviction of both military and civilian leaders that Germany could not win the arms race against its continental neighbours." Similarly, Patrick McDonald concludes that "Germany launched a preventive war in July 1914 because it could not keep pace with an accelerating arms race that was rapidly shifting the balance of military power on the continent to its detriment."[59]

Several factors contributed to Germany's inability to hold its own in the arms race. The Dual Alliance was at a disadvantage in terms of key demographic and economic indicators. They had only 46 percent of the population and 61 percent of the gross national product (GNP) of the Entente.[60] In addition, since 1890 Russia had been outpacing Germany in terms of rates of growth in population, GNP, and iron and steel production.[61] However, other economic indicators were more favorable to Germany. Germany was growing faster than any of its adversaries in terms of exports and in terms of gross domestic capital formation, and faster than Britain and France (but not Russia) in GNP and steel production.[62] Ferguson concludes from his comparative analysis of the political economies of Germany, Austria-Hungary, and their main rivals that

---

[57] Holger H. Herwig, "Germany," in Richard F. Hamilton and Holger H. Herwig (eds.), *The Origins of World War I* (Cambridge University Press, 2003), pp. 150–187, at 165.

[58] Mombauer, *Helmuth von Moltke*, p. 108.

[59] Ferguson, "Public Finance," p. 143; McDonald, *Invisible Hand of Peace*, p. 232.

[60] The importance of the demographic dimension was reinforced in the eyes of those influenced by Social Darwinism and the school of geopolitics. See Thomas Lindemann, *Die Macht der Perzeptionen und Perzeptionen von Mächten* (Berlin: Duncker & Humblot, 2000), pp. 228–251.

[61] Ferguson, "Public Finance," pp. 147–148; also Paul Kennedy, *The Rise and Fall of the Great Powers: Economic Change and Military Conflict from 1500 to 2000* (New York: Random House, 1987), pp. 249–254; Stevenson, *Armaments and the Coming of War*, pp. 1–14.

[62] Ferguson, "Public Finance," p. 148.

Germany had the economic capability to spend considerably more on defense, and thus in principle to keep up with the arms race. The problem was that there were domestic constraints on Germany's ability to tax and borrow. Ferguson concludes that "the domestically determined financial constraint on Germany's military capability was a – perhaps *the* – crucial factor in the calculations of the German General Staff in 1914."[63]

Ferguson argues that Germany could not win the arms race because it was "Unable to borrow as much as the Russian or French states, unable to raise as much in direct taxation as the British, and unable to reduce the large shares of the states and local government in total public revenue ..."[64] Germany's creditworthiness had been declining, and its short-term indebtedness was growing.[65] Germany's politically more centralized adversaries were less constrained in securing tax increases, while decentralized Austria-Hungary was even more constrained. Underlying Germany's financial constraint were a number of institutional and political constraints.[66]

Institutionally, Germany's federal structure left most control over taxation to individual German states, to the extent that only about a third of total public revenues went to the Reich. The states, not the Reich, could impose income taxes, but they generally opposed the funding of the army.[67] Politically, the Reichstag also posed constraints on both conscription and taxation. The Social Democrats, the leading party by 1912, along with their many allies in the center left, opposed conscription and the taxation necessary to support it because their costs would fall disproportionately on the working classes. This made it very difficult for the government to put together a legislative coalition that would facilitate an increase in defense spending and in the size of the army.[68]

---

[63] Niall Ferguson, *The Pity of War: Explaining World War I* (New York: Basic Books, 1999), p. 140. On the theoretical relationship between credit and war, see Karen A. Rasler and William R. Thompson, "Global Wars, Public Debts and the Long Cycle," *World Politics* 35(4) (1983): 489–516; Patrick Shea, "Financing Victory: Sovereign Credit, Democracy, and War," *Journal of Conflict Resolution* (2013): DOI: 10.1177/0022002713478567.

[64] Ferguson, "Public Finance," p. 164.

[65] Ferguson, "Public Finance," p. 164; David Stevenson, "Was a Peaceful Outcome Thinkable? The European Land Armaments Race before 1914," in Holger Afflerbach and David Stevenson (eds.), *An Improbable War? The Outbreak of World War I and European Political Culture before 1914* (New York: Berghahn, 2007), pp. 130–148, at 138.

[66] For a theoretical analysis of institutional sources of financial constraints on the ability of politically decentralized states to prepare for war, see McDonald, *Invisible Hand of Peace*.

[67] Ferguson, "Public Finance," pp. 155–156.

[68] McDonald, *Invisible Hand of Peace*, pp. 212–217. On the impact of globalization on conscription, see David M. Rowe, "The Tragedy of Liberalism: How Globalization Caused the First World War," *Security Studies* 14(3) (2005): 407–447.

Requests for army expansion also generated concerns among the military about the consequences of substantial increases in military spending. The War Ministry cut the December 1912 Moltke–Ludendorff request for a 50 percent increase in defense expenditures by over half because they feared the social and political consequences. One War Ministry bureau chief said that "If you continue with these armaments demands, then you will drive the German people to revolution."[69] The military also had long-standing concerns about the impact of army expansion on the social composition of the army, and its political consequences. The main fear was a dilution of the aristocracy's dominance over the officer corps and an increasingly "bourgeois" General Staff. War Minister Heeringen stated that the Moltke–Ludendorff request would result in the "'democratization' of the army."[70]

These constraints complicated Bethmann-Hollweg's efforts to pass the army law of 1913 and forced him to take politically risky actions. His decision to fund the increases through property taxes won him the support of the Socialist left, but alienated conservatives, traditional allies of the kaiser and a core base of his own parliamentary support. As McDonald concludes, "the arms race on land had thus pushed Germany to its financial limits and threatened the government's capacity to sustain it."[71]

German leaders had been expressing their concerns about the security consequences of financial constraints on rearmament for a number of years. In 1909, the kaiser lamented that Germany did not have the financial capabilities to improve the readiness of the fleet because of the "inexorable constraints of the tightness of funds."[72] In his argument for war at the December 1912 "War Council," Moltke argued that "the army would get into an increasingly unfavourable position, for the enemies are arming more strongly than we, as our money is very tied up." An article in a September 1913 General Staff journal focused on "Russia's growing financial strength after 1906."[73]

The final straw for Moltke came in July 1914, when German War Minister Falkenhayn opposed his request for additional troops, largely on financial grounds. Moltke concluded that no army increases would be forthcoming in the immediate future. This meant

---

[69] Holger H. Herwig, "Strategic Uncertainties of a Nation-State: Prussia–Germany, 1871–1918," in Williamson Murray, MacGregor Knox, and Alvin Bernstein (eds.), *The Making of Strategy: Rulers, States, and War* (Cambridge University Press, 1994), pp. 242–277, at 264.

[70] Ferguson, "Public Finance," p. 155; Gordon A. Craig, *The Politics of the Prussian Army, 1640–1945* (Oxford University Press, 1955), pp. 232–238.

[71] McDonald, *Invisible Hand of Peace*," p. 215.   [72] *Ibid.*, p. 83.

[73] Fischer, *War of Illusions*, pp. 162, 371.

that Germany's position could only decline, while Russian and French armies continued to grow, further undercutting the Schlieffen Plan. As Mombauer argues, "The debate over army increases is thus crucial background to understanding Moltke's decision-making during the July crisis."[74]

These concerns were reflected in more general pessimism about the future among German leaders. In Moltke's last meeting with Conrad at Carlsbad on May 12, 1914, he said that "To wait any longer meant a diminishing of our chances; as far as manpower is concerned we cannot enter into a competition with Russia." He later told Jagow that:

Russia will have completed her armaments in two or three years. The military superiority of our enemies would be so great that he [Moltke] did not know how we might cope with them. In his view there was no alternative to waging a preventive war in order to defeat the enemy as long as we could still more or less pass the test."[75]

Bethmann-Hollweg shared many of Moltke's concerns.[76] On July 6–7, he told his personal secretary Kurt Riezler that "The future belongs to Russia ... as it grows and grows and weighs upon us like an ever-deepening nightmare."[77] Austria was becoming "weaker and more immobile," "increasingly undermined from north and south-east, at any rate incapable of going to war for German interests as our ally." Bethmann-Hollweg was particularly worried about the completion of the Russian railroad system, concerns that had been reinforced by two recent General Staff studies: "The Completion of the Russian Railroad Network" and "The Growing Power of Russia." He said that "After the completion of their strategic railroads in Poland our position [will be] untenable."[78] Several years later, when pressed about his earlier motivations, he said (in February 1918), "Lord yes, in a certain sense it was a preventive war," motivated by "the constant

---

[74] Mombauer, *Helmuth von Moltke*, p. 181.
[75] Ferguson, *Pity of War*, p. 100. Also Imanuel Geiss (ed.), *July 1914: The Outbreak of the First World War: Selected Documents* (New York: Scribner, 1967), pp. 46–47.
[76] Bethmann-Hollweg's fears were greatly enhanced by news in May–June 1914 that Britain and Russia were holding secret naval talks. For two years Bethmann-Hollweg had relied on détente with Britain to restrain Russia, minimize Germany's sense of encirclement, and help to maintain peace and stability in Europe. With intelligence reports of the naval talks, and with additional mistrust generated by Grey's public denial of the talks, Bethmann-Hollweg lost faith in the restraining effects of détente, gave greater weight to the alliance with Austria, and embarked on a more assertive policy. See Mulligan, *Origins of the First World War*, pp. 88–90; Clark, *Sleepwalkers*, p. 421.
[77] Cited in Herrmann, *Arming of Europe*, p. 214. Bethmann-Hollweg had expressed a similar pessimism two years earlier when he said that there was no use planting new trees on his estate because the Russians would be there within a few years. Fischer, *War of Illusions*, p. 224.
[78] Jarausch, "Illusion of Limited War," p. 57; Herrmann, *Arming of Europe*, p. 214.

threat of attack . . . its inevitability in the future, and by the military's claim: today war is still possible without defeat, but not in two years!"[79]

Foreign Secretary Jagow had similar fears. He told Lichnowsky on July 18 that "Russia will be ready to fight in a few years. Then she will crush us by the number of her soldiers; then she will have built her Baltic fleet and her strategic railroads. Our group, in the meantime, will have become weaker right along."[80] Max Warburg recounts the kaiser's remarks in a June 21, 1914 meeting between the two friends: "Russia's armaments, the big Russian railway constructions were in his view preparations for a great war which could start in 1916 . . . oppressed by his worries he even considered whether it might not be better to attack than to wait."[81]

German fears that the military situation would continue to decline, and that financial and domestic factors would prevent a German army expansion and rearmament that might preserve the existing distribution of power on the Continent, created enormous pressure for a strategy of preventive war while the odds of winning were reasonably good. This preventive logic was exacerbated by additional factors, including preemptive logic driven by the growing belief that war was inevitable and imminent.

Preemptive pressures

Given the Schlieffen Plan's requirement for a quick victory in the west, if war ever came to be perceived as imminent, Germany had strong military incentives to secure first-mover advantages by preempting. Those incentives were enhanced by Moltke's modifications in Schlieffen's original plan. Rejecting Schlieffen's assumption that France would pursue a purely defensive strategy, Moltke modestly reduced the ratio of the enveloping forces on the right wing to the defensive forces in the south.[82] He also modified Schlieffen's original plan to outflank France's eastern fortresses by going through Holland as well as through Belgium. Moltke had grown increasingly skeptical of the widespread assumption that a European war would be short.[83] He calculated that by avoiding Holland

---

[79] Jarausch, "Illusion of Limited War," p. 48.

[80] Max Montgelas and Walter Schücking (eds.), *The Outbreak of the World War: German Documents*, collected by Karl Kautsky (New York: Oxford University Press, (1919), trans. in one volume, Carnegie Endowment for International Peace, 1924), No. 72, pp. 131–132.

[81] Fischer, *War of Illusions*, p. 471.   [82] Mombauer, *Helmuth von Moltke*, pp. 90–92.

[83] Stig Förster, "Dreams and Nightmares: German Military Leadership and the Images of Future Warfare, 1871–1914," in Manfred F. Boemeke, Roger Chickering, and Stig Förster (eds.), *Anticipating Total War: The German and American Experiences, 1871–1914* (Washington, DC: German Historical Institute, 1999), pp. 343–376. The extent to which this realization of the likelihood of a long war was shared by the rest of the German

he could secure Dutch neutrality and use that country as a "windpipe" that would allow Germany to "breathe" by securing access to outside markets during the long struggle against economically stronger opponents.[84]

These changes had enormous consequences for military planning and consequently for crisis stability. Avoiding Holland meant that additional forces had to be routed through Belgium without creating extra delays. Moltke's plans required a *coup de main* on Liége so that the First and Second armies could pass quickly through a narrow 12-mile corridor. Because the invasion of France could not proceed until the vital forts and railroad lines of Liége had been secured, the Moltke–Schlieffen Plan required that German armies would advance into Belgium as an integral part of mobilization, even prior to a declaration of war.[85] This magnified the belief that small delays could be enormously costly, cutting further into the narrow temporal window of opportunity required by the Moltke–Schlieffen Plan. This added to Germany's military incentives to preempt once war became likely.[86]

These considerations explain German military leaders' concerns when their intelligence revealed that on July 29 Belgium had called up reservists (more than doubling the size of the Belgian standing army), reinforced the garrison at Liége, and begun defensive military preparations. As Stevenson argues, the Belgian action "set a time bomb ticking under the German Schlieffen Plan . . ."[87]

Of even greater concern to the German military, however, were early Russian military actions in the form of the secret "period preparatory to war" that was approved on July 24, begun the next day, and quickly observed by German intelligence. The geographic scope of the actions

military leadership is not clear. Moltke did not share his doubts about the likely duration of the war and the odds of Germany winning it with Bethmann-Hollweg, the kaiser, or other civilian leaders. Mombauer, *Helmuth von Moltke*, pp. 85, 288.

[84] Mombauer, *Helmuth von Moltke*, pp. 93–95.

[85] The political consequences were substantial. Bethmann-Hollweg strove for British neutrality without realizing (because he was unaware of the details of mobilization) that mobilization itself would draw Britain into the war. In addition, because mobilization meant war, it further reduced Germany's diplomatic options in a crisis. On the political rigidity of the Schlieffen Plan, and links to theories of organizational processes and politics, see Jack S. Levy, "Organizational Routines and the Causes of War," *International Studies Quarterly* 30(2) (1986): 193–222.

[86] Stephen Van Evera, "The Cult of the Offensive and the Origins of the First World War," *International Security* 9(1) (1984): 58–107, at 71–79; Levy, "Preferences, Constraints, and Choices," p. 182. For a more skeptical view of the importance of Liège, see Marc Trachtenberg, "The Meaning of Mobilization in 1914," *International Security* 15(3) (1990/1): 120–150, at 144.

[87] David Stevenson, "Militarization and Diplomacy in Europe before 1914," *International Security* 22(1) (1997): 125–161, at 152; Ulrich Trumpener, "War Premeditated? German Intelligence Operations in July 1914," *Central European History* 9(1) (1976): 58–85, at 80; Mombauer, *Helmuth von Moltke*, p. 203.

(in districts opposite Germany as well as Austria-Hungary, and in the Baltic as well as by the Black Sea Fleet) significantly added to German insecurities.[88] To Moltke, this looked like the early stages of a Russian mobilization, helping Russian armies to threaten Germany's thinly guarded eastern frontier before Germany could achieve a decisive victory over France.[89]

Despite its military incentives to move quickly, and contrary to theories of the cult of the offensive, German political and military leaders did not rush to take preemptive action or otherwise escalate the crisis, at least not until July 31.[90] They did not respond in kind to Russian pre-mobilization actions. When Falkenhayn proposed on July 29 to declare *Kriegsgefahrzustand*, the "threatening danger of war," Moltke objected, and the war minister backed off.[91] Later that evening, after receiving news of the Russian partial mobilization, Bethmann-Hollweg rejected a call for German mobilization. After receiving new information about the progress of Russian military preparations, by noon on July 30 Moltke had joined Falkenhayn and other generals in pushing for *Kriegsgefahrzustand*, but Bethmann-Hollweg refused.

Up to this point, preemptive logic had little impact on German decision-making. Pressure from the military continued to escalate, however, and by 9 pm that night Bethmann-Hollweg agreed to declare *Kriegsgefahrzustand* by noon on July 31 unless Russia reversed course. Bethmann-Hollweg issued a 12-hour ultimatum to Russia to stop all military preparations, but Russia rejected the ultimatum and announced a general mobilization before noon on July 31. The Russian mobilization was a sufficient condition for German mobilization, and German mobilization was a sufficient condition for war because the Schlieffen Plan required the seizure of Liège as part of mobilization.[92]

Berlin's cautious responses to events in the week before July 31 raise questions about the argument that German preemption played a central

---

[88] Trumpener, "War Premeditated?" pp. 66–72.
[89] Stevenson, "Militarization," pp. 152–153; Bobroff (Chapter 9) and Williamson (Chapter 2), this volume.
[90] Levy, "Preferences, Constraints, and Choices," pp. 181–182; Trachtenberg, "Meaning of Mobilization," pp. 137–138.
[91] *Kriegsgefahrzustand* would make mobilization more likely, but not automatic. Albertini, *Origins of the War of 1914*, vol. 2, p. 599.
[92] Levy, "Preferences, Constraints, and Choices," pp. 179–182. This leads many to regard the Russian mobilization as the decisive act leading to war, though taking place in a causal chain in which German actions also played a critical role. Paul M. Kennedy (ed.), *The War Plans of the Great Powers, 1880–1914* (Boston, MA: Allen & Unwin, 1979), p. 15; Albertini, *Origins of the War of 1914*, vol. 3, p. 31. On Russia, see Lieven, *Russia*, ch. 5; McMeekin, *Russian Origins*, chs. 1–2; Bobroff, Chapter 9, this volume.

causal role in the processes leading to war.[93] One of the problems with the sizable theoretical literature on "offense–defense theory" is that it generally defines first-strike advantages in strictly military terms.[94] For Germany, however, calculations about the costs and benefits of preemption (and military action in general) were significantly shaped by domestic and diplomatic considerations.

Domestic and diplomatic constraints on German mobilization

When Moltke invoked preventive logic in arguing for war at the December 1912 "War Council," he emphasized the importance of gaining the support of public opinion.[95] Moltke, along with other German leaders, was convinced that domestic unity was a key to military victory, and that unity required a war that was publicly perceived to be legitimate.[96] With that goal in mind, he proposed a press campaign. He later told Bethmann-Hollweg that prospects were bright "if we manage to formulate the *casus belli* in such a way that the nation will take up arms unitedly and enthusiastically."[97]

This required convincing the public – particularly socialists, liberals, and left-wing Catholics, who were a political majority, and who had opposed armament increases and hard-line foreign policies in the absence of a clear threat – that Germany was fighting a defensive war started by Russia. Moltke recognized that it would be necessary for Germany to delay its military actions and let Russia mobilize first. From the beginning, Moltke insisted that "the attack must come from the Slavs."[98] Late on July 29, 1914, Moltke, with unanimous support, instructed Conrad: "Do not declare war on Russia but wait for Russia's attack." Similarly, Bethmann-Hollweg insisted that Germany wait for a state of war between Russia and Austria, "because otherwise we should not have

---

[93] If Russian leaders had delayed the Russian mobilization without accepting the terms of the German ultimatum, and if Bethmann-Hollweg had gone ahead with his promise to declare *Kriegsgefahrzustand* by noon on July 31, we would be giving greater causal weight to German preemptive logic at the end of the crisis.

[94] Michael E. Brown, Owen R. Coté, Jr., Sean M. Lynn-Jones, and Steven E. Miller (eds.), *Offense, Defense, and War* (Cambridge, MA: MIT Press, 2004).

[95] There is a substantial literature on the domestic sources within Germany pushing for war. See Fischer, *War of Illusions*; Wolfgang J. Mommsen, "Domestic Factors in German Foreign Policy before 1914," *Central European History* 6(1) (1973): 3–43. The focus here is different: on domestic constraints on an early German mobilization for war.

[96] See Mulligan, Chapter 5, this volume.   [97] Mombauer, *Helmuth von Moltke*, p. 145.

[98] Moltke to Conrad, February 10, 1913, cited in Fischer, *Germany's Aims*, p. 33.

public opinion with us either at home or in England."[99] As Crown Prince Rupprecht of Bavaria stated in August 1914, "Everyone knows what this war, which is forced upon us, is all about; it is a true people's war (*Volkskrieg*), whereas if war had resulted from the Moroccan matter, this would not have been understood among the people."[100]

The people's war argument was easier to make after the First Balkan War than before. Although the German left and center had long shared the image of Russia as autocratic, backward, and barbaric, until 1913 they did not view Russia as their primary threat. That changed with the First Balkan War. This shift in definition of the enemy helped the German leadership convince the center left to support a defensive "people's war" against a Tsarist Russia they had always held in contempt.[101]

Still, Bethmann-Hollweg was very concerned about the domestic consequences of war. Whereas some believed that war would generate a "rally round the flag effect" and diffuse the political threat from the left, Bethmann-Hollweg believed that war would "strengthen tremendously the power of Social Democracy . . . and would topple many a throne." War would lead to "a revolution of everything existing."[102]

The kaiser, Bethmann-Hollweg, and other civilian leaders saw additional diplomatic reasons for insisting that Germany did not act until Russia had mobilized first. Although there is substantial debate about whether Bethmann-Hollweg and other German civilian decision-makers *expected* Britain to enter the early stages of a continental war, they certainly *hoped* that Britain would stay out.[103] Bethmann-Hollweg believed that British neutrality was contingent on the British perception that Germany was fighting a defensive war in response to Russian aggression, and he repeatedly insisted to the kaiser and to the military that

---

[99] In Trachtenberg, "Meaning of Mobilization," p. 138.

[100] Mombauer, *Helmuth von Moltke*, p. 107.

[101] Hewitson, *Germany*, pp. 130, 188; Stevenson, *Cataclysm*, pp. 30–31.

[102] Quoted in Geiss (ed.), *July 1914: Outbreak*, p. 471; David E. Kaiser, "Germany and the Origins of the First World War," *Journal of Modern History* 55(3) (1983): 442–474, at 470. On "rally effects" and the diversionary theory of war, see Jack S. Levy, "The Diversionary Theory of War: A Critique," in Manus I. Midlarsky (ed.), *Handbook of War Studies* (Boston, MA: Unwin Hyman, 1989), pp. 259–288.

[103] See the exchange in Jack S. Levy, Thomas J. Christensen, and Marc Trachtenberg, "Correspondence: Mobilization and Inadvertence in the July Crisis," *International Security* 16(1) (1991): 189–203. See also Levy, "Preferences, Constraints, and Choices," p. 165, and Copeland, Chapter 7, this volume. The issue was not whether Britain would intervene at all – surely it would if France was about to get crushed by Germany – but whether any intervention would come too late to affect the outcome of the war in the west. This was the meaning of Bethmann-Hollweg's reassurance to the kaiser on July 23, 1914, that "It is improbable that England will *immediately* enter the fray." Cited in Jarausch, "Illusion of Limited War," p. 62.

"Russia must ruthlessly be put into the wrong."[104] Bethmann-Hollweg also undertook several diplomatic initiatives to secure British neutrality. Those efforts failed because Bethmann-Hollweg insisted that Britain stay neutral regardless of how a war started, whereas Britain offered neutrality only in the event of an unprovoked attack on Germany.[105]

In my view, Bethmann-Hollweg not only hoped that Britain would stand aside in a continental war, but he continued to believe there was a good chance it would do so if Russia incurred the blame for the war.[106] Bethmann-Hollweg based his policies on that assumption, at least until the evening of July 29–30.[107] Along with most German political leaders, Bethmann-Hollweg hoped for a localized war in the Balkans, and was willing to risk a war with Russia and France that was confined to the Continent, but believed that the worst outcome for Germany would be a world war triggered by British intervention.[108] Throughout much of the July Crisis Bethmann-Hollweg was reasonably confident that Britain would stay out of the early stages of a continental war and, given his preferences, that expectation reinforced his hard-line policies until the end of the July Crisis.[109]

Bethmann-Hollweg's behavior changed dramatically on the evening of July 29, after he learned of Russia's partial mobilization and of the strong likelihood that Britain would enter the war. The information about Britain was particularly compelling, and Bethmann-Hollweg's initial response was predictable given his preferences.[110] After three weeks of urging Austria-Hungary to undertake immediate military action against Serbia,

---

[104] Jarausch, "Illusion of Limited War," p. 67.   [105] Fischer, *Germany's Aims*, p. 27.

[106] The real question is not whether or not German leaders expected British neutrality, but the probability they attached to that outcome.

[107] Moltke had assumed since 1912 that Britain would intervene. Mombauer, *Helmuth von Moltke*, pp. 77, 104, 109.

[108] Levy, "Preferences, Constraints, and Choices," pp. 159–161.

[109] I develop my argument about German expectations of British neutrality in "Preferences, Constraints, and Choices," pp. 163–170. See also Fischer, *Germany's Aims*, ch. 2; Scott D. Sagan, "1914 Revisited: Allies, Offense, and Instability," *International Security* 11(2) (1986): 151–175, at 171–172; Sean M. Lynn-Jones, "Detente and Deterrence: Anglo-German Relations, 1911–1914," *International Security* 11(2) (1986): 121–150. This argument is reinforced by Moltke's comment in May 1914 that "Our people unfortunately still expect a declaration from Britain that it will not join in." Fischer, *War of Illusions*, p. 400. It is also reinforced by the fact that serious political divisions in the British Cabinet meant that as late as July 29–30 the British had not decided what they would do in the event of a continental war. I read Clark, *Sleepwalkers*, as generally supporting this interpretation of the views of Bethmann-Hollweg and of the kaiser. For dissents, see Trachtenberg, "Meaning of Mobilization"; Copeland, Chapter 7, this volume.

[110] See my argument in Levy, Christensen, and Trachtenberg, "Correspondence." For a more cynical explanation of Bethmann-Hollweg's behavior, see Copeland, *Origins of Major War*, and Chapter 7, this volume.

Bethmann-Hollweg reversed course and in a flurry of telegrams tried to hold back Austrian leaders. He urged them to adopt some version of the Halt in Belgrade plan, and hinted that Germany might abandon its Austrian ally rather than be drawn into a world war. Bethmann-Hollweg's efforts to restrain Vienna lasted less than a day, but his radical shift in behavior in response to the new information about Britain suggests the importance he attached to British intentions. Röhl makes a similar argument about the kaiser. He notes that from July 27–31 the kaiser's mood "flip-flopped from wild aggression to half-baked attempts at mediation and back again. The key to explaining these mood swings . . . is to be found . . . in Wilhelm's perception of Britain's attitude," which Röhl goes on to document.[111]

Interaction effects between shifting power and other variables

As I emphasized earlier, whether states respond to adverse shifts in relative power usually depends on the presence of other conditions or beliefs. One important variable is expectations about the costs and risks of war now. The greater the expected probability of victory with minimal costs in war now, the greater the incentives for a preventive war strategy.[112] An analysis of this factor for Germany in 1914 is complicated by the existence of some variation in views among both German military and political leaders, with the latter being somewhat more optimistic.

The idea that the military shared a "short war illusion" is no longer the conventional wisdom among historians. Moltke in particular recognized that a general war was likely to be a long and enormously destructive war of attrition.[113] As Mombauer emphasizes, however, Moltke never made his fears widely known, and as a result German political leaders were quite confident of a decisive victory at minimal cost.[114] This suggests that some causal role in German decision-making needs to be given to

---

[111] John C. G. Röhl, "The Curious Case of the Kaiser's Disappearing War Guilt: Wilhelm II in July 1914," in Holger Afflerbach and David Stevenson (eds.), *Improbable War? The Outbreak of World War I and European Political Culture before 1914* (New York: Berghahn, 2007), pp. 75–95, at 83.

[112] Levy, "Declining Power," pp. 99–100.

[113] Förster, "Dreams and Nightmares." Moltke believed that war "would destroy the culture of almost the whole of Europe for decades to come." Mombauer, *Helmuth von Moltke*, p. 202. This is not to say that Moltke and his colleagues feared a military defeat. As Hewitson (*Germany*, p. 121) argues, there was little talk of that possibility, even in private.

[114] Mombauer, *Helmuth von Moltke*, pp. 95, 211–212. This optimism was reinforced by the belief that neither Russia nor France was ready for war, and by accounts of the July 13

organizationally driven misperceptions of political leaders. In the end, however, the German decision was shaped more by fears of the future than by confidence in war now. They were convinced that things would only get worse, and that it was essential for Germany to seize the opportunity before it vanished. On July 26, 1914, Moltke said that "We shall never again strike as well as we do now, with France's and Russia's expansion of their armies incomplete."[115]

Another theoretical condition contributing to the preventive use of military force is expectations that a future war is inevitable or highly likely.[116] This increases the fear of the future, and the costs and risks of inaction now, and it reduces both the attractiveness of alternative strategies for dealing with decline and decision-makers' incentives to try to manage the crisis to avoid war. Expectations of inevitable war also undercut internal opponents of preventive war, who can no longer claim that avoiding preventive war will avoid war. A number of factors mentioned earlier contributed to growing German estimates of the likelihood of a future war. These include increasingly belligerent Russian policies; the departure of more moderate voices from the Russian government; Russian sponsorship of the Balkan League; the acceleration of the arms race through the Great Programme; the Anglo-Russian naval talks; and Russian pre-mobilization measures. Expectations of a high probability of war constitute a causal variable in its own right, but it gains added causal weight through its interaction effects with declining power.

Conclusion

One can find enough evidence to provide some support for nearly every interpretation of the outbreak of the First World War. This helps to explain why historians have debated the origins of the war for nearly a century, and why political scientists have used the war to test or illustrate a wide range of theoretical models of war at nearly every level of analysis. My aims have been more modest: to identify the sources of preventive war thinking in Germany, and in the process to raise some analytic issues surrounding the concept of preventive war. I see these theoretical and empirical tasks as necessary first steps before tackling the larger objectives

---

discussion in the French parliament detailing a wide range of French military weaknesses. See John F. V. Keiger, *France and the Origins of the First World War* (London: Macmillan, 1983); Keiger, Chapter 10, this volume; Clark, *Sleepwalkers*, p. 440.

[115] Ferguson, "Public Finance," p. 146.

[116] Levy, "Declining Power," pp. 98–99. Expectations that war is imminent increase incentives for preemption.

of assessing the precise causal role of preventive logic in German decision-making leading up to the war, and of assessing the role of shifting power and preventive logic in the outbreak of the war as a whole.

Recent research has made it increasingly clear that a more satisfactory interpretation of the causes of the war will require more attention to the role of the other Great Powers and of Serbia. One interesting theme that emerges is that it was not only German and Austrian political leaders who feared that their states had reached the peak of their influence and who saw some advantages in a war sooner rather than later. Even French leaders were concerned about the growing power and assertiveness of Russia, feared that they might be abandoned by their stronger ally, and worried that they were "working against the clock."[117] The current Austro-Serbian crisis engaged Russian interests and ensured that France would not face Germany alone. Russian leaders feared that their strategic position was becoming increasingly fragile, and that their opportunities for influence in the Straits would soon diminish.[118] The causal strength of this better-now-than-later thinking for many of the Great Powers is an important question for further research.

As for Germany, although there is little doubt that preventive logic played an important role, attaching a precise causal weight to this factor raises difficult historical and conceptual issues. Minimal criteria for such an assessment include identifying the influence of preventive logic on each of the leading decision-makers, and specifying the influence of each actor on the decision-making process.[119] Even if we focus our attention on the three leading decision-makers (the kaiser, Bethmann-Hollweg, and Moltke), it is clear that the influence of preventive logic and the impact of other factors that pushed for a less aggressive policy varied in each of these actors. In addition, historians continue to debate the relative influence of each of these actors in the German decision-making process.

In terms of policy preferences, Moltke was the most consistently and most powerfully driven by preventive logic, though even he was insistent that Germany must allow Russia to mobilize first. Bethmann-Hollweg shared Moltke's concerns, but was generally restrained by other factors. Bethmann-Hollweg's primary strategy for eliminating, or at least mitigating, the security threat to Germany was not preventive war, but instead the promotion of a localized Austro-Serbian war, which would precipitate a

---

[117] Clark, *Sleepwalkers*, p. 313; Schmidt, *Frankreichs*.
[118] McMeekin, *Russian Origins*; Clark, *Sleepwalkers*, pp. 328, 484.
[119] Vasquez, Chapter 8, this volume.

diplomatic realignment in the Balkans and relieve pressure on Austria-Hungary. Bethmann also believed (perhaps aided by some wishful thinking) that a localized war might lead to a break-up of the Entente, ending Germany's problem of encirclement. From 1911 to 1914, he relied heavily on détente with Britain to restrain Russia. It was only after he learned of the Anglo-Russian naval talks in May 1914 that Bethmann-Hollweg was willing to seriously contemplate war. He also feared the potentially revolutionary domestic consequences of a European war. Bethmann-Hollweg's temporary pressure on Austria to hold back early on July 29–30 suggests that he preferred a peaceful resolution of the crisis once it became clear that Britain would intervene.[120]

Although preventive logic driven by fears of the rising power of Russia exerted a powerful push toward war for the kaiser, there were other factors that restrained him. He had not supported the military's recommendations for war in the 1911 Moroccan Crisis, and the military feared that the kaiser might back away again in the July Crisis.[121] When the kaiser learned of Serbia's conciliatory response to the Austrian ultimatum, he stated that the grounds for war had evaporated. When he learned from London early on July 28 that Britain would probably enter the war, he immediately called for Great Power mediation based on the Halt in Belgrade proposal. As Röhl notes, the kaiser's flip-flops are "not easy to interpret."[122] Though changing news from Britain explains some of this variation, psychological factors undoubtedly also played a role.[123]

All this leads me to the provisional conclusion that although shifting power and preventive logic were among the most important motivations influencing German leaders in 1914, the evidence falls short of substantiating the argument that Germany had a consistent strategy of preventive war in the year or two leading up to the July Crisis.[124] If it had, we would see more evidence of German preparation for war and for a war economy. Fear of decline may have led Germany to a coercive and high-risk foreign policy, but during the July Crisis Bethmann-Hollweg and the kaiser were still hoping to localize the war. As Clark notes, in military terms Germany remained "an island of relative calm throughout the crisis."[125]

---

[120] Bethmann-Hollweg's failure to follow through with his pressure on Austria was due to Austria's resistance and to pressure from the German military driven (by that time) by short-term preemptive logic based on the fear of imminent war.

[121] Mombauer, *Helmuth von Moltke*, p. 181.

[122] Röhl, "William II in July 1914," p. 86.

[123] On psychological approaches to the study of politics, see Leonie Huddy, David O. Sears, and Jack S. Levy (eds.), *Oxford Handbook of Political Psychology*, 2nd edn. (Oxford University Press, 2013).

[124] Clark, *Sleepwalkers*, pp. 520, 523.   [125] *Ibid.*, p. 510.

The primary causal influence of preventive logic came through pressure from Moltke and the military, but that pressure did not have a strong impact until the very end of the July Crisis. A satisfactory evaluation of the causal impact of preventive logic will undoubtedly involve identifying its interaction effects with other variables in the complex processes leading to the First World War.

International relations theory and the three great puzzles of the First World War

Dale C. Copeland*

The First World War continues to this day to be a source of great controversy among theorists of international relations (IR). Aside from its decisive role in shaping the twentieth century, there is probably one main reason why this particular war, above all others, seems to provoke such heated debate in the IR field: pretty well every major theory of international relations has a dog in this fight. Defensive realists and bargaining theorists, who believe wars occur because of spirals of mistrust and an inability to locate a mutually preferred negotiated peace, consider the First World War to be *the* preeminent case of actors falling into a war they would otherwise have wanted to avoid. Liberals and constructivists, who see wars arising from unit-level pathologies in the heads of leaders and their societies, can look to 1914 as a case where hypernationalism, class warfare, cartel politics, and psychological distortions led actors to race to the front in the hope of satisfying unmet domestic and personal needs. Structural neorealists, who argue that multipolar systems force great powers to support critical allies in a crisis, even at the risk of total war, view the First World War as their main example of such chain-gaining dynamics.[1]

This chapter challenges each of these broad approaches to explaining the First World War. Consistent with dynamic versions of systemic realism founded upon the logic of preventive war, I argue that the war that broke out in that fateful summer of 1914 had one, and only one, primary cause: the profound fear among German leaders that their nation was in irreversible decline relative to a rising Russian colossus.[2] For the key

---

* This chapter draws from and extends arguments and evidence first laid out in Dale C. Copeland, *The Origins of Major War* (Cornell University Press, 2000), chs. 3–4.

[1] See below for references.

[2] For references to the now vast preventive war literature, see Jack S. Levy, "Preventive War and Democratic Politics," *International Studies Quarterly* 52(1) (2008): 1–24. For a critique of the First World War as solely a preventive war, see Vasquez, Chapter 8, this volume. For references to the strong support for the preventive war thesis in recent diplomatic history, see Keir A. Lieber, "The New History of World War I and What it Means for International Relations Theory," *International Security* 32(2) (2007): 155–191, and Levy, Chapter 6, this

decision-makers in Berlin, all other apparent "causes" were either not important or only secondary to this preventive logic. Elsewhere, I have laid out a new approach to thinking about preventive war, one that differentiates between the effects of decline across bipolar and multipolar systems, and between decline that is inevitable versus temporary and reversible.[3] Here my purpose is not to belabor the details of this theoretical logic or the logic of any other IR theory, but rather to plunge into the documentary evidence supporting the preventive war position relative to competing arguments. In this sense, I am not trying to uphold the superiority of my own particular take on preventive war, but rather to show the superiority of any perspective that views the war as one driven primarily by German actions, actions undertaken out of a belief that a rising Russia would pose an unacceptable security threat to Germany within a decade.[4]

I will demonstrate the power of a preventive explanation of the war relative to its main competitors through the posing of three critical historical puzzles. First, why did a crisis in the Balkans in 1914 lead to system-wide war when on at least three occasions in 1912 and 1913 similar crises in the Balkans did not lead to war between the Great Powers? Second, why did German leaders on the night of July 29, 1914 seem to back away from their hard-line pressuring of Austria-Hungary, only to return to this hard-line stance by the next day? Did they really get cold feet and yet were unable to stop the ball from rolling, as Chancellor Theobald von Bettman-Hollweg later claimed? The third puzzle is one that has been almost completely ignored by the IR literature, but is perhaps the most intriguing: why did Germany surprise Russia with a declaration of war on August 1, and yet delay a similar declaration of war for France until August 4? German military plans called for an initial quick and decisive attack on France, and for offensive operations against Russia only after France had been dispatched (that is, weeks later). So why not declare war on France first to justify the plunge into Belgium required by those plans?

Any IR theory worth its salt must be able to answer all three of these puzzles in a coherent and empirically supported manner. If a particular theory J has an explanation for only one or perhaps two of the puzzles, and an alternative theory K can explain all three, then logic would dictate that theory K must be preferred to theory J. Much of the blame for the lack of scholarly consensus on the First World War must be traced to a tendency

---

volume. Given Lieber's and Levy's admirable overviews of the new literature, I will not repeat their summaries here, but rather focus on what the documentary record reveals about German preventive thinking and decision-making.

[3] Dale C. Copeland, *The Origins of Major War* (Ithaca, NY: Cornell University Press, 2000).

[4] See, for example, Patrick McDonald, *The Invisible Hand of Peace: Capitalism, the War Machine, and International Relations Theory* (Cambridge University Press, 2008), ch. 7.

by IR theorists to pick isolated pieces of evidence from specific moments in this complex case to support a preferred perspective, and to ignore evidence from other moments that goes against an argument's larger logic.[5] By focusing on what I believe are the three biggest puzzles of the war, we can avoid this tendency, and perhaps put ourselves on the road to a true scholarly consensus. At the very least, we can narrow down the range of "remaining" debates by taking disconfirmed or implausible explanations out of the running. In this way, some modest accumulation of knowledge might still be possible in the notoriously divided IR field.

This chapter proceeds as follows. I will first briefly lay out the main arguments that compete with this chapter's view that German leaders used the July Crisis of 1914 to bring about a preventive war at the best possible moment, both politically and in terms of German military power. I will then discuss the evidence that supports this preventive perspective for the 1912–1914 period, with special attention to the providing of answers to the above three puzzles. Space constraints preclude a full consideration of all the empirical problems facing the existing literature. But it will hopefully be clear by the chapter's end that competing arguments provide plausible accounts for at most only one of the three puzzles posed, namely, for German behavior on the night of July 29, and that even here their explanations face inconsistencies that force us to reevaluate their merits. As we eliminate alternative perspectives and leave the preventive explanation standing, we gain confidence that this complicated war perhaps did have a single overarching cause: not crazy leaders or spiraling dynamics, but the existential pressure exerted on Germany by the growth of Russian power.

Competing arguments

The preventive war perspective competes with three broad groups of explanations for the First World War. The first, drawn from the spiral model, would see the war as inadvertent: no state wanted major war, yet the pre-1914 arms race had put the Great Powers on a hair-trigger. Hence, when the crisis began in the Balkans in July 1914, all states mobilized and then went to war to preempt what they perceived to be the impending attacks of their adversaries.[6] Misperceptions, cults of the offensive, and

---

[5] For example, by ignoring the question of why the 1912–1913 Balkan crises did not create incentives for preemptive war, spiral theorists can keep us focused on July 1914, where evidence for preemptive motivations seems more plausible.

[6] See esp. Robert Jervis, *Perception and Misperception in International Politics* (Princeton University Press, 1976), ch. 3; Charles Glaser, *Rational Theory of International Politics* (Princeton University Press, 2010).

military timetables are seen to reinforce this basic spiral dynamic. Richard N. Lebow argues that decision-making pathologies led Berlin to expect others to back down, so that German objectives could be achieved without war. By late July, when it was clear that all states, including Britain, would oppose Germany, German leaders were so incapacitated by the shock of the new information that they were unable to avert catastrophe.[7] Stephen Van Evera argues that the pervasive belief among European leaders that the offensive was dominant led states to rush to preemptive war for fear their adversaries would strike first.[8] This view is underpinned by the argument that military leaders, particularly in Germany, seized the reins of power, putting states on mobilization schedules which made preventive war inevitable.[9]

The second category of explanations rejects the idea that no one wanted war, but locates the causal source of aggression at the domestic level rather than (as in my argument) at the systemic level. Certain states, most importantly Germany, were indeed aggressive, not due to misperceptions and security fears, but because of domestic pathologies. One such argument is that hypernationalism, fed through a rapacious press, pressured leaders to adopt aggressive, expansionary postures.[10] Others argue that as after 1890 Germany moved to a policy of belligerent self-assertion to achieve its "place in the sun," it could not help but act aggressively in the core.[11] Jack Snyder contends that Germany's tendency to overexpansion reflects the strategic ideology shaped by a cartelized political system: the sharing of power between interest groups led to expansion through domestic log-rolling.[12] Perhaps the most influential domestic-level explanation is Fritz Fischer's argument that German leaders initiated war to solve their internal crisis. Berlin, he argues, sought "to consolidate the position of the ruling classes with a successful imperialist foreign policy." Germany's

[7] Richard N. Lebow, *Between Peace and War* (Baltimore, MD: Johns Hopkins University Press, 1981), ch. 5.

[8] Stephen Van Evera, "The Cult of the Offensive and the Origins of the First World War," *International Security* 9(1) (1984): 58–107. See also Jack N. Snyder, "Civil–Military Relations and the Cult of the Offensive," *International Security* 9(1) (1984): 108–146; Jack N. Snyder, *The Ideology of the Offensive* (Ithaca, NY: Cornell University Press, 1984).

[9] See esp. Luigi Albertini, *The Origins of the War of 1914*, 3 vols., trans. and ed. Isabella M. Massey (London: Oxford University Press, 1952–1957); Van Evera, "Cult of the Offensive."

[10] Paul Kennedy, *The Rise of Anglo-German Antagonism, 1860–1914* (London: Allen & Unwin, 1980), ch. 14.

[11] See esp. Woodruff D. Smith, *The Ideological Origins of Nazi Imperialism* (Oxford University Press, 1986), chs. 4 and 8.

[12] Jack Snyder, *Myths of Empire* (Ithaca, NY: Cornell University Press, 1991).

declining military power only affected the timing of German actions; the core objectives were still social imperialist.[13]

The third category of explanations includes systemic explanations other than preventive war. For neorealists, the war was one of rational miscalculation caused by multipolarity. Since states could not abandon their allies without endangering their security, once Russia moved to support Serbia, Germany was forced to defend Austria and France to defend Russia. A small crisis in the Balkans thus dragged all the Great Powers into major war.[14] This argument can be supplemented by the belief that the Austro-Hungarian government did indeed want war, but only a localized conflict that would help to stem the disintegration of its imperial realm. In the process of seeking this limited aims objective, it unleashed the chain-ganging tendencies of the multipolar system.[15]

Before turning to the evidence for the First World War as a German-initiated preventive war, it is worth noting some of the main problems with the above explanations.[16] For the spiral model to argue that war was caused by incentives to preempt, it must show that German leaders thought Russian mobilization meant that St. Petersburg had a possible desire for war. Yet German leaders knew with essential certainty that the tsar and Russian officials were desperate to avoid war in 1914, if only because Russia had not completed its rearmament.[17] The argument that Berlin reacted with preemptive strikes because of its belief in offense dominance is also suspect. If true, why did Germany threaten Russia with war on July 29 in response only to initial preparations against Austria, when in the winter of 1912/13 it had done nothing after a much more extensive Russian mobilization against Austria? More broadly, the

---

[13] Fritz Fisher, *War of Illusions: German Policies from 1911 to 1914*, trans. Marian Jackson (New York: W. W. Norton, 1975), p. 8. On the primacy of domestic politics, see esp. Wolfgang J. Mommsen, "Domestic Factors in German Foreign Policy Before 1914," in Wolfgang J. Mommsen (ed.), *Imperial Germany, 1867–1918* (London: Arnold, 1995); Michael Gordon, "Domestic Conflict and the Origins of the First World War," *Journal of Modern History* 46(2) (1974): 191–226.

[14] Kenneth N. Waltz, *Theory of International Politics* (New York: McGraw-Hill, 1979), p. 167; Thomas J. Christensen and Jack Snyder, "Chain Gangs and Passed Bucks," *International Organization* 44(2) (1990): 137–168. As with the first explanation, war is seen as inadvertent. Note, however, that states are drawn into war less as a function of irrational beliefs, and more as a rational response to systemic imperatives. See Scott D. Sagan, "1914 Revisited: Allies, Offense, and Instability," *International Security* 11(2) (1986): 151–175.

[15] See esp. Samuel R. Williamson, Jr., *Austria-Hungary and the Origins of the First World War* (New York: Macmillan, 1991) and Williamson, Chapter 2, this volume.

[16] For full coverage of these problems, see Copeland, *Origins of Major War*, chs. 3–4.

[17] For a nice critique of Sean McMeekin's more Machiavellian view of Russia, see Bobroff, Chapter 9, this volume.

shift from Germany's restraint of Austria in previous cases to German pressure in July 1914 must be explained.

Integral to the issue of preemption is whether Germany truly could not stop its war machine once it got rolling, either because the military seized the reins of power or because logistical schedules produced some sort of technical determinism. Yet if so, why on August 2 would Chancellor Bethmann-Hollweg tell the kaiser that he was delaying a declaration of war and an attack on France "in the hope that the French will attack us," and then proceed to war only when the French would not oblige?[18] If the military controlled the situation, why on July 29 did the chancellor's opinion that Germany should delay general mobilization win the day? Why was the crucial decision to declare war on Russia, made on July 31 and implemented on August 1, kept secret from all the military leaders except Army Chief of Staff Helmut von Moltke?[19]

The Fischer thesis that Germany initiated war to solve its domestic crisis is also problematic. It is clear that Bethmann-Hollweg and the other key officials believed both before and during the July Crisis that major war would only *increase* the possibility of social revolution in Germany, even if Germany was victorious.[20]

Finally, if German civilian leaders were truly seeking a negotiated peace by late July, including one giving Austria almost everything it wanted, why would they cut off all possible last-minute negotiations by declaring war on Russia on August 1? Since Russia was the slowest mobilizer, why not give Austria and Russia a bit more time to find a mutually acceptable deal, one that avoided a big war that both clearly had no interest in? Furthermore, if Berlin hoped St. Petersburg would cave in under pressure, why not inform the Russians that a declaration of war was pending, instead of designing a declaration that would take them by surprise and give them no chance to back down? These questions are crucial, since essentially every argument out there, even Fischer's, ultimately accepts that things got out of control in the last days of the crisis (why else would Berlin not have chosen a favorable negotiated settlement to a world war that included Britain?).

In the rest of this chapter, I show how an explanation rooted in German fears of deep and inevitable decline relative to Russia helps to clear up these outstanding issues. German leaders were so convinced of the necessity of preventive war by 1914 that once they had secured the support of the

---

[18] Max Montgalas and Walther Schücking (eds.), *The Outbreak of the World War: German Documents*, collected by Karl Kautsky (New York: Oxford University Press, [1919] 1924), doc. No. 629. Herein, as per convention, the Kautsky documents will be referred to as *DD*.
[19] See below.   [20] See below, and Copeland, *Origins of Major War*, pp. 75–78, 83–85.

German masses and of Austria by blaming Russia for the coming war, they deliberately undermined all chances of peace.

Postponing the First World War: German war planning, 1911–1913

Through 1912, fear of Russian growth began to pervade the civilian leadership. Bethmann-Hollweg was greatly sobered by his visit to Russia in July 1912. A meeting with Tsar Nicholas reinforced his belief that the Russians had no desire for war, at least while they were rebuilding: "Russia needs peace to consolidate itself. For this reason … its present rulers want to be on good terms [with Germany]." Yet he was worried about Russia's "wealth of mineral resources and solid physical man-power," noting "Russia's rising industrial power, which will grow to over-whelming proportions."[21] His pessimism would only deepen over time: overlooking his estate before the war, he told his son that there was little reason to plant new trees, since "in a few years the Russians would be here anyway."[22]

It was Bethmann-Hollweg's growing recognition that a general war would have to be fought sooner rather than later that pushed him to support the army's call for a massive increase in war readiness.[23] In late 1911, the ministry made its case that this time had come. On November 19, Minister of War Josias von Heeringen wrote to Bethmann-Hollweg that despite recent setbacks, he and Moltke were convinced that Germany's army was still equal to the combined strength of its opponents in the near term, but its long-term ability to deter its adversaries was falling.[24] Ten days later, on November 29, General Franz von Wandel, the individual responsible for drafting the new army bill, produced a memorandum outlining the army's logic. The situation was not favorable. Even if Germany was mili-tarily superior in the short term, "Russia is working with gigantic financial resources on the reconstruction of its army," and having solved its prob-lems with Japan, it could now intervene in a European war.[25]

---

[21] Quoted in Fischer, *War of Illusions*, p. 139.

[22] Quoted in Volker R. Berghahn, *Germany and the Approach of War in 1914* (New York: St. Martin's Press, 1973), p. 186.

[23] He supported the 1912 and 1913 military laws that would increase standing land forces by 25 percent, even though it was clear that it would spark a competition with Germany's neighbors. David Herrmann, *The Arming of Europe and the Making of the First World War* (Princeton University Press, 1996), pp. 161, 165.

[24] Quoted in *ibid.*, p. 166; David Stevenson, *Armaments and the Coming of War: Europe, 1904–1914* (Oxford University Press, 1996), pp. 201–202.

[25] Herrmann, *Arming of Europe*, pp. 166–167.

With general war looming, the chancellor initiated discussion through British Minister of War Richard Haldane to see if any hope of British neutrality remained. When Haldane arrived in February 1912, it was soon apparent that Berlin sought Britain's promise of unconditional neutrality: even if Germany were the aggressor, Britain had to agree to stay out of a continental conflict. Needless to say, if Berlin had no intention of initiating major war, it would not have had to insist on unconditional neutrality, something which the British quickly recognized. London responded that it could agree never to join an offensive attack on Germany, but this was rejected. Combined with Berlin's inability in 1905 and 1911 to split Britain from France, the failure of the Haldane mission confirmed the need to prepare for a world war that included Britain.[26] This conclusion was bolstered on December 3, 1912, when Berlin received a telegram from Max von Lichnowsky, German ambassador in London, relaying a message from Haldane. Referring to the Balkan crisis that had begun in October, Haldane told Lichnowsky that Britain would not remain a bystander should Austria invade Serbia. British policy was based, according to Haldane, on the conviction that the balance of power must be preserved.[27]

On December 8, the kaiser called his military leaders to a secret meeting to discuss the dilemma of almost certain British intervention in a continental war. This infamous War Council (so named by Bethmann-Hollweg) and the events that immediately followed are highly significant. They show that German leaders, both military and civilian, had begun actively preparing for a preventive war to be initiated within one to two years.[28]

Admiral George von Müller recorded the council's proceedings in his diary. The kaiser began by arguing that Austria, to survive, must deal energetically with the Serbian problem. Yet "if Russia supports the Serbs, which she evidently does ... then war would be unavoidable for us too." From Haldane's statements it was clear that war could not be contained on the Continent. Hence, "the fleet must naturally prepare itself for the war against England." Moltke, who had sought preventive war since 1909, readily agreed, arguing: "I believe a war is unavoidable and the sooner the better."[29] The stumbling block was once again the navy. Chief of Naval Staff Alfred von Tirpitz, as in 1909 and 1911, argued that the navy was still not quite ready, and hence "would prefer to see the postponement of

---

[26] Fischer, *War of Illusions*, pp. 124–125.

[27] *Die Grosse Politik der Europäishen Kabinette, 1871–1914* (*GP*), 39 vols. (Berlin: Deutsche Verlagsgesellschaft für Politik und Geschichte, 1922–1927), vol. 39, doc. No. 15612.

[28] See Fischer, *War of Illusions*, ch. 9; John C. G. Röhl, *The Kaiser and his Court: Wilhelm II and the Government of Germany* (Cambridge University Press, 1996), ch. 7.

[29] From Admiral Müller's diaries, quoted in Röhl, *Kaiser*, p. 162.

the great fight for one and a half years," by which time the Kiel Canal and the Heligoland U-boat harbor would be complete. Moltke responded that "the navy would not be ready even then and the army would get into an increasingly unfavorable position."[30] Since Britain's involvement was now seen as a given, however, Tirpitz's argument for postponing war won the day.

Three important conclusions fall out of this meeting. First, no one disagreed with the thrust of Moltke's argument, namely, that a preventive war for hegemony had to be fought, and soon. Rather, the decision was only postponed, due mainly to Tirpitz's insistence that the German fleet was not ready. Reinforcing the decision to postpone was War Minister Heeringen's argument that Germany's land forces still needed more time to prepare. When asked by the kaiser to prepare a new army bill for 1913, on top of the one in 1912, Heeringen demanded the postponement of its introduction until autumn because the army "could not digest yet more big increases; all troop exercising areas were overfilled, the armaments industry could not keep pace."[31] The kaiser accepted the need to wait. Two days after the War Council, he confidentially told the Swiss ambassador that the "racial war ... of Slavdom against Germandom" could be postponed but not avoided, and "will probably take place in one or two years."[32]

Second, all participants understood that Britain would oppose a German attack on France. Not even the chancellor, the individual often seen to have the greatest faith in British neutrality, put much hope in it. On December 20, 1912, the chancellor wrote privately to a colleague that:

Haldane's disclosure to Lichnowsky was not all that serious. It merely reflected what we have long known: that Britain continues to uphold the policy of the balance of power and that it will therefore stand up for France if in a war the latter runs the risk of being destroyed by us.[33]

After December 1912, Bethmann-Hollweg would still make some effort to secure British neutrality. Yet it is clear he did not *count* on British neutrality when he pushed for war in July 1914; it would have been an added bonus, but general war would have to be chosen even if Britain fought.

Third, every key leader seemed to agree on the necessity of motivating Germany's population for a war directed against Russia. Moltke had argued in the meeting that "we ought to do more through the press to

---

[30] Quoted in *ibid.*, pp. 161–163, 177.
[31] Quoted in John C. G. Röhl, "V. Admiral Müller and the Approach of War," *Historical Journal* 12(4) (1969): 651–673, at 663.
[32] Röhl, *Kaiser*, pp. 175–176.   [33] Fischer, *War of Illusions*, p. 166 (see also p. 69).

prepare the popularity of a war against Russia." Müller's diary notes speak
of the need to provoke Germany's enemies into war, a technique used so
effectively in July 1914:

The Chief of the Great General Staff says: War the sooner the better, but he does
not draw the logical conclusion from this, which is to present Russia or France or
both with an ultimatum which would unleash the war with right on our side.[34]

After the War Council meeting, the chancellor "now impressed upon the
Emperor the need to prepare for a great war."[35] On December 4, four days
before the meeting, he had called for a new army bill; this bill was approved
by the kaiser on January 1 for submission to the Reichstag. The diplomatic
ground for war at the most favorable moment also had to be prepared.
Most importantly, as I discuss shortly, Austria had to be restrained from
taking any action in the Balkans that would precipitate war with Russia
before the completion of German army and navy preparations.

The sense of inevitable decline continued to grow through 1913–1914.
In the spring of 1913, the chancellor warned the Reichstag of Russian
growth, as his personal secretary Kurt Riezler relates: "A huge, ever
lengthening wave grows steadily. Once the mass of the Russian people
becomes aware of its nationalism the world will see the greatest movement
ever as regards extent and unused intensity."[36] By 1914, the sense that
Russia was translating its massive potential power into overwhelming
economic and military power began to crystallize into a tangible fear. In
late 1913, the tsar had approved what was called the "Great Programme,"
a plan to increase the Russian army by 470,000 men, or approximately
40 percent, by 1917.[37] In early 1914, the German military attaché in
St. Petersburg passed on a report concerning Russian growth. This became
the basis for an important memorandum from Moltke to the Foreign Office
in March 1914, emphasizing Russia's growing preparedness for war since
its 1905 defeat by Japan.[38]

The early part of 1914 was used to solidify alliance arrangements with
Austria so that it could play its proper role in the coming conflict. Yet
Berlin knew that the others did not want war. Moltke wrote to Conrad on
March 13 that the news from Russia "suggests that at present they have no

---

[34] Röhl, *Kaiser*, p. 163.   [35] From Fischer's summary, *War of Illusions*, p. 164.
[36] Quoted in Fischer, *War of Illusions*, p. 262, see also p. 371 on fears of Russian financial
reforms.
[37] William C. Fuller, *Strategy and Power in Russia, 1600–1914* (New York: Free Press, 1992),
p. 437. On Russia's massive industrial/military growth before the war, see Peter Gatrell,
Government, Industry, and Rearmament in Russia, 1900–1914: The Last Argument of Tsarism
(Cambridge University Press, 1994), chs. 3–7.
[38] Fischer, *War of Illusions*, p. 371.

intention of adopting an aggressive attitude."[39] By late spring, there was little question that both German political and military leaders were in agreement as to the necessity of preventive war. On May 29, after a private discussion with Moltke, Foreign Minister Gottlieb von Jagow wrote that:

The prospects for the future weighed heavily upon him. In two to three years Russia would have finished arming. Our enemies' military power would then be so great that he did not know how he could deal with it ... In his view there was no alternative but to fight a preventive war so as to beat the enemy while we could still emerge fairly well from the struggle. [Moltke] therefore put it to me that our policy should be geared to bringing about an early war.[40]

Note that the army chief was not calling for a bolt from the blue, but rather for the active manipulation of the diplomatic environment so as to make war appear justified. As he had told Conrad in early 1913, Russia "must appear to be the aggressor" if Germany was to have an "effective slogan" for the war at home.[41]

The Balkan crises of 1912–1913: avoiding inadvertent war

A good theory should not only explain why war broke out in August 1914, but also why it did not break out earlier under apparently similar circumstances. The German leadership, this section shows, was aware that any Austrian move against Serbia posed a high risk of reputation-driven escalation to major war. Russia, due to commitments to its Serbian ally and previous humiliations, would have to respond to uphold its image among its allies. Yet if the Russian and Austrian armies clashed directly, France would feel compelled to act should Germany support Austria, dragging all states into war. The conditions for inadvertent spiraling, as per the story often told about July 1914, were indeed present. What is significant, however, is that Berlin recognized these risks. It thus deliberately restrained Vienna through three Balkan crises from 1912 to 1913 whenever events threatened to draw Russia in. Yet in July 1914, German policy dramatically switched to pushing Vienna to attack Serbia as soon as possible.

There is a straightforward reason for German leaders' moderate Balkans policy up until 1914: they did not believe that conditions were yet ripe for preventive war. So while they did want to help Austria mitigate decline by shoring up its regional position, Vienna was permitted to make aggressive moves only when it was clear that Russia would not intervene. By July

---

[39] Quoted in *ibid.*, p. 397.   [40] Quoted in *ibid.*, p. 402.
[41] Albertini, *Origins of the War of 1914*, vol. 1, p. 437.

1914, with Germany's military power at its peak, Berlin's Balkans policy shifted to a hard-line stance which would force Russia to mobilize, thus thrusting the blame for major war onto Russian shoulders.

The First Balkan War, which began in October 1912, had its roots in an earlier offensive alliance formed by Greece, Montenegro, Serbia, and Bulgaria against Turkey. Montenegro declared war on Turkey on October 8, with Bulgaria, Serbia, and Greece joining soon after. By early December, Turkey was close to being pushed out of Europe, increasing Austria's worry that Russia would expand its influence in the region. A Great Power brokered armistice requiring the states to hold their positions was signed on December 3. Negotiations and intermittent fighting continued for another six months, however, and only on May 30, 1913 was a peace treaty signed. This treaty was immediately undermined by the start of the Second Balkan War in June.

The First Balkan War witnessed two periods of marked tension when Great Power war was at least a possibility: from October to the peace conference in December; and from January to March, when Austria and Russia stood eye-to-eye in states of partial mobilization. In each crisis, German policy was to support Austria, but never to the point where Austrian actions might bring in Russia and thus provoke a general war. Bethmann-Hollweg and Austrian Foreign Minister Leopold von Berchtold met on September 7–8 to discuss the growing Balkan tension. German Foreign Minister Alfred von Kiderlen, irritated by Vienna's willingness to make diplomatic moves without consulting Berlin, advised Bethmann-Hollweg to tell Berchtold that he must inform Berlin of his intentions and not just present it with a *fait accompli*. Germany had no obligation "to support Austria-Hungary in her Near Eastern plans, let alone adventures, all the less so as Austria-Hungary has not promised outright her support against France."[42] In November, however, two cornerstones of Austria's Balkan policy – an independent Albania as a check on Serbia and the prevention of Serbian access to the sea – were threatened by the successes of the Balkan League. Austria mobilized, while Russia, in support of Serbia, responded by deploying 220,000 troops along the Galician border. In late November, Vienna increased its troop strength in Galicia by 50 percent, called up more reserves, and told the fleet to prepare for mobilization.[43]

Recognizing the risks of escalation, German leaders were cautious. On December 11, three days after the German War Council, Berchtold met with the heir-apparent Franz Ferdinand, and advised him against war.

---

[42] Quoted in *ibid.*, p. 381.   [43] Williamson, *Austria-Hungary*, p. 128.

As Samuel Williamson summarizes, Berchtold's central point "was his well-founded belief that Berlin would never agree to a unilateral move by Vienna." Later that day, the civilian ministers made the same argument to Emperor Franz Joseph.[44] The monarch agreed, and by the end of December a fragile peace still held.

From January to March, however, Austria and Russia remained in states of partial mobilization across their borders. This fact alone led to the second Great Power crisis of the First Balkan War. Austria had decided against attacking Serbia, but the Russians did not know this. Hence, both sides maintained a state of high military readiness until March. Yet an uncontrolled escalation to war was again avoided. Why was the German military machine not mobilized in response to Russian mobilization, as in 1914?

The answer is clear: given the War Council decision of December 1912, Germany still needed more time to maximize its superiority. In January 1913, Berchtold sent Count Friedrich von Szápáry on a secret mission to Berlin to clarify the German perspective. Szápáry was told that the Germans had no desire for war.[45] Just to make sure Vienna got the message, however, both Bethmann-Hollweg and Moltke sent letters to their respective Austrian counterparts. The chancellor's letter, dated February 10, reminded Berchtold that "for Russia, with her traditional relationship to the Balkan states, it is almost impossible without an immense loss of prestige to be an inactive spectator of a military action on the part of Austria-Hungary against Serbia." Hence, "to bring about a forcible solution – even if many interests of the Austro-Hungarian Monarchy were to urge it – at a moment when a prospect, even if only a distant one, opens up of settling the conflict in conditions essentially more favourable to us, would in my opinion be an error of incalculable magnitude."[46] Moltke's letter to Austrian Army Chief of Staff Franz Conrad, also dated February 10, like the chancellor's, did not advise the Austrians to abandon thoughts of war, but only to hold off until it could be fought under better circumstances. Significantly, Moltke's main concern was that Russia should be blamed for any war so as to find an effective basis for the propaganda campaign back in Germany. "A European war must come sooner or later in which ultimately the struggle will be one between Germanism and Slavism," he wrote to Conrad. "But the aggression must come from the Slavs."[47] Thus, the crisis that, in terms of mobilization, bore the closest parallel to July 1914, was resolved without war by mid-March 1913.

---

[44] *Ibid.*, p. 130.   [45] *Ibid.*, p. 133.
[46] Quoted in Albertini, *Origins of the War of 1914*, vol. 1, p. 436.
[47] Quoted in *ibid.*, p. 437.

A third crisis arose as a complication of the Second Balkan War, started by Bulgaria in late June when it attacked Serbian and Greek forces. Berchtold felt that Austria needed to attack Serbia in support of Bulgaria, and this was communicated to Berlin in early July.[48] Once again, German officials reacted quickly, going straight to Austrian Ambassador Szögyény to inform him that they saw no reason for Vienna "to give up the waiting attitude [it] has till now maintained." Alfred Zimmermann, Germany's undersecretary of state for foreign affairs, also advised the kaiser that Vienna should be persuaded "to take no decision without German advice."[49] The kaiser agreed.

Bethmann-Hollweg, out of town during the first few days of the crisis, returned to Berlin on July 5 and was soon informed of Austria's hard-line position. Clearly concerned, he told Szögyény that Austria should be satisfied that its two southern Slav neighbors were destroying themselves in war. But if Austria attempted to use force, then it "would mean a European war. This would most seriously affect the vital interests of Germany and I must therefore expect that before Count Berchtold makes any such resolve, he will inform us of it."[50] We see again the common theme in the 1912–1913 Balkan crises. When there was little possibility of Russian intervention, Berlin allowed Austria to act forcefully; but whenever it seemed that Russia might be forced, for the sake of its reputation, to oppose Austrian actions, Berlin withheld support and advised Vienna to maintain its "waiting attitude." By July 1914, this policy would be reversed.

July 29, 1914: the night of the cold feet?

This section and the next argue that Germany actively sought war in July 1914, and that by the end of July German leaders preferred world war to a negotiated peace, even to one that gave Austria most of what it wanted. Berlin thus took all steps necessary to prevent any kind of negotiated solution, while at the same time ensuring that Russia was blamed for the war. This argument goes a few steps beyond Fritz Fischer, whose argument that Germany preferred continental war over a return to the status quo sparked a heated controversy which is still with us.[51] Fischer contends that Bethmann-Hollweg, the German chancellor, expected Britain to

---

[48] *Ibid.*, p. 454.
[49] The first quote is Albertini's paraphrase; the second is from the documents, *ibid.*, p. 455.
[50] *Ibid.*, p. 456.
[51] See John Langdon, *July 1914: The Long Debate, 1918–1990* (New York: Berg, 1991), chs. 4–5; H. W. Koch (ed.), *The Origins of the First World War*, 2nd edn. (London: Macmillan, 1984).

remain neutral, and therefore would not have pushed Austria to act against Serbia had he known that Britain would intervene. He is also vague as to whether Germany preferred a localized war, giving Austria a victory over Serbia, to a continental war.[52]

In the above discussion, we saw that German leaders by late 1912 saw the chances of Britain remaining neutral as being very low, given Britain's balance of power tradition. Hence, while continental war was certainly preferred to world war, and while diplomacy in a crisis might help to keep Britain out – at least in the early stages of war – it is clear that no leader in Berlin counted on British neutrality in pursuing a hard-line strategy. In this regard, we can put to rest one of the most persistent myths surrounding the First World War, namely, that Bethmann-Hollweg and his associates got cold feet on July 29 when they realized that Britain would fight for France. Even Fischer accepts this view of July 29, and thus, like Albertini, falls back on the notion that things did get out of hand after that date. Yet as I show below, Bethmann-Hollweg knew two days earlier that little hope remained that London would stay out of the war. In the face of this knowledge, he simply continued forward to war. In short, given a choice between world war and a negotiated peace, the German leadership preferred the former and did nothing to achieve the later.

The German preference for general war from the start of the July Crisis is shown by a comment made by Chancellor Bethmann-Hollweg to his personal secretary Kurt Riezler on July 6, 1914, the day after Germany had given Austria a "blank check" to destroy Serbia. Bethmann-Hollweg's news, Riezler recorded, "gives me a unnerving picture":

Russia's military power [is] growing rapidly; with the strategic extension [of Russian railroads] into Poland the situation is untenable. Austria increasingly weaker and immobile ... An action against Serbia can lead to a world war [*Weltkrieg*]. From a war, regardless of the outcome, the chancellor expects a revolution of everything that exists ... Generally, delusion all around, a thick fog over the people ... The future belongs to Russia, which grows and grows, and thrusts on us a heavier and heavier nightmare.[53]

---

[52] See Jack S. Levy, "Preferences, Constraints, and Choices in July 1914," *International Security* 15(3) (1990/1): 151–186.

[53] Kurt Riezler, *Tagebücher, Aufsätze, Dokumente*, ed. Karl D. Erdmann (Göttingen: Vandenhoeck & Ruprecht, 1972), pp. 182–183. While there is some historical debate as to whether Riezler's diaries for the July 1914 period were edited down prior to publication, the consensus is that the more objectionable material was removed to make Germany appear in a somewhat better light. What remains, therefore, is particularly damning, insofar as it shows a chancellor consciously leading his nation into war, rather than simply responding to events beyond his control. For more on what Riezler's notes suggest about Bethmann-Hollweg's role, see Copeland, *Origins of Major War*, pp. 83–92, 102.

This passage highlights three points. First, and most importantly, is the clear statement that general war was critical due to Russia's growth. Second, Bethmann-Hollweg was not pushing Germany toward war to solve a domestic crisis. Instead, he expected that war, regardless of whether Germany won or lost, would only increase the likelihood of social revolution at home. Third, Bethmann-Hollweg was aware even by July 6 that any Great Power war would likely be a world war, not a continental war; that is, Britain would be involved.

These revelations align with his thinking up to July. Bethmann-Hollweg had written to his ambassador in London in June that "not only the extremists, but even level-headed politicians are worried at the increase in Russian strength."[54] On July 20, three days before Austria's ultimatum to Serbia, Riezler writes of another talk with Bethmann-Hollweg. The feeling was that Russia, with her "tremendous dynamic power" could "no longer be contained within a few years, especially if the present European constellation continues."[55] Bethmann-Hollweg's subordinates thought similarly. On July 25, Foreign Minister Jagow smiled as he confidentially told Theodore Wolff, editor of the *Berlin Tageblatt*, that war would certainly occur soon if things continued as they were, "and in two years' time Russia would be stronger than it is now." Wolff heard this logic reiterated later that day in conversations with Wilhelm von Stumm, political director of the Foreign Office.[56]

The above discussion indicates that by early July, Berlin was seeking to bring on a preventive war, even a preventive world war, before it was too late. When we examine the most critical seven days of the crisis, Sunday, July 26 to Saturday, August 1, we can see exactly how the German leadership brought this about. Interpretations of this week have been driven by the universally accepted view that German civilian leaders – specifically Chancellor Bethmann-Hollweg – got cold feet on the night of July 29–30, and then tried, but failed, to keep Austria from pulling the system into war. This view – critical to almost every explanation of the war – grows out of two crucial telegrams, sent at 2.55 am and 3.00 am on the morning of July 30.[57] These so-called "world-on-fire" telegrams seem to show a

---

[54] Quoted in Norman Stone, *The Eastern Front, 1914–1917* (New York: Scribner, 1975), p. 42.

[55] Riezler, *Tagebücher*, p. 187.

[56] Theodor Wolff, *Tagebücher 1914–1919*, ed. Bernd Sösemann (Boppard: Harald Boldt, 1984), p. 64.

[57] Inadvertent war theories need it to show that German leaders did not want war, but could not prevent events from getting out of hand. Fischer needs it because he believes that Bethmann-Hollweg, counting on British neutrality, panicked when he saw that Britain would indeed oppose Germany.

German chancellor, worried that world war was about to occur, pleading with Austria to reach an agreement with Russia to keep the peace.

Yet if one puts these telegrams within the context of everything that happened that night, on the previous two nights, and the next day, a very different picture emerges. As it should become clear, these telegrams represent only one thing: Bethmann-Hollweg's effort to get the Austrians to moderate their position as it appeared to the world, such that Russia would still be blamed for the general war that followed. Pinning responsibility on Russia, as noted, was essential to build domestic support, to ensure that Austria fought, and to, hopefully, delay British intervention. Yet to achieve this, Russia had to be perceived to be poised to attack the German homeland. Austria also had to be convinced not to back out through a negotiated solution with Russia. Finally, the world, and the German people in particular, had to believe that Russia had mobilized while Germany and Austria were still seeking a peaceful outcome to the dispute. If any of these elements failed, the preventive war could not be waged successfully.

By Monday evening, July 27, as is shown elsewhere, it was becoming apparent that an Austro-Serbian conflict could not be contained to even a continental war.[58] Britain would indeed support France and Russia.[59] Some scholars argue that German leaders discounted this evidence, since they were convinced that war would remain localized.[60] Berlin's behavior on Monday and Tuesday, however, shows that these leaders were determined to get a war even if it meant a world war that included Britain. Their only concern was to shift the blame for the general war to Russia. On Monday night, Bethmann-Hollweg wrote to German Ambassdor Heinrich von Tschirschky in Vienna, stating that since Berlin had already rejected British Foreign Minister Sir Edward Grey's proposal for a European conference, it could not now ignore the new British suggestion that Germany act as mediator. He went on:

By refusing every proposition for mediation, we should be held responsible for the conflagration by the whole world, and be set forth as the original instigators of the war. That would also make our position impossible in our own country, where we must appear as having been forced into the war.[61]

---

[58] Copeland, *Origins of Major War*, ch. 4.
[59] Riezler's diary on Monday shows that Berlin was perfectly aware of Britain's new stand: "The reports all point to war ... England's language has changed. Obviously London has suddenly realized that a rift will develop in the Entente if it is too lukewarm [in its support] of Russia." Riezler, *Tagebücher*, p. 192.
[60] See esp. Lebow, *Between Peace and War*, ch. 5.   [61] *DD*, doc. No. 277.

This passage indicates that Bethmann-Hollweg was not only seeking to shift the blame; he was assuming war as a given, despite the fact that Austria had not yet declared war on Serbia, nor had Russia moved to even partial mobilization. Moreover, the issue of blame is critical not because of any need for British neutrality, but simply to ensure domestic support for the war.

On Tuesday night, Bethman sent a long, detailed telegram to Tschirschky that was even more revealing of German thinking. It begins by noting that Serbia's conciliatory reply to Austria's ultimatum posed a problem, since "in case of a completely uncompromising attitude on the part of [Vienna], it will become necessary to reckon upon the gradual defection from its cause of public opinion throughout all Europe." The next paragraph focuses on the need to blame Russia for the war to come. As with the telegram the previous night, this had nothing to do with keeping Britain neutral; war with Britain is assumed as a given. Berlin, Bethmann-Hollweg states, is concerned about statements suggesting that Austria's military might delay its attack on Serbia for two weeks rather than attacking immediately, as the Germans had requested. As a result,

[Germany] is placed in the extraordinarily difficult position of being exposed in the meantime to the mediation and conference proposals of the other Cabinets, and if it continues to maintain its previous aloofness in the face of such proposals, it will incur the odium of having been responsible for a world war [*Weltkrieg*], even, finally among the German people themselves. A successful war on three fronts cannot be commenced and carried on on any such basis. It is imperative that the responsibility for the eventual extension of the war among those nations not originally immediately concerned should, under all circumstances, fall on Russia.[62]

Austria is then asked to open up negotiations with Russia on the basis of an Austrian occupation of Belgrade and other parts of Serbian territory, using as a model the settlement imposed on France after the Franco-Prussian War(!). If St. Petersburg failed to see the justice in this position, "it would have against it the public opinion of all Europe, which is now in the process of turning away from Austria."[63]

Thus, by Tuesday night, the groundwork in the campaign to blame Russia was being laid. Much more was to come. In the mid-afternoon of Wednesday, July 29, Berlin received its first confirmation that Russia had

---

[62] *DD*, doc. No. 323.

[63] *DD*, doc. No. 323. As I show elsewhere, Bethmann-Hollweg carefully altered the kaiser's suggestion for a halt in Belgrade alone in order to make any Austrian suggestions to St. Petersburg unacceptable to the Russian government. Copeland, *Origins of Major War*, pp. 93–94.

ordered partial mobilization.[64] Although this was an encouraging development, it was still not the optimal scenario. Germany could go to war over
partial mobilization, but to truly blame Russia, Berlin needed a Russian
general mobilization. In a conference later that afternoon, Bethmann-
Hollweg was able to convince the military to delay even public "risk of
war" preparations until word of Russian general mobilization. Without
this Russian action, he argued, "we would not have public opinion on our
side."[65] Moltke supported Bethmann-Hollweg, which is not surprising
considering his point in February 1913 that the aggression must be seen
to come from Russia.

The night of July 29–30, most historians would agree, is probably the
most pivotal of the crisis. It is generally interpreted as the night that
German civilian leaders confirmed British opposition, got cold feet, and
hurriedly scrambled to find a last-minute solution. This interpretation
is based on the two world-on-fire telegrams sent to Vienna in the early
morning of Thursday, July 30, telegrams that seem to show Bethmann-
Hollweg desperately seeking to rein in Austria to prevent world war. From
the perspective of this chapter, nothing could be further from the truth. As
with Bethmann-Hollweg's policy over the two previous nights, he was
only attempting in the face of Austrian intransigence to push Germany's
ally to appear more conciliatory. Thrusting blame onto Russia remained
his prime objective.

At 5.07 pm on Wednesday, a telegram was received from London
reinforcing what Berlin had known since Monday, namely, that the British
were convinced that unless Austria entered into discussions on the Serbian
question, "a world war is inevitable."[66] At 8.29 pm, a telegram was received
from St. Petersburg. Russian Foreign Minister S. D. Sazonov had been
notified that Vienna had refused direct Austro-Russian talks, and had
replied that there was now nothing left but to return to the British proposal
for conversations à quatre (that is, European-wide). Sazonov made it clear
that he was not expecting Austria "to submit to a sort of European court
of arbitration," but that "he was only looking for a way out of the present
difficulties, and that in doing so he was grasping at every straw."[67]
Bethmann-Hollweg now had to be careful. He had heard nothing from
Vienna regarding his instructions the previous night, and he needed Austria
to appear to be negotiating with Russia. But in Sazonov's desperate state of

---

[64] *DD*, doc. No. 343.
[65] See Imanuel Geiss (ed.), *Julikrise und Kreigsausbruch 1914*, 2 vols. (Hanover: Verlag für
Literatur & Zeitgeschenen, 1964), vol. 2, doc. No. 676.
[66] *DD*, doc. No. 357. See *DD*, doc. No. 355 for a similar telegram received at 4.34 pm.
[67] *DD*, doc. No. 365.

mind, he might accept an Austrian offer if it allowed him to save face. Thus, at 10.18 pm and then again at 10.30 pm, Bethmann-Hollweg sent two one-sentence messages to Vienna. The first asked if the July 28 instructions – the long telegram reiterating the importance of appearing to open negotiations with St. Petersburg – had arrived; the second said simply that he "expect[ed] immediate carrying out" of these instructions. His urgency is shown by the fact that the first message went out uncoded to speed up transmission.[68]

The above discussion helps to put into context the two world-on-fire telegrams sent to Vienna at 2.50 am and 3.00 am. It is typically argued that they reflect the chancellor's realization that Britain would indeed fight, based on the 5.07 pm telegram from London and another that arrived at 9.12 pm, and on a meeting with the British ambassador at 10.00 pm. Yet this view cannot explain why Bethmann-Hollweg's telegrams to Vienna for the almost six hours between 9.12 pm and 2.50 am show no signs of nervousness about Germany's situation. Instead, they show Berlin pressing Austria to appear to be negotiating with St. Petersburg in order to blame Russia for war. At the same time, they are carefully manipulated to mislead Vienna as to Russian resolve, and thus the real possibility of world war. In behavior perfectly consistent with the previous two nights, Bethmann-Hollweg sought to avoid the appearance of responsibility, while simultaneously ensuring that Austria did not back out for fear of general war.

At 12.30 am, the chancellor sent a message to Vienna. Instead of communicating the text of the 9.12 pm telegram from Ambassador Lichnowsky in London – the clearest statement yet that Great Britain would fight with France – Bethmann-Hollweg sent only selective parts of the Lichnowsky telegram that had arrived at 5.07 pm. Since he was completely informed of the 9.12 pm telegram, this move was evidently designed to avoid scaring Vienna unless it was absolutely necessary. Of the 5.07 pm telegram, Bethmann-Hollweg relayed only two small parts: that Russia was aware that Vienna had refused direct talks; and that Grey was forwarding a proposal suggesting Serbia might accept harsher demands if Austria agreed to Britain's suggestion.[69] Conveniently, Bethmann-Hollweg left out the part where Grey warned that Russia "could not and would not stand by quietly" while Serbia was destroyed.[70] The chancellor instructed Tschirschky to inform the Austrian leaders that Berlin considered compliance to the proposal to be a basis for negotiations "if founded on an occupation of a portion of Serbian territory as a hostage."[71] Bethmann-Hollweg

---

[68] See *DD*, doc. No. 377 and its n. 3.   [69] *DD*, doc. No. 384.
[70] See *DD*, doc. No. 357.   [71] *DD*, doc. No. 384.

had still heard no word on whether Vienna would agree to appear to negotiate with Russia. He thus reiterated the German proposal from the night before.

At the same moment, at 12.30 am, Bethmann-Hollweg sent another message to Vienna relaying the German ambassador in St. Petersburg Friedrich von Pourtalès' message that Russia had gone to partial mobilization. This telegram nicely demonstrates Bethmann-Hollweg's technique of relaying the text from other ambassadors either word for word or with his own paraphrasing, depending on the desired impact. Here, instead of quoting Pourtalès' text, he simply states that:

> Russian mobilization, however, is far from meaning war, as in western Europe; the Russian army might be a long time under arms without crossing a frontier; relations with Vienna not broken off, and Russia wants to avoid war, if in any way possible.[72]

These lines are actually Sazonov's, but Bethmann-Hollweg presents them as *Berlin's* opinion of the situation! The chancellor was obviously trying to convince Vienna not to be too worried by Russian partial mobilization.[73] The chancellor ends the telegram by stating that:

> Russia complains that ... the conferences [have not] made any headway. Hence we must urgently request, in order to prevent a general catastrophe, or at least to put Russia in the wrong, that Vienna inaugurate and continue with the conference according to telegram 174.[74]

Telegram 174 was the one that went out Tuesday night with the proposal for occupying parts of Serbia, and imposing on it a peace equivalent to that forced on France in 1871. So here we have the German chancellor, more than three hours after final confirmation of British opposition, telling Tschirschky to carry out instructions that he knew had little chance of success, in order to "at least put Russia in the wrong."[75] Where are the cold feet that Bethmann-Hollweg should have had at this time? Is it at all conceivable, since the world-on-fire telegrams did not go out until 2.50/3.00 am, that the information from Britain somehow had a delayed psychological effect on Bethmann-Hollweg, enough to then prompt a change of mind? Of course not. If it had not hit him by 12.30 am that his policy was leading to world war, there is no reason why it would hit

---

[72] *DD*, doc. No. 385.
[73] *DD*, doc. No. 342. This passages shows that Bethmann-Hollweg knew that Russian mobilization was different, that it did not force Germany to preempt. See also Geiss, *Julikrise*, doc. No. 676, on Bethmann-Hollweg's July 29 conference with the generals, when he told them that he was "of the opinion that ... the mobilization of Russia did not mean war."
[74] *DD*, doc. No. 385.   [75] *DD*, doc. No. 323.

him two and a half hours later, especially since no new troubling information had been received during that time. Indeed, the very fact that Bethmann-Hollweg stayed up until the small hours of the morning indicates that he was waiting for some other piece of crucial information.

So what information did arrive that led to the world-on-fire telegrams? Finally, at 1.30 am, after sending three telegrams that evening seeking information on Vienna's response to Berlin's proposal, Bethmann-Hollweg received a short message from Tschirschky.[76] It noted that Austrian Foreign Minister Berchtold had thanked Berlin for its "suggestion," but was not ready to give a reply, and that in spite of the ambassador's urgent pleas, he had received "no further communication" from the government in Vienna.[77] This telegram could not have pleased the chancellor. That Vienna was continuing to show resolve was heartening. But it had not implemented his proposal from the Tuesday night telegram. As Bethmann-Hollweg had stated in that telegram, such an uncompromising attitude from Austria would make it impossible to carry out a successful war on three fronts.

The chancellor was thus in a bind: having pushed Vienna into a hard-line posture, Austria was now so convinced it could destroy Serbia – or that Berlin would accept nothing less – that it would not even go through the motions of appearing to be willing to compromise. To shift responsibility, Berlin had to be seen to favor the British proposals for a mediated solution. This was especially so now that Russia, after Austria's intransigence, had turned to Britain and its idea of European-wide conversations.[78]

Yet here was the dilemma. If Bethmann-Hollweg suggested that Austria accept the idea of European-wide mediation, as had occurred in December 1912, Austria would likely refuse, and the odium for world war would fall on Germany's shoulders. Even worse, Austria, fearing general war, might *accept* the idea. Russia would then agree, and preventive war would have to be postponed. Berlin therefore needed something to satisfy the British request, make Austria appear to want peace, and at the same time ensure that no diplomatic solution could ever be achieved. The solution: direct Austrian–Russian talks around an unacceptable proposal based on Austria's partial occupation of Serbia, with Germany playing the role of mediator.

It is this objective that led to the two telegrams sent to Vienna at 2.55 am and 3.00 am. The first began by providing the first three paragraphs of the Lichnowsky telegram that had arrived at 9.12 pm on Wednesday (the last two paragraphs being studiously left off). The first two paragraphs

---

[76] At 10.15 pm, 10.30 pm, and 12.30 am.   [77] *DD*, doc. No. 388.
[78] *DD*, doc. No. 365 from St. Petersburg, arriving at Berlin at 8.29 pm, July 29.

concerned Sazonov's request that Grey again take up mediation efforts. Grey saw two possibilities: mediation either *à quatre* or by Bethmann-Hollweg himself. It would be a suitable basis for mediation, Grey said, if Austria, after occupying Belgrade, should announce her conditions. The third paragraph contained Grey's warning that if Germany and France were to become involved, Britain could not stand aside, and the resulting war would be the greatest catastrophe ever experienced.[79] After the presentation of Lichnowsky's message, Bethmann-Hollweg writes that if Austria continued to refuse all mediation, Austria and Germany would stand alone against all other Great Powers, including Britain. Austria could satisfy her honor and claims against Serbia by the occupation of Belgrade or of other places:

Under these circumstances we must urgently and impressively suggest to the consideration of the Vienna Cabinet the acceptance of mediation on the above-mentioned honourable conditions. The responsibility for the consequences that would otherwise follow would be an uncommonly heavy one both for Austria and for us.[80]

This grim picture of an impending world war, with a suggestion for a diplomatic way out, seems to demonstrate a sudden desire for peace on the part of the chancellor. Yet note that Vienna is not asked to accept a limited occupation of Serbia, but only "*mediation* on the above-mentioned conditions," that is, negotiations with the partial occupation of Serbia as a potential point of discussion. The beginning of such negotiations would deflect blame from Germany, while ensuring that no solution could be found quickly.[81] And what kind of mediation was Berlin pushing for here? This message is vague as to whether Vienna should accept mediation *à quatre* or only through Germany. The second telegram to Tschirchsky at 3.00 am resolves this ambiguity: Austria should choose the second.

This telegram starts off by reproducing most of the Pourtalès telegram that had arrived in Berlin at 8.29 pm, July 29. Sazonov had told Pourtalès of Vienna's categorical refusal to enter into direct negotiations, and that therefore it seemed necessary to return to British proposals for conversations *à quatre*.[82] Bethmann-Hollweg told Tschirschky that this did not agree with Tschirschky's previous reports indicating that Count

---

[79] From *DD*, doc. No. 368.   [80] *DD*, doc. No. 395.
[81] This interpretation may seem less plausible than the simpler explanation: that Bethmann-Hollweg truly wanted Austria to back down and agree to a deal with Russia. Yet while both interpretations are possible, the latter remains inconsistent with all Bethmann-Hollweg's actions surrounding this telegram.
[82] *DD*, doc. No. 365.

Berchtold and the Russian ambassador in Vienna had begun discussions (that is, bilaterally, not *à quatre*):

[Vienna's] refusal to hold any exchange of opinions with Petersburg ... [is] a serious error, as it would be direct provocation of Russia's armed interference, which Austria-Hungary is beyond all else interested to prevent. We are, of course, ready to fulfill the obligations of our alliance, but must decline to be drawn wantonly into a world conflagration by Vienna, without having any regard paid to our counsel.[83]

Berlin was clearly pushing Austria to accept direct Russian–Austrian talks with German mediation, as opposed to European-wide intervention. Yet this proposal did not represent any real change from what Berlin had been suggesting since Monday evening. By controlling the mediation process, Germany could not only appear as the honest broker; it could also ensure any Austrian offer to occupy parts of Serbia remained harsh enough to preclude Russian agreement.

If any doubt remains that the chancellor and the Foreign Office conspired to unleash general war under favorable conditions, it is dispelled by their other actions from July 29 to August 1. The trick was to maneuver Germany and German public opinion into position so that as soon as Russian general mobilization was announced, war could be instantly initiated. As Admiral Müller nicely summarized on July 27, the "tendency of our policy [is] to keep quiet, letting Russia put itself in the wrong, but then not shying away from war."[84]

On July 29, as noted, Bethmann-Hollweg had secured the military's agreement to delay even the announcement of "risk of war" preparations until after Russian general mobilization. That same day, in meetings with the top officials of the Social Democratic Party, he secured their support for a general war against the Slavic threat.[85] By the next day, Bethmann-Hollweg could tell his colleagues that the "general public feeling was good in Germany," with "[nothing] particular to fear from Social Democracy or from the leadership of the Social Democratic Party."[86] Riezler had noted on July 27 that the chancellor was going to "work the Social Democrats from all sides."[87] The strategy was evidently paying off.

On Thursday morning, Bethmann-Hollweg employed the kaiser himself as a tool to get war going under the best circumstances. At 11.15 am, he sent two telegrams to Wilhelm. In the first, he noted that he had instructed

---

[83] *DD*, doc. No. 396.
[84] From his diary, quoted in Röhl, "V. Admiral Müller," p. 669.
[85] K. H. Jarausch, *The Enigmatic Chancellor: Bethmann-Hollweg and the Hubris of Imperial Germany* (New Haven, CT: Yale University Press, 1973), p. 169.
[86] *DD*, doc. No. 456.   [87] Riezler, *Tagebücher*, p. 193.

Tschirschky to demand an immediate explanation of Austrian behavior from Count Berchtold:

> in order that this episode may be closed in one way or another. I also called his attention to the fact that every declaration by Vienna to St. Petersburg concerning the purpose and extent of Austria's action against Serbia would only emphasize and openly label Russia's responsibility before the entire world.[88]

This language is hard to reconcile with the view that the chancellor sought peace when he sent the world-on-fire telegrams. Here he is, a mere eight hours later, talking again about thrusting blame onto Russia.

In the second 11.15 am message, Bethmann-Hollweg tells Wilhelm that he should send a message to the tsar stating that if Russia continues with partial mobilization, "then the role of mediator which I [the kaiser] took upon myself at your request will be endangered, if not made impossible. Yours alone is for the moment the responsibility of deciding." Bethmann-Hollweg ends his telegram with the following:

> As this telegram will be a particularly important document historically, I would most humbly advise that Your Majesty do not – as long as Vienna's decision is still outstanding – express in it the fact that Your Majesty's role as mediator is ended.[89]

Why would Bethmann-Hollweg say such an odd thing just when he should have been seeking a negotiated solution? The answer, of course, is that he wanted no such solution. Hence, he was already planning ahead to when the German people would be given documented evidence on Russian aggression. It is no coincidence that the German White Book – entitled *Germany's Reasons for War with Russia* – was published just three days later on August 2, and then presented to the Reichstag on August 3 (before hostilities with France began).[90] Considering simple publishing logistics, the book must have been in preparation throughout the previous week, when Berlin was supposedly seeking a mediated solution. It is also not by accident that Exhibit 23 of the White Book is Wilhelm's very telegram to the tsar that Bethmann-Hollweg notes will be a "particularly important document historically."

The machinations do not end there. In the White Book, the telegram's time of sending is given as 1.00 am, July 30. But it was actually sent at 3.30 pm Berlin time that day, and arrived in St. Petersburg only at 5.30 pm. The final version of the telegram, and the one appearing in the White Book, ends: "the whole weight of the decision lies solely on your [the tsar's] shoulders now, who have to bear the responsibility for peace or

---

[88] *DD*, doc. No. 407.   [89] *DD*, doc. No. 408.   [90] Geiss, *Julikrise*, doc. No. 1089.

war."[91] Given that Russian general mobilization was not ordered until 5.00 pm, an earlier dispatch time had to be put on the published document to make it appear that the Russians, despite being given plenty of fore-warning, had still aggressively moved to mobilization against Germany. A "particularly important document historically" indeed![92]

The situation was now primed for war. On the morning of Friday, July 31, the chancellor and the military gathered to wait for word of Russian general mobilization. At 11.40 am, confirmation was received.[93] General Karl von Wenninger recorded the reaction at the German War Ministry: "Everywhere beaming faces, people shaking hands in the corridors, congratulating one another on having cleared the hurdle."[94] The hurdle here is obviously the risk that Russia would not go to general mobilization, thus preventing Germany from blaming Russia for the war. Berlin now had the war it wanted under close to perfect conditions. Only one hurdle now remained: the possibility that Austria and Russia might make a last-minute deal to avert a direct conflict that both greatly feared.

The declaration of war on Russia, August 1, 1914

By Friday afternoon, Bethmann-Hollweg was prepared to execute the final diplomatic instruments to ensure Russian responsibility. An ultima-tum with a 12-hour deadline was prepared for dispatch to St. Petersburg, telling the Russians to back down or face German mobilization. The wording of this ultimatum and Bethmann-Hollweg's subsequent actions toward St. Petersburg constitute perhaps his most subtle manipulation in the crisis, so subtle that it has been missed by almost every historical account.[95] On Friday afternoon at 3.30 pm, an ultimatum was sent to St. Petersburg, stating:

In spite of the still pending negotiations for mediation and although we ourselves have up to the present hour taken no mobilization measures of any kind, Russia has mobilized her entire army and navy, thus against us also. For the security of the Empire, we have been compelled by these Russian measures to declare a state of threatening danger of war, which does not yet mean mobilization. Mobilization must follow, however, in case Russia does not suspend every war measure against

---

[91] *DD*, doc. No. 420; German White Book in *Collected Diplomatic Documents Relating to the Outbreak of the European War (CDD)* (London: Fischer Unwin, 1915), exhibit No. 23.

[92] This is not the only tampering with times in the White Book to show Russia's responsi-bility. Compare Exhibits 20 and 21 of *CDD* to *DD*: docs. Nos. 335 and 332, respectively.

[93] *DD*, doc. No. 473.

[94] From "Neue Dokumente zu Kriegsausbruch und Kriegsverlauf," documents collected by B. Schulte, *Militärgeschichtliche Mitteilungen* 25 (1979): 140.

[95] Albertini, *Origins of the War of 1914*, vol. 3, ch. 1, is the sole exception I could find, although he draws different conclusions.

Austria-Hungary and ourselves within twelve hours and make us a distinct declaration to that effect.[96]

The first sentence is deliberately deceptive. Negotiations were not "still pending"; Berlin had asked Tschirschky to cease pursuing them the previous night (July 31). And while Germany had not yet gone to mobilization, it had secretly taken all measures needed to achieve it within days (indeed, it was able to cross into Luxembourg on August 2).

The critical aspect of this telegram, however, lies in what it does not say. There is no mention that Berlin was preparing to follow a Russian rejection of the ultimatum with a declaration of war, as was already planned as the ultimatum was being drawn up. Moreover, even though on July 26 and 29 Berlin had threatened war in response to mere Russian preparations, there was now not even a hint that German mobilization would lead to war.

Yet Berlin had to worry that Russia might back out by capitulating to Austrian demands. There was one sure way to prevent this, namely, a declaration of war on Russia. Germany's premature declaration of war on August 1 provides the final proof that by the end of July world war was preferred over all possible negotiated solutions, even one giving Austria everything it wanted. Through Bethmann-Hollweg's diplomacy, German workers were ready to fight a war of self-defense against the Slavic aggressors, and with Austrian help. Such favorable conditions, with Germany at the peak of its military power, would be hard to ever recreate.

Thus, we have the puzzle that confounds other theories: why would German civilian leaders plan for a declaration of war on Russia as soon as the 12-hour ultimatum was up, and yet not warn anyone, including the Russians? Military strategy would argue against declaring war until one's forces were ready to attack. Recognizing this, the civilian leaders kept the decision to declare war secret from all the top military leaders (except one) until after it was a *fait accompli*. It also makes no sense to argue, as Bethmann-Hollweg tried to do with his outraged military, that Germany was compelled to follow international law, which required declarations of war before attacking. Considering the unannounced plunge into neutral Belgium three days later, this argument is clearly absurd. Moreover, Berlin deliberately held back the declaration of war against France, even though France was to be attacked weeks before Russia. Nor can it be argued that the declaration of war had a diplomatic or political value. If anything, the declaration would hurt Bethmann-Hollweg's own efforts to blame Russia for the war.

[96] *DD*, doc. No. 490.

Finally, we have two important pieces of direct evidence. A senior official in the German Foreign Office made a slip on July 31. He admitted to a representative of a neutral power, who then told George Buchanan, British ambassador in St. Petersburg, that "the only thing which [the German] Government fears was that Russia would, at the eleventh hour, climb down and accept [the ultimatum]."[97] Even more damning is a comment by Army Chief of Staff Moltke, the only individual in the military informed of the plan to declare war on Russia. On August 1, just after the kaiser had signed the mobilization order, Moltke was recalled and told of a British promise to keep France neutral. Wilhelm, overjoyed with the idea that France would stay out of the war, called for an immediate halt to deployment in the west. Admiral Müller's diary records Moltke's emotional response:

This we cannot do; the whole army would fall into disarray and we would end all chances of winning. Besides, our patrols have already invaded Luxembourg and the division from Trier is immediately following up. All we need now is for Russia to back off as well [*Jetzt fehlte nur noch, dass auch Russland abschnappt*].[98]

Far from fearing a Russian attack, Moltke is worried that Russia might also want peace. The fact that Moltke could say this in the presence of Germany's most important civilian and military leaders, and that Müller records no reaction, suggests either that his opinion was already well known, or that they agreed with it. Either way, combined with the evidence presented below, it is clear that the biggest fear in Berlin in the last days of peace was not that war might occur, but that it might not.

We have seen that the German ultimatum to Russia mentioned only that mobilization would follow its rejection, not war. One might suppose that on the afternoon of July 31 when the ultimatum was sent, Berlin still sought peace, and therefore worried that stronger threats might make Russia hostile to negotiation. Yet on the same day that the ultimatum was sent, a telegram that would be used to instruct Pourtalès to hand over a declaration of war rather than the promised word of German mobilization was being drafted in the Foreign Office.[99] In short, it was not as though on August 1, due to the emotions of the moment, the civilian leaders panicked and declared war. They had already decided *the day before* to surprise Russia with the declaration of war immediately after the deadline.

The telegram with the declaration of war went out at 12.52 pm on August 1. It again pinned all blame on Russia, stating that Germany

---

[97] Buchanan's paraphrase, in *My Mission to Russia*, vol. 1 (Boston: Little, Brown, 1923), p. 209.
[98] Geiss, *Julikrise*, doc. No. 1000(d).   [99] *DD*, doc. No. 542, n. 3.

would have to declare war for purely defensive reasons. So that Russia did not try to prolong negotiations by simply not responding to the ultimatum (as opposed to an outright refusal) the declaration of war had written into it both possibilities, neither of which could change the outcome.[100] Bethmann-Hollweg and his cohorts also carefully planned the timing of its hand-over to prevent any intervention by Wilhelm and the German military, both of whom were kept in the dark regarding the impending declaration. Hence, while the original telegram said that Pourtalès should present the declaration "immediately upon the expiration of the respite, at the latest, however, this afternoon at five o'clock," Jagow and Bethmann-Hollweg crossed this out and substituted the much more precise statement: "at 5 o'clock this afternoon, according to Central European time,"[101] or five hours after the actual deadline. It is surely not coincidental that this was the exact time that military and civilian leaders were to meet with Wilhelm to get his signature on the order for general mobilization. The civilians were making it physically impossible for either the kaiser or the military to stop the declaration of war from being presented, even if they somehow got wind of it at this meeting.

The evening of August 1 was a nerve-racking one for Moltke. The kaiser had put the Schlieffen Plan on hold as Berlin awaited word on the possible British offer to keep France neutral. Around 11.00 pm, word was received that the British proposals were a misunderstanding.[102] Wilhelm recalled Moltke, telling him, "now you can do as you will."[103] The Schlieffen Plan was thus back on, with the invasion of Luxembourg to take place early the next morning.

The view that after July 30 the civilians gave up control to the military and their mobilization schedules – a myth Bethmann-Hollweg helped to foster, and one accepted not only by inadvertent war scholars, but even by Albertini and Fischer – has been shaken by the above evidence. It is now time to put it in its final resting place. Far from controlling the process, only one military leader – Army Chief of Staff Moltke – knew of the plan that would have a much greater effect on military actions than on civilian operations: the surprise declaration of war on Russia. When Navy Chief of Staff Tirpitz found out in the late evening of August 1, he was outraged. Aside from the obvious military reasons for not declaring war until Germany was ready to attack Russia, Tirpitz felt that the move would undermine efforts to blame German adversaries for the war.[104] Minister of War Erich von Falkenhayn was also up in arms. To smooth

---

[100] *DD*, doc. No. 542.   [101] *DD*, doc. No. 542, n. 5.   [102] *DD*, doc. No. 612.
[103] Quoted in Albertini, *Origins of the War of 1914*, vol. 3, p. 177.   [104] *Ibid.*, pp. 191–192.

ruffled feathers, at 2.30 am on August 2, Bethmann-Hollweg met with Tirpitz and the generals to discuss the issue, as well as the timing of the declaration of war on France.

From records of the meeting, it is clear that many in the military were still wondering whether the declaration of war on Russia had actually been served. Bethmann-Hollweg admitted that the telegram containing the declaration had already been sent. But by failing to mention that it was delivered to Sazonov at 5.00 pm on the previous day, he evidently sought to keep them confused on this point. In yet another example of Bethmann-Hollweg's and Moltke's insidious collaboration, Moltke informed the group that Russia had fired shots across the border. Tirpitz then records Bethmann-Hollweg's response: "then, of course, the case is clear, that means the Russians have been the first to start and I shall have the declaration of war handed over the frontier by the nearest general." The military left the meeting still believing that the declaration of war was in the process of being delivered, even though the Russians had received it more than eight hours before. Thus, Falkenhayn grabbed Jagow just after the meeting, pleading with him "to prevent the foolish and premature declaration of war on Russia." Jagow's reply was that it was now too late.[105]

It is surely revealing that Moltke knew the whole time of the plan to declare war on Russia, yet said nothing to his colleagues.[106] As the only military leader privy to this plan, there can be little doubt that Moltke conspired with the civilian leaders – Bethmann-Hollweg, Jagow, and the others in the Foreign Office – to bring about war while minimizing last-minute interference from either the kaiser or the German military. The declaration of war on Russia was a brilliant stroke, as Moltke surely understood: as with Austria's declaration of war against Serbia (pressed by Berlin), it would end any possibility of diplomatic intervention. Preventive war could then proceed. It is not surprising therefore that Moltke would confide to a friend a year later, just after being dismissed:

---

[105] Quoted in *ibid.*, pp. 195–196.

[106] We know this from Moltke's interchanges with Conrad up to August 1. Moltke's key objective over the previous two days had been to ensure that Austria played its role of diverting Russian forces in the early stages of the war. Yet Conrad, believing that he had time, had been hinting that Austria would focus on Serbia and stay on the defensive against Russia. To force Conrad's hand, at 2.20 am on August 1, Moltke told him that Germany had demanded Russia's suspension of all military measures, and that if Russia refused, "German declaration of war follows immediately" (quoted in *ibid.*, p. 48). Conrad now knew localized war against Serbia was out, and that he had to concentrate forces against the Russian colossus. For more on this, see Copeland, *Origins of Major War*, pp. 113–114.

"It is dreadful to be condemned to inactivity in this war which I prepared and initiated."[107]

On August 4, as German troops were crossing into Belgium, London sent an ultimatum to abstain or face a British declaration of war. It was ignored. The intricate maneuverings of the chancellor, the Foreign Office, and Moltke had delivered a war under favorable conditions: with Russia taking the blame, the German public supported a war for the survival of the fatherland; and Vienna had been cornered not only into fulfilling its alliance obligations, but into concentrating its troops on the Russian, rather than the Serbian border. British neutrality was not secured, but no one, including Bethmann-Hollweg, had ever thought it was likely in the first place. Yet by stringing London along, Berlin had at least delayed by a few days the deployment of the British Expeditionary Forces. It is no wonder that Admiral Müller would write in his diary on August 1:

> The morning papers carry the speeches of the Emperor and of the Reich Chancellor to the enthusiastic crowd assembled outside the Palace and the Chancellor's Palais respectively. The mood is brilliant. The government has managed brilliantly to make us appear the attacked.[108]

Bethmann-Hollweg and his cohorts had indeed succeeded in the difficult task of making others seem responsible for a war that only Germany wanted. Their activities were so effective that almost a century later, we still debate who or what caused the First World War.

Conclusion

This chapter's purpose has been a simple one: to show that only a preventive war perspective can explain why war broke out in July 1914, and not earlier or not at all. Established theories of IR that use the First World War as a primary case, especially arguments based on spiral–preemptive dynamics and domestic pathologies, have been shown to hold little water across this chapter's three puzzles. Spiral theorists stressing pressures to mobilize have trouble explaining why three Balkans Crises in 1912–1913 did not lead to Great Power war, or why Germany would declare war on Russia but hold off on a declaration against France. Arguments based on the pathologies of German leaders cannot explain why Berlin would restrain Vienna in 1912–1913 and then push it into war in 1914, nor the

---

[107] Quoted in John C. G. Röhl, "Germany," in Keith Wilson (ed.), *Decisions for War, 1914* (New York: St. Martin's Press, 1995). On Moltke's role in bringing about preventive war, see Annika Mombauer, *Helmuth von Moltke and the Origins of the First World War* (Cambridge University Press, 2005).

[108] Quoted in Fischer, *War of Illusions*, p. 505.

skillful machinations of German civilian leaders during the July Crisis to bring on general war exactly at the peak of Germany's relative military power.

Let me be clear as to what this chapter's argument really means. It does not mean that theories competing with the preventive war explanation cannot find documents to support their interpretations of specific moments in the crisis. Nor does it mean that all German officials were free of pathologies, or that leaders of other powers had absolutely no desire for war.[109] But it does mean that if alternative theories cannot explain anomalies for their arguments, they cannot stand as plausible explanations, especially when the preventive logic works well and faces no apparent contradictions. And it means that those individuals within Germany who did not want a preventive war in 1914 were either insignificant players or were, like the evidently unstable kaiser, kept out of the loop so that they would not interfere with the overall plan. Finally, it means that even if one could show that certain Austrian, Russian, or French leaders countenanced the possibility of a general war, there is no evidence that they preferred general war to a localized war or a negotiated peace. Thus it was up to the German leaders to decide whether to seek such a peace or to work actively to undermine any chance that peace might break out through diplomacy. Bethmann-Hollweg and his associates chose the latter, to the point of having to declare war on Russia to prevent any last-minute Austro-Russian deal.

Once we make the mental shift away from the overarching view that "no one wanted general war" – the singular assumption that unifies all the various defensive-realist, liberal, and psychological arguments – we can see exactly why the preventive war explanation works so well, and why competing logics necessarily fall by the wayside. German leaders understood that they needed a major war sooner rather than later because without such a war, the Russian colossus would overwhelm the system once it had completed its industrialization program. A localized crisis won by Austria would not do the job. Only a total war that would eliminate the French threat in the west to give the Germans time to reduce Russian power in the east would permanently solve Germany's security problem. By July 1914, all other options were off the table.

---

[109] Cf. Vasquez, Chapter 8, this volume.

8   Was the First World War a preventive war?
Concepts, criteria, and evidence

John A. Vasquez

The preventive motivation for war has long been a concern among political scientists and numerous scholars who have seen Germany as the key actor in bringing about the First World War.[1] The clearest exponent of this position is Dale Copeland.[2] In this analysis I want to raise the question of how we know when a given war should be characterized as a preventive war, providing evidence in support of a preventive theory of war. When a war is regarded as a preventive war varies by how scholars define that term. For some, the mere presence of a preventive motivation anywhere in the initiating state is sufficient. For others, the preventive motivation must be seen as the main causal factor making for the decision to go to war or for bringing it about. I outline some criteria for making this inference and apply them in detail to specific decision-makers within Germany in the summer of 1914. I argue that only when the preventive motivation is the primary cause of the war and other causes are either not present or clearly subservient can the war be seen as a preventive war.

Once Germany is treated, I briefly look at Austria-Hungary and its role as a basis for an alternate explantion of the war. The dynamics of the Austrian-Hungarian–Serbian case raises conceptual issues not present in the German case. Looking at this dyad and the others that enter in 1914 places Germany's role within a larger context.

The concept

The preventive theory of war grows out of a realist perspective that sees international politics as a struggle for power. If it is assumed that the struggle for power is the primary focus of foreign policy, then the question

---

[1] See Jack S. Levy, "Declining Power and the Preventive Motivation of War," *World Politics* 40(1) (1987): 82–107.

[2] Dale C. Copeland, *The Origins of Major War* (Ithaca, NY: Cornell University Press, 2000), but see also Jack Snyder, *The Ideology of the Offensive: Military Decision Making and the Disasters of 1914* (Ithaca, NY: Cornell University Press, 1984) and Annika Mombauer, *Helmuth von Moltke and the Origins of the First World War* (Cambridge University Press, 2001).

arises as to why states would permit rising challengers to catch up. Why not attack to prevent that and, more importantly, avoid placing oneself in a position where one's enemy or principal rival could attack from an advantageous power position?

A preventive war should be defined in this theoretical context. I will first analyze a definition most consistent with the realist theoretical foundation of the concept. I will then review definitions that stretch the concept and make it highly elastic so that it includes wars that have little to do with an ascendant power challenge. Jack Levy best captures the emphasis on a rising challenger surpassing one's power:

> Preventive war is a state strategy to use military force to forestall an adverse shift in the distribution of power between two states. It is driven by the perception of a rising adversary, the anticipation of a decline in relative power, and the fear of the consequences of decline, which include diminishing bargaining leverage, the likelihood of escalating demands by an increasingly powerful adversary, and the risk of war under worse circumstances later.[3]

What this definition makes clear is that a preventive war is one in which decision-makers try to stem or reverse long-term decline.[4] Although this sort of a concern has a long tradition within classical realism,[5] it is most discussed in the literature with regard to the power transition school[6] and Copeland's theory of preventive war. Organski and Kugler initially see a power transition as the ascendant power catching up and leap-frogging the hegemon. It is this phenomenon that a preventive war is trying to prevent and, therefore, it can be expected to occur at any time that the more powerful state makes the projection. Although Organski and Kugler and others focus only on the most powerful states in a system, this theory has also been applied to regions.[7] In principle I see no reason why

---

[3] Jack S. Levy, "Preventive War: Concept and Propositions," *International Interactions* 37(1) (2011): 87–96, see also Levy, Chapter 6, this volume, p. 139.

[4] On the concept and similar definitions, see Robert Jervis, "Cooperation under the Security Dilemma," *World Politics* 30(2) (1978): 167–214, at 188–189, Levy, "Preventive War: Concept and Propositions"; Stephen Van Evera, *Causes of War: Power and the Roots of Conflict* (Ithaca, NY: Cornell University Press, 1999), p. 40; Dan Reiter, "Exploding the Powder Keg Myth: Preemptive Wars Almost Never Happen," *International Security* 20(2) (1995): 5–34, at 6–7; as well as Jack S. Levy, "Preventive War and Democratic Politics," Presidential Address to the International Studies Association, *International Studies Quarterly* 52(1) (2008): 1–24.

[5] See Hans J. Morgenthau, *Politics among Nations: The Struggle for Power and Peace*, rev. 5th edn. (New York: Alfred A. Knopf, 1978), pp. 215–216. He states that, "Preventive war is in fact a natural outgrowth of the balance of power," p. 216.

[6] A. F. K. Organski and Jacek Kugler, *The War Ledger* (University of Chicago Press, 1980).

[7] Organski and Kugler apply their theory only to the most powerful state in the system and the next two most powerful, which they see as possible contenders, Organski and Kugler, *The War Ledger*, pp. 44–45. On the application of power transition theory to regions, see Douglas Lemke, *Regions of War and Peace* (Cambridge University Press, 2002).

preventive war theory cannot be applied to any two rivals regardless of their place in a given status order.

Such an emphasis makes preventive war a strategic and not a tactical consideration, which is what realist theory is addressing. It is not concerned with short-term shifts, like an increase in the annual military expenditures, or the building of new ships, or the mobilization of reserves. Only if these occur with a long-term shift in the distribution of capability that will be difficult to overcome once it is achieved does a tactical consideration become a strategic one. Hence, military shifts are often seen as most dangerous when they are coupled with demographic and economic shifts.

In recent years the prospect of nuclear proliferation has superseded concern with economic shifts. An opponent that acquires nuclear weapons and a delivery system, even if it does not reach nuclear parity, can inflict a devastating blow. The longer the more powerful state waits, the more the rival's nuclear capability grows, the greater the potential blow and the greater the political equality. From the perspective of the logic of preventive war, this military and political shift can be seen as a decline in strategic power that should be prevented if possible. Israel's 1981 attack on Iraq and its current threats toward Iran would thus fit the definition.

The idea of a preventive war arises from a specific theoretical problem about shifts in power from a realist perspective and a logical solution to that problem: attack now while one has an advantage. The latter prescription has sometimes been used to stretch the concept to include any policy that is based on fighting war sooner rather than later. Such "language hooks," which are used to make a concept overly elastic, need to be resisted because they make a concept ambiguous by introducing multiple empirical referents. The "better-now-than-later" logic includes preventive war, but it can also include things other than attempts to avoid adverse shifts in the long-term distribution of power. For one thing, it would include all preemptive wars – that is, attacking the other side because you suspect that it is about to attack you and you want to gain the advantage of striking first.[8]

It would also include all attempts to time one's war to occur at the most opportune moment. Once decision-makers decide to go to war, it is in

---

[8] A preemptive war is one where one side expects an imminent attack from the other and therefore attacks first to gain a military advantage. This is primarily a tactical consideration and the long-term power distribution has nothing to do with the immediate situation. On preemptive wars and the difference with preventive wars, see Reiter, "Exploding the Powder Keg Myth," pp. 6–7.

their interest to time the initiation of the war to their advantage, if they can. Questions of timing arise in many decisions about war initiation whether they are related to avoiding a long-term shift in power or not. Matters of timing, therefore, are not a sufficient basis for identifying preventive wars. To define preventive war as any war that a decision-maker would prefer "to fight now rather than later" is much too broad a definition and would mix tactical considerations with strategic ones. Such a definition would make it considerably more likely to find a preventive motivation.[9] At the same time, unless the preventive motivation is the primary reason for a war such instances are apt to reflect matters of timing, that is, reflect concerns about when to attack and not indicate the reason for attacking.

Likewise, in the case of long-term rivals where one side is generally weaker than the other because of demographic imbalances and/or economic ones, and an opportunity arises where the more powerful actor is now temporarily weaker also violates the preventive war condition that such wars must be a reaction to a long-term (and fairly) permanent shift in power. An example here would be the 1980 Iran–Iraq War, where Iraq sought to take advantage of the Iranian Revolution to initiate a war (along with apparently at least the tacit support of the United States). Such a case is theoretically different from those discussed so far, but because of the temporary nature of the advantage it cannot be a relevant case to any realist theory of preventive war because it is not concerned with a long-term power shift.

The reason for a war from a realist preventive theory of war has to be the projected power distribution. This is made explicit by Levy when he states, "Specific conflicts of interest at stake are secondary in the preventive path to war. The primary issue is power."[10] This is an important insight and nicely captures the difference between the realist paradigm, which sees power at the heart of politics, and the issue politics paradigm, which sees disagreements over the disposition of issues (and political grievances) and not power as the heart of politics.[11] Discerning the goal and objectives of a war is not easy, in part because they change; nonetheless, it should be discernible whether a decision-maker is primarily motivated by power concerns, such as long-term future shifts, or challenges to

[9] See Levy, "Preventive War and Democratic Politics," pp. 2, 5, particularly his discussion of Jonathan Renshon, who includes within wars of "prevention," wars dealing with any grave national security threat. Jonathan B. Renshon, *Why Leaders Choose War: The Psychology of Prevention* (Westport, CT: Praeger, 2006).

[10] Levy, Chapter 6, this volume, p. 139.

[11] On the issue politics paradigm, see Richard W. Mansbach and John A. Vasquez, *In Search of Theory: A New Paradigm for Global Politics* (New York: Columbia University Press, 1981).

hegemony, or specific substantive issues, like the disposition of Bosnia or the leadership of Iraq.

There are two sorts of criticism of preventive war theory. First, there are those that question the extent to which such wars actually occur within history. Are they as frequent as the theory would predict?[12] Second, there are those who see the causes of war as coming from other sources, with the preventive motivation being unimportant, confined to a few wars, or even when present of only secondary or tertiary importance. The latter position is the one held here.

For preventive war theory to hold it must show that states do in fact fight under the conditions that it stipulates. Since the theory is a decision-based theory, this evidence must consist not simply of shifts in capability (as power transition does), but also of decision-makers' perceptions and policy objectives. Copeland's *The Origins of Major War* is an exemplar in terms of addressing both these issues and presenting case evidence along these lines. At the same time, a proper test must treat cases where a preventive war could have occurred, but did not, and show in such circumstances why war did not occur when it should have (or as Lebow, puts it, "do states jump through windows of opportunity?").[13]

Criteria

How can we determine whether a war is a preventive war? One way to develop such criteria is to look at some of the concerns of critics and then see if both supporters and critics can agree on a set of procedures for settling their disagreements. Given that the theory is a decision theory, the evidence must show that decision-makers have a concern about shifting power and decide to meet this concern by deciding to launch a war. There are two criteria that need to be satisfied: first, the material conditions of a power shift; and, second, dealing with the problem of decline by deciding to go to war while one is still more powerful than one's challenger. Technically, the latter is a preventive *motivation*. An important assumption for any truly realist theory is that objective conditions (that is, material conditions) produce interests that naturally give rise to a preventive motivation.

It is also important to recognize that within classical realism itself (as well as the power transition school) a steady shift in power need not be

---

[12] See Richard N. Lebow, "Windows of Opportunity: Do States Jump Through Them?" *International Security* 9(1) (1984): 147–186; Reiter, "The Powder Keg Myth," asks this question with regard to preemptive wars, which share a kinship with preventive wars, but are conceptually different.
[13] Lebow, "Windows of Opportunity."

met solely by a preventive war. More typically, the recommendation and expectation within classical realism is that declining power will be dealt with by increasing one's own power either by making alliances (as Britain did from 1902 to 1907) and/or by building up one's military (as Britain also did in reaction to the German naval build-up). In the literature this is seen as the problem of substitutability, that is, more than one policy can be used to deal with a problem.[14]

Looking at the logic of the theory as we have above helps to specify various hypotheses embedded within the theory that are not always explicit. It also points out potential difficulties in interpreting evidence and evaluating the scientific adequacy of a theory, because these other possibilities (that is, making alliances or building up arms) can serve as *ad hoc* explanations for why a test did not work out. To avoid the problem of too many *ad hoc* explanations, preventive war theory can specify in advance the conditions under which a preventive motivation will emerge vis-à-vis these other policy options. In other words, given a long-term decline, or the perception thereof, when do decision-makers opt for a policy of preventive war, for a military build-up, or the making of an alliance? To my knowledge this question has not been addressed by theorists, and it is an important theoretical gap in the literature. One way of assessing preventive war theory that has not received much attention is to look at what kind of policies states choose to deal with a problem of decline, and under what conditions they choose one option(s) over another. Given the rational cost–benefit approach of realism, it is reasonable to expect that a preventive war would be launched only if decision-makers believe that the decline cannot be reversed by other less costly and risky means, specifically, increasing one's strength through alliances or a military build-up.

Another reason preventive wars might be rare and why states do not jump through windows of opportunity is that preventive war requires decision-makers to take on the immediate costs and risks of war to solve a problem that is still in the future. In the long run many things may happen to correct the decline. The decline involves uncertainty, but going to war is immediate. War is also risky; it often involves unanticipated costs and events. This arouses concerns among those who are risk-averse and those who are more prudent. Inertia is on the side of doing nothing. All this forms a psychological barrier against deciding for war. In addition, the norms of the existing political order and international system may also place barriers to the launching of a preventive war that add costs to taking

---

[14] Benjamin Most and Harvey Starr, "International Relations Theory, Foreign Policy Substitutability and 'Nice' Laws," *World Politics* 36(3) (1984): 383–406.

this option, including the possibility of a countervailing hostile coalition.[15] There are then three barriers to preventive war that make it rare: first, substitutability may provide less costly and risky options; second, there is a psychological and political barrier to taking on the immediate costs of war to solve a future problem that may not materialize; and, third, the international system is apt to have strong normative barriers to preventive wars.

Of course, some members of the elite, or those who influence policy outside the government, may adopt a preventive motivation because they see it as an effective rationale (that is, an effective rhetorical device) for persuading others to go to war (even if they do not believe it is the main reason for going to war, that is, they want to go to war for other reasons). Thus, scholars who take bureaucratic politics or the military–industrial complex hypotheses seriously might argue that sometimes when a preventive motivation is present, it is really a rhetorical device employed by these actors to advance their own particular bureaucratic (or economic) interests in order to persuade other members of the elite of the need to go to war.

Rather than look at such detail, preventive war theory just wants to see if the preventive motivation is present prior to going to war. This has important advantages. One can ignore the material conditions and the problem of substitutability, and simply predict war whenever the preventive *motivation* is present. This seems to be Copeland's tack, and as a first-cut it is not unreasonable, but to establish empirically whether preventive war grows out of objective material conditions or is better seen as a perceptual variable one will need tests on the earlier stage.[16]

Examining just the presence of preventive motivation is the minimum criterion that needs to be satisfied. But why is this just a minimum criterion and what would be the other criteria? There are two other criteria: (a) the decision-makers who hold this view must be the ones in charge of foreign policy or, failing that, those in charge must be persuaded to adopt a preventive motivation; and (b) those who adopt a preventive motivation must believe that it is the true reason for going to war, that is, it must not be a rhetorical device to just gain support for going to war for some other real motivating reason. In other words, it must be shown that the presence of a preventive motivation is causally connected to the war decision.

Lastly, even if all of the above are present two additional criteria need to be satisfied. The presence of a preventive motivation does not mean that it is the only or most important causal factor. If the preventive motivation is just one of ten reasons for going to war, then its causal significance is

---

[15] See Mulligan, Chapter 5, this volume, pp. 119, 138.
[16] See also Copeland, Chapter 7, this volume.

not great. If it is just one more reason that a good debater has thrown into the "pro" side of the ledger, then this is not weighty evidence that the war in question is a preventive war. In order for a war to be considered a preventive war, the preventive motivation must be a key, if not *the* fundamental, motive in the decision to go to war. How important is a preventive motivation compared with other motives, such as previous or ongoing grievances?

This last point raises the problem of multiple motivations. If a preventive motivation is present with other motivations, it may not be evident which is primary. Lindblom in his analysis of public policy in the United States goes as far as to argue that a policy may not have any intrinsic goal because different actors may support it because they see it as satisfying different goals.[17] For Lindblom, collectivities do not support a goal, but simply a policy. Policies, then, are difficult to evaluate because there may be different reasons for supporting them. The same processes may be going on in decisions to go to war; if the motivation to enter them differs, then it may be difficult to determine whether a war is a preventive war or a case of something else. This is particularly difficult if the decision-makers responsible for a war have multiple motives or, what is more likely, ambivalent motives. Ultimately, however, this is an empirical question.

A final criterion is whether the preventive motivation, or any motive, is the real causal factor operating. The reasons that decision-makers go to war may not be the actual causes of the war. Decision-makers may not fully understand why they go to war; other factors, such as long-held grievances, alliance commitments, military doctrine, or less conscious factors like systemic anarchy, stress, and accident, may be much more important.[18] The mere presence of a preventive motivation is not in and of itself sufficient evidence to conclude that a given war is a preventive war; the analyst must also show that it is the main, or only, cause operating to bring about the war.

A failure to take the last two criteria seriously is one of the main deficits of much of what is written about preventive motivation. Too often analysts will show that a preventive motivation was present and seriously

---

[17] Charles E. Lindblom, "The Science of Muddling Through," *Public Administration Review* 19(2) (1959): 79–88.

[18] On the complexity of the causes of the First World War, see Rasler and Thompson, Chapter 3, this volume; Manus I. Midlarsky, *The Onset of World War* (Boston, MA: Allen & Unwin, 1988); William R. Thompson, "Powder Kegs, Sparks and World War I," pp. 147–193, and Paul W. Schroeder, "Necessary Conditions and World War I as an Unavoidable War," pp. 113–135, both in Gary Goertz and Jack S. Levy (eds.), *Explaining War and Peace: Case Studies and Necessary Condition Counterfactuals* (London: Routledge, 2007).

considered as a reason to go to war, but no attempt is made by the analyst to assess its relative impact against other reasons or factors.

The above discussion delineates what a preventive war is; it is equally important given the ambiguity with which the term is used to specify what is *not* a preventive war. General statements that it is better to fight now rather than later do not constitute a preventive motivation if they are not specifically offered as a solution to a perceived long-term decline in power that will leave the state vulnerable to losing its current ranking and to an attack that will lead to a major defeat. The reason for this is that the concept of a preventive war arises as a solution to a specific realist problem in realist theory and must be confined to that theoretical problem if it is not to become overly elastic. Statements arguing for war now rather than later that are made primarily in order to gain a tactical advantage by attacking first or to gain political advantage need not in and of themselves indicate a policy of preventive war; so too are all concerns relating to the timing of the war and/or preemption.

We are now in a position to formally list these criteria. In order to determine if a given war is a preventive war, all the following must hold:

(1) A state must experience a long-term decline in capability compared with a rival or challenger, or have evidence for anticipating one.
(2) Decision-makers must seek to deal with the power shift by a realist policy of preventive war.
(3) The decision-makers who have a preventive war motivation must be those in charge of foreign policy or, failing that, be able to convince those who are to adopt a preventive motivation.
(4) Those that hold a preventive motivation must not be using it as a rhetorical device to persuade others, but must genuinely believe it is the key reason for going to war.
(5) The preventive motivation must be the only, or the main, motive in their belief system that impels decision-makers to go to war.
(6) Belief in a preventive motivation must be more important than other causal factors operating to bring about war, including grievances, previous interactions, structural factors, and non-conscious factors.

Wars that do not meet all these criteria cannot be considered preventive wars; specifically, wars that are fought now rather than later, but not for the purpose of stopping a projected decline in power vis-à-vis a challenger are not preventive wars. In other words, timing the initiation of a war to gain an advantage is not in and of itself *prima facie* evidence that this is a preventive war or that a preventive motivation is present. In addition, establishing the existence of a genuine preventive motivation does not mean a war is a preventive war if criteria (3)–(6) are not satisfied.

We now turn to the First World War to see if it was a preventive war.

The First World War

Germany

As with historians, the views of political scientists with regard to the First World War have been varied. There have been two major views of those who see power as the key causal variable. Both views place Germany as the key actor in bringing about the war. The first, and now somewhat dated, view is the power transition position in which the First World War is associated with a rising Germany challenging the power of Britain as the hegemon of the system.[19] From this point of view the First World War was primarily a war between Germany and Britain, brought about by the challenging state. Because the war is brought about by the challenger, as the power transition hypothesis typically argues, it could not be by definition a preventive war. The latter has to be brought about by the leading or hegemonic state not the ascendant state. More central to the substance of the argument is that this view cannot be accepted because both Bethmann-Hollweg and the kaiser did not want war with Britain and sought to avoid it.[20]

The preeminent view that explains the First World War as a preventive war brought about by Germany is that of Copeland,[21] although others such as Snyder place emphasis on the preventive nature of the war mostly because they place emphasis on offensive military doctrine and, hence, Moltke's views.[22] Copeland has subjected the war to extensive analysis to support his preventive theory of war. He provides a review of numerous documents, and argues that the First World War was a preventive war brought about by a preventive motivation. He maintains that Germany and its decision-makers held a preventive motivation for several years and used the July 1914 crisis to go to war with Russia.

Our question is whether it is historically and theoretically accurate to characterize the First World War as a preventive war. Copeland has presented the best case in literature that it is. He addresses a number of the criteria, especially the first two, in an almost exemplary fashion.

---

[19] Organski and Kugler, *The War Ledger*, pp. 57–60.

[20] See Jack S. Levy, "The Role of Necessary Conditions in the Outbreak of World War I," in Gary Goertz and Jack S. Levy (eds.), *Explaining War and Peace: Case Studies and Necessary Condition Counterfactuals* (London: Routledge, 2007), p. 71. For a contrary view that it was not British neutrality but Russian partial mobilization that is key, see Marc Trachtenberg, "The Meaning of Mobilization in 1914," *International Security* 15(3) (1990/1): 120–150.

[21] Copeland, *Origins of Major War*, chs. 3–4; Copeland, Chapter 7, this volume.

[22] Snyder, *Ideology of the Offensive*; see also Van Evera, *Causes of War*; Mombauer, *Helmuth von Moltke*.

Nonetheless, this study will raise serious questions about the case he makes and will suggest that the debate is far from over. The analysis will begin by going through the first two criteria.

It is reasonable to begin by seeing what evidence is consistent with the preventive war thesis. The strongest part of Copeland's case is that he does show that a preventive motivation was present among certain decision-makers, namely, Moltke, Chief of the General Staff, and elements of the army going back at least to the famous 1912 "War Council."[23] Most of the evidence on Moltke's views and his insistence on a preventive war have been marshaled by Mombauer.[24] There is no doubt that Moltke adopted a preventive motivation. Under the criteria outlined here, Moltke had a preventive motivation because he was concerned not just with tactical matters and questions of timing, but with the long-term increase in Russian power, although it must be admitted that the building of the railroads weighed more heavily on his mind than more fundamental economic trends. Moltke pushed for war even before the July Crisis.[25]

The military are not all of one cloth, however. A preventive motivation was not held by Tirpitz or the navy, who felt, rightly, that they were still weaker than Britain and needed more time. Tirpitz was not averse to going to war, but not until the navy was prepared. Note, however, that Tirpitz does not fit the picture that Germany was fighting a preventive war against Russia, since he was more concerned with Britain than with Russia. What is important is that in 1912 (the year that Fischer sees as critical), and even later, Tirpitz argued against Moltke and against a war.[26] Copeland maintains that the preparations Tirpitz wanted were completed by 1914, and it is true that in 1912 Tirpitz wanted to postpone the war for at least eighteen months.[27] Others argue that even in 1914 Tirpitz still wanted

---

[23] See also David Stevenson, *Cataclysm: The First World War as Political Tragedy* (New York: Basic Books, 2004), p. 20.

[24] Mombauer, *Helmuth von Moltke*.

[25] What Copeland does not address, and needs to be addressed to satisfy criterion (4), is how important the preventive motivation was to Moltke compared with other possible reasons he might have had for going to war, such as the doctrine of the offensive (see Snyder, *Ideology of the Offensive*), or a particular war plan, such as the Schlieffen Plan. On the latter, see Keir A. Lieber, "The New History of World War I and What it Means for International Relations Theory," *International Security* 32(2) (2007): 155–191, for recent historiography that questions the importance of the Schlieffen Plan). Lastly, are there any personal reasons that motivated Moltke to want war and how important are they? For example, did he feel the need to prove himself, especially in light of the reputation of his uncle, the elder Moltke?

[26] See Fritz Fischer, *War of Illusions: German Policies from 1911 to 1914*, trans. Marion Jackson (New York: W. W. Norton, 1975), pp. 161–164.

[27] Copeland, *Origins of Major War*, pp. 62–63, 65; on Tirpitz, see Fischer, *War of Illusions*, p. 162.

more time.[28] The latter makes more sense, because by 1914 it was clear that Germany had lost the naval race to Britain;[29] this was even conceded by budget shifts in 1911–1912 that scaled down naval building and shifted funds to the army in Germany's 1912 army law.[30]

What is important here is that the key decision-makers were not united in their views, and the decision to go war and the reason(s) for it vary. Once the black box (of Germany) is opened things are more complicated, and it is clear that whether and why war occurs will be a product of the hauling and pulling of politics (as Lindblom characterizes most political decisions).[31] Having said that, it can also be said in defense of Copeland that Tirpitz had less influence than Moltke, both because the army was so much more important than the navy by 1913–1914, and because of his personal weight in the decision-making process.

"Constitutionally" the key actor was the kaiser. He is a complicated figure and treatments of him as a "coward" or as psychologically unbalanced due to his withered arm do not really improve our understanding and will be set aside here.[32] What can be said is that the kaiser exhibited a pattern of bellicosity and bluster followed by a pulling back from war as it came closer.[33] Two things are important for our discussion here. First,

[28] David E. Kaiser, "Germany and the Origins of the First World War," *Journal of Modern History* 55(3) (1983): 442–474.

[29] Michael Epkenhans, "Was a Peaceful Outcome Thinkable? The Naval Race before 1914," in Holger Afflerbach and David Stevenson (eds.), *An Improbable War? The Outbreak of World War I and European Political Culture before 1914* (New York: Berghahn, 2007), pp. 113–129, at 125–126, argues that the realization came as early as 1913, when Tirpitz had lost the confidence of the kaiser when he realized he had no more money to compete, so by 1914 he was not ready. See also J. Paul Harris, "Great Britain," in Richard F. Hamilton and Holger H. Herwig (eds.), *The Origins of World War I* (Cambridge University Press, 2003), pp. 266–299, at 292

[30] David Stevenson, "Was a Peaceful Outcome Thinkable? The European Land Armaments Race before 1914," in Holger Afflerbach and David Stevenson, *An Improbable War? The Outbreak of World War I and European Political Culture before 1914* (New York: Berghahn, 2007), pp. 130–148, at 134, 144.

[31] Lindblom, "The Science of Muddling Through," pp. 79–88.

[32] On the kaiser's alleged cowardice, see Paléologue's (the French ambassador to Russia) comment to the tsar, from his *Memoirs*, November 21, 1914, reprinted in Samuel R. Williamson, Jr. and Russel Van Wyk (eds.), *July 1914: Soldiers, Statesmen, and the Coming of the Great War: A Brief Documentary History* (Boston, MA: Bedford/St. Martin's Press, 2003), p. 145, where he remarks: "The Emperor William is not a man of courage . . ." On his alleged mental illness, see the discussion in John C. G. Röhl, *The Kaiser and His Court: Wilhelm II and The Government of Germany* (Cambridge University Press, 1996), pp. 20–27. On p. 26 there is even a quote by Freud psychoanalyzing Wilhelm, which in our post-Freudian age seems at best quaint, but at the time was taken seriously. On the withered arm and related problem, see p. 25.

[33] See Luigi Albertini, *The Origins of the War of 1914*, 3 vols., trans. and ed. Isabella M. Massey (London: Oxford University Press, 1952–1957; New York: Enigma Books, 2005 edn.),

the kaiser's support for war varied during the entire July period. At first he was very supportive of Austria-Hungary doing something, including going to war, and, after checking with Bethmann-Hollweg, he pledged Germany's support in what was later called by historians a "blank check."[34] This is a stark reversal from Germany's position during the Balkan Wars, where it had restrained Austria-Hungary.[35] No doubt his personal relationship with Franz Ferdinand played some part in this, but how much is unclear.[36] Later, after the Serbian reply to the ultimatum, he writes in the margin that given this response there is no need for war, presumably not even a local war.[37]

On the whole, it is assumed by most observers that the kaiser supported a local war and even a continental one, but did not want a war with Britain (the so-called world war). As British neutrality appeared less likely, the kaiser became very active in trying to avoid a larger war and, with Edward Grey, vigorously pushed the Halt in Belgrade proposal.[38] What is clear from this overall picture, which is not controversial, is that the kaiser, unlike Moltke, did not see the assassination as an opportunity to fight a preventive war. Further evidence of the kaiser's unwillingness to support a preventive war comes from Moltke, who throughout the July Crisis regarded him as an opponent and an obstacle to going to war.

vol. 3, pp. 4–5, for some illustrations of this pattern and its impact on Bethmann-Hollweg. See also John C. G. Röhl, "The Curious Case of the Kaiser's Disappearing War Guilt: Wilhelm II in July 1914," in Holger Afflerbach and David Stevenson (eds.), *An Improbable War? The Outbreak of World War I and European Political Culture before 1914* (New York: Berghahn, 2007), pp. 75–94.

[34] Graydon A. Tunstall, Jr., "Austria-Hungary," in Richard F. Hamilton and Holger H. Herwig (eds.), *The Origins of World War I* (Cambridge University Press, 2003), pp. 112–149, at 136.

[35] See Albertini, *Origins of the War of 1914*, vol. 1, pp. 380–381, 466–467.

[36] The kaiser had visited the archduke just two weeks before the assassination and was "profoundly shaken" by his death, Williamson and Van Wyk (eds.), *July 1914: Soldiers*, p. 11. Williamson sees the visit, and presumably their friendship, as playing a role in the kaiser's determination to back Austria-Hungary; Samuel R. Williamson, Jr., "Aggressive and Defensive Aims of Political Elites? Austro-Hungarian Policy in 1914," in Holger Afflerbach and David Stevenson (eds.), *An Improbable War? The Outbreak of World War I and European Political Culture before 1914* (New York: Berghahn, 2007), pp. 61–74, at 65.

[37] See Sidney B. Fay, *The Origins of the World War*, rev. 2nd edn. (New York: Macmillan, 1966), vol. 2, p. 420, for the actual annotation, see also Röhl, "The Curious Case," p. 84. On this incident Williamson and Van Wyk (eds.), *July 1914: Soldiers*, p. 102, state: "For Wilhelm now believed the Serbs' response to Vienna's ultimatum was sufficient. He thus proposed that Bethmann-Hollweg get Vienna to agree to halt in Belgrade and take no further military action."

[38] On the kaiser's belief that Britain would remain neutral and his efforts to avoid war once it was clear she would not, see Röhl, "The Curious Case," pp. 79, 86. Fay, *Origins of the World War*, pp. 420–426, refers to the Halt in Belgrade proposal as the "Kaiser's Pledge Plan."

Copeland is prepared to concede most of this with regard to the kaiser, stating, "Thus we see that of the key participants, only the Kaiser was worried about the prospects of general war."[39] What this means is that along with Tirpitz, criterion (2) is not fully satisfied, but this can be superseded if criterion (3) is satisfied.[40] Copeland deals with the analytical problem of the kaiser by arguing that Chancellor Bethmann-Hollweg did accept the preventive motivation of war and initially tried to isolate the kaiser and keep him from playing a major role, subsequently manipulating the kaiser into a position where he must accept war and could not stop it.[41]

The pivotal decision-maker in this debate therefore becomes Bethmann-Hollweg. Is he the hard-liner who supported a preventive war, the way Copeland portrays him? Since Copeland fails to show that the kaiser had accepted the preventive motivation, then in order to satisfy criterion (3) he must show that Germany went to war because Bethmann-Hollweg was guided by the preventive motivation and was able to get the kaiser to go to war. There are two issues here: did the chancellor support war, and did he support war from a preventive motivation?

The open question for me, and I suspect others, is whether Bethmann-Hollweg was really guided right through to the end by a preventive motivation. Copeland admirably lays out this case in detail. To believe the case requires two things. First, it requires that we believe that Bethmann-Hollweg manipulated and undercut his own kaiser, siding with Moltke to bring about a war that, in the final days of July, the kaiser was scrambling to prevent. Second, it requires, as Copeland states, that Bethmann-Hollweg was able to manipulate Austria-Hungary to bring about a continental war with Russia that was primarily in Germany's interest (Austria preferred the local war, with Germany coercively preventing Russian intervention).[42]

More importantly, one has to believe the interpretative story Copeland tells of how the various telegrams Bethmann-Hollweg sent were meant to bring about a Russian mobilization (so Russia would seem to be at fault) and simultaneously to undercut any peace plan, including the kaiser's and Germany's own Halt in Belgrade proposal. In Copeland's own words, such an effort by Bethmann-Hollweg "attribute supreme Machiavellian

---

[39] Copeland, *Origins of Major War*, p. 83, see also p. 93.
[40] For criterion (2) this means that the key decision-makers do not seek to deal with the power shift by a policy of preventive war, but criterion (3) means that the war can be seen as a preventive war if those in charge can be convinced to adopt a preventive motivation.
[41] Röhl, "The Curious Case," pp. 82–83, argues that despite efforts to do so the kaiser was not isolated.
[42] Copeland, *Origins of Major War*, p. 63; on preference orderings in general, see Jack S. Levy, "Preferences, Constraints, and Choices in July 1914," *International Security* 15(3) (1990/1): 151–186.

dexterity to German officials."[43] Ultimately, the accuracy of Copeland's interpretation is a question that historians will have to arbitrate, but at this point I do not find the interpretation persuasive. There is no smoking gun, and the evidence provided is not the sort of evidence that would hold up in a court of law. While history and political science can have lower standards than a court of law, the stretches here are multiple and require us to believe in a well-orchestrated cabal that so successfully hid Germany's role that, as Copeland states, "eighty years later we still debate who or what caused the First World War."[44]

At the same time, other scholars, namely, David Kaiser, deny that the preventive motive was a very powerful motive for Bethmann-Hollweg by the spring of 1914. Kaiser states: "But only a few weeks before the assassination of Franz Ferdinand, Bethmann had agreed with the Bavarian minister to Berlin that the moment for a preventive war had passed and added that the emperor would never consent to one."[45] In addition, Kaiser makes it evident that Bethmann-Hollweg had specific foreign policy goals in mind for which he wanted to go to war, specifically to fulfill the agenda of expansion and *Weltpolitik*, to gain Germany's rightful place in the sun, and to break up the entente.[46]

In a similar vein, William Mulligan does not see the preventive motivation as primary:

German civilian and (some military) decision-makers did not perceive Russia's financial and military weakness in 1914 as a window of opportunity to launch a preventative war, justified on the flimsy pretext of the assassination of the Archduke. Instead, in Berlin's view, Austria-Hungary had a legitimate opportunity to strike at Serbia.[47]

In fact, contrary to Copeland, who sees the assassination as an opportunity to fight the preventive war, Mulligan argues that civilian leaders saw Russian weakness as a restraint that would work to keep Russia out of the war and permit Germany to intimidate Russia.[48] From this point of view, far from seeing Russian weakness as an opportunity for a preventive war,

---

[43] Copeland, *Origins of Major War*, p. 90, see also pp. 81, 115. In contrast, Herwig characterizes Germany this way: "Chaos and confusion rather than direction and design were the hallmarks of German decision making in late July 1914," Holger H. Herwig, "Germany," in Richard F. Hamilton and Holger H. Herwig (eds.), *The Origins of World War I* (Cambridge University Press, 2003), pp. 150–187, at 183; see also Röhl "The Curious Case," p. 83 on the kaiser's shifts,

[44] Copeland, *Origins of Major War*, p. 116.   [45] Kaiser, "Germany," p. 469.

[46] *Ibid.*, pp. 463, 471–472.

[47] William Mulligan, *The Origins of the First World War* (Cambridge University Press, 2010), p. 212, see also Mulligan, Chapter 5, this volume.

[48] Mulligan, *Origins of the First World War*, p. 213.

it was seen as enabling Germany to use coercion to win without a continental war, although such a war would be risked.[49]

The critical days are July 29–31.[50] The height of Bethmann-Hollweg's
attempt to force Austria-Hungary to accept the Halt in Belgrade proposal
comes on the evening of July 29 with his instruction to Tschirschky,
Germany's ambassador to Vienna, to indicate to Berchtold that they
would not "be dragged by Vienna wantonly and without regard to our
advice into a world conflagration," which Albertini interprets as, "This
meant that either Vienna must be reasonable and agree to yield or
Germany would leave her to her fate."[51] It is on this day that Bethmann-
Hollweg also thought that the Halt in Belgrade proposal would permit
Austria to dispense with the one major condition that Serbia rejected
in the ultimatum.[52] On July 30, however, the language is less forceful.
Copeland takes this as an indicator of Bethmann-Hollweg's true feelings,
while Albertini sees this as the beginning of Bethmann-Hollweg, and ultimately the kaiser, giving way to Moltke's demand for a declaration of an
"imminent danger of war" in response to Russian partial mobilization.[53]
This culminates in Zimmerman's telegram to Tschirschky ordering him not
carry out Instruction No. 200, which again urged Vienna to accept Grey's
proposal, but in softer language.[54] What we learn from Albertini's review is
that Bethmann-Hollweg shifted or gave in to the press of events and failed
to increase the pressure on Austria-Hungary, as Albertini says he should
have.[55] This is hardly evidence that he was in favor of a preventive war,
quite the contrary. It is the view of a man who, in his own words, said that
despite all the governments being pacific "the situation had got out of
hand and the stone had started rolling."[56]

While it is true that Moltke got his war, this does not satisfy criterion
(3) because he did not convince Bethmann-Hollweg or the kaiser to adopt
a preventive motivation as the main reason for the war. If anything, it was
the concern with Russian preemption and their own failure to preempt
successfully due to Russian mobilization that moved them (and leads
some analysts to see Russia as the critical actor in bringing about the

---

[49] Interestingly, according to Otte, Chapter 4, this volume, p. 108, Berchtold said that
Szápáry, the Austrian-Hungarian ambassador to Russia, thought that Russia would not
intervene if it came to war.
[50] For a detailed review of these days, see Albertini, *Origins of the War of 1914*,
vol. 3, ch. 1.
[51] *Ibid.*, vol. 3, p. 18.
[52] See his minute to the Pourtalès telegram, quoted in Albertini, *Origins of the War of 1914*,
vol. 3, p. 19.
[53] *Ibid.*, vol. 3, pp. 18–29; on the kaiser giving way, see *ibid.*, vol. 3, p. 38.
[54] *Ibid.*, vol. 3, p. 22.   [55] *Ibid.*, vol. 3, pp. 5, 22.   [56] *Ibid.*, vol. 3, p. 15.

war).[57] This detailed analysis also reveals that criterion (4) is satisfied in that the preventive motivation does not seem to be used as a rhetorical device by anyone.

Another piece of evidence that neither Bethmann-Hollweg nor the kaiser were fundamentally hard-liners, but accommodationists who were willing to work together, is their behavior in the 1911 Second Moroccan Crisis.[58] Despite his willingness to engage in bluster at the beginning of the crisis to intimidate, the kaiser was not willing to risk war with France by going to the brink of war in the the way that State Secretary Kiderlen wanted. When Bethmann-Hollweg became aware of Kiderlen's position, he alerted the kaiser and the two of them openly opposed Kiderlen's stance. Wilhem felt that Morocco was not worth a war, let alone the French Congo. In this crisis both Bethmann-Hollweg and the kaiser showed themselves to be true accommodationists and not hard-liners.[59] This is very unlike Moltke or Conrad in Austria-Hungary, who were always hard-liners and advocated war. As a result, both the chancellor and the kaiser were heavily criticized in the press and the Reichstag. Moltke wrote bitterly to his wife about the peaceful outcome.[60]

The lack of a consistent hard-line, not to mention advocating a preventive war, is also present in the Balkan Wars. This was not seen as an opportunity to support Austria-Hungary to get into a situation where war with Russia might result. Why is that? What is the main difference between Germany's position here, where it restrains Austria-Hungary, and later if Bethmann-Hollweg and the kaiser were in favor of a preventive war with Russia? One possibility is that by 1914 the window for a preventive war was closing and so pressure was mounting.[61] This is a logical possibility. But another is that the two decision-makers were not thinking

---

[57] See *ibid.*, vol. 3, p. 31. For a brief review of the early literature on Russia's mobilization as a factor in bringing about the war, see David Alan Rich, "Russia," in Richard F. Hamilton and Holger H. Herwig (eds.), *The Origins of World War I* (Cambridge University Press, 2003), pp. 188–226, at 188–189; see also Bobroff, Chapter 9, this volume. For an analysis of the mobilization and how it was viewed, see Sean McMeekin, *The Russian Origins of the First World War* (Cambridge, MA: Belknap Press of Harvard University Press, 2011), pp. 59–75.

[58] The material on the Second Moroccan Crisis is based on James L. Richardson, *Crisis Diplomacy: The Great Powers since the Mid-Nineteenth Century* (Cambridge University Press, 1994), pp. 170–180.

[59] Bethmann-Hollweg was seen in this way among nationalist hard-liners, see Herwig, "Germany," p. 178.

[60] He wrotes in a personal letter: "If we slink out of this affair again with our tail between our legs . . . then I despair of the future of the German Reich. Then I shall quit. But before that I shall propose that we do away with the army and place ourselves under the protection of Japan," quoted in *ibid.*, p. 91.

[61] Levy, "The Role of Necessary Conditions," pp. 83–84, argues something like this when he says that German fears of Russian power were growing in 1914 because of the anticipated growth in Russian armaments and the completion of its railroad system.

about a preventive war opportunity, but simply looking at their interests and were not willing to risk a war for Austria-Hungary during the Balkan Wars, whereas given the assassination they were willing to do so in 1914 because Austria-Hungary was in the right.

It must also be kept in mind, as Otte shows, that the view of Russia in Germany was not as an implacable rival with whom war was inevitable, rather there were several options for dealing with Russia and these were centered on Russia's foreign policy goals and not its growing power *per se*.[62] Many thought that an alliance with Russia would break Germany's encirclement, which was seen as the real foreign policy problem, not the projected growth of Russian power.[63] The kaiser had long sought such an alliance and it had affected his behavior in the First Moroccan Crisis.[64] The general possibility of détente, which made Bethmann-Hollweg optimistic about future Russo-German relations, and the kaiser's confidence that he could solve the July Crisis if only the ministers would leave it to him,[65] are all indicators that preventive war was not the prevailing mood among all the decision-makers, even though it was for Moltke.

As Mulligan points out, the occurrence of the war tends to make observers interpret history in this light rather than in light of the views of the time.[66] At the time, détente and belief in the improbability of war were a common, if not the prevailing, view.[67] Also, as Mulligan demonstrates, preventive war had been viewed in a negative light for some time both in Germany and Austria-Hungary as a violation of existing norms and political order.[68] In 1905, when the German military advantage was greater, there was a fear that a preventive war would place Germany outside the international system and might provoke a hostile coalition against it.[69] These fears persisted.

However, he says what made the pressure much more intense now than in previous years was the fear that Germany could no longer win a two-front war, especially if Russia mobilized quickly. This is more of a preemptive motivation. Levy also states that the Russian mobilization was a necessary condition for the war, which implies that without the fear of preemption there would have been no war.

[62] Otte, Chapter 4, this volume.

[63] Indeed, the growth in Russian power instilled fears in France that they would not be needed as an ally and that Russia might depart their alliance and join with Germany, Otte, Chapter 4, this volume, p. 94.

[64] He actually reached agreement for an alliance with Tsar Nicolas II at Björkö in 1905, but this did not stand.

[65] Otte, Chapter 4, this volume, p. 102.   [66] Mulligan, Chapter 5, this volume.

[67] See Holger Afflerbach, "The Topos of Improbable War in Europe before 1914," in Holger Afflerbach and David Stevenson (eds.), *An Improbable War? The Outbreak of World War I and European Political Culture before 1914* (New York: Berghahn, 2007), pp. 161–182.

[68] Mulligan, Chapter 5, this volume, pp. 134–135.

[69] Mulligan, Chapter 5, this volume, pp. 119, 138.

Still, this is not to say that Bethmann-Hollweg was not concerned with the growth of Russian power over the long term, and gloomy about it. It is unclear, however, how much this personal sentiment found its way into Bethmann-Hollweg's foreign policy. I would argue that in the end Bethmann-Hollweg's gloom about the future of Russian power really has to do with timing and is not the main goal of the war. If war was inevitable or necessary to attain certain political objectives, then the current distribution of capability was an *added* reason for going to war now. It was not the primary reason for going to war. The primary reason lay with the very real substantive grievances Bethmann-Hollweg felt, not the issue of power (see Levy's distinction).[70] Nonetheless, it seems that once it was clear that his long and persistent policy of trying keep Britain neutral had collapsed he did indeed get cold feet and tried to prevent a continental war because it would become a world war involving Britain.[71] Thus, neither criteria (3) (decision-makers in charge must have the preventive motivation) nor (5) (it must be the main reason for war) are satisfied. Without satisfying these two criteria the First World War should not be labeled a preventive war.[72]

Alternate explanations and Austria-Hungary

One of the problems with much of the discussion of the causes of the First World War is that sometimes scholars have treated the war too much as a single unit with a single set of causes, and Copeland adds to this by concluding that the First World War "turns out to be one of the most mono-causally driven major wars in history."[73] Even though many have recognized that there were several causes operating, there has not been much effort to distinguish which are more important. One way to begin this discussion is to look at some of the assumptions Copeland makes about the war. He assumes that the war was brought about by Germany and principally because of its concerns about Russia. Copeland, like Fischer, accepts the position that Germany was primarily responsible for

---

[70] Levy, Chapter 6, this volume, p. 139; see also Levy, "Preventive War," p. 87.

[71] See also Levy, "Preferences," pp. 155, 160, 162, 175. On his cold feet, see Albertini, *Origins of the War of 1914*, vol. 3, p. 19, who remarks, "He had traveled a long way in the twenty-four hours since the arrival of the English warning."

[72] Still some might come back and argue that Austria-Hungary had a preventive motivation in going to war with Serbia, even though Copeland does not argue that. The Austrian-Hungarian attack on Serbia cannot be seen as a preventive war because Serbia could never catch up to Austria-Hungary's power. Austria-Hungary attacked because of a severe territorial threat not because Serbia might surpass its power.

[73] Copeland, *Origins of Major War*, p. 116.

bringing about the war.[74] One must ask whether the German–Russian dyad is the principal dyad (or rivalry) responsible for the war. As Williamson has pointed out on numerous occasions, the role of Austria-Hungary needs to be taken more seriously, in which case the primary dyad that brought about the war was that of Austria-Hungary–Serbia.[75]

Copeland does not see Austria-Hungary as the prime actor. He argues that Germany dragged in Austria-Hungary, actually manipulating Austria into its own war and not vice versa.[76] Recently, there has been more attention given to Austria-Hungary and the role it played in bringing about the war.[77] There is a great deal of *prima facie* evidence that Austria-Hungary was crucial, if not primary. It was, of course, Austria-Hungary that started the war. Germany's role is also critical in that it provided the famous "blank check," but why it provided a blank check, and whether it could have been later withdrawn, are important questions for determining just how responsible Germany was for the entire war. If Germany was supporting an ally that had to be supported if it hoped to keep that ally, and its support was meant to replay basically the successful coercive diplomacy game of 1908 (in the Bosnian crisis), then Austria-Hungary brought Germany into its war and not vice versa.[78] In this case, diffusion and alliance commitments were what brought about the war, and the preventive motivation in Germany was not a primary cause.

A focus on Austria-Hungary sees the First World War as a third Balkan war that gets out of hand. The alliance commitments of the major states and the alignment of Russia with Serbia, coupled with previous crises like the 1908 Bosnian crisis, led a local two-party war to spread in part because of a failure of crisis management. The approach in this chapter is to separate the war into two distinct phases: the war between the originators (in this case only Austria-Hungary and Serbia); and the war that expanded (to the others).[79] This is an analytical stance first emphasized by Bremer,

---

[74] Fritz Fischer, *Germany's Aims in the First World War* (New York: W. W. Norton, 1967); Fischer, *War of Illusions*.

[75] Samuel R. Williamson, Jr., *Austria-Hungary and the Origins of the First World War* (New York: Macmillan, 1991); Williamson, "Aggressive and Defensive Aims," pp. 61–74.

[76] Copeland, *Origins of Major War*, p. 63.

[77] See Williamson, Chapter 2, this volume, and Samuel R. Williamson, Jr., "Austria-Hungary and the Coming of the First World War," in Ernest R. May, Richard Rosecrance, and Zara Steiner (eds.), *History and Neorealism* (Cambridge University Press, 2010), pp. 103–128, esp. pp. 126–127 where he challenges the claim that a German desire to be the hegemon was a main cause of the war.

[78] See Holger H. Herwig, "Why did it Happen?" in Richard F. Hamilton and Holger H. Herwig (eds.), *The Origins of World War I* (Cambridge University Press, 2003), pp. 443–468, at 456.

[79] See John A. Vasquez, Paul F. Diehl, Colin Flint, Jürgen Scheffran, Sang-Hyun Chi, and Toby J. Rider, "The ConflictSpace of Cataclysm: The International System and

Table 8.1 *Dyadic participants in the First World War, July 1914–May 1915*

State A	State B	Date	Year	Arms.	Number of MIDs
Austia-Hungary	Serbia	July 28	1914	1	4
Germany	Russia	August 1	1914	0	3
Germany	France	August 3	1914	1	14
Germany	Belgium	August 4	1914	1	2
Germany	Great Britain	August 4	1914	0	8
Austria-Hungary	Russia	August 6	1914	0	4
Germany	Serbia	August 6	1914	1	1
Austria-Hungary	France	August 12	1914	1	5
Austria-Hungary	Great Britain	August 12	1914	0	2
Germany	Japan	August 23	1914	0	2
Austria-Hungary	Japan	August 25	1914	0	1
Austria-Hungary	Belgium	August 28	1914	1	1
Turkey	Serbia	November 2	1914	0	2
Turkey	Russia	November 2	1914	0	19
Turkey	France	November 5	1914	0	10
Turkey	Great Britain	November 5	1914	0	10
Austria-Hungary	Italy	May 23	1915	1	10

who argued that the causes of war onset are likely to be fundamentally different from the causes of war expansion.[80] Before it can be concluded that the First World War was a preventive war brought about by Germany, this alternate explanation that emphasizes Austria-Hungary and war diffusion must be considered.

An attempt to move in that direction is taken in Table 8.1, which presents a list of all the dyads (pairs of states) that enter the war from July 28, 1914 until May 23, 1915.[81] The table is intended to highlight the potential complexity of the war by asking why each dyad fights each other.

the Spread of War 1914–1917," *Foreign Policy Analysis* 7(2) (2011): 143–168; David Stevenson, "From Balkan Conflict to Global Conflict: The Spread of the First World War." *Foreign Policy Analysis* 7(2) (2011): 169–182.

[80] Stuart A. Bremer, "Advancing the Scientific Study of War," in Stuart A. Bremer and Thomas R. Cusack (eds.), *The Process Of War: Advancing the Scientific Study of War* (Amsterdam: Gordon & Breach, 1995), pp. 1–34; see also Yoshinobu Yamamoto and Stuart A. Bremer, "Wider Wars and Restless Nights: Major Power Intervention in Ongoing War," in J. David Singer (ed.), *The Correlates of War, vol. 2: Testing some Realpolitik Models* (New York: Free Press, 1980), pp. 199–229.

[81] The list is confined to those dyads who participate at a certain level of involvement (based on criteria used by the Correlates of War project, see Brandon Valeriano and John A. Vasquez, "Identifying and Classifying Complex Wars," *International Studies Quarterly* 54(2) (2010): 561–582, for details). Thus, dyads that are merely legally at war have been excluded.

Three major points can be made from the data displayed in Table 8.1. First, it can be seen that those who argue that the First World War was a preventive war focus on only one of the several dyads. This assumes that of the several dyads who entered the war in the first week this single dyad is the key dyad. Second, the originating dyad, which one would think is the key dyad, is not Germany–Russia, but Austria-Hungary–Serbia.

Third, Germany–Russia do not seem to have as many grievances (with each other) as some of the other dyads and not as many hostile interactions. Since 1816, it can be seen from the table (in the last column: number of militarized interstate disputes (MIDs) since 1815) that Germany and Russia had only three MIDs compared with eight with Britain and fourteen with France. If one takes a threshold of six MIDs as an indicator of an enduring rivalry, then the latter have an enduring rivalry, but Germany and Russia do not.[82] Lastly, Germany and Russia did not have an ongoing arms race in 1914; whereas, France and Germany did, and Britain and Germany previously had a naval race.[83] Given these indicators it seems that one would think that Germany would have had more reason to fight France or Britain rsther than than Russia.

The lack of serious grievances is one reason to suspect (or at least question) the idea that the onset of the First World War lies with the German–Russian dyad. Could we go so far as to say that without the tie to Austria-Hungary, Germany and Russia would not have fought at this time? That is not an unreasonable position. We can ask what were Germany's grievances against Russia, and were they sufficient to bring about a two-party war if the kaiser did not need to worry about domestic opposition from the left. The issues dividing Germany and Russia seem less serious than those dividing Germany and Britain, and less serious than the latent issue (of Alsace-Lorraine) dividing Germany and France. Also, it is France and Britain, not Russia that are blocking Germany from attaining its "rightful place in the sun."

Indeed, if one is willing to speculate in a counterfactual vein, it could be argued that one way for Germany to deal with Russian growth would have been simply to move closer to Russia and away from Austria-Hungary,

---

[82] The concept of enduring rivalry is based on Paul F. Diehl and Gary Goertz, *War and Peace in International Rivalry* (Ann Arbor, MI: University of Michigan Press, 2000). However, unlike their work, which requires that the MIDs be clustered within twenty years, the data in the table simply count the number of MIDs.

[83] The arms race designation is taken from data provided by Susan G. Sample based on a measure developed by Michael Horn, see her "Military Buildups: Arming and War," in John A. Vasquez (ed.), *What do We Know about War?* (Lanham, MD: Rowman & Littlefield, 2000), pp. 165–195, at 193–194, fns. 3, 7, for a discussion of Horn's measure in comparison with others.

and as we have seen such a rapprochement and alliance was a serious option.

The alternative explanation focuses more on the Austria-Hungary–Russian rivalry and sees the war starting because of the territorial threat Serbian nationalism posed to the Austro-Hungarian Empire. Russia is drawn in because of its support of Serbia. Germany is drawn in because of its support of Austria-Hungary. Both Germany and Russia fail to manage the crisis in a manner that would have prevented a world war. As Williamson says, "Germany gave Vienna a 'blank check,' Paris gave Russia a 'blank check,' and France and Russia gave Belgrade a 'blank check.'"[84] From a crisis management perspective, the failure of the Halt in Belgrade proposal is crucial. Unlike Copeland, I do not think this was just a ruse by Bethmann-Hollweg as part of an elaborate scheme to place the blame on Russia and circumvent the kaiser, but a sincere attempt that failed under the pressure of events.[85] The causally significant factors bringing about the world war lie not *just* with Germany, but with powerful diffusion effects that brought in Germany and all the major states that entered in 1914.

If we think of Germany's role in the First World War in terms of joining an ongoing war rather than as bringing it about in the first place, then the Austro-Hungarian–Serbian conflict was an opportunity to pursue some of the grievances that Bethmann-Hollweg had (until it seems that Britain will intervene). Such an analysis suggests that the grievances with Russia alone were not sufficient for Germany to start a war, *but* in the presence of the right crisis could be sufficient to draw Germany into a war. David Kaiser's comment is prescient:

The chronic paralysis over questions of war and peace within the German government makes it unlikely that Berlin ever would have provoked a war out of the blue; to a certain extent the Germans had to be pushed into the war by exogenous impulses. Yet the chancellor's reactions to the crisis reflected his own longstanding foreign policy goals. If Vienna made the initial decisions to fight, Berlin followed for its own reasons.[86]

What role, if any, is there for preventive motivation in this alternate scheme? I do not think the evidence presented by Copeland is sufficient to warrant accepting his argument that preventive motivation brought about the war. It fails to satisfy criterion (3), and the diffusion explanation suggests that it cannot satisfy criteria (5) and (6), that is, the preventive

---

[84] Williamson, Chapter 2, this volume, p. 50.
[85] Copeland, *Origins of Major War*, pp. 97ff.   [86] Kaiser, "Germany," p. 466.

motivation is the main reason for the war and that it is more important than other causal factors.

What can be concluded about the First World War? First, in Germany the documents and the consensus among historians indicate that the preventive motivation is most clearly present in Moltke and the army. Second, the kaiser did not seem to be guided by a preventive motivation in 1914, although he may have entertained it in earlier years. At the end of July as the crisis came to a head, he seemed to want to avoid war, much as Moltke worried that he would do. Third, Bethmann-Hollweg was in fact worried about the looming increase in Russian power, but whether he sought to bring about war because of a preventive motivation after he became convinced that Britain would intervene is questioned by this analysis. Copeland's interpretation of the documents requires one to believe that Bethmann-Hollweg successfully carried out an elaborate Machiavellian scheme that entrapped not only the kaiser, but Austria, Russia, and France as well. Therefore, we can conclude that the First World War was not a preventive war, but caused by something else. Fifth, the best way to understand the war is to see it as a local war between Austria-Hungary and Serbia that erupted in the presence of several diffusion mechanisms that drew in the other participants from 1914 to 1917.

Conclusion

This chapter has laid out criteria to determine if any particular war is a case of preventive war and applied them to the First World War. Of the six criteria, the most important is to show when a preventive motivation actually operates. The First World War should not be taken as a case of preventive war because the decision-maker(s) in charge of Germany's foreign policy (Bethmann-Hollweg and the kaiser) were not guided by this policy as the July Crisis unfolded. Bethmann-Hollweg, with the kaiser, tried to avoid a world war in which Britain would fight.

An explanation that focuses on the role of Austria-Hungary in starting the war and diffusion factors bringing in the major states is presented as an alternative. From this perspective the First World War is analyzed in terms of the causes of war onset (between Austria-Hungary and Serbia) and subsequent war expansion along the German–Russian (French) axis. Alliance commitments (including Russia's alignment with Serbia) are seen as the initial set of diffusion mechanisms that bring in other major states in 1914. Germany does not become involved in the First World War because of an overriding fear of future Russian power. While this may be a concern of Moltke and many in the army, it did not appear to be a sufficient reason for war for the kaiser. Nor did Germany's grievances with

Russia seem as great as those with France and Britain. Rather, the war occurred because Germany gets dragged into a coercive game with Russia (in support of its only real ally) that breaks down. The First World War, then, is not a preventive war because the preventive motivation was not a causally significant factor that brought about the war, let alone the main factor (criterion (5)).

Preventive war is a serious theoretical and policy question. It is important, therefore, that we have an accurate idea of its prevalence in international history. The criteria laid out and applied in this analysis are offered to make that determination as rigorous as possible. In doing so, it is hoped that a widespread misconception within political science that the First World War was primarily about Germany and its attempt to fight a preventive war will be corrected.

Part IV

The role of the other powers

9   War accepted but unsought

Russia's growing militancy and the July Crisis, 1914

Ronald P. Bobroff

In July 1914, the Russian government reacted to developments in a fashion that transformed a local Balkan war into a continental conflict.[1] While concerns about the sovereignty and security of Serbia and about Austrian intentions in the Balkans played their roles, by the summer of 1914, the Russian leadership acted in an atmosphere of real distrust of Germany that had built up over a decade of misunderstanding and rivalry. A string of diplomatic crises increased Russia's suspicions of German intentions in the Near East, a region of strategic, economic, and cultural interest to Russians. Vital trade relations between the two were increasingly strained as Russia grew to resent German economic power, especially in the context of a renegotiation of a major trade treaty. In this context, Russia's changing leadership perceived German manipulation of Austria during July 1914 and thought that the only way to preserve its prestige in Europe, as well as to slow German penetration into a region vital to its interests, would be to deter action by the Central Powers through a strong show of resolution via the mobilization of its army. While these measures increased the threat of a war that Russia did not want, it felt only such a demonstration could make an impression on German leaders. The failure of the Russian deterrent helped to bring the outbreak of the First World War.

---

[1] Russia at this time still used the Julian calendar. All the dates given in this chapter, however, are by the Gregorian calendar used everywhere else in Europe. Names in the body of the chapter are given in their English or Western form if there is a common one. Names in the footnotes are strict transliterations from the documents.

Research for this chapter was funded in part by a grant from the International Research and Exchanges Board (IREX), with funds provided by the National Endowment for the Humanities, and the US Department of State. Funding for research was also provided by the following divisions of Duke University: Graduate School, History Department, Center for Slavic, Eurasian, and East European Studies, and Center for International Studies; and of Wake Forest University: the Griffen Fund of the History Department and Archie Fund for Arts and Humanities.

Historiography

The debate over the causes of the war has been among the most voluminous in all European history.[2] After the war, the Bolshevik government in Russia published many documents from the tsarist archives in order to expose the bankruptcy of the Romanov regime and capitalism as a whole. Using published and unpublished documents, Communist historians faulted Russia for grasping at the Turkish Straits – the Bosphorus and Dardanelles. M. N. Pokrovskii made that case the most aggressively, though some contemporaries disagreed about the level of imperial acquisitiveness.[3] By the Stalinist era, many Soviet historians presented Russia as a victim of colonial exploitation by states such as France. After Stalin's death, some diversity returned to Soviet scholarship, though it continued to be hemmed in by the strictures of Marxism–Leninism.

In the West during the interwar period, scholars examined Russia closely, looking especially at the role of the Straits. While Sidney Fay pointed to Russia's "historic aims" at the Straits and its desire to come to a "final reckoning with Germany,"[4] Bernadotte E. Schmitt, pointed to the need to defend Serbia and a failure to understand the importance of a Russian mobilization to Germany.[5] Subsequently, Dominic Lieven offered the major test of the Fischer thesis for Russia, and his 1983 analysis remains the best work on the topic. Ultimately, Lieven found the Fischer thesis wanting in Russia's case, arguing that while internal factors contributed, the predominant influences on Russia's decisions were alliance politics and balance of power considerations.[6]

Recently, research on Russia has tended to focus on two areas: mobilization and the Turkish Straits. L. C. F. Turner examined the Russian mobilization and found it to be a significant step toward war, taken because of "chauvinism, corruption, and political and military incompetence" in

---

[2] Annika Mombauer, *The Origins of the First World War: Controversies and Consensus* (London: Longman, 2002). See also Joshua Sanborn, "Russian Historiography on the Origins of the First World War since the Fischer Controversy," *Journal of Contemporary History* 48(2) (2013): 350–362.

[3] Mikhail N. Pokrovskii, *Vneshniaia politika Rossii v XX veke: populiarnyi ocherk* (Moscow: Izd-vo Kommun. un-ta im IA. M. Sverdlova, 1926); Ia. Zakher, "Konstantinopol' i prolivy," *Krasnyi arkhiv* 6 (1924): 48–76, 7 (1924): 32–54; Valeriĭ I. Bovykin, *Iz istorii vozniknoveniia pervoi mirovoi voiny (Otnosheniia Rossii i Frantsii 1912–1914 kummun period after im. 1914 gg.)* (Moscow: Izd-vo Mosk. universiteta, 1961).

[4] Sidney B. Fay, *The Origins of the World War* (New York: Macmillan, 1929), vol. 2, p. 304

[5] Bernadotte E. Schmitt, *The Coming of the War 1914*, 2 vols. (New York: Scribner, 1930), vol. 2, pp. 480–481.

[6] Mombauer, *Origins of the First World War*, pp. 127–174; D. C. B. Lieven, *Russia and the Origins of the First World War* (London: Macmillan, 1983), p. 154.

Russia.[7] Marc Trachtenberg looked at German and Russian mobilizations, and in the latter case found that there was no stumble, no inadvertent entry into war by misusing mobilization or having civilians pushed into it by the military. Instead, the civilians knew what mobilization meant – war – but pursued it anyway.[8] More recently, David Alan Rich confirmed the military mistakes in advising the civilians, but insisted that the latter understood the details better than has been suggested.[9] In contrast, two authors have recently argued that the Turkish Straits were a major factor in Russia's willingness to fight in 1914. Both Iu. V. Luneva and Sean McMeekin, however, overstate the role of the Straits in Russian thinking and fail to incorporate a broader range of causes into their interpretations.[10] Interestingly, Michael Reynolds, in his recent, groundbreaking study of Russo-Ottoman relations before and through the war, does not discuss the July Crisis at all, much as this chapter's author chose not to discuss it in his own work on Russian policy toward the Turkish Straits, implicitly suggesting that the Straits little influenced the development of the crisis.[11]

Long-term radicalization

The Russian Empire of 1914 operated in a sort of controlled chaos. A constitution, a legislature, and even the framework for cabinet-style government existed, but none of these fulfilled the expectations of their founding during the troubles surrounding the loss in the Russo-Japanese War and concurrent revolution.[12] The Fundamental Laws of 1906

---

[7] L. C. F. Turner, "The Russian Mobilisation in 1914," in Paul Kennedy (ed.), *The War Plans of the Great Powers, 1880–1914* (Boston, MA: Allen & Unwin, 1979), pp. 252–268, at 266.

[8] Marc Trachtenberg, "The Meaning of Mobilization in 1914," *International Security* 15(3) (1990/1): 120–150, at 147–148.

[9] David Alan Rich, "Russia," in Richard F. Hamilton and Holger H. Herwig (eds.), *The Origins of World War I* (Cambridge University Press, 2003), pp. 188–226, at 220–226. On Russian mobilization, see Bruce Menning, "Pieces of the Puzzle: The Role of Iu. N. Danilov and M. V. Alekseev in Russian War Planning before 1914," *International History Review* 25(4) (2003): 775–798; Bruce Menning, "War Planning and Initial Operations in the Russian Context," in Richard F. Hamilton and Holger H. Herwig (eds.), *War Planning 1914* (Cambridge University Press, 2010), pp. 80–142.

[10] Iu. V. Luneva, *Bosfor i Dardanelly: Tainye provokatsii nakanune Pervoi mirovoi voiny (1908–1914)* (Moscow: Kvadriga, 2010); Sean McMeekin, *The Russian Origins of the First World War* (Cambridge, MA: Belknap Press of Harvard University Press, 2011).

[11] Michael A. Reynolds, *Shattering Empires: The Clash and Collapse of the Ottoman and Russian Empires 1908–1918* (Cambridge University Press, 2011); Ronald P. Bobroff, *Roads to Glory: Late Imperial Russia and the Turkish Straits* (London: I. B. Tauris, 2006).

[12] Geoffrey A. Hosking, *The Russian Constitutional Experiment: Government and Duma, 1907–1914* (Cambridge University Press, 1973), pp. 2–12, 74–105; Andrew Verner, *The Crisis of Russian Autocracy: Nicholas II and the 1905 Revolution* (Princeton University Press, 1990).

provided that the tsar retain executive power while some legislative power passed to the new State Duma, including the responsibility to approve any increase in the budgets of the armed services and the Foreign Ministry.[13] The Council of Ministers remained responsible to the tsar, and military and foreign affairs remained solely the tsar's prerogative. After the 1908–1909 Bosnian Crisis, however, the chairman of the council, P. A. Stolypin, succeeded in drawing foreign policy under his purview as he tried to unify governmental policy, especially to maintain peace to allow rebuilding. Subsequent chairmen, V. N. Kokovtsov and I. L. Goremykin, possessed decreasing influence.[14]

Between 1905 and 1914, European international relations became increasingly strained as successive crises regularly found the rival Triple Alliance and Triple Entente on opposite sides. David Stevenson has argued that this string of crises, intensifying the tension in Europe, increased the militarization of diplomacy in Europe, inclining most Great Power governments to take greater risks that culminated in the decisions of July 1914.[15] But while Stevenson concentrates on the diplomatic crises, there are other factors that contributed to this development. For Russia, not only did the string of crises have a militarizing effect on the Council of Ministers, but they also increased concern about Germany. Worsening economic relations between Russia and Germany compounded St. Petersburg's hostility toward Berlin. Given these developments, Russian leaders chose to make a bolder diplomatic stand in July 1914 than they had before.

The Bosnian Crisis in 1908 set the foundation for Russian decision-making in July 1914. Russian Foreign Minister A. P. Izvolskii bungled his attempt to trade Russian approval of Austrian annexation of the Ottoman provinces of Bosnia and Herzegovina for Austrian support in changing the rules for the passage of Russian warships through the Turkish Straits, closed at this time to all non-Ottoman warships in peacetime. It gave the appearance of Russia coldly trading the fate of Balkan Slavs to the

---

[13] David MacLaren McDonald, *United Government and Foreign Policy in Russia, 1900–1914* (Cambridge, MA: Harvard University Press, 1992), p. 124.

[14] McDonald, *United Government*, pp. 89, 106, 161; Dominic Lieven, *Nicholas II: Emperor of All the Russias* (London: Pimlico, 1993), pp. 182–186; V. N. Kokovtsov, *Iz moego proshlogo. Vospominaniia. 1903–1919 gg.*, 2 vols. (Moscow: Nauka, 1992), vol. 2, pp. 127–128; Hosking, *Russian Constitutional Experiment*, pp. 203–204; William C. Fuller, Jr., "The Russian Empire," in Ernest R. May (ed.), *Knowing One's Enemies: Intelligence Assessment before the Two World Wars* (Princeton University Press, 1984), pp. 98–126, at 99–102.

[15] David Stevenson, "Militarization and Diplomacy in Europe before 1914," *International Security* 22(1) (1997): 125–161, at 160.

advantage of its own geostrategic interests, embarrassing the Russian government, the traditional protector of the Slavic peoples.[16] St. Petersburg tried to support the Serbians diplomatically as Belgrade mobilized its forces to protest the Austrian action, but a German ultimatum forced St. Petersburg to relent, causing great humiliation.[17]

Under Sazonov's leadership at the Foreign Ministry from the autumn of 1910, Russia had a brief détente with Germany, but tensions rose somewhat during the Balkan Wars of 1912–1913 during the difficult negotiations among the ambassadors of the Great Powers over the future borders of the victorious Balkan states, including whether Serbia would get a port on the Adriatic Sea as Belgrade and St. Petersburg desired.[18]

In November 1913, St. Petersburg learned that the sultan had invited Germany to send new advisors to the Ottoman Empire to modernize further the Ottoman army. The new military commander, General Otto Liman von Sanders, would have wider responsibilities, worst of which for Russia was his command of an army corps in Constantinople itself. Russia demanded that the general's brief be changed, and ultimately Germany relented. St. Petersburg remained concerned, however, that the Germans would possess more influence over the Ottoman officer corps than earlier. A press war ensued between the newspapers of Russia and Germany, feeding off these slights and heightened by testy negotiations for the renewal of a major trade agreement between the two empires. It was at this juncture that a Bosnian Serb assassinated the Austrian archduke in Sarajevo, and Austria sought retribution, at whatever cost.

The Austrian road to its July 1914 ultimatum provides an instructive parallel to the Russian developments. As both Samuel R. Williamson, Jr. and David Stevenson have shown, the government in Vienna became radicalized by the events of the previous years, especially the Balkan Wars, as well as by personnel changes in the leadership. Two parallel processes increased the willingness of the Austro-Hungarian Common Ministerial Council to take bolder steps against Serbia in 1914.[19] First, in a series of three war–peace crises during and after the Balkan Wars, Austria-Hungary insisted that Serbia (and Montenegro in the second) agree

---

[16] Luigi Albertini, *The Origins of the War of 1914*, 3 vols., trans. and ed. Isabella M. Massey (London: Oxford University Press, 1952–1957), vol. 1, p. 22: M. S. Anderson, *The Eastern Question, 1774–1923* (Basingstoke: Macmillan, 1966), pp. 210–218

[17] Anderson, *Eastern Question*; Barbara Jelavich, *Russia's Balkan Entanglements, 1806–1914* (Cambridge University Press, 1991).

[18] Richard Hall, *The Balkan Wars, 1912–1913: Prelude to the First World War* (London: Routledge, 2000), p. 11; Andrew Rossos, *Russia and the Balkans: Inter-Balkan Rivalries and Russian Foreign Policy 1908–1914* (University of Toronto Press, 1981), pp. 34–36.

[19] Samuel R. Williamson, Jr., *Austria-Hungary and the Origins of the First World War* (New York: Macmillan, 1991), p. 14; Stevenson, "Militarization and Diplomacy."

232   *Ronald P. Bobroff*

to its demands, backing its action with the threat of military force, via mobilizations and/or ultimata. Most Austrian leaders, including Foreign Minister Leopold Berchtold, took the lesson that only diplomacy backed by force offered decisive influence over events.[20]

Second, the strongest voice advocating peace had disappeared from the Austrian leadership by July 1914. Archduke Franz Ferdinand had typically provided a strong voice for moderation, but his assassination removed that influence.[21] Thus, when the Austro-Hungarian leaders considered their options in July, remembering the successes of their mobilizations and ultimatum and missing the moderating voice of the heir to the throne, they chose not only to present an extreme ultimatum to Serbia, but also to follow up with war when they received the expected unsatisfactory response.

The Russian Council of Ministers similarly developed. Stevenson notes that by the Balkan Wars, Russia's government possessed a "new willingness for brinkmanship," and that inclination shifted attitudes among the influential ministers and changing membership to one weighted toward bellicosity.[22]

In looking at developments among the ministers, two of them who played central roles in July 1914 must be considered: Minister of Agriculture A. V. Krivoshein, recognized as the most influential voice in the council; and Foreign Minister Sazonov, at the center of the diplomatic storm during the crisis.[23] Krivoshein is often remembered as a hawk because of his aggressive reactions to the Austrian ultimatum of July 23, 1914, and then his advocacy of general mobilization on July 30. Key to this was not his hostility to Austria-Hungary, but instead his growing suspicion of Germany. Early in his ministerial career, however, Krivoshein had been more pro-German.[24] Soon after the Russian humiliation over Bosnia, in April 1909, the German ambassador reported that Krivoshein was one of a couple of ministers most interested in a rapprochement with Germany, though Krivoshein insisted that this was because Russia needed to rely on a strong power. Krivoshein apparently believed that when choices were limited, "it was necessary to have the courage 'to benefit from necessity.'"[25] During the Balkan Wars, however, Krivoshein's belief

---

[20] Williamson, *Austria-Hungary*, pp. 141–142, 151–155.

[21] *Ibid.*, pp. 130, 133–134, 146, 152, 163, 176, 214.

[22] Stevenson, "Militarization and Diplomacy," p. 147.

[23] P. L. Bark, "Iiul'skie dni 1914 goda: nachalo velikoi voiny," *Vozrozhdenie* 91 (1959): 22.

[24] I. V. Bestuzhev, *Bor'ba v Rossii po voprosam vneshnei politiki 1906–1910* (Moscow: Nauka, 1961), p. 46; Hosking, *Russian Constitutional Experiment*, p. 229.

[25] K. A. Krivoshein, *A. V. Krivoshein (1857–1921 gg.). Ego znachenie v istorii Rossii nachala XX veka* (Paris: P.I.U.F., 1973), p. 195.

that Austro-Hungarian stubbornness depended on German support made him more antagonistic toward Germany.[26] While discussing the renegotiation of the trade treaty with Germany, Krivoshein insisted that "Russia had groveled before the Germans enough and had humbly tried enough to get any little concession in exchange for direct contempt for our national interests."[27] Indeed, what appeared to have been a "war party" began to emerge in the Council of Ministers, with Krivoshein at its center.[28]

Sazonov, too, became more belligerent and more anti-German as his ministerial term continued. After Stolypin's death, Sazonov continued to avoid international complication in order that Russia could concentrate on its internal redevelopment and pursue détente with Berlin in his first months.[29] However, during the Balkan Wars, Sazonov became willing to consider military options. Several times in October and November, as Balkan forces defeated the Ottoman army, Sazonov declared that if Austria intervened militarily, Russia could not stand idly by. On October 10, 1912, as Russia feared Austrian interference in the newly begun conflict, Sazonov warned that an Austro-Hungarian occupation of the Sanjak between Serbia and Montenegro "would inevitably entail Russian intervention."[30] As Serbia seemed more likely to seize and hold Albanian territory in November, which could elicit Austrian preventive action, Sazonov told the British ambassador, Sir George Buchanan, that if Austria "took any military action against Servia [sic], Russia could not keep out of the war."[31] But there were limits to the lengths he would go. On November 23, 1912, he and Kokovtsov joined a late-called meeting with the War Minister, the tsar, and a couple of other ministers and generals in which they learned that General Sukhomlinov planned an immediate partial mobilization of the army along the Austrian frontier. The civilian ministers spoke out strongly against such a measure, insisting that it contained a great threat of war not just with Austria-Hungary but with Germany, too, for which

---

[26] *Ibid.*

[27] Kokovtsov, *Iz moego prozhlogo*, vol. 2, p. 107. See also H. H. Fisher (ed.), *Out of My Past: The Memoirs of Count Kokovtsov*, trans. Laura Matveev (Stanford University Press, 1935), p. 349.

[28] McDonald, *United Government*, p. 185.

[29] *Ibid.*, pp. 158–162; Bestuzhev, *Bor'ba*, pp. 81–85.

[30] Buchanan to Grey, October 10, 1912, tel. 359, G. P. Gooch, Harold Temperley, and Lillian Penson (eds.), *British Documents on the Origins of the War 1898–1914*, 11 vols. (London: HMSO, 1926–1938), vol. 9:II, No. 13; Bertie to Grey, October 13, 1912, des. 439, *ibid.*, No. 25.

[31] Buchanan to Grey, November 17, 1912, tel. 435, *ibid.*, No. 216. See also Buchanan to Grey, November 13, 1912, des. 334, *ibid.*, No. 195.

Russia was unprepared. These arguments persuaded the tsar to withdraw his approval, and in private Sazonov lambasted the general for his myopic actions.[32] A personal letter in early December 1912 confirmed Sazonov's deep distaste for war at this time. He wrote that "the vital interests of the Russian people [demand] . . . peace for its development and for putting it in good order . . . Almost everyone [in Russia] behaves in a way that they create the impression that a European war is inevitable. That is foolish and dangerous."[33]

But over the next year, Sazonov's caution lessened. Although he had carried on friendly talks with the German leadership in early November 1913, the foreign minister became far more hostile to the Germans in December because of the dispatch of the Liman von Sanders mission to the Porte.[34] For Sazonov, the significance lay in the general's new command over Turkish troops in Constantinople. Once in place, "the German Government would be in a position to assume complete control of the Turkish capital, whenever it might consider such a move desirable."[35] Given the strategic and cultural importance of the city and the nearby Straits, this development appeared to be a direct threat to Russian interests.[36] In his memoirs, Sazonov suggested that the mission wrought a critical change in Russian thinking:

If there were people in Russia who still entertained any doubts as to the real aims of Germany's Near Eastern policy, the conditions under which General Liman von Sanders' mission was conceived and executed put an end to all uncertainty and misunderstanding on the subject.[37]

Sazonov was among those convinced by these events.[38] Baron M. F. Schilling, the head of the Foreign Ministry's chancellery, echoed Sazonov's views when he suggested to a British diplomat on December 12, 1913 that the German step was only the beginning of a move to take control of the Ottoman Empire. Schilling insisted that it was better to end this now rather than farther down "this dangerous path."[39]

---

[32] Kokovtsov, *Iz moego prozhlogo*, vol. 2, pp. 102–106. See also McDonald, *United Government*, pp. 182–186; Turner, "Russian Mobilisation," pp. 254–256.

[33] Sazonov to Volkova, December 6, 1912, letter, State Archive of the Russian Federation (Gos. arkhiv Rossiiskoi federatsii, hereafter GARF), f. 887 op. 1 d. 384 ll. 109–110.

[34] On Sazonov's description of those talks, see Sazonov to Nicholas II, November 6, 1913, rep., Archive of the Foreign Policy of the Russian Empire (Arkhiv vneshnei politiki Rossiiskoi imperii, hereafter AVPRI), f. 138 op. 467 d. 718/777 ll. 3–9.

[35] Sergei D. Sazonov, *Fateful Years, 1906–1916* (New York: Stokes, 1928), p. 118.

[36] *Ibid.*, p. 119.   [37] *Ibid.*, p. 124.

[38] Hosking, *Russian Constitutional Experiment*, p. 238.

[39] Diary of Baron M. Schilling, GARF f. 813 op. 1 d. 127 ll. 2–5.

Furthermore, the Liman von Sanders crisis made Sazonov more willing
to use military means to achieve diplomatic objectives.[40] During the First
Balkan War, he had suggested moving troops to Constantinople to prevent a Bulgarian seizure of the city, but that proposal was not followed up,
partly, because the means of moving troops quickly enough did not exist
and, partly, because the Bulgarians did not ultimately attack the city.[41]
Such an operation, however, only minimally threatened Great Power
involvement, as Bulgaria was a minor power. But in the 1913–1914 crisis,
on Sazonov's suggestion, the Russian leadership considered the seizure
of Ottoman ports to force the sultan to accede to Russian demands about
Liman von Sanders. The problem here was that Germany's intimate
involvement in the crisis carried a much higher risk of European complication. In seeking Nicholas II's permission to confer with the relevant
ministers about the problem, Sazonov cited German duplicity and insin-
cerity on the Liman question and his own doubt about the success of the
continuing negotiations.[42] He acknowledged that seizure of Ottoman
ports entailed a serious risk of a European war, but argued that if Russia
again conceded, the Central Powers' pretensions would grow and the trust
of the Entente partners in Russia would decline.[43] In the conference of
January 13, 1914, the military and naval leaders, Sazonov, and Kokovtsov,
sorted through the options.[44] Kokovtsov insisted repeatedly that Russia
must avoid war. On being asked whether Russia could fight, the army
commanders said that Russia was prepared for a one-on-one clash with
either Germany or Austria-Hungary, but it was more likely that the whole
Triple Alliance would fight. Sazonov insisted that if Britain made clear
its intention to side with France and Russia, Germany would not challenge
a Russian seizure. The conference concluded that if continuing negotiations yielded no compromise, then, *only* with French and British support,
could the measures discussed be implemented. Germany resolved the
crisis by promoting Liman von Sanders to a rank that made corps command impossible, obviating the need for the measures discussed at the
conference. But Sazonov's memorandum and the conference reveal how
far he had moved toward accepting the risk of war.

Beyond the radicalization of Krivoshein and Sazonov, the loss of dovish
voices in the Council of Ministers also increased Russia's preparedness
to back its diplomacy with armaments. From 1906 to 1914, the Council

---

[40] McDonald, *United Government*, pp. 190–196; David Stevenson, *Armaments and the Coming of War: Europe, 1904–1914* (Oxford University Press, 1996), pp. 345–349.
[41] Bobroff, *Roads to Glory*, pp. 43–66.
[42] E. A. Adamov (ed.), *Konstantinopol' i prolivy Po sekretnym dokumentam b. ministerstva inostrannykh del*, 2 vols. (Moscow: Izdanie Litizdat NKID, 1925), p. 62.
[43] *Ibid.*, p. 63.   [44] *Ibid.*, pp. 65–68.

of Ministers moved a remarkable distance, starting from an insistence on peace at almost any price. Stolypin understood that a relationship existed between foreign and domestic affairs, and "he was determined to avoid new foreign entanglements that could undermine his domestic program."[45] After the Bosnian Crisis and the subordination of Izvolskii to his will, Stolypin could more effectively shape a foreign policy that would avoid dangerous complications. This is not to say that Stolypin desired a supine Russia: in 1908 and 1910 he called for stronger forces in the Caucasus and even small-unit action in Persia because of instability there, and in 1909 and 1910 he agreed to the inclusion of capital ships in the southern Russian fleet, especially to maintain superiority over the Ottoman navy.[46] But caution was the watchword. As Rich observes, Stolypin's assassination in 1911 "removed that moderating hand from Russian foreign policy."[47]

Kokovtsov, serving as finance minister and chairman of the Council of Ministers, worked hard to keep Russia from war, as we have seen above. He lost some leverage against the hawks, however, when the Russian economy improved after 1911, depriving him of the specter of bankruptcy, but he could still threaten financial calamity with some effectiveness. But the frustrations of other ministers with Kokovtsov were increasing, especially as their inclination to take military measures grew. Nicholas II dismissed him in early February 1914, thanks in part to the machinations of Krivoshein, who wanted Kokovtsov out of the way, and in part to Nicholas' desire to have less interference from the chairman of the council.[48] Furthermore, the British ambassador reported that Kokovtsov was removed "to prepare the way for the adoption of a stronger and more consistent policy both at home and abroad."[49] Indeed, Kokovtsov's replacement as finance minister, P. L. Bark, had limited ability to resist the demands for greater funding and himself supported a strong stand. Furthermore, the new chairman of the Council of Ministers, I. L. Goremykin, had little backbone of his own.[50]

---

[45] Abraham Ascher, *P. A. Stolypin: The Search for Stability in Late Imperial Russia* (Stanford University Press, 2001), p. 251.

[46] Andrei N. Mandelstam, "La politique russe d'accès à la Méditerranée au XXe siècle," *Recueil des cours* 47 (1934): 603–802, at 661; Jennifer Siegel, *Endgame: Britain, Russia, and the Final Struggle for Central Asia* (London: I. B. Tauris, 2002), p. 87; K. F. Shatsillo, *Russkii imperializm i razvitie flota: nakanune pervoi mirovoi voiny (1906–1914 gg.)* (Moscow: Nauka, 1968), pp. 82, 323–327; Stolypin to Voevodskii, August 2, 1910, ltr. 3834, Russian State Archive of the Navy (Rossiiskii gos. arkhiv voenno-morskogo flota, hereafter RGAVMF), f. 418 op. 1d. 668 ll. 5–6; Bobroff, *Roads to Glory*, pp. 16–19.

[47] Rich, "Russia," p. 195.

[48] Lieven, *Nicholas II*, p. 184; McDonald, *United Government*, pp. 197–198.

[49] Buchanan to Grey, February 25, 1914, des. 44, National Archives, United Kingdom, Foreign Office files (hereafter FO), 371 2091 Russia 1914 8009, p. 99.

[50] Hosking, *Russian Constitutional Experiment*, pp. 203–204.

The negotiations for a new Russo-German trade treaty also created resentment and suspicion among the Russians toward the Germans. By the 1890s, Germany had become Russia's biggest trading partner.[51] Because of the chaos caused by the Russo-Japanese War during the final negotiations for the treaty in 1904, Finance Minister Sergei Iu. Witte had to make many concessions on agricultural and industrial tariffs to the German benefit. The Russians had been trying to improve on the 1894 agreement, since both sectors in Russia voiced dissatisfaction with the disadvantageous tariffs Berlin was trying to push on them, but the German Chancellor Prince Bernhard von Bülow appeared to take advantage of St. Petersburg's sudden weakness.[52] By raising doubts about continued German loans and benevolent neutrality during the war, Bülow politicized Russo-German trade relations. Even though mutual trade grew sharply over the next decade, Bülow's tactic created substantial resentment within Russia and thus "a disastrous effect on subsequent political relations" between them.[53] Adding to Russian frustration, observers understood that Germany was a more important market for Russian goods than the reverse and blamed the treaty for this. Thus, attacks on the agreement, and on the Germans for their approach, grew.[54]

The significance of this frustration increased in the last years before the outbreak of war, especially as the Russian economy grew strongly, and both industrial and agricultural sectors continued to modernize.[55] Increased economic strength reduced the willingness to accept inferior terms. When Chancellor Theobald von Bethmann-Hollweg and Kokovtsov met during Nicholas II's visit to Kaiser Wilhelm II, Bethmann-Hollweg remarked that he had observed the storm brewing in the Russian press over the negotiations and wondered if Kokovtsov expected trouble. The latter replied that such protests should not be a surprise given the way the 1904 treaty was negotiated and the restrictions put on Russia. Kokovtsov voiced hopes that in the upcoming talks they would be able to work toward their mutual

---

[51] Dietrich Geyer, *Russian Imperialism: The Interaction of Domestic and Foreign Policy 1860–1914*, trans. Bruce Little. (New Haven, CT: Yale University Press, 1987), p. 163.

[52] Robert Mark Spaulding, *Osthandel and Ostpolitik: German Foreign Trade Policies in Eastern Europe from Bismarck to Adenauer* (Providence, RI: Berghahn, 1997), pp. 81–83. Geyer suggests that the Russians did not actually do that much worse in 1904 than they would have done without war, but Witte could parry complaints by pointing to wartime necessity. Geyer, *Russian Imperialism*, pp. 165–168.

[53] Spaulding, *Osthandel and Ostpolitik*, p. 84.   [54] *Ibid.*, pp. 88–89.

[55] Peter Gatrell, "Poor Russia, Poor Show: Mobilising a Backward Economy for War 1914–1917," in Stephen Broadberry and Mark Harrison (eds.), *The Economics of World War I* (Cambridge University Press, 2005), pp. 235–275, at 237. For data, see Paul R. Gregory, *Russian National Income, 1885–1913* (Cambridge University Press, 1982), pp. 56–59, 73.

advantage.[56] Indeed, as new advocacy groups for the agricultural sector emerged, they used the complaints about German tactics in 1904, complaints that reached the level of hysteria according to one historian, to try to influence the tariff levels of the next treaty.[57] Kokovtsov remembers that when, in late 1912, Krivoshein surveyed local leaders about the changes they wanted in the revised treaty, his letter dripped with hostility to Germany.[58] Krivoshein, overseeing the implementation of the Stolypin reforms in agriculture, would have been quite concerned with markets for the peasants' produce, and this rivalry would only have compounded his anti-Germanism discussed above. German signals that they would press for the same tariffs as before, however, only stoked up the public storm in 1914.[59] Thus, as the council faced the July Crisis, its members were readier to take a strong stand, were more hostile to the Central Powers, and were missing crucial voices for peace.

Hindrances

In contrast, the strategic preoccupation with the Turkish Straits was indubitably a long-term concern, but a desire to seize them did not directly influence decision-making in July 1914. Since the time of Tsar Nicholas I, the Russian government had believed that Ottoman control of the Straits sufficiently secured Russian interests, but if the Porte's hold were threatened, only Russian rule could replace it. In the twentieth century, the Russians understood that they could seize the Straits only during a continental war lest other Great Powers opposed the move and coalesced against St. Petersburg. At times, the preoccupation with the Straits neared panic in the two years before the First World War whenever the sultan's control seemed threatened. Whether during the Balkan Wars, when Bulgaria seemed on the verge of attacking Constantinople, or later when Liman von Sanders appeared about to gain command of the shores of the Bosphorus, Russia feared new influences there. Germany's broader engagement in Ottoman affairs, including not only military reform, but also concerns like the Berlin–Baghdad railroad added to Russian worries of German ascendancy.

In the year before the outbreak of world war, these threats led St. Petersburg to again begin planning an operation to seize the Bosphorus

---

[56] Kokovtsov, *Iz moego prozhlogo*, vol. 2, pp. 67–68; Kokovtsov, *Out of My Past*, pp. 322–323.

[57] Geyer, *Russian Imperialism*, p. 308.

[58] Kokovtsov, *Iz moego prozhlogo*, vol. 2, pp. 106–107; Kokovtsov, *Out of My Past*, pp. 348–349.

[59] Spaulding, *Osthandel and Ostpolitik*, p. 90; Volker R. Berghahn, *Germany and the Approach of War in 1914*, 2nd edn. (London: Macmillan 1993), pp. 156–174.

and Constantinople. But preparation was only preliminary in July 1914. Neither troops nor transport were readied. Major exercises for a landing on a hostile beach were planned for fall 1914 on Russia's Black Sea coast; without such training, an operation in the summer of 1914 would have been an even bigger gamble. While McMeekin argues that Russia used the July Crisis to engineer a war to facilitate the capture of the region, there is no sign in the correspondence of the Foreign Ministry, navy, and army, nor in the extant records of the Council of Ministers meetings on July 24 and 25, 1914, that suggests that these leaders sought to manipulate the crisis for these purposes.[60] Indeed, one can see in the memoranda of Navy Minister Admiral I. K. Grigorovich in July that he did not expect war, but instead continued to plan for the maneuvers in the fall.[61] In his writing one can detect no sense of urgency that might reveal a diabolical plot to maneuver other states into a war to Russia's benefit. Instead, he calmly reviewed plans and discussed expectations of further revision to landing plans after the maneuvers. On July 7, 1914, Grigorovich even learned from the chief of the Naval General Staff that, while the February 1914 conference on Straits planning had called for the launch date of the operation to be moved up from ten days after mobilization (M+10) to M+5, the state of the necessary ships was such that it would actually take more than two weeks.[62] Additionally, in that February 1914 conference, army commanders explained that they did not want to pare off forces for such an attack from the main battle on Russia's western front; they believed that the battle for Constantinople would be won in Berlin and Vienna.[63] Given the lack of preparation, Sazonov could not have expected the army and navy to be ready to seize the moment. If anything, the low readiness spoke to a need to *delay* war, in order to have the military and naval units able to act when the opportunity actually arose.

Furthermore, looking at Sazonov's policies between the outbreak of the war and the entry of the Ottoman Empire in late October 1914, one finds Sazonov desperate to keep the Porte *out* of the war, not draw it in. He refused naval requests to mine the exit from the Bosphorus to prevent German warships from entering the Black Sea, and he delayed Russian arming of anti-Ottoman minorities in Anatolia to avoid provoking Constantinople into war.[64] These are not the choices of a foreign minister

[60] McMeekin, *Russian Origins*, pp. 41–75.
[61] Neniukov to Grigorovich, June 26, 1914, rep. 360, "Scheme for Black Sea Fleet Maneuvers," RGAVMF, f. 418 op. 1 d. 5564 ll. 69–74; Sukhomlinov to Grigorovich, June 26, 1914, let. 799, RGAVMF f. 418 op. 2 d. 260 l. 200; Grigorovich to Nicholas II, July 5, 1914, rep., RGAVMF, f. 418 op. 2 d. 196.
[62] Rusin to Grigorovich, July 7, 1914, let. 382, RGAVMF, f. 418 op. 1, d. 784 ll. 160–161.
[63] Adamov, *Konstantinopol'*, vol. 1, p. 78.   [64] Bobroff, *Roads to Glory*, pp. 100–111.

recklessly focused on conquest. While Sazonov and others made the Straits a priority once the Ottoman Empire was at war, one cannot judge motivations for entering the war by the war aims declared once in it. Overall, while apprehension about German intentions in the Near East added to Russian distrust of Berlin, planning for an eventual seizure of the Turkish Straits worked against an aggressive stance in July 1914.

More generally, a major reason that the Russians should have delayed war was that neither branch of their armed forces had made significant progress in major expansion programs that had begun over the year before the July Crisis. For the army, the State Duma only a few months earlier had funded the "Great Programme" to add almost half a million men (an increase of nearly 40 percent) to the military, as well as to improve organization and mobilization, artillery and aviation.[65] This development represented a definitive shift to a concentration on the threat posed by Germany, especially given the greater tension within Europe and pressure from the French. This followed several years of compromises symbolized by mobilization plans that tended to focus on the Austro-Hungarian front as the primary theater of operations, or awkwardly hedging between mobilizing against Germany or Austria-Hungary, depending on developments.[66] But these changes would not be complete before 1917, and probably later than that given the inefficiencies of the Russian system.[67] That the army leadership recognized the ill-prepared condition of the Russian army is suggested by one of Sazonov's closest advisors, who spoke with Sukhomlinov just before news of the Austrian ultimatum arrived. The War Minister wanted Sazonov to know that the Great Programme:

cannot be completed until 1917, and its fulfillment would necessarily be hindered if war should break out now ... In these conditions, even with France's support, we would find ourselves until 1917, and perhaps even until 1918, in a position of indisputable inferiority to the combined forces of Germany and Austria. Consequently, we should do everything in our power to avoid war.[68]

Sukhomlinov thus recognized the inferior state of the Russian army and privately expressed a fear of premature war.

[65] Rich, "Russia," p. 213; William C. Fuller, Jr., *Strategy and Power in Russia, 1600–1914* (New York: Free Press, 1992), p. 437.

[66] Peter Gatrell, *Government, Industry and Rearmament in Russia, 1900–1914: The Last Argument of Tsarism* (Cambridge University Press, 1994), pp. 133–134; Rich, "Russia," pp. 206–214; Bovykin, *Iz istorii*, pp. 81–102; Menning, "Pieces of the Puzzle"; Menning, "War Planning," pp. 81–126; Fuller, *Strategy*, pp. 423–433, 440–445.

[67] Rich, "Russia," p. 213.

[68] Nicolas de Basily, *Memoirs: Diplomat of Imperial Russia, 1903–1917* (Stanford, CA: Hoover Institution Press, 1973), p. 91.

Russian leaders had to cope with a similar lag in naval expansion. After much argument, significant funding for warship construction on both the Baltic Sea and the Black Sea was approved by 1914.[69] With several battleships and more subsidiary vessels planned for both fleets, a significant increase in the strength of the Russian navy was forecast. But on the Baltic Sea, the two squadrons would not be complete before 1919. On the Black Sea, in April 1914, the French naval attaché reported that the Russians had increased the pace of construction, pushed "by the events in Constantinople, by the augmentation of Turkish naval strength, and by the continual provocation by Germany."[70] Even so, Russia would suffer a period of inferiority to the growing Ottoman navy, since the first Russian dreadnoughts would not be available before 1915, while Ottoman battleships under construction in England were expected to arrive in summer 1914.[71] Here again, then, the imbalance of forces called for patience until Russian construction could provide the navy with the superiority necessary to defend the southern coastline, to say nothing of mounting offensive operations near the Bosphorus.

Beyond these internal concerns, an external concern that should have made Russian leaders more cautious in July 1914 was doubt about the intentions of Great Britain in case of continental war between the Triple and the Franco-Russian alliances. Britain had been tightening its relationships with its Entente partners ever since those understandings were concluded in 1904 with France and 1907 with Russia. While the two Moroccan crises in 1905–1906 and 1911 served to push Britain and France closer together, relations between Britain and Russia remained more distant, especially as nagging problems reemerged between them, including disagreement in Persia, British left-wing displeasure with Russia as a partner, and Russian conservative distaste for the British agreement.[72]

In Russian discussions of foreign policy in 1914, the uncertainty about British intentions in case of war often loomed large. For example, in the

[69] Shatsillo, *Russkii imperializm*; Gatrell, *Government*, pp. 135–138.
[70] Gallaud to Gauthier, April 7, 1914, dep. 269, Service historique de la Marine, SS Ea 157; Stevenson, *Armaments and the Coming of War*, p. 349.
[71] Bobroff, *Roads to Glory*, pp. 89–90; Naval General Staff to Main Administration for Ship Construction, April 25, 1914, RGAMF f. 418 op. 1 d. 33 l. 129.
[72] Samuel R. Williamson, Jr., *The Politics of Grand Strategy: Britain and France Prepare for War, 1904–1914* (London: Ashfield, 1990), pp. 167–342; Zara Steiner and Keith Neilson, *Britain and the Origins of the First World War*, 2nd edn. (Basingstoke: Palgrave Macmillan, 2003), pp. 84–116, 151–153; Stevenson, *Armaments and the Coming of War*, pp. 212–216; J. F. V. Keiger, *France and the Origins of the First World War* (London: Macmillan, 1983), pp. 104–116; Keiger, Chapter 10, this volume; Siegel, *Endgame*; Keith Neilson, *Britain and the Last Tsar: British Policy towards Russia, 1894–1917* (Oxford: Clarendon Press, 1995), pp. 267–316; McDonald, *United Government*, pp. 199–203; Lieven, *Origins*, pp. 74–83.

January 1914 conference about Liman von Sanders, a key consideration was whether Britain would fight with Russia and France against the Central Powers. Sazonov argued that Germany did not believe a war against only Russia and France would be particularly dangerous. Only with the participation of Britain would Germany shrink from a fight. Given the doubt about London's involvement, however, the conference agreed that pushing the Ottoman Empire and Germany overly hard was too risky.[73]

In the months that followed, Sazonov insisted to Paris and London that the key to holding back Germany and keeping the peace was turning the Triple Entente into a new Triple Alliance. Out of frustration over Britain's lack of commitment, on February 19, 1914, Sazonov wrote to his ambassador in London, A. K. Benckendorff, that:

> world peace will be assured only on the day when the Triple Entente, the actual existence of which is no more proven than that of the Serpent of the Sea, is transformed into a defensive alliance, without secret clauses and made public by all the world's newspapers. On that day, the danger of German hegemony will be definitively eliminated.[74]

Six weeks later, Sazonov wrote to Izvolskii that creating a new Triple Alliance was an "urgent task," and was "the best means of preserving peace in Europe."[75] He also wondered if perhaps Paris and London could share the nature of their political agreement with St. Petersburg, as a model for an agreement between Russia and Britain. The French replied that there was no such political arrangement and suggested that Russia seek a naval understanding, as the French had, with Britain.[76]

Sazonov sought more, however, suggesting to Buchanan that the two states come to a defensive agreement in Europe. Sazonov contended that, "unless something was done, the Triple Entente would soon become a quantité négligeable. Germany . . . was bent on establishing her hegemony in Turkey and she would one day push matters too far, with the result that we should all be dragged into war."[77] Sazonov, aware that London never concluded peacetime alliances in Europe, pointed to the treaty Great

---

[73] Adamov, *Konstantinopol'*, vol. 1, pp. 67–69.

[74] Sazonov to Benkendorf, February 19, 1914, let., AVPRI, f. 138 op. 467 d. 323/327 ll. 7–8. Sazonov continued that the three allies could then look to their own concerns in peace: England to its social problems; France to enhancing its security against outside threats; and Russia "to consolidate and work at our economic reorganization." It is worth noting that Sazonov does not refer to any external goal, including the Straits, but instead focuses, like Stolypin, on Russia's continued internal recovery.

[75] Sazonov to Izvol'skii, April 2, 1914, let. 23, AVPRI, f. 138 op. 467 d. 323/327 ll. 15–16.

[76] Izvol'skii to Sazonov, April 9, 1914, let., AVPRI f. 138 op. 467 d. 323/327 ll. 24–25.

[77] Buchanan to Nicolson, April 16, 1914, let., FO 800 373 pp 52–53.

Britain had with Japan. "Why could we not then conclude an agreement with Russia that would guarantee us both against German aggression. He did not care what form that agreement took; but if we wished to maintain peace, we must proclaim to the world the solidarity of the Triple Entente."[78] The tsar spoke likewise to Buchanan about the German danger in the Near East and the need for an Anglo-Russian treaty.[79]

The British refused, but the French convinced them to engage in naval talks with Russia, along the lines of the Anglo-French understanding.[80] To the Russians' frustration, however, the British approached these talks in a dilatory fashion, and no substantive start had been made as the summer began. The British had decided that the First Sea Lord, Prince Louis of Battenberg, would negotiate in St. Petersburg in August 1914. Both Sazonov and Nicholas II pressed Buchanan in late June for talks as soon as possible, implicitly threatening trouble on Persian and Tibetan questions if satisfaction was not given.[81] Thus, as the July Crisis intensified, the position of Great Britain had not been resolved.[82] When the Russians made their crucial decisions of the crisis on July 24 and 25, the British position remained unclear. Buchanan could not assure Sazonov about London's ultimate decision. Given how important the Russians considered British participation in a war with Germany, such uncertainty would give the Russians pause about the prospects of such a conflict.[83]

The crisis and decision to mobilize

These factors all offered good reasons for the Russian government to react cautiously to the Austrian ultimatum to Belgrade of July 23, 1914. Instead, in the Council of Ministers meetings on July 24 and 25, the Russians committed to strong measures that they hoped would support their diplomatic efforts to prevent war, but at the same time prepare them for the opening of possible hostilities. Krivoshein and Sazonov offered the most persuasive arguments for a strong stand, and the service chiefs

---

[78] Ibid.
[79] Paléologue to Doumergue, April 18, 1914, tels. 154–155, AVPRI f. 138 op. 467 d. 323/327 l. 31.
[80] Stevenson, *Armaments and the Coming of War*, pp. 349–350; Asquith to George V, May 14, 1914, CAB 41/35/13; Viscount Grey of Fallodon, *Twenty-Five Years, 1892–1916* (New York: Stokes, 1925), pp. 273–278; Steiner and Neilson, *Britain*, pp. 105–111, 128–132; Williamson, *Politics of Grand Strategy*, pp. 284–293, 337–339; Paul G. Halpern, *The Mediterranean Naval Situation 1908–1914* (Cambridge, MA: Harvard University Press, 1971), pp. 86–110, 311–313.
[81] Buchanan to Grey, June 25, 1914, tel., FO 800 74, pp. 285–289.
[82] Siegel, *Endgame*, pp. 175–196; Steiner and Neilson, *Britain*, pp. 125–127.
[83] Bovykin, *Iz istorii*, p. 180.

concurred in the civilians' assessments, assuring the council that the military could fight if necessary. The tsar agreed to the ministers' recommendations, and so the Russian Empire planned a partial mobilization against Austria-Hungary, if the latter declared war on Serbia. Furthermore, given the heightened concern about war, they decided that the military should engage in pre-mobilization preparations (those associated with the declaration of the Period Preparatory to War). Once war with Germany looked likely by July 29, the leadership sought a general mobilization, agreement to which the tsar grudgingly gave the next day, which historians argue forced the Germans to start war lest their war plan should lose the advantages of speed of mobilization and concentration that they enjoyed over the Russians. Understanding the Russian choices requires an examination of their thinking in the last week of July in the context of the long-term developments that we have reviewed above. Increased suspicions of the Central Powers, especially Germany, when combined with the increasing willingness to consider military options, thanks to the changing composition of the council and the opinions and attitudes of those remaining, facilitated the decision to mobilize.

While concerns about the British might have given the Russians pause, France encouraged St. Petersburg's resolute stance during the crisis. Indeed, the French had been encouraging Russia's strengthening especially since 1912, when Raymond Poincaré became prime minister. After several years of drift in the alliance, Poincaré sought to pull the two allies closer together and encouraged Russia to develop its security apparatus in a fashion that would better serve French security.[84] Paris wanted an enlargement of the Russian army, the development of more strategic railroads, and an earlier date for the Russian invasion of Germany after mobilization. The French expected most of Germany's forces to invade France, so they needed a rapid Russian attack westward to force Berlin to redeploy units.[85] Poincaré also replaced the aging, ineffective Georges Louis as ambassador to Russia with Théophile Delcassé, a former foreign minister who possessed a stalwart pro-alliance and anti-German identity.[86] During the Balkan Wars, Poincaré strongly supported the Russians, if in part to restrain the Russians from intervention in the conflict.[87]

In the July Crisis that firm support continued. Poincaré, now France's president, visited St. Petersburg with members of the Cabinet from July 20 to 23, 1914. Remarkably, we still have little information about the

---

[84] *Ibid.*, pp. 87–102; Keiger, *France and the Origins*, pp. 90–102.
[85] Fuller, *Strategy*, pp. 441–442; Turner, "Russian Mobilisation," pp. 257–258.
[86] Keiger, *France and the Origins*, pp. 102, 138.
[87] *Ibid.*, pp. 98–100; Turner, "Russian Mobilisation," p. 256.

details of the Franco-Russian discussions, but the French likely expressed their support for whatever measures Russia thought necessary to resist aggression by the Triple Alliance.[88] Demands on Serbia were expected from Vienna, so the allied leaders would have been able to concert their response in a general fashion. On July 23, 1914, the French government sailed for home, and immediately after their departure, the Austrians delivered their ultimatum to the Serbians. This deliberate timing undermined the French ability to communicate about the crisis for several days. But the ambassador in St. Petersburg, Maurice Paléologue, stridently supported Sazonov, repeatedly insisting that France would fulfill its alliance responsibilities, even appearing at times to urge Sazonov to take a stronger stand than that to which the latter was personally inclined.[89] Once the French leaders returned to Paris, however, they counseled caution in order to avoid provoking the Germans. Paris suggested continuing with military preparations, but more covertly, avoiding large movements of troops for the time being in case there were any hopes of preserving peace, or at least putting off the breakdown for a time.[90] Overall, Sazonov could make decisions believing that the French stood with Russia regardless of the outcome.

Most obviously, and most talked about in the literature, the Russian leadership feared for Serbian independence and their own prestige.[91] In the crises of 1908–1913, Serbian independence had not been threatened.[92] With the 1914 ultimatum, however, Vienna seemed to threaten Serbia's sovereignty itself. Given the long history of Russian pan-Slav advocacy, and the particularly close connection between Russia and Serbia, Russian prestige in Europe, and especially in the Balkans, depended on Russia's stance before this new threat.[93] It can be seen that, even in 1912, Sazonov recognized the connection between Russian defense of Slavic interests and Russia's own prestige and influence in the region when he told Benckendorff that its goal in the diplomatic struggle over the resolution

---

[88] Bovykin, *Iz istorii*, pp. 192–193; Keiger, *France and the Origins*, pp. 150–152; Turner, "Russian Mobilisation," p. 260.

[89] Buchanan to Grey, July 24, 1914, tel. 166, BD XI, No. 101, and Buchanan to Grey, July 25, 1914, tel. 169, BD XI, No. 125; Irwin Halfond, *Maurice Paléologue: The Diplomat, the Writer, the Man, and the Third French Republic* (Lanham, MD: University Press of America, 2007), pp. 83–99; Jean Stengers, "1914: The Safety of Ciphers and the Outbreak of the First World War," in C. Andrew and J. Noakes (eds.), *Intelligence and International Relations* (University of Exeter Press, 1987), pp. 29–48.

[90] Izvol'skii to Sazonov, July 30, 1914, tels. 208, 210; *Mezhdunarodnye otnosheniia v epokhu imperializma* 3rd series (Moscow: Gos. sots., 1931–1940) (hereafter MO) 3/V Nos. pp. 289, 291; Ignat'ev to General-Quartermaster Section of the General Staff, July 28, 1914, tel. 227, MO 3/V No. 293; Bovykin, *Iz istorii*, p. 206.

[91] Jelavich, *Balkan Entanglements*, pp. 248–265; Lieven, *Russia*, pp. 147, 153.

[92] Stevenson, "Militarization and Diplomacy," p. 156.   [93] Bovykin, *Iz istorii*, p. 180.

of the Balkan Wars was to "provide itself the possibility of preferential or even exclusive influence" in the region; this was "the red thread across all the questions which require resolution."[94] To lose this influence would be to sacrifice its position as a Great Power.

But perhaps more worrying, St. Petersburg interpreted Vienna's wider demands as an unwillingness on Vienna's part to compromise. Thanks to intelligence sources, St. Petersburg knew that Vienna would serve Belgrade with demands over the murder of the Habsburg heir.[95] This knowledge itself did not evince any particular alarm among the Russians. While Sazonov warned the Austrians against such a move, the Russians did not begin any special preparations before learning the actual wording of the ultimatum. But by July 22, Sazonov tried to caution Vienna in a friendly but firm fashion about the possible consequences of harsh demands.[96] More warnings as well as vague news from Belgrade arrived on July 23, but when, on July 24, Sazonov learned of the ultimatum's timeframe and terms, in shock he exclaimed, "It's the European war!"[97] Later that morning, when the Austrian ambassador brought him a copy of the demands, Sazonov reacted by accusing Austria of seeking war against Serbia that would spread to the whole of Europe.[98] Demands infringing on Serbia's sovereignty, as well as the aggressively short 48-hour deadline, suggested that this time Vienna would not allow a diplomatic resolution.[99] While Sazonov continued to search for a way to work with Vienna, the Austrians withdrew their delegation from Belgrade on the expiry of the ultimatum's deadline, having not received complete satisfaction of their demands, and declared war on Serbia on July 28, 1914.[100]

The German attitude during this time was of graver consequence, however, for the Russians. As has been shown, by the summer of 1914, many Russian leaders had grown quite suspicious of German intentions and had come to see Berlin as a greater threat to Russian interests in Europe and especially in the Near East than Vienna. The string of crises

---

[94] Sazonov to Benkendorf, December 13, 1912, let. 848, AVPRI, f. 151 op. 482 d. 131 ll. 119–123.

[95] Rich, "Russia," pp. 215–216; Shebeko to Sazonov, July 16, 1914, tel. 88, MO 3/IV No. 247.

[96] Sazonov to Shebeko, July 22, 1914, tel. 1475, MO 3/IV No. 322.

[97] Daily Journal, MID, July 24, 1914, MO 3/V No. 25; M. F. Schilling, *How the War Began in 1914* (London: Allen & Unwin, 1925), pp. 28–29.

[98] Szápáry to Berchtold, July 24, 1914, tels. 157, 159, in Imanuel Geiss (ed.), *July 1914: The Outbreak of the First World War: Selected Documents* (New York: Scribner, 1967), No. 51. British Foreign Secretary Sir Edward Grey found the ultimatum so alarming that he described it as "the most formidable document that was ever addressed from one State to another." Mensdorff to Berchtold, July 24, 1914, tel. 108, in Geiss (ed.), *July 1914: Outbreak*, No. 50.

[99] Rich, "Russia," p. 218.   [100] Geiss (ed.), *July 1914: Outbreak*, Nos. 37 and 72.

ratcheted up St. Petersburg's distrust, which was exacerbated by hostility in the negotiations for a new trade treaty. Germany seemed to be trying to undermine Russia's position at every turn. Thus, by 1914, the Russians believed that Germany lurked behind Austrian moves. After the ultimatum emerged, the Russians believed Germany to be instrumental in its provision. When Sazonov informed Nicholas II of the details of the ultimatum, he added "undoubtedly ... this note was drawn up by prior agreement between Vienna and Berlin."[101] Before the Council of Ministers meeting started on July 24, Finance Minister Bark consulted with Baron Schilling, and they agreed that Bark should immediately withdraw the large deposits the Treasury had in Berlin.[102] This decision is significant in how soon after the delivery of the ultimatum the Russians feared war not just with Austria-Hungary, but also with Germany.

Sazonov and Krivoshein dominated the ministers' meeting that afternoon. Sazonov stressed Germany's drive for hegemony in Europe and how Berlin sought the right time to push this forward with war. He argued that the ultimatum presented to Serbia by Austria was likely composed not just in agreement with Germany, but under Berlin's direct influence. If Russia did not stand up for Serbia, it would be abandoning its historic role and be reduced to "a second-rank power."[103] Furthermore, if Russia did not resist "Germany's armored fist" at this time, German demands would only grow.[104] Although Britain's position remained uncertain, making the possibility of war more alarming, Sazonov insisted that "the only way for Russia to maintain its authority in international affairs is to take a harder line than earlier and stand up for Serbia."[105] Krivoshein, generally considered the most influential member of the council, also argued for a less compromising policy toward the Central Powers, since a passive stance taken out of fear of war would not prevent war if the Central Powers wanted it, and it had not achieved the empire's goals in its relations with Berlin and Vienna so far. He suggested that "more forceful and energetic behavior" was required.[106] While his comments in the meeting evinced no greater concern for either of the Central Powers, right after the meeting, Krivoshein told Bark that he viewed Germany as the primary threat, stating that "The only hope of stopping Germany is calm resolution and preparedness to begin military operations."[107] Other ministers, including the service chiefs, spoke more briefly, agreeing with Sazonov's and Krivoshein's position. No one at

---

[101] Bark, "Iiul'skie dni 1914," p. 17; Lieven, *Russia*, pp. 141–144.
[102] Bark, "Iiul'skie dni," p. 18; Schilling, *How the War Began*, p. 29.
[103] Bark, "Iiul'skie dni," pp. 19–20.   [104] *Ibid.*, p. 20.   [105] *Ibid.*, p. 21.
[106] *Ibid.*, p. 22.   [107] *Ibid.*, p. 25.

the meeting spoke strongly against such measures, which was a big change from previous discussions. Stolypin's assassination had removed one moderating influence from the council, Kokovtsov's dismissal another. Neither Goremykin nor Bark opposed a hard line now. The ministers thus resolved to continue with diplomacy backed by military measures to win more time for negotiations and to find a compromise that would avoid war, as well as to advise the Serbian government to go as far as it could in meeting the Austrian demands without violating its own sovereignty. At the same time, in case these measures failed, the army was to prepare to mobilize four military districts along the Austrian border and the navy was to prepare to mobilize its Black and Baltic fleets.[108]

This meeting reflects more, of course, than the increased distrust for Germany that had been building over several years, though this distrust should not be discounted. One sees in the ministers' comments a readiness to resist German encroachment by backing their diplomatic measures with military posturing. Just as Austria became more extreme in its treatment of Serbia from 1912 to 1914, believing the military measures made the difference, so too do we see the Russians more willing to risk war by brandishing the sword to provide more backbone to their negotiations.[109] For five days the leadership hoped that a partial mobilization would suffice to achieve their diplomatic objectives.

There has been extensive discussion in the literature about the pitfalls of a partial mobilization.[110] For one, the four districts that were to be mobilized did not include the Warsaw military district. Such an omission, while avoiding provocative Russian activity on the German border, would leave the northern border of Austria-Hungary unprepared. Second, the Russian army in fact possessed no detailed plans prepared for a partial mobilization. The General Staff had used partial mobilizations during the Russo-Japanese War in 1904–1905 and made up plans for the mobilizations as they went, with disastrous results.[111] Finally, and perhaps most problematic, as General Iu. N. Danilov, who was intimately familiar with mobilization, told a close advisor of Sazonov, by the second day of a partial mobilization, switching to a general mobilization in an orderly fashion would be impossible. Most of the experienced generals thus strongly opposed such half-measures.[112]

---

[108] Special Journal of the Council of Ministers, July 24, 1914, MO 3/V No. 19.
[109] Stevenson, "Militarization and Diplomacy," pp. 155–160.
[110] The following discussion of partial mobilization relies heavily on Fuller, *Strategy*, pp. 446–450, and Rich, "Russia," pp. 220–224.
[111] Fuller, *Strategy*, pp. 403–404.   [112] Basily, *Memoirs*, p. 99.

It has been assumed that the partial mobilization was chosen out of ignorance of the realities described above by Sazonov in consultation with Sukhomlinov and Chief of the General Staff, General N. N. Ianushkevich, none of whom understood mobilization well, or, in Sazonov's case, much at all.[113] But there are no documents that definitively show whose idea it was or what they expected beyond warning Austria-Hungary and not provoking Germany.[114] Another possibility is that the officers at least knew enough to understand the complications of a partial mobilization, but in concert with Sazonov, they chose to offer it in the July 24 meeting for exactly the overt purpose described – to signal seriousness to Vienna and Berlin – but did not expect to actually have to implement it. It is likely that the one person who took the option seriously was Tsar Nicholas II. On July 25, 1914, he approved the plans for partial mobilization in case diplomatic efforts failed. Once most had given up hope by July 29, 1914 that peace would be preserved, the only person still interested in the partial option was the tsar. That evening Nicholas at first grudgingly approved general mobilization, after Germany warned Russia that if it continued its preparations Germany would have to mobilize, which the Russians took as a sign that war with Germany was inevitable.[115] But when the kaiser sent the tsar a telegram that instilled more hope in the latter, the tsar rescinded his approval of general mobilization and ordered a partial one instead.[116] Thus, the confusion that has been ascribed to the top generals and the foreign minister may have been largely the product of wishful thinking by a tsar who wished to avoid war.

But while using partial mobilization for diplomatic purposes, an intriguing element of the Russian preparations is that not only did they plan for partial mobilization, but they resolved at the July 24 council meeting to begin the preparations associated with the Period Preparatory to War, a set of pre-mobilization measures that, unlike mobilization, were not public and would allow the army to speed general mobilization once it was declared.[117] These began in the evening of July 25/26, 1914. The army, through the Period Preparatory to War, essentially proceeded with preparations for general mobilization, having long expected Germany to fight alongside Austria-Hungary. Furthermore, the army leadership may have feared being surprised by a mobilization in Germany, after being caught unawares by the Austrian mobilization of their forces in Galicia during the First Balkan War. "The generals were determined

---

[113] Rich, "Russia," p. 222.   [114] Fuller, *Strategy*, p. 446.
[115] Sazonov to Izvol'skii, July 29, 1914, tel. 1551, MO 3/V No. 221.
[116] Lieven, *Nicholas II*, p. 202.   [117] Stevenson, *Armaments and the Coming of War*, p. 383.

not to be caught napping again."[118] The weaker level of Russian intelligence-gathering in Germany compared with that in Austria-Hungary would only have reinforced those fears.[119] Already on July 26, 1914, the chief of the mobilization section of the General Staff, General S. K. Dobrorolskii, could present orders for both partial and general mobilizations.[120] The next day, Dobrorolskii alerted the head of military communications that if diplomacy failed, *all* forces designated for the western front would be mobilized. And on July 28, Ianushkevich telegraphed a warning to his commanders that on July 30, 1914, general mobilization would begin, pending appropriate further notification, though this last measure may have been under the influence of Sazonov, who Dobrorolskii remembered had come to the conclusion that a continental war was unavoidable and told Ianushkevich that mobilization could no longer be delayed.[121] All these measures suggest how little the army actually expected to implement a partial mobilization.

The last gasp of the diplomatic offensive started on July 28, 1914. With the Austrian declaration of war, Russia had to declare partial mobilization according to the plan of July 24. But Sazonov continued to hope that partial mobilization would give him leverage. He instructed the chargé d'affaires in Berlin to tell the German government of the Russian partial mobilization and stress that it was not directed at them. He also made sure Berlin knew that Russia was not withdrawing its ambassador from Vienna, another signal that Russia did not wish to go to war.[122] Early on July 29, Sazonov told the German ambassador of the partial mobilization, emphasizing both that it was only on the Austrian frontier and that Russian mobilization would not lead automatically to war.[123] But by July 29, the Russian authorities had heard news of German preparatory military and naval measures.[124] And that afternoon, the German ambassador returned to warn Sazonov that if Russia did not cease its military preparations, Germany would have to mobilize. Such a declaration, on top of Berlin's foot-dragging during the intense week of negotiations since the ultimatum, would only have confirmed the Russian suspicions of Germany that had been growing for so many years and thus the need

---

[118] Lieven, *Russia*, p. 149.   [119] Fuller, "Russian Empire," p. 115.

[120] Dobrorol'skii to Ianushkevich, July 26, 1914, Report 3645/668, MO 3/V No. 112.

[121] Ianushkevich to Nikolai Nikolaievich, Vorontsov-Dashkov, *et al.*, July 28, 1914, tel. 1785, *ibid.*, No. 210; Stevenson, *Armaments and the Coming of War*, p. 385.

[122] Sazonov to Bronevskii, July 28, 1914, tel. 168, MO 3/V No. 168.

[123] Pourtalès to Jagow, July 29, 1914, tel. 183; Geiss (ed.), *July 1914: Outbreak*, No. 124a; Daily Journal of the Foreign Ministry, July 29, 1914, MO 3/V No. 224.

[124] Ignat'ev to General-Quartermaster Section of the General Staff, July 28, 1914, tel. 217, *ibid.*, No. 182; Demerik to Sazonov, July 28, 1914, *ibid.*, No. 187.

for general mobilization. Informing his ambassadors in Paris and London of the German demand, Sazonov indicated that Russia would have to hasten its preparations as war now appeared inevitable.[125] The tsar, however, proved resilient in his hope for localization of the war. As noted above, late on July 29 he countermanded an earlier order for general mobilization, returning to plans for partial mobilization because he thought that Wilhelm II was willing to work with him. Only the next day under the weight of evidence piling up against Germany was Sazonov able to persuade Nicholas II to commit Russia to general mobilization.[126]

In these ways, then, Russia entered into conflict with the Central Powers aware of what was at stake and, at least in the short term, aware of the potential costs. Russia did not stumble into war, nor engineer it for its own gain, but turned to military measures as a show of strength that it hoped would resolve its diplomatic quandary. Much appeared to be at stake in July 1914: the independence of Serbia; Russian prestige and honor, its position as a Great Power in Europe; and a balance of power in Europe that would prevent German hegemony. While some of these concerns had arisen before, Russia had not stood as firmly because its leaders had not agreed that it was yet necessary or even possible. Only after Germany's repeated challenges to Russia in both diplomatic and economic arenas, and after a hawkish shift in the position of Russian leadership to one ready to back negotiations with force, did Russia make its stand in July 1914. In the face of other states seeking war for gain or survival, the Russians reluctantly stood their ground, because they could no longer see any alternative.

---

[125] Sazonov to Izvol'skii, July 29, 1914, tel. 1551, *ibid.*, No. 221.
[126] Sazonov, *Fateful Years*, pp. 201–205.

10 France's unreadiness for war in 1914 and its implications for French decision-making in the July Crisis

J. F. V. Keiger

The French specialist in international history, Jean-Baptiste Duroselle, asked whether political leaders caught up in the complexities of a process that in the end leads to war have a clear view of what they are seeking to achieve: maybe the avoidance of war; maybe the most propitious circumstances for war?[1] Do they continually calculate or measure the impact of each decision on the possible outbreak of conflict, as historians do with the benefit of hindsight? Similarly, do decision-makers have in their minds a running calculus of their state's readiness for war – a risk analysis? If so, do they act upon it at every turn? In short, do they act rationally with each decision in what might be called the fog of pre-war? Whatever the degree of calculation per decision, it is reasonable to assume, however, that leaders apply a minimum of rationality in their decision-making when success or failure in conflict is at stake.

Well before its end the First World War raised the question of state responsibility for its outbreak. But behind the charge of intentional provocation lies the assumption that before they act decision-makers engage in a minimum of strategic analysis, "that leaders' decisions for war are generally based on some kind of cost–benefit calculation of the consequences of war."[2] Leaders might be assumed to attach different probabilities to different choices and outcomes.[3] In modern parlance, they engage in a risk assessment of the consequences of war, identifying, assessing, and prioritizing the risks to the national interests that encouraging war might bring. Rationality suggests that leaders seek to encourage war only if it is in the national interest to do so. A key component in the risk assessment must be whether a state is strong and ready for war.

---

[1] J-B. Duroselle, "Preface," in Georges-Henri Soutou, *L'or et le sang. Les buts de guerre économiques de la première guerre mondiale* (Paris: Fayard, 1989), p. ii.

[2] Jack S. Levy, "The Initiation and Spread of the First World War: Interdependent Decisions," *Foreign Policy Analysis* 7(2) (2011): 183–188; see also the classic political science text, Bruce Bueno de Mesquita, *The War Trap* (New Haven, CT: Yale University Press, 1981).

[3] Levy, "Initiation and Spread of the First World War," p. 186.

The great strategist and theoretician of war, Karl von Clausewitz, writing at the beginning of the nineteenth century, made the mundane, but crucial, point that in order to wage war "The best strategy is always to be very strong; first in general, and then at the decisive point."[4] He also described war as "'a remarkable trinity,' in which the directing policy of the government, the professional qualities of the army, and the attitude of the population all played an equally significant part."[5] For Clausewitz, readiness for war meant aligning those three key elements. By 1900, there was a veritable craze for Clausewitz in France, with his leading disciple being the future Marshal Ferdinand Foch, whose *Principles of War*, published in 1903, borrowed widely from the master. French civilian authorities, though perhaps not directly cognisant of Clausewitz's work, understood that for France to begin a conflict with her principal rival Germany she should at least be in a state of readiness for war in terms of government policy, military preparation, and public opinion. Furthermore, although Clausewitz afforded little attention to economic factors in questions of strategy, France's political leaders considered finance to be an important element should France wish to wage war.

This chapter will seek to do two things. First, it will examine whether France was sufficiently strong and ready to wage war in August 1914 as an indication of the likelihood of her having encouraged war. Second, in the light of her apparent state of unreadiness, it will seek to evaluate the decision-making of her leaders against some broader theoretical debates on why nations go to war.

How "ready" was France for war in 1914?

The question of French responsibility in the outbreak of war has never been far from controversy since the First World War began.[6] But with the opening up of the French archives in the late 1970s and work on French decision-makers since the early 1980s France's role was demonstrated to have been more passive than that of other Great Powers.[7] This line of research posits that the French government did not want or seek war

---

[4] Quoted in Michael Howard, *Clausewitz: A Very Short Introduction* (Oxford University Press, 2002), p. 40.

[5] Howard, *Clausewitz*, p. 20.

[6] See John F. V. Keiger, *Raymond Poincaré* (Cambridge University Press, 1997), pp. 193–201; on the politicization of historical interpretations more generally, Annika Mombauer, *The Origins of the First World War: Controversies and Consensus* (New York: Longman, 2002).

[7] Jean-Jacques Becker, *1914: Comment les français sont entrés dans la guerre* (Paris: Presses de la Fondation nationale des sciences politiques, 1977); John F. V. Keiger, *France and the Origins of the First World War* (London: Macmillan, 1983).

in 1914, was not following a policy of revanche for 1871 and the loss of Alsace-Lorraine, and did not inflame the July Crisis. In the last few years some challenges have been made to that position by suggesting that French leaders, notably the President of the Republic, Raymond Poincaré, were more active in encouraging war.[8] But none produce any "smoking gun" documentary evidence that Poincaré was willing to risk war or encouraged Russia recklessly. It is timely therefore to revisit the question of France's responsibility in the origins debate from a different angle: to study her state of readiness for war as an indicator of the rationality of her having potentially willed war.

It is now more widely known that many of the accusations of French responsibility for the outbreak of the First World War had less to do with the events of 1914 than with the vagaries of post-war domestic and international politics. That blame was generated principally in the period after 1918 (and partly during the war) inside France for reasons related to domestic politics, and abroad to attenuate German responsibility, to minimize reparations payments, and to bolster the legitimacy of the new Bolshevik and Soviet regimes.[9]

Joseph Caillaux, the senior French Radical Party leader who had been premier at the time of the 1911 Agadir Crisis and was favorable to a Franco-German entente, included in his memoirs, published in 1947, an alleged account of the French Cabinet meeting of August 1, 1914. Caillaux, a former close friend turned arch rival of Raymond Poincaré, the President of the Republic of the time and by that token chairman of Cabinet meetings, claimed that in Cabinet on August 1, Poincaré had uttered the words: "It is not at the moment when we are ready that we are going to renounce profiting from the situation ... If necessary we will create a frontier incident. It isn't difficult..."[10]

Given that French Cabinet minutes were not taken at this time (unlike in Britain), there is no evidence pointing to Poincaré making any such statement; indeed, the record shows that at Poincaré's behest everything was done to *avoid* a frontier incident by ordering that French covering

[8] Stefan Schmidt, *Frankreichs Außenpolitik in der Julikrise 1914: ein Beitrag zur Geschichte des Ausbruchs des Ersten Weltkriegs* (Munich: Oldenbourg, 2009); Christopher Clark, *The Sleepwalkers: How Europe Went to War in 1914* (London: Allen Lane, 2012).

[9] For further details, see Keiger, *Poincaré*, pp. 193–201, 271–272, 279–285; see also the article by Andrew Barros and Frédéric Guelton, "Les imprévus de l'histoire instrumentalisée: le livre jaune de 1914 et les documents diplomatiques français sur les origines de la Grande Guerre, 1914–1928," *Guerres mondiales et conflits contemporains*, 2006.

[10] Caillaux, *Mes mémoires*, 1947, vol. 3, pp. 175–176, quoted in Daniel Amson, *Poincaré l'acharné de la politique* (Paris: Tallandier, 1997), p. 203.

troops remain 10 km back from the Franco-German border.[11] Caillaux
was not a member of the government and consequently not present at the
Cabinet meeting. But such remarks were typical of the post-1918 domestic campaign of rumor and innuendo targeted at "Poincaré-la-guerre"
for party political reasons on the left by the French Communist Party,
the Socialists, and the more moderate Radicals, who wished to stop
him returning to power as premier in the 1920s. They echoed German-
inspired and financed propaganda intended to counter Article 231 of the
Versailles Treaty acknowledging Germany's guilt, by emphasizing France
and Poincaré's own guilt in terms of revanchism, military build-up, the
Franco-Russian treaty, and a push for war.[12] But most ironical of all,
Caillaux was incorrect in attributing to Poincaré the comment that it was
because France was "ready" for war that she should take advantage of
the situation. The crux of the matter was that France and the French were
not at all ready for war on August 1, 1914, or at any time in July. Indeed,
everything pointed to them not being ready in a number of critical areas
for some three years.

Of course, it could be argued that diplomatic victory, not war, was what
was desired by all the powers, and that France, like others, overplayed her
hand. However, it is not the intention of this chapter to study the detailed
management of the July Crisis, which I have done elsewhere.[13] What it
will attempt to show is that, more than for most powers, certain objective
conditions in 1914 gave French decision-makers neither the desire nor
the inclination to pursue a policy likely to lead to conflict. A decision to
encourage war on the basis of readiness for war was therefore not a
reflection of rational choice. Indeed, if anything, France's lack of readiness should, from a rational point of view, have pointed her politicians

[11] There is no mention in the manuscript version of Poincaré's secret diaries, despite their
being a detailed and copious record of his daily activities and meetings; indeed, he
considered the diaries so intimate that he had them locked in the Elysée safe when he
was absent on state visits. See Keiger, *France and the Origins*, p. 120.

[12] See Keiger, *Poincaré*, pp. 198–199. On German propaganda, see Sally Marks, "Smoke-
filled Rooms and the Galerie des Glaces," in Manfred Boemeke, Gerald Feldman, and
Elisabeth Glaser (eds.), *The Treaty of Versailles: A Reassessment after 75 Years* (Cambridge
University Press, 1998), pp. 337–370; Wolfgang Mommsen, "Max Weber and the Peace
Treaty of Versailles," in Manfred F. Boemeke, Gerald D. Feldman, and Elisabeth Glaser
(eds.), *Treaty of Versailles: A Reassessment after 75 Years* (Cambridge University Press,
1998), pp. 535–546; on the success of German propaganda in the United States and the
perpetuation of the myth of the unfair Versailles treaty, see William Keylor, "Versailles and
International Diplomacy," in Manfred Boemeke, Gerald Feldman, and Elisabeth Glaser
(eds.), *The Treaty of Versailles: A Reassessment after 75 Years* (Cambridge University Press,
1998), pp. 469–505.

[13] See Keiger, *France and the Origins*; John F. V. Keiger, "France," in Keith Wilson (ed.),
Decisions for War, 1914 (New York: St. Martin's Press, 1995), pp. 121–149; Keiger,
Poincaré.

and soldiers in the direction of wishing to avoid war in the near future for reasons to do with alliances, military preparations, finances, and public opinion, each of which will be discussed in turn.

Unready allies

The first reason concerned the three powers, Britain, Russia, and Italy. In the summer of 1914, it was by no means clear to French leaders that France's friend, Britain, or her ally, Russia, would, or could, come to France's assistance effectively in the event of a war with Germany; the former was not formally committed to France in the event of war, and the latter appeared militarily unprepared to do so. A third power conditioning France's behavior in the last days of July 1914 was Italy, formally a member of the opposing Triple Alliance with Germany and Austria-Hungary, but Rome's commitment to the Central Powers was conditional on them not committing any act of aggression.

Despite the 1904 Entente Cordiale and the commitment since 1905 to secret military talks between London and Paris as to what might be done if either was threatened by war, Britain expressly reserved her decision, as she repeatedly warned France. Just three days before Germany declared war on France, on August 3, the French ambassador in London, Paul Cambon, was still complaining that Britain would not make a commitment. On July 31, 1914, Poincaré wrote a personal letter to George V in which he admitted that Britain was not committed to France by any agreement: "Without doubt our military and naval agreements leave Your Majesty's government with complete freedom" ("*laissent entière la liberté du gouvernement*"). He added that it was his deep conviction that "the more Britain, France and Russia gave a strong impression of unity in their diplomatic action . . . the more likely it would be to count on peace being maintained."[14]

In the meantime, French political leaders refused to take any *preparatory military measures*. As is well known, Poincaré, Viviani (premier and foreign minister), and the political director of the French Foreign Ministry were at sea in the Baltic when the July Crisis blew up with the Austrian ultimatum to Serbia on July 23, 1914, which had deliberately been held back by Austria until the French had left St. Petersburg. Even when French Chief of the General Staff and Commander-in-Chief designate, Joseph Joffre, learned to his annoyance on July 28 from War Minister Adolphe Messimy that the Quai d'Orsay had been informed by their

---

[14] Raymond Poincaré, *Au service de la France, vol. IV: l'union sacrée 1914* (Paris: Plon, 1927), Friday, July 31, 1914, p. 439.

ambassador in Berlin on July 21 that Germany had taken preliminary steps toward mobilization and that French preparatory measures needed to be taken, Messimy preferred to wait until Poincaré and Viviani had returned from the Russian state visit on July 29. Even then, it was only on July 30, following a request from Joffre, that the Cabinet ordered deployment of covering troops along France's eastern border. But even that authorization was granted only as long as it did not involve troop movement by rail, calling up reservists, or requisitioning horses.[15] Furthermore, the Cabinet insisted that French covering troops in the east be held back 10 km from the border and that general mobilization be further delayed. Such restraint, which some considered reckless, was intended as a general indication of French peacefulness, a sign of good faith to Britain of France's reasonableness, and as a practical measure to avoid any border incident that might provide a pretext to Germany for war.

The significance of this sacrifice can be measured by its likely impact on French military preparations. First, the 10-km withdrawal did not figure in France's Plan XVII and so risked disorganizing mobilization, should it be declared. Second, Joffre warned the Cabinet that every 24-hour delay in mobilizing the eastern army corps was equivalent to a 15–20 km loss of French territory. But the Cabinet would not budge; the moral and diplomatic argument prevailed over the military. Even then, the impact on London was unclear. Poincaré's request to George V fell on stony ground; the British government was still unable to make a commitment to side with France. It is not surprising, then, that Raymond Poincaré noted in his memoirs that "until the last moment, the French government did not know what England's position would be."[16] As late as August 3, Poincaré wrote in his diary of Viviani's anguish at Britain's delay in committing to France, and of the French premier excitedly exclaiming: "All is lost," and "England betrays us."[17] Though perhaps not decisive in military terms, a British commitment to France was considered morally essential from a domestic and international perspective and no less important for its potential naval, financial, and economic aid.

Russia was an official ally bound by the 1892–1894 Franco-Russian treaty. It is well known that France had provided Russia with vast amounts of capital, and it has often been assumed that this had altered the military

---

[15] Marshal Joseph Joffre, *Mémoires du Maréchal Joffre 1910–1917* (Paris: Plon, 1932), vol. 1, pp. 216–218, quoted in Eugenia Kiesling, "France," in Richard F. Hamilton and Holger Herwig (eds.), *The Origins of World War I* (Cambridge University Press, 2003), p. 251.

[16] Poincaré, *Au service de la France*, vol. IV, Friday, July 31, 1914, p. 437.

[17] Poincaré diary, Bibliothèque nationale de France, August 3, 1914, Poincaré papers, nouvelles acquisitions françaises 16027, vol. 36, p. 144.

balance, and created in both France and Russia a new confidence in their military strength. But if we look closer the French military continued to have serious concerns about Russia's ability to mobilize quickly enough to be of assistance to France in the initial stages of a war. Since coming to power as premier and foreign minister, Poincaré had been adamant about revitalizing the Franco-Russian alliance, which had proven so ineffective in the 1911 Franco-German Agadir incident, while at the same time ensuring that Russia did not use it in the Balkans to drag France into a war. An attempt had been made to improve Russia's very slow mobilization speed. To that end, France had financed Russia's strategic rail network, but little practical progress had been made, despite the efforts of Poincaré, Joffre, and Théophile Delcassé (French ambassador in Russia) in 1913 to pressure the Russian government and General Staff into building more strategic lines.

France's foreign minister and French financial authorities had approved a program of loans to St. Petersburg on the express condition that "the railway works whose necessity the French and Russian Chiefs of Staff recognized in the conferences in August 1913 will be undertaken as soon as possible, so as to be completed within four years."[18] But David Herrmann has shown that French loans to Russia for strategic railroads were nearly all spent on commercial lines and Russia did next to nothing for the strategic lines in the west. The French knew this only too well. Even the Russian Chief of Staff, General Zhilinski, admitted this to the French military attaché, General Laguiche, on June 26, 1913.[19] On November 6, 1913, the French assistant military attaché in St. Petersburg, Major Wherlin, reported that "It seems difficult to foresee the execution of major strategic works in Europe for another two years."[20]

Thus, for all the symbolic importance of Russian railroads speeding up Russian mobilization in the event of war, it was clear that no decisive benefit could be derived from the French loans before 1917–1918, much to French decision-makers' disappointment. As things stood in July 1914,

[18] Minutes of conference at the Foreign Ministry, November 10, 1913, Ministère des affaires etrangères (MAE), CP Russie NS 65 Nos. 425(bis)–425(5); see also Russian embassy typescript, Paris, July 2, 1913, MAE CP Russie NS 42, No 45; Sazonov–Delcassé agreement, December 30, 1913, MAE CP Russie NS 42 Nos. 208–209. Cited in David Herrmann, *The Arming of Europe and the Making of the First World War* (Princeton University Press, 1996) p. 196; also David Stevenson, *Armaments and the Coming of War: Europe, 1904–1914* (Oxford University Press, 1996).

[19] Herrmann, *Arming of Europe*, p. 197.

[20] Cited in Herrmann, *Arming of Europe*, p. 197; for confirmation of Russia's incomplete military modernization, rearmament, and lack of readiness for war, see David Alan Rich, "Russia," in Richard F. Hamilton and Holger Herwig (eds.), *The Origins of World War I* (Cambridge University Press, 2003), p. 219.

according to a barely twelve-month-old French General Staff report, Russian troops could not make contact with the Germans until fifteen days after mobilization, and could not launch a general offensive until the twenty-third day. French decision-makers were aware that Russia would be of no assistance for two to three weeks during the crucial early battles of what was expected to be a short war.[21] Just as it was in Germany's interest to begin war before Russia's strategic position improved, so it was in France's to delay for at least a couple of years.

Italy was by no means an ally of France in 1914, but neither was she an enemy, merely a potential one. What was most important about Italy's position for France in July 1914 was that, although formally a member of the Triple Alliance and therefore an ally of Austria and Germany, in 1900–1902 France and Italy had signed a secret agreement whereby Italy would not side against France in any war by the Triple Alliance powers if France were attacked. Thus, France had every incentive not to act aggressively toward the Central Powers; the prize being Italian neutrality and potentially the possibility of winning Italy to the French side should France be embroiled in a defensive war. Consequently, the French Cabinet was anxious to avoid France appearing to act in a manner that the Italians might construe as aggressive. This, together with fear of alienating Britain, was a further guarantee of French restraint in the July Crisis. As the French ambassador in Rome, Camille Barrère, informed Paris on July 30, 1914, "Italy's attitude in the event of a general conflict is uncertain."[22] French uncertainty about Italy obliged Paris to maintain several army divisions along the southeastern frontier until August 4 when Rome finally declared official Italian neutrality precisely because the Central Powers, not France, had acted aggressively.

Military unreadiness

It was not only France's ally, Russia, that was militarily unprepared for war at the end of July 1914. France's own state of military readiness for an eventual war indicated that August 1914 was by no means an ideal moment for her to begin a conflict. Despite a French report of September 1912 pointing to a victory of the Triple Entente over the Central Powers, the findings were premised on Britain siding with France. One might have expected the French position to have improved since that date,

---

[21] John F. V. Keiger, *France and the World since 1870* (London: Arnold, 2001), p. 86.
[22] Barrère to Paris, July 30, 1914, No. 229, quoted in Poincaré, *Au service de la France*, vol. IV, p. 491.

particularly with the passing of the three-year military service law in August 1913. However, in the short term the introduction of the three-year law, far from being a benefit, was a clear source of disorganization for French military preparedness. The three-year law was only officially scheduled to have its full positive effect by 1916. Worse still, in the first year or so the passage from two to three years would clearly destabilize French army organization, as German military reports in 1913 and 1914 pointed out in some detail.[23] What the Germans observed, French decision-makers – military and civilian – experienced only too vividly. Thus, by the time of the July Crisis France's military position was far from optimal: overcrowded barracks, insufficient uniforms and equipment, a lack of officers and NCOs to instruct and train the new troops, and a woefully inadequate number of large training camps. The hoped-for benefit of larger numbers, quicker mobilization, and greater unit cohesion could not be expected for three years.[24]

Even though French military leaders continued to demonstrate optimism, their German counterparts spotted the opportunity provided by French weakness. During the summer of 1914, Chief of the German General Staff, Helmuth von Moltke, campaigned to convince the kaiser, the civilian authorities, and the Austrians that as a result of their new armaments programs, France and Russia would only possess more formidable forces in a few years' time. On July 25, 1914, the journalist Theodor Wolff was told by the German Secretary for Foreign Affairs, Gottlieb von Jagow, that although "neither Russia nor France wanted war ... The Russians were not ready with their armaments, they would not strike; in two years time, if we let matters slide, the danger would be much greater than at present."[25] On July 26, 1914, von Moltke remarked: "We shall never again strike as well as we do now, with France's and Russia's expansion of their armies incomplete."[26] As John Röhl has explained, the kaiser had also pointed out on July 6 that France and Russia were ill-prepared militarily and financially for conflict. The Bavarian military attaché in Berlin reported meetings with Moltke and other military leaders between July 26 and 28 in which Moltke had pointed "to the fact that France

---

[23] For example, Schoen to Bethmann-Hollweg, August 8, 1913; Winterfelt to Kriegsministerium, August 20, 1913; report on the impact of the three-year law from Chef des Generalstabes der Armee, February 1914, cited in Herrmann, *Arming of Europe*, p. 202.

[24] Herrmann, *Arming of Europe*, pp. 202–203

[25] T. Wolff, *Eve of 1914*, p. 448, quoted in Niall Ferguson, *The Pity of War: Explaining World War I* (New York: Basic Books, 1999), p. 151.

[26] Quoted in *ibid.*, p. 152.

finds herself in nothing less than military difficulties [and] that Russia feels everything but secure."[27]

Lack of military preparation and organizational deficiencies were not merely a perception of France's potential enemy. On July 13, 1914, the former army officer, Lorraine senator, and *rapporteur* for the Senate Army Commission, Charles Humbert, produced a grim catalog of France's military shortcomings. He warned of the inferiority of French field artillery compared with Germany's, the inadequacies of French fixed artillery, mortars, and the general shortage of munitions. Lack of preparation extended to the absence of neutral-color uniforms for the troops, outdated field equipment, and a deficiency of 2 million pairs of military boots. He pointed out that in the event of war the French soldier would have only one pair of boots, the reserve pair in his pack being thirty years old. Georges Clemenceau, France's future wartime leader, summed up on Bastille Day the Senate's shock and disbelief at the findings: "Since 1870, I have never attended as moving, as anguishing, as sorrowful a session of Parliament as I have today."[28]

Humbert's report caused a general stir across France. Even though senior officers, such as General Michelet, might disagree with the way Humbert had publicly aired his findings, he agreed about the poor state of the French army. On July 14, Michelet wrote a long letter to his regular correspondent, Antonin Dubost, President of the Senate, commenting on Humbert's findings and noting that "L'armée est un malade" and lamenting the terrible lack of army leaders.[29] War Minister Adolphe Messimy, in responding to Humbert's report compounded the problem by broadcasting to the world from the French Parliament the all too candid promise that most of France's military weaknesses would be addressed by 1917. That such forebodings about France's preparation for war were not mere exaggerations or the psychodramas of political opponents engaged in political point-scoring would be made clear, albeit too late, when by the end of August 1914 the German armies had swept across northern France to threaten Paris itself and bring France within a whisker

---

[27] Volker Berghahn, *Germany and the Approach of War in 1914*, 2nd edn. (London: Macmillan, 1993), p. 213.

[28] *Sénat*, July 13, 1914, 1199–1210; July 14, 1914, 1261–1272, quoted in John F. Godfrey, *Capitalism at War: Industrial Policy and Bureaucracy in France 1914–1918* (Oxford: Berg, 1987), pp. 46–47.

[29] General Michelet to Antonin Dubost, July 14, 1914, "Lettres adressées à Antonin Dubost Président du Sénat, par le Général Michelet (1914–19)," in Papiers Antonin Dubost, Archives départementales de l'Isère, Grenoble. For other clear examples of France's lack of readiness, see also General R. Alexandre, *Avec Joffre d'Agadir à Verdun* (Paris: Éditions Berger-Levrault, 1932), pp. 13–109, and especially the chapter "La loi de trois ans, la campagne de Charles," pp. 95–104.

of defeat. Although less directly implicated in the international train of events, Britain had at least begun to make initial preparations for war in July1914, according to the story current in London. British officials had done their preparatory work with respect to the army, navy, transport, and provision, and were finally to turn to finance when war began.[30]

One might therefore ask how France's Commander-in-Chief designate assessed France's readiness for war in 1914, as Joffre had advised against war at the time of Agadir for lack of readiness. Despite some improvements, France was not much better placed militarily in 1914 than it had been in 1911. But this did not appear to affect Joffre's assessment of France's ability to fight a war. The "offensive strategy" he had developed in the notorious Plan XVII – only itself completed in May 1914 – and the mentality that accompanied it, whereby, as some have sardonically remarked, even the customs officers attack, was the panacea for any weakness and blinded him to harsher realities. Joffre appears not to have been concerned by fundamental problems to do with France's readiness for war, even though he confessed to a lack of time to rejuvenate the high command, to complete infantry training, and to rectify inadequacies in heavy artillery.[31]

This position was exacerbated by France's assessment of Germany, which was far from accurate. The French High Command misjudged both the strength and direction of the German attack, as well as her use of reserves and heavy artillery, and quite wrongly based French strategy on an all-out early victory. Thus, as Christopher Andrew has pointed out, in the final years of peace "intelligence assessments were accepted by Operations and by Joffre only when they reinforced their 'pre-conceived ideas.'"[32] At the heart of those ideas was a blind faith in France's ability to win that transcended purely material preparation and was fairly conveyed in the Napoleonic dictum: "the morale is to the physical as two to one."[33] This mentality was partly a reflection of the civil–military divide in French society since the Dreyfus affair, whereby the military, and finally its strategic doctrine, had become isolated from mainstream society. A further contributor was that intelligence highlighting French inferiority to Germany was often dismissed as defeatist. Consequently, the French

---

[30] Barry J. Eichengreen, *Golden Fetters: The Gold Standard and the Great Depression, 1919–1939* (Oxford University Press, 1996), pp. 74–75.

[31] For Joffre's nonchalance, see Kiesling, "France," pp. 252–259; Gerd Krumeich, *Armaments and Politics in France on the Eve of the First World War* (Oxford: Berg, 1984), p. 23.

[32] C. M. Andrew, "France and the German Menace," in Ernest May (ed.), *Knowing One's Enemies: Intelligence Assessment before the Two World Wars* (Princeton University Press, 1984).

[33] For more on this, see Keiger, *France and the World*, pp. 86–87.

High Command was not encouraged to tailor strategy to French means, leading Joffre to take risks beyond the capabilities of his armies.[34]

French decision-makers, however, were less infected by Joffre's over-confidence and wishful thinking in July 1914, and more focused on the need to avoid war, or at least delay it, for as long as possible. On July 27 former premier, Charles Jonnart, wrote to ex-premier Alexandre Ribot, explaining what he had gleaned from just reading the newspapers. He expressed considerable anxiety at the international situation and France's vulnerable position, warning that: "It is obviously in Germany's interest to surprise us in the midst of our reorganization and before Russia has had time to construct the railways that will allow her to speed up her mobilisation."[35] Consistent with the war minister's confession to Parliament three weeks earlier on French military shortcomings, Poincaré described how on August 5, Minister of War Messimy had broken down in tears in Cabinet, head in his hands, when asked whether French officer and troop preparation and training could compensate for armament deficiencies, only to pull himself together and claim that victory would be France's.[36]

Financial unreadiness

France's lack of financial readiness was laid bare for her decision-makers in late July 1914. At that time France was seriously hamstrung by large structural debt brought on principally by increasing defense expenditure. In 1913, French defense expenditure as a percentage of net national product was the highest of the major powers (with the exception of Russia) at 4 percent, with defense representing 42 percent of public sector spending. Furthermore, France's national debt was higher than that of Britain, Germany, and Russia, so that by 1913 national debt as a percentage of net national product was a vertiginous 86.5 percent (compared with 27.6 percent for Britain, 44.4 percent for Germany and 47.3 percent for Russia). As a consequence, debt servicing accounted for the largest proportion of central government spending and was the highest of all the Great Powers.[37] French leaders were all too conscious of this, given its importance since the three-year law debate and its impact on the burning political question of whether an income tax should be implemented to pay for the additional expenditure.

---

[34] *Ibid.*, and for more on French military shortcomings compared with Germany, p. 53.
[35] Dr. A. Ribot (ed.), *Journal d'Alexandre Ribot et correspondances inédites, 1914–22* (Paris: Plon, 1936), p. 20.
[36] Poincaré, *Au service de la France*, vol. IV, p. 4.   [37] Ferguson, *Pity of War*, p. 128.

Heavy structural debt was compounded by short-term debt: France had a forecast deficit for 1914 of 794 million francs as a result of her latest military and naval expenditure. A loan was seen as the only means of paying for the three-year law, other than recourse to the very thorny political issue of the introduction of a much delayed and needed income tax. The extremely well-respected and experienced former Minister of Finance Alexandre Ribot, who would resume that portfolio at the outbreak of war, noted in his diary on May 15, 1914 that any government would have great difficulty in raising a loan given the present feeling in the French money markets.[38] In June, Ribot formed a new government and was able to see first hand the "critical" state of French finances. On June 11, he noted in his diary that "by the beginning of July there will be no resources available." On that day he decided to raise a loan of 800 million francs; but two days later the government had resigned.[39] A new government was formed and a loan floated. But on the eve of war, the parlous state of France's public finances was worsened by the failure of the July 1914 internal funding loan. Though intended to give the French government some financial headroom, it failed to do so because the loan was too small and a large proportion of the issue remained controlled by speculators. Ribot later described France's public finances on the eve of war as "singularly embarrassing."[40] France was financially unprepared for war.

A measure of the poor state of French finances in the last days of peace can also be taken from the much greater slump in French bonds than those of other major powers, except Russia. Whereas between July 18 and August 1 (the last day that quotations were published) the French 3 percent bond fell 7.8 percent, that of Germany fell by only 4 percent. Niall Ferguson claims that this allows us to infer what the City expected to happen in a purely continental war: the defeat of France and the victory of Germany, as in 1870. Such warnings of how others perceived France's chances in a war (without Britain) would not have gone unnoticed among French decision-makers in the last days of peace, and would certainly have led them to err on the side of caution, indeed, to try to avoid war altogether. On July 31, Lord Rothschild, the London banker, urged his French banking cousins to get Poincaré to impress upon the Russian government two things: first, that the outcome of the war, however powerful their ally might be, was doubtful and certain to produce enormous misery and sacrifice; and, second, that France was Russia's greatest creditor. Indeed, he went on, the financial and economic conditions of the two countries

[38] Ribot, *Journal*, p. 5.   [39] *Ibid.*, p. 16.
[40] Martin Horn, *Britain, France, and the Financing of the First World War* (Montreal: McGill-Queen's University Press, 2002), p. 20.

were intimately connected and, therefore, everything should be done to prevent a hideous struggle. Unlike political leaders, the bankers did not believe the war would be short.[41] The threat of French financial collapse was clear. France's "financial armament" was by no means primed for war.

What gave French leaders some financial reassurance for prosecuting a war was the excessive reliance that was placed on the 1911 agreement with the Bank of France, whereby France's large gold reserves would be used to advance funds to the French state to finance a short war, along the lines of the six-month 1870–1871 Franco-Prussian War. But even then not everybody was convinced that France's gold reserves would be enough. Nor was everyone convinced, including a number of French economists of the time, that the war would be that short. Some like the influential Polish-born banker Jean de Bloch, who predicted that the next war would be long, believed that France should pursue a pacific foreign policy that reflected her wealth, her foreign investments, and her stagnating population.[42] Although French political leaders might not necessarily have been aware of the views of bankers and economists, successive French finance ministers could not have failed to be concerned about France's precarious financial position.

Of course, the financial world had everything to lose from war and thus always shied from it. But financial exigencies exerted even more pressure on French leaders to secure wealthy Britain's entry into the war. The combined national income of France and Russia was roughly 15 percent smaller than that of Germany and Austria-Hungary without Britain. With Britain, the Triple Entente suddenly leapt to 60 percent superiority.[43] Hence, the need to defer to British sensibilities by not acting aggressively if France hoped to win Britain as an ally.

Unreadiness of French political leadership

Coming on top of France's lack of readiness for war in terms of allies, and military and financial preparation, was the widely publicized and almost complete absence from Paris of all her principal decision-makers: the President of the Republic, the premier, foreign minister, and the director of the Foreign Ministry; it was the justice minister who stood in for them in Paris. The cause was a state visit scheduled to last for over two weeks

---

[41] Ferguson, *Pity of War*, p. 193.
[42] For a fine explanation of the debate among economists in pre-war France on the likely financial effects of war and its duration, see Talbot Imlay and Martin Horn, "Thinking about War: French Financial Preparations and the Coming of the Two World Wars," *International History Review* 27(4) (2005): 709–753.
[43] Ferguson, *Pity of War*, p. 248.

from July 16 to July 31, and organized six months previously, to Russia, Sweden, Denmark, and Norway, by sea at a time when ship-to-shore radio transmission was in its infancy. This meant that France's key decision-makers were to a large extent isolated from crucial moments in the international crisis of late July until their forced return on July 29, only three days before French general mobilization and a mere five days before France had war declared on her. The Central Powers certainly perceived this as conferring an advantage on them and deliberately withheld issuing the Austrian ultimatum to Serbia until July 23, precisely because the state party would set sail from Russia that day for Scandinavia and would not be able to communicate with Russia, or France for that matter, while at sea. The diplomatic record shows that the occasional cable that did reach the ship *France* on which the French state party were travelling was often garbled. Until they finally cut short their trip to Denmark and Norway at the request of the Cabinet and returned to Dunkirk harbor on July 29, French leaders were less well informed of events, less able to communicate with other powers, in short, less ready for a conflict than any of their counterparts. It is unlikely that given this state of affairs, and France's poor state of readiness for war militarily and financially, that her leaders would have indulged in the luxury of encouraging or supporting war.[44]

Unreadiness of the French people

Added to the lack of readiness on all these fronts were doubts about the readiness of the French people to accept war. For some time French leaders had had concerns about the likelihood of the French population at large being ready to fight in the event of war being declared. The army General Staff calculated that up to 10 percent of French conscripts might fail to respond to the mobilization order.[45] Certainly, labor unrest was predicted if war did come about. France's major trade unions were committed to the idea of a general strike to stop mobilization and conflict until only a short time before war broke out. The assassination of France's erstwhile anti-war socialist leader, Jean Jaurès, on July 31, 1914, risked producing grave social unrest and anti-war demonstrations, according to the Paris Préfet de Police. As a precautionary measure two regiments of cavalry scheduled for departure to the east were kept back in Paris to deal

---

[44] Jean-Jacques Becker notes: "It is hard to imagine the leaders of the country indulging in the joys of tourism, even political, having plotted the outbreak of a European war," *1914: Comment les français sont entrés dans la guerre* (Paris: Fondation nationale des sciences politiques, 1977), p. 140.

[45] P. J. Flood, *France 1914–18: Public Opinion and the War Effort* (London: Macmillan, 1990), p. 15.

with any unrest. By August 1, the labor movement and parties of the left were undergoing a sea-change in their attitude to a potential war; anti-war sentiment was being replaced by that old Republican reflex and national rallying cry of "la patrie en danger."[46]

But this put even more pressure on French leaders to act cautiously and avoid giving the impression of France acting aggressively as conflict loomed. Poincaré acted and spoke to that effect on the night of August 1–2 when visited urgently by the Russian ambassador, who had come to ask what France would do now that Germany had declared war on Russia, a clear indication that no commitment had been made to Russia. Poincaré told Isvolsky that France "would naturally meet her commitments and would respect the alliance," but he did not want to be forced into declaring war on Germany. Poincaré advised that "it would be better if we were not forced to declare it and that it be declared on us. All that for both military reasons and for domestic political motives: a defensive war would lift the whole country; a declaration of war by us could leave doubts about the alliance with part of public opinion."[47]

This author has found no evidence to show that this means of proceeding was part of some cunning entrapment of Germany; on the contrary, given the fragile condition of France's domestic opinion and the uncertain position of Britain, it was a continuation of the prudent, defensive, and cautiously reactive measures France continued to take during the crisis. Certainly, the Germans believed that France had been, and continued to be, a restraining influence on Russia. As German Chancellor Bethmann-Hollweg explained on July 16, 1914:

We have grounds to assume and cannot but wish, that France, at the moment burdened with all sorts of cares, will do everything to restrain Russia from intervention ... If we succeed in not only keeping France quiet herself but in getting her to enjoin peace on St. Petersburg, this will have a repercussion on the Franco-Russian alliance highly favourable to ourselves.[48]

Even as late as July 29, Germany continued to believe that France was "setting all levers in motion at St. Petersburg to exercise a moderating influence there."[49]

---

[46] For more detail on how French leaders skillfully handled the assassination of Jaurès, see Keiger, "France," pp. 130–131; also A. Kriegel and J-J. Becker, *1914: La guerre et le mouvement ouvrier français* (Paris: Armand Colin, 1964), pp. 114–133.

[47] Poincaré diary, Bibliothèque nationale de France, August 2, 1914, Poincaré papers, nouvelles acquisitions françaises 16027, vol. 36, p. 138.

[48] Luigi Albertini, *The Origins of the War of 1914*, 3 vols., trans. and ed. Isabella M. Massey (London: Oxford University Press, 1952–1957), vol. 2, p. 160.

[49] *Ibid.*, p. 161.

Even Germany's diplomatic representatives in Paris felt that France wanted to avoid war. Following a meeting with French Premier and Foreign Minister René Viviani on July 29, 1914, the German ambassador, von Schoen, telegraphed his report to Berlin. The despatch was intercepted by the French authorities and later deciphered. Von Schoen concluded his report with the words: "Viviani does not wish to abandon the hope of maintaining peace that is deeply wished for here."[50] The Bavarian minister in Paris wrote on August 4, 1914, to the king before leaving France: "I had until the last moment the impression that the French government wanted to avoid war at any cost."[51]

France had neither the inclination nor the incentive to seek war in July or August 1914. She was intent on maintaining the Franco-Russian alliance, but as I have attempted to demonstrate elsewhere, not at any price. Ever since 1912 in his dealings with St. Petersburg Poincaré had feared that Russia could drag France into a war that France's population was unlikely to accept and that might shatter the nation's brittle unity.[52] There was also the knowledge that neither France nor Russia were ready militarily or financially to fight a war in the short term, and would not be so for another two years or more.

Almost a century before the First World War, the strategic military thinker Clausewitz insisted that a "trinity" of the people, the state and the armed forces all had to play their correct parts for the successful conduct of war. In July 1914, French political leaders were all too conscious of France's lack of readiness for war in four essential areas: allies, arms, finance, and public opinion. Two days after war had been declared on France by Germany, Poincaré recorded in his diaries his "serious apprehensions" as to France's future.[53] His *post hoc* risk assessment does not convey great optimism. Other than the grim prospect of the devastation of war itself, Poincaré's apprehension was stimulated by a series of questions as to France's readiness for war. The diplomatic situation was better than it had been with Russia and Britain on side, he reflected, but was not German military preparation superior to that of France? He recognized that the three-year law had helped to remedy France's inferiority, but "it is still, however, a long way from having produced all its effects." He added that pre-war criticism in the French Senate from the likes of

---

[50] Quoted in Poincaré, *Au service de la France*, vol. IV. The despatch was intercepted by French intelligence and deciphered later when the French had rebroken the German code.

[51] *Le Temps*, March 7, 1922, in MAE, *Europe 1918–1940*, sous série Allemagne, vol. 327, f. 113; for other German assessments of France's reluctance for war, see Kiesling, "France," p. 239, n. 52.

[52] Keiger, *France and the Origins*, especially chapter on Russia.

[53] Poincaré, *Au service de la France*, vol. IV, p. 2.

Georges Clemenceau and Charles Humbert on France's readiness for war "were not, unfortunately, without foundation." He lapsed into a catalog of France's military shortcomings: the lack of heavy artillery; the French Parliament's delay in voting through the loan and the exceptional line of credit which had delayed the rebuilding of military hardware; the disadvantages of France's 75-mm canon displayed in the recent Balkan wars, whose flat trajectory, unlike that of its German counterpart, denied French gunners the ability to drop shells over hillsides; Germany's considerable numerical superiority in heavy artillery and munitions. Poincaré confessed on August 5: "If I myself feel some doubt, can I admit it to myself? Most of all can I let it be detected by others?"[54] While declaring his morale to be optimistic, his spirit, he wrote, was less so and he concluded: "it is not without anxiety that I await the first clashes." All this he summed up with a reference to his old Republican hero and former premier, Jules Simon, who had written twenty years previously almost to the day that although Frenchmen were repeatedly told that their army was invincible in the face of Germany this ignored the fact that Germany had worked as hard as France and "it was no longer a case of heroic war, but of scientific war. Glory, which used to be won by courage, is now only won by tools and numbers."[55] Poincaré reflected that such words were all the more poignant today. Compared with German military preparations, those of France had been "very mediocre and very lazy." France might have on her side "our courage and our right,"[56] but clearly for Poincaré, France was not ready for war and had not been since well before the conflict began. As late and as unsystematic as it was, this risk assessment confirmed France's lack of readiness, and thus implicitly the irrationality of France and Poincaré having willed or encouraged conflict.

French decision-making in a theoretical context

Whether political leaders caught up in the complexities of a process that leads to war measure the impact of each decision on the possible outbreak of war, as Jean Baptiste Duroselle asks, is unlikely. But all rationality does not evaporate in such a context. Given the non-existence of French Cabinet minutes it is hard to know whether the French government conducted any systematic risk assessment of the perils of going to war. What can be said is that precisely because French leaders were aware that France was not physically or psychologically prepared for war and would not be so for two to three years, it made no sense to encourage war, rather

---

[54] *Ibid.*, pp. 4–5.   [55] *Ibid.*   [56] *Ibid.*

to delay it. This held France back in the July Crisis politically and militarily; her actions were largely reactive and defensive. In so doing her leaders were behaving rationally; rational choice was aligned with objective material conditions. France followed the path of restraint in this way partly because she risked losing a war if one did break out, but also because without a clear demonstration to the outside world of self-restraint she might have one more enemy (Italy), one less ally (Britain), and a recalcitrant population with which to wage war. That was enough to make any leader proceed cautiously. It is reasonable to conclude that given the logic of their own perceptions and fears, as well as their recorded fears and actions, French leaders did not seek a conflict; indeed, they clearly sought to avoid one. However, post-war international and domestic agendas would see to it that the self-restraint view of France's role in the origins of the war was hotly contested.

The question remains as to why France, seemingly unready for conflict, did in the end go to war in 1914. The short answer is that war was declared on her by Germany on August 3. It is hard to see how this could have been avoided without deliberately placing French security at the mercy of Germany – for example, by ceasing mobilization and surrendering defensive fortifications, as Germany demanded. She was now fighting a defensive war against German aggression. But, even if the decision had not been made for her, French leaders would probably still have felt compelled to fight. Like Britain, it was for negative reasons – because not to have done so would have been a threat to her national security in the short and long term. It was not simply a case of wishing slavishly to honor the Franco-Russian alliance, but because she was not willing to live, as she had done from 1871 to 1892, in the shadow of German domination of the Continent, which would have reemerged from the defeat of Russia. This would have been a more complete domination than after 1871, and won by a more powerful, more unpredictable, and more aggressive Germany than that of Bismarck. In the end, France was constrained by events into going to war. She was forced to fight, however reluctantly, not only because the long-term threat of German domination outweighed France's lack of preparation, but also because the immediate demands that Germany was making in July 1914 were such that no French politician of any party, and no soldier, could possibly concede them, whatever the consequences. To insist that they somehow could or should have behaved differently seems unhistorical, even unreasonable.

The example of the French case in the outbreak of the First World War raises in more general historical terms the fundamental question as to whether leaders do always conduct a serious risk analysis before embarking on paths that might lead to war. Indeed, it is legitimate to ask whether the choices clear to the historian with hindsight are necessarily evident to the leader in the fog of pre-war, whether decision-makers do look many moves ahead of the game, or even if they know, unlike the historian, what is the nature of the game.[57] In his recent excellent work on the outbreak of the 1914 war, the historian Christopher Clark leaves, however, little room for the fog of pre-war when he states that:

The key decision-makers walked towards danger in watchful, calculated steps. The outbreak of war was the culmination of chains of decisions made by political actors with conscious objectives who were capable of a degree of self-reflection acknowledged by a range of options and formed the best judgments they could on the basis of the information they had to hand.[58]

This conforms to the "rational actor model" developed by Allison in 1971, whereby states have certain "national interests" that political leaders seek to maximize through careful weighing of costs and benefits.[59] If such rationality did characterize the French case, then lack of readiness for war should equate to French self-restraint and passivity during the July Crisis.

Even if the rational actor model supports the argument of this chapter, it provides an incomplete picture of decision-making in July 1914 and especially in France. Rational actor theory allows little room for a major preoccupation of the historian, as distinct from the social scientist – the human dimension and the particular case. It does not give sufficient place *inter alia* to the vagaries of political leaders' personalities, emotional states, or their flawed information-processing.[60] Nor does it allow for what is of particular relevance to the French case in the July Crisis: the extent to which decision-makers suffer stress during international crises and make flawed judgments. Were French decision-makers able to take decisions at optimal levels given the stress of being isolated from events as a result of their visit to Russia and Scandinavia at the height of the crisis, and given the pressure of having to assimilate a host of information from multiple sources on their return from Russia? Unlike other nations' leaders the degree to which the French were playing catch-up, or ought to have been doing so, cannot be underestimated in their assessment and decision-taking. This was a high stakes game for all parties, but for the French

---

[57] Levy, "Initiation and Spread of the First World War," p. 186.

[58] Clark, *Sleepwalkers*, pp. xxv–xxvi.

[59] Graham Allison, *Essence of Decision: Explaining the Cuban Missile Crisis* (New York: Little, Brown, 1971).

[60] Jack S. Levy, "Political Psychology and Foreign Policy," in David O. Sears, Leonie Huddy, and Robert Jervis (eds.), *Oxford Handbook of Political Psychology* (New York: Oxford University Press, 2003), pp. 253–284.

leaders stress, shorter decision times, and information overload were more acute than for most powers. Both historians and social scientists would do well to consider the political psychology of decision-making in 1914.[61]

How else might psychological theory help us to comprehend French decision-making and attitudes in July 1914? With respect to the all-important question of leaders' willingness to take risks, "prospect theory" suggests that risk propensity varies with the situation. In situations involving choices among positive outcomes (relative to a reference point), people tend to be risk averse. In choices among bad outcomes, people tend to be risk acceptant.[62] But different individuals in the same situation will behave differently. France's dominant decision-maker in 1914 was the Lorrainer Raymond Poincaré, whose personality and temperament were highly unsuited to risk. Poincaré was risk averse. For him decision-taking was a very slow process that could be completed only when all possible consequences had been weighed, and even then hesitancy or fence-sitting was a common feature of his behavior. From early in his political career his friends nicknamed him "Prudence Lorraine." "He hurries to abstain!" was how colleagues had characterized his behavior since the 1880s.[63] More than most Great Power leaders at this time, Poincaré was by nature temperamentally the least likely to risk war or to encourage it, and all the more so given the country's clear lack of readiness for war.

It is a truism that the promotion or willing of war involves risk. But how particular states assess that risk and react to it at any one time varies considerably. Even within those states how individual leaders, permanent officials, and soldiers assess the risk individually and collectively is of similar variability. As rationally as individuals might theoretically be assumed to behave, they might be making the right decisions for the wrong reasons, or vice versa. The interaction of psychological variables with political and strategic conditions needs to be at the heart of any analysis of foreign policy decision-taking, and all the more so of decisions for war. Without it any understanding of the process by which the Great Powers assessed the risk of war and embarked on it in 1914 will be incomplete.

---

[61] Levy, "Political Psychology and Foreign Policy," p. 262.
[62] For a summary of the theory and applications to international relations, see Jack S. Levy, "Prospect Theory, Rational Choice, and International Relations," *International Studies Quarterly* 41(1) (1997): 87–112.
[63] Keiger, *Poincaré*, pp. 22–23.

References

Adamov, Evgeniĭ Aleksandrovich (ed.). *Konstantinopol' i prolivy po sekretnym dokumentam b. ministerstva inostrannykh del*, 2 vols. Moscow: Izdanie Litizdat NKID, 1925.

Afflerbach, Holger. "The Topos of Improbable War in Europe before 1914," in Holger Afflerbach and David Stevenson (eds.), *An Improbable War? The Outbreak of World War I and European Political Culture before 1914*. New York: Berghahn, 2007, pp. 161–182.

Der Dreibund: Europäische Großmacht- und Allianzpolitik vor dem Ersten Weltkrieg. Vienna: Böhlau, 2002.

Afflerbach, Holger and David Stevenson (eds.). *An Improbable War? The Outbreak of World War I and European Political Culture*. New York: Berghahn, 2007.

Albertini, Luigi *The Origins of the War of 1914*, trans. and ed. Isabella M. Massey, 3 vols. London: Oxford University Press, 1952–1957.

Alexandre, General R. *Avec Joffre d'Agadir à Verdun*. Paris: Éditions Berger-Levrault, 1932.

Allain, Jean Claude. *Joseph Caillaux: le défi victorieux*. Paris: Imprimerie Nationale, 1978.

Allison, Graham. *Essence of Decision: Explaining the Cuban Missile Crisis*, New York: Little, Brown, 1971.

Amson, Daniel. *Poincaré l'acharné de la politique*. Paris: Tallandier, 1997.

Anderson, Matthew S. *The Eastern Question, 1774–1923*. Basingstoke: Macmillan, 1966.

Andrew, C. M. "France and the German Menace," in Ernest May (ed.), *Knowing One's Enemies: Intelligence Assessment before the Two World Wars*. Princeton University Press, 1984.

Angelow, Jürgen. *Der Weg in die Urkatastrophe: Der Zerfall des Alten Europa 1900–1914*. Berlin: be.bra verlag, 2010.

Kalkül und Prestige: Der Zweibund am Vorabend des Ersten Weltkrieges. Cologne: Böhlau, 2000.

Ascher, Abraham. *P. A. Stolypin: The Search for Stability in Late Imperial Russia*. Stanford University Press, 2001.

Astafiev, I. I. *Russko–Germanskie Diplomaticheskie Otosheni'ia, 1905–1914: Ot Portsmutskogo Mira do Potsdamskogo Soglashenia*. Moscow: n.p. 1972.

Bark, P. L. "Iul'skie dni 1914 goda: nachalo velikoi voiny," *Vozrozhdenie* 91 (1959): 17–45.

Barnes, Harry Elmer. *The Genesis of the World War*, 2nd edn. New York: Alfred A. Knopf, 1927.

Barros, Andrew and Frédéric Guelton. "Les imprévus de l'histoire instrumentalisée: le livre jaune de 1914 et les documents diplomatiques français sur les origines de la Grande Guerre, 1914–1928," *Guerres mondiales et conflits contemporains*, 2006.

Bartlett, C. J. *Peace, War, and the European Powers, 1814–1914*. Basingstoke: Palgrave Macmillan, 1996.

Basily, Nicolas de. *Memoirs: Diplomat of Imperial Russia, 1903–1917*. Stanford, CA: Hoover Institution Press, 1973.

Baumgart, Winfried. *Europäisches Konzert und nationale Bewegung. Internationale Beziehungen 1830–1878*. Paderborn: Schöningh, 1999.

Becker, Jean-Jacques. *1914: Comment les français sont entrés dans la guerre*. Paris: Presses de la Fondation nationale des sciences politiques, 1977.

Berghahn, Volker R. *Germany and the Approach of War in 1914*. New York: St. Martin's Press, 1973 (2nd edn. London: Macmillan, 1993).

Bestuzhev, Igor V. *Bor'ba v Rossii po voprosam vneshnei politiki 1906–1910*. Moscow: Nauka, 1961.

Bismarck, Otto von. *Gesammelte Werke, 1874–1876*, ed. Bendick Rainer. Paderborn: Schöningh, 2005.

Bittner, Ludwig, Alfred F. Pribram, Heinrich Srbik, and Hans Uebersberger (eds.). *Österreich-Ungarns Außenpolitik von der Bosnischen Krise bis zum Kriegsausbruch*, 9 vols. Vienna: Österreichischer Bundesverlag für Unterricht, Wissenschaft & Kunst, 1930.

Bled, Jean-Paul, *François-Joseph*. Paris: Fayard, 1987.

Bobroff, Ronald P. *Roads to Glory: Late Imperial Russia and the Turkish Straits*. London: I. B. Tauris, 2006.

Bosworth, R. J. B. "Italy and the End of the Ottoman Empire," in Marion Kent (ed.), *The Great Powers and the End of the Ottoman Empire*. London: Allen & Unwin, 1984, pp. 51–72.

Italy, the Least of the Great Powers: Italian Foreign Policy before the First World War. Cambridge University Press, 1979.

Bovykin, Valerii I. *Iz istorii voznikno veniia pervoi mirovoi voiny (Otnosheniia Rossii i Frantsii 1912–1914 kummun period after im. 1914 gg.)*. Moscow: Izd-vo Mosk. universiteta, 1961.

Bremer, Stuart A. "Advancing the Scientific Study of War," in Stuart A. Bremer and Thomas R. Cusack (eds.), *The Process of War: Advancing the Scientific Study of War*. Amsterdam: Gordon & Breach, 1995, pp. 1–34.

Brett, Maurice V. (ed.). *Journals and Letters of Reginald Viscount Esher*, 4 vols. London: Nicholson & Watson, 1934–1938.

Bridge, F. R. *The Habsburg Monarchy among the Great Powers, 1815–1918*. New York: Berg, 1990.

Great Britain and Austria-Hungary, 1906–1914: A Diplomatic History. London: Littlehampton Book Services, 1972.

Brock, Michael. "Britain Enters the War," in R. J. W. Evans and Hartmut P. von Strandmann (eds.), *The Coming of the First World War*. Oxford: Clarendon Press, 1988, pp. 145–178.

Brose, Eric Dorn. *A History of the Great War: World War One and the International Crisis of the Early Twentieth Century*. Oxford University Press, 2010.

Brown, Michael E., Owen R. Coté, Jr., Sean M. Lynn-Jones, and Steven E. Miller (eds.). *Offense, Defense, and War*. Cambridge, MA: MIT Press, 2004.

Buchanan, George. *My Mission to Russia*, vol. 1. Boston, MA: Little, Brown, 1923.

Bueno de Mesquita, Bruce. *The War Trap*. New Haven, CT: Yale University Press, 1981.

Caldwell, C. E. *Field-Marshal Sir Henry Wilson: His Life and Diaries*, 2 vols. London: Cassell, 1927.

Canis, Konrad. *Der Weg in den Abgrund: Deutsche Außenpolitik 1902–1914*. Paderborn: Ferdinand Schöningh, 2011.

Carter, Miranda. *George, Nicholas and Wilhelm: Three Royal Cousins and the Road to World War I*. New York: Random House, 2009.

Choucri, Nazli and Robert C. North. *Nations in Conflict*. San Francisco, CA: W. H. Freeman, 1975.

Christensen, Thomas J. and Jack Snyder. "Chain Gangs and Passed Bucks," *International Organization* 44(2) (1990): 137–168.

Clark, Christopher. *The Sleepwalkers: How Europe Went to War in 1914*. New York and London: HarperCollins and Allen Lane, 2012/2013.

Kaiser Wilhelm II: Profiles in Power. London: Longman, 2000.

Colaresi, Michael P., Karen Rasler, and William R. Thompson. *Strategic Rivalry: Space, Position and Conflict Escalation in World Politics*. Cambridge University Press, 2007.

Conze, Eckart. "'Wer von Europa spricht, hat unrecht': Aufstieg und Verfall des vertraglichen multilateralismus im Europäischen Staatensystem des 19. Jahrhunderts," *Historisches Jahrbuch* 121 (2001): 214–241.

Copeland, Dale C. "A Tragic Choice: Japanese Preventive Motivations and the Origins of the Pacific War," *International Interactions* 37(1) (2011): 116–126.

The Origins of Major War. Ithaca, NY: Cornell University Press, 2000.

Cornwall, Mark. "Serbia," in Keith Wilson (ed.), *Decisions for War, 1914*. New York: St. Martin's Press, 1995, pp. 55–96.

Craig, Gordon A. *The Politics of the Prussian Army, 1640–1945*. Oxford University Press, 1955.

Dedijer, Vladimir. *The Road to Sarajevo*. New York: Simon & Schuster, 1966.

DiCicco, Jonathan M. and Jack S. Levy. "Power Shifts and Problem Shifts: The Evolution of the Power Transition Research Program," *Journal of Conflict Resolution* 43(6) (1999): 675–704.

Diehl, Paul F. and Gary Goertz. *War and Peace in International Rivalry*. University of Michigan Press, 2000.

Doering-Manteuffel, Anselm. "Internationale Geschichte als Systemgeschichte des 19. und 20. Janhrhunderts," in Wilfried Loth and Jürgen Osterhammel (eds.), *Internationale Geschichte: Themen–Ergebnisse–Aussichten*. Munich: Oldenbourg, 2000.

Doughty, Robert A. *Pyrrhic Victory: French Strategy and Operations in the Great War*. Cambridge, MA: Harvard University Press, 2005.

Duroselle, J-B. "Preface," in Georges-Henri Soutou, *L'or et le sang. Les buts de guerre économiques de la première guerre mondiale*. Paris: Fayard, 1989.

Eichengreen, Barry J. *Golden Fetters: The Gold Standard and the Great Depression, 1919–1939*. Oxford University Press, 1996.

Ekstein, Michael G. "Great Britain and the Triple Entente on the Eve of the Sarajevo Crisis," in F. H. Hinsley (ed.), *British Foreign Policy under Sir Edward Grey*. Cambridge University Press, 1977, pp. 342–348.

Elman, Colin and Miriam Fendius Elman. "Introduction: Negotiating International History and Politics," in Colin Elman and Miriam Fendius Elman (eds.), *Bridges and Boundaries: Historians, Political Scientists and the Study of International Relations*. Cambridge, MA: MIT Press, 2001, pp. 1–36.

Epkenhans, Michael. "Was a Peaceful Outcome Thinkable? The Naval Race before 1914," in Holger Afflerbach and David Stevenson (eds.), *An Improbable War? The Outbreak of World War I and European Political Culture before 1914*. New York: Berghahn, 2007, pp. 113–129.

Fallodon, Viscount Grey of. *Twenty-Five Years, 1892–1916*. New York: Stokes, 1925.

Fay, Sidney B. *The Origins of the World War*, 2 vols., rev. 2nd edn. New York: Macmillan, 1930.

The Origins of the World War, 2 vols. New York: Macmillan, [1928] 1966.

Fearon, James D. "Rationalist Explanations for War," *International Organization* 49(3) (1995): 379–414.

Fellner, Fritz. "Die 'Mission Hoyos'" [1976] and "Zwischen Kriegsbegeisterung und Resignation – ein Memorandum des Sektionschefs Forgách von Jänner 1915" [1975], in Heidrun Maschl and Brigitte Mazohl-Wallnig (eds.), *Vom Dreibund zum Völkerbund: Studien zur Geschichte der internationalen Beziehungen, 1882–1919*. Vienna: Verlag für Geschichte und Politik, 1994, pp. 112–141 and 142–154.

(ed.). *Schicksaljahre Österreichs, 1908–1919: Das politische Tagebuch Josef Redlichs*, 2 vols. Graz: Böhlau, 1953.

Ferguson, Niall. "Virtual History: Toward a 'Chaotic' Theory of the Past," in Niall Ferguson (ed.), *Virtual History: Alternatives and Counterfactuals*. New York: Basic Books, 1999, pp. 1–90.

The Pity of War: Explaining World War I. New York: Basic Books, 1999.

"Public Finance and National Security: The Domestic Origins of the First World War Revisited," *Past and Present* 142(1) (1994): 141–168.

Fischer, Fritz. *Krieg der Illusionen: Die deutsche Politik von 1911 bis 1914*. Düsseldorf: Droste, 1969; translated as *War of Illusions: German Policies from 1911 to 1914*, trans. Marian Jackson. New York: W. W. Norton, 1975.

Griff nach der Weltmacht. Düsseldorf: Droste, 1961; English edition: *Germany's Aims in the First World War*. New York: W. W. Norton, 1967.

Griff nach der Weltmacht: Die Kriegsziele des Kaiswerlichen Deutschland, 1914/18, 3rd edn. Düsseldorf: Droste, 1964.

Fisher, H. H. (ed.). *Out of My Past: The Memoirs of Count Kokovtsov*, trans. Laura Matveev. Stanford University Press, 1935.

Flood, P. J. *France 1914–18: Public Opinion and the War Effort*. London: Macmillan, 1990.

Foley, Robert (ed.). *Alfred von Schlieffen's Military Writings*. Routledge: London, 2002.

Förster, Stig. "Im Reich des Absurden: Die Ursachen des Ersten Weltkrieges," in Bern Wegner, Ernst Willi Hansen, Kerstin Rehwinkel, and Matthias Reiss (eds.), *Wie Kriege entstehen: Zum historischen Hintergrund von Staatenpolitik.* Paderborn: Ferdinand Schöningh, 2000, pp. 211–252.

"Dreams and Nightmares: German Military Leadership and the Images of Future Warfare, 1871–1914," in Manfred F. Boemeke, Roger Chickering, and Stig Förster (eds.), *Anticipating Total War: The German and American Experiences, 1871–1914.* Washington, DC: German Historical Institute, 1999, pp. 343–376.

"Der deutsche Generalstab und die Illusion des kurzen Krieges, 1871–1914. Metakritik eines Mythos," *Militärgeschichtliche Mitteilungen* 54(10) (1995): 61–95.

Der doppelte Militarismus: Die deutsche Rüstungspolitik zwischen Status-Quo-Sicherung und Aggression. Wiesbaden: Steiner, 1985.

Frantz, Günther. *Russlands Eintritt in den Weltkrieg: Der Ausbau der russischen Wehrmacht und ihr Einsatz bei Kriegsausbruch.* Berlin: Deutsche Verlagsgesellschaft für Politik & Geschichte, 1924.

Fromkin, David. *Europe's Last Summer: Who Started the Great War?* New York: Alfred A. Knopf, 2004.

Fuller, William C., Jr. *Strategy and Power in Russia, 1600–1914.* New York: Free Press, 1992.

"The Russian Empire," in Ernest R. May (ed.), *Knowing One's Enemies: Intelligence Assessment before the Two World Wars.* Princeton University Press, 1984, pp. 98–126.

Gatrell, Peter. "Poor Russia, Poor Show: Mobilising a Backward Economy for War 1914–1917," in Stephen Broadberry and Mark Harrison (eds.), *The Economics of World War I.* Cambridge University Press, 2005, pp. 235–275.

Government, Industry and Rearmament in Russia, 1900–1914: The Last Argument of Tsarism. Cambridge University Press, 1994.

Geiss, Imanuel. "Kurt Riezler und der erste Weltkrieg," in Imanuel Geiss, Fritz Fischer, and Bernd Jürgen Wendt (eds.), *Deutschland und die Weltpolitik des 19. und 20. Jahrhundert.* Düsseldorf: Bertelsmann Universitätsverlag, 1973, p. 401.

(ed.). *July 1914: The Outbreak of the First World War: Selected Documents.* New York: Scribner, 1967.

(ed.). *Julikrise und Kreigsausbruch 1914,* 2 vols. Hanover: Verlag für Literatur & Zeitgeschenen, 1964.

George, Alexander L. (ed.). *Avoiding Inadvertent War: Problems of Crisis Management.* Boulder, CO: Westview Press, 1991.

George, Alexander L. and Andrew Bennett. *Case Studies and Theory Development in the Social Sciences.* Cambridge, MA: MIT Press, 2005.

George, Alexander L. and Richard Smoke. *Deterrence in American Foreign Policy: Theory and Practice.* New York: Columbia University Press, 1974.

Geyer, Dietrich. *Der Russisiche Imperialismus: Studien über den Zusammenhang von Innerer und Auswärtiger Politik, 1860–1914.* Göttingen: Vandenhoeck & Ruprecht, 1977; translated as *Russian Imperialism: The Interaction of Domestic and Foreign Policy, 1860–1914,* trans. Bruce Little. New Haven, CT: Yale University Press, 1987.

Gilbert, Arthur N. and Paul Gordon Lauren. "Crisis Management: An Assessment and a Critique," *Journal of Conflict Resolution* 24(4) (1980): 641–644.

Gilpin, Robert. *War and Change in World Politics*. New York: Cambridge University Press, 1981.

Girault, René. *Emprunts russes et investissements français en Russie, 1887–1914*. Paris: Colin, 1973.

Glaser, Charles. *Rational Theory of International Politics*. Princeton University Press, 2010.

Godfrey, John F. *Capitalism at War: Industrial Policy and Bureaucracy in France 1914–1918*. Oxford: Berg, 1987.

Goertz, Gary and Jack S. Levy. "Causal Explanation, Necessary Conditions, and Case Studies," in Gary Goertz and Jack S. Levy (eds.), *Explaining War and Peace: Case Studies and Necessary Condition Counterfactuals*. London: Routledge, 2007, pp. 9–45.

Gooch, George P. *Franco-German Relations, 1871–1914*. London: Longman, Green, 1923.

Gooch, George P., Harold Temperley, and Lillian Penson (eds.). *British Documents on the Origins of the War 1898–1914*, 11 vols. London: HMSO, 1926–1938.

Gordon, Michael. "Domestic Conflict and the Origins of the First World War," *Journal of Modern History* 46(2) (1974): 191–226.

Gregory, Paul R. *Russian National Income, 1885–1913*. Cambridge University Press, 1982.

Gutsche, Willibald. *Aufstieg und Fall eines kaiserlichen Reichskanzlers: Theobald von Bethmann Hollweg, 1856–1921. Ein politisches Lebensbild*. East Berlin: Akademie Verlag, 1973.

Haber, Stephen, David M. Kennedy, and Stephen D. Krasner. "Brothers Under the Skin: Diplomatic History and International Relations," *International Security* 22(1) (1997): 34–43.

Halfond, Irwin. *Maurice Paléologue: The Diplomat, the Writer, the Man, and the Third French Republic*. Lanham, MD: University Press of America, 2007.

Hall, Richard. *The Balkan Wars, 1912–1913: Prelude to the First World War*. London: Routledge, 2000.

Halpern, Paul G. *The Mediterranean Naval Situation 1908–1914*. Cambridge, MA: Harvard University Press, 1971.

Hamilton, Richard F. and Holger H. Herwig (eds.). *The Origins of the First World War*. Cambridge University Press, 2003.

War Planning 1914. Cambridge University Press, 2010.

Harris, J. Paul. "Great Britain," in Richard F. Hamilton and Holger H. Herwig (eds.), *The Origins of World War I*. Cambridge University Press, 2003, pp. 266–299.

Hayne, M. B. *The French Foreign Office and the Origins of the First World War*. Oxford: Clarendon Press, 1993.

Helmreich, E. C. *The Diplomacy of the Balkan Wars, 1912–1913*. Cambridge, MA: Harvard University Press, 1938.

Herrmann, David G. *The Arming of Europe and the Making of the First World War*. Princeton University Press, 1996.

Herwig, Holger H. "Germany," in Richard F. Hamilton and Holger H. Herwig (eds.), *The Origins of World War I*. Cambridge University Press, 2003, pp. 150–187.

"Why Did It Happen?" in Richard F. Hamilton and Holger H. Herwig (eds.), *The Origins of World War I*. Cambridge University Press, 2003, pp. 443–468.

The First World War: Germany and Austria-Hungary, 1914–1918. London: Arnold, 1997.

"Strategic Uncertainties of a Nation-State: Prussia–Germany, 1871–1918," in Williamson Murray, MacGregor Knox, and Alvin Bernstein (eds.), *The Making of Strategy: Rulers, States, and War.* Cambridge University Press, 1994, pp. 242–277.

Hewitson, Mark. *Germany and the Causes of the First World War.* Oxford: Berg, 2004.

Hildebrand, Klaus. *Das Vergangene Reich: Deutsche Außenpolitik zwischen Bismarck und Hitler.* Stuttgart: Deutsche Verlags-Anstalt, 1995.

Hillgruber, Andreas. *Deutsche Großmacht- und Weltpolitik im 19. und 20. Jahrhundert.* Düsseldorf: Droste, 1979.

Höbelt, Lothar. *Franz Joseph I. Der Kaiser und sein Reich: Eine politische Geschichte.* Vienna: Böhlau, 2009.

Hoffmann, Dieter. *Der Sprung ins Dunkle: Oder Wie der 1. Weltkrieg entfesselt Wurde.* Leipzig: Militzke, 2010.

Höhne, Heinz. *Der Krieg im Dunkeln: Macht und Einfluß der deutschen und russischen Geheimdienste.* Munich: C. Bertelsmann, 1985.

Holsti, Ole R. "Historians, Social Scientists, and Crisis Management: An Alternative View," *Journal of Conflict Resolution* 24(4) (1980): 665–682.

Crisis, Escalation, War. Montreal: McGill-Queens University Press, 1972.

Hopman, Albert. *Das ereignisreiche Leben eines "Wilhelminers": Tagebücher, Briefe, Aufzeichnungen 1901 bis 1920,* ed. Michael Epkenhans. Munich: Oldenbourg, 2004.

Horn, Martin. *Britain, France, and the Financing of the First World War.* Montreal: McGill-Queen's University Press, 2002.

Horne, John. *Labour at War: France and Britain, 1914–1918.* Oxford University Press, 1991.

Hosking, Geoffrey A. *The Russian Constitutional Experiment: Government and Duma, 1907–1914.* Cambridge University Press, 1973.

Hötzendorf, Franz Conrad von. *Aus meiner Dienstzeit, 1906–1918,* 5 vols. Vienna: Rikola, 1921–1925.

Howard, Michael. *Clausewitz: A Very Short Introduction.* Oxford University Press, 2002.

Huddy, Leonie, David O. Sears, and Jack S. Levy (eds.). *Oxford Handbook of Political Psychology,* 2nd edn. Oxford University Press, 2013.

Imlay, Talbot and Martin Horn. "Thinking about War: French Financial Preparations and the Coming of the Two World Wars," *International History Review* 27(4) (2005): 709–753.

Janorschke, Johannes. *Bismarck, Europa, und die "Krieg in Sicht"-Krise von 1875.* Paderborn: Schöningh, 2010.

Jarausch, Konrad H. "Statesmen versus Structure: Germany's Role in the Outbreak of World War One Reconsidered," *Laurentian University Review* 5(3) (1973): 133–160.

The Enigmatic Chancellor: Bethmann-Hollweg and the Hubris of Imperial Germany. New Haven, CT: Yale University Press, 1973.

"The Illusion of Limited War: Chancellor Bethmann-Hollweg's Calculated Risk, July 1914," *Central European History* 2(1) (1969): 48–76.

Jeismann, Karl-Ernst. *Das Problem des Präventivkrieges im europäischen Staatensystem mit besonderem Blick auf die Bismarckzeit.* Freiburg: Alber, 1957.

Jelavich, Barbara. *Russia's Balkan Entanglements, 1806–1914.* Cambridge University Press, 1991.

"What the Habsburg Government Knew about the Black Hand," *Austrian History Yearbook* 22(10) (1991): 131–150.

Jeřábek, Rudolf. *Potiorek: General im Schatten von Sarajevo.* Graz: Verlag Styria, 1991.

Jervis, Robert. *System Effects: Complexity in Political and Social Life.* Princeton University Press, 1997.

"Cooperation under the Security Dilemma," *World Politics* 30(2) (1978): 167–214.

Perception and Misperception in International Politics. Princeton University Press, 1976.

Joffre, Marshal Joseph. *Mémoires du Maréchal Joffre 1910–1917.* Paris: Plon, 1932, vol. 1, pp. 216–218.

Joll, James. *The Origins of the First World War.* New York: Longman, 1984.

Joly, Bertrand. "La France et la revanche, 1871–1914," *Revue d'histoire moderne et contemporaine* 46(2) (1999): 325–347.

Kahneman, Daniel. "The Surety of Fools," *New York Times Magazine,* October 23, 2011, pp. 30–33, 62.

Thinking, Fast and Slow. New York: Farrar, Straus & Giroux, 2011.

Kahneman, Daniel and Jonathan Renshon. "Why Hawks Win," *Foreign Policy* 158 (2007): 34–38.

Kaiser, David E. "Germany and the Origins of the First World War," *Journal of Modern History* 55(3) (1983): 442–474.

Keiger, John F. V. *France and the World since 1870.* London: Arnold, 2001.

Raymond Poincaré. Cambridge University Press, 1997.

"France," in Keith Wilson (ed.), *Decisions for War, 1914.* New York: St Martin's Press, 1995, pp. 121–149.

France and the Origins of the First World War. London: Macmillan, 1983.

Kennan, George F. *The Decline of Bismarck's European Order: Franco-Russian Relations, 1875–1890.* Princeton University Press, 1979.

Kennedy, Paul M. *The Rise and Fall of the Great Powers: Economic Change and Military Conflict from 1500 to 2000.* New York: Random House, 1987.

"The First World War and the International Power System," *International Security* 9(1) (1984): 7–40.

The Rise of the Anglo-German Naval Rivalry, 1860–1914. London: Allen & Unwin, 1982.

The Rise of Anglo-German Antagonism, 1860–1914. London: Allen & Unwin, 1980.

(ed.). *The War Plans of the Great Powers, 1880–1914.* Boston, MA: Allen & Unwin, 1979.

Keylor, William. "Versailles and International Diplomacy," in Manfred F. Boemeke, Gerald D. Feldman, and Elisabeth Glaser (eds.), *The Treaty of Versailles: A Reassessment after 75 Years.* Cambridge University Press, 1998, pp. 469–505.

Kiesling, Eugenia. "France," in Richard F. Hamilton and Holger Herwig (eds.), *The Origins of World War I.* Cambridge University Press, 2003.

Kießling, Friedrich, *Gegen den "Großen Krieg"? Entspannung in den internationalen Beziehungen, 1911–1914.* Munich: Oldenbourg, 2002.

Kloster, Walter. *Der deutsche Generalstab und der Präventivkriegsgedanke.* Stuttgart: Kohlhammer, 1932.

Koch, H. W. (ed.). *The Origins of the First World War*, 2nd edn. London: Macmillan, 1984.

Kokovtsov, Vladimir N. *Iz moego prozhlogo. Vospominaniia. 1903–1919 gg.*, 2 vols. Moscow: Nauka, 1992.

Korelin, A. P. (ed.) (for Rossiskaya Akademiya Nauk/Institut Rossiiskoi Istorii). *Rossiya 1913 God: Statistiko-dokumental'nyi Spravochnik.* St. Petersburg: Blits, 1995.

Kriegel, A. and J-J. Becker. *1914: La guerre et le mouvement ouvrier français.* Paris: Armand Colin, 1964.

Krivoshein, K. A. *A. V. Krivoshein (1857–1921 g.). Ego znachenie v istorii Rossii nachala XX veka.* Paris: P.I.U.F., 1973.

Kronenbitter, Günther. *"Krieg im Frieden": Die Führung der k.u.k. Armee und die Großmachtpolitik Österreich-Ungarns, 1906–1914.* Munich: Oldenbourg, 2003.

Krüger, Peter. "Von Bismarck zu Hitler? Die Agonie des Europäischen Staatensystems 1938/1939," in Peter Krüger (ed.), *Kontinuität und Wandel in der Staatenordnung der Neuzeit.* Marburg: Hitzeroth, 1991, pp. 69–85.

Krumeich, Gerd. *Armaments and Politics in France on the Eve of the First World War.* Oxford: Berg, 1984.

Lambert, Nicholas A. *Planning Armageddon: British Economic Warfare and the First World War.* Cambridge, MA: Harvard University Press, 2012.

Sir John Fisher's Naval Revolution. Columbia, SC: University of South Carolina Press, 1999.

Langdon, John. *July 1914: The Long Debate, 1918–1990.* New York: Berg, 1991.

Lappenküper, Ulrich. *Die Mission Radowitz: Untersuchungen zur Rußlandspolitik Otto von Bismarcks 1871–1875.* Göttingen: Vandenhoeck & Ruprecht, 1990.

Lebow, Richard N. "Franz Ferdinand Found Alive: World War I Unnecessary," in *Forbidden Fruit: Counterfactuals and International Relations.* Princeton University Press, 2010, ch. 3.

A Cultural Theory of International Relations. Cambridge University Press, 2008.

"Contingency, Catalysts, and Nonlinear Change: The Origins of World War I," in Gary Goertz and Jack S. Levy (eds.), *Explaining War: Case Studies and Necessary Condition Counterfactuals.* London: Routledge, 2007, pp. 85–111.

"Contingency Catalysts and International System Change," *Political Science Quarterly* 115(4) (2000): 591–616.

"Windows of Opportunity: Do States Jump through Them?" *International Security* 9(1) (1984): 147–186.

Between Peace and War. Baltimore, MD: Johns Hopkins University Press, 1981.

LeDonne, John P. *The Russian Empire and the World, 1700–1917: The Geopolitics of Expansion and Contraction.* Oxford University Press, 1997.

Lemke, Doug. *Regions of War and Peace.* Cambridge University Press, 2002.

Lepsius, Johannes, Albrecht Mendelssohn-Bartholdy, and Friedrich Thimme (eds.). *Die Grosse Politik der Europäischen Kabinette, 1871–1914,* 40 vols. Berlin: Deutsche Verlagsgesellschaft für Politik & Geschichte, 1922–1927.

Leslie, John. "The Antecedents of Austria-Hungary's War Aims: Policies and Policy-Makers in Vienna and Budapest before and during 1914," in Elisabeth Springer and Leopold Kammerhold (eds.), *Archiv und Forschung: Das Haus-, Hof- und Staatsarchiv in seiner Bedeutung für die Geschichte Österreichs und Europas.* Vienna: Verlag für Geschichte & Politik, 1993, pp. 307–394.

"Österreich-Ungarn vor dem Kriegsausbruch: Der Ballhausplatz in Wien im Juli 1914 aus der Sicht eines Österreichisch-Ungarischen Diplomaten," in Ralph Melville, Claus Scharf, Martin Vogt, and Ulrich Wengenroth (eds.), *Deutschland und Europa in der Neuzeit.* Stuttgart: Franz Steiner, 1988, pp. 661–684.

Levy, Jack S. "The Initiation and Spread of the First World War: Interdependent Decisions," *Foreign Policy Analysis* 7(2) (2011): 183–188.

"Preventive War: Concept and Propositions," *International Interactions* 37(1) (2011): 87–96.

"Counterfactuals and Case Studies," in Janet Box-Steffensmeier, Henry Brady, and David Collier (eds.), *Oxford Handbook of Political Methodology.* Oxford University Press, 2008, pp. 627–644.

"Preventive War and Democratic Politics," Presidential Address to the International Studies Association, *International Studies Quarterly* 52(1) (2008): 1–24.

"The Role of Necessary Conditions in the Outbreak of World War I," in Gary Goertz and Jack S. Levy (eds.), *Explaining War and Peace: Case Studies and Necessary Condition Counterfactuals.* London: Routledge, 2007, pp. 47–84.

"Political Psychology and Foreign Policy," in David O. Sears, Leonie Huddy, and Robert Jervis (eds.), *Oxford Handbook of Political Psychology.* New York: Oxford University Press, 2003, pp. 253–284.

"Explaining Events and Developing Theories: History, Political Science, and the Analysis of International Relations," in Colin Elman and Miriam Fendius Elman (eds.), *Bridges and Boundaries: Historians, Political Scientists, and the Study of International Relations.* Cambridge, MA: MIT Press, 2001, pp. 39–84.

"Prospect Theory, Rational Choice, and International Relations," *International Studies Quarterly* 41(1) (1997): 87–112.

"Preferences, Constraints, and Choices in July 1914," *International Security* 15(3) (1990/1): 151–186.

"The Diversionary Theory of War: A Critique," in Manus I. Midlarsky (ed.), *Handbook of War Studies.* Boston, MA: Unwin Hyman, 1989, pp. 259–288.

"Declining Power and the Preventive Motivation for War," *World Politics* 40(1) (1987): 82–107.

"Organizational Routines and the Causes of War," *International Studies Quarterly* 30(2) (1986): 193–222.

Levy, Jack S. and Joseph R. Gochal. "Democracy and Preventive War: Israel and the 1956 Sinai Campaign," *Security Studies* 11(2) (2001/2): 1–49.

Levy, Jack S. and William R. Thompson. *Causes of War.* Chichester: Wiley-Blackwell, 2010.

Levy, Jack S., Thomas J. Christenson, and Marc Trachtenberg. "Correspondence: Mobilization and Inadvertence in the July Crisis," *International Security* 16(1) (1991): 189–203.

Lieber, Keir A. "The New History of World War I and What it Means for International Relations Theory," *International Security* 32(2) (2007): 155–191.

War and the Engineers: The Primacy of Politics over Technology. Ithaca, NY: Cornell University Press, 2005.

Lieven, Dominic. *Nicholas II: Emperor of All the Russias*. London: Pimlico, 1993.

Russia and the Origins of the First World War. New York: Macmillan, 1983.

"Pro-Germans and Russian Foreign Policy, 1890–1914," *International History Review* 2(1) (1980): 34–54.

Lindblom, Charles E. "The Science of Muddling Through," *Public Administration Review* 19(2) (1959): 79–88.

Lindemann, Thomas. *Die Macht der Perzeptionen und Perzeptionen von Mächten*. Berlin: Duncker & Humblot, 2000.

Lloyd George, David. *War Memoirs*, 2 vols. London: Odhams Press, 1938.

Lobell, Steven E. "Bringing Balancing Back In: Britain's Targeted Balancing, 1936–1939," *Journal of Strategic Studies* 35(6) (2012): 747–773.

Louis, Georges. *Les carnets de Georges Louis, 1908–1917*, 2 vols. Paris: F. Rieder, 1926.

Luneva, Iu. V. *Bosfor i Dardanelly: Tainye provokatsii nakanune Pervoi mirovoi voiny 1907–1914*. Moscow: Kvadriga, 2010.

Lustick, Ian. "History, Historiography, and Political Science: Multiple Historical Records and the Problem of Selection Bias," *American Political Science Review* 90(3) (1996): 605–618.

Lynn, John. "The Embattled Future of Academic Military History," *Journal of Military History* 61(4) (1997): 777–789.

Lynn-Jones, Sean M. "Detente and Deterrence: Anglo-German Relations, 1911–1914," *International Security* 11(2) (1986): 121–150.

MacKenzie, David. *The "Black Hand" on Trial: Salonika, 1917*. New York: East European Monographs, 1995.

Apis, the Congenial Conspirator: The Life of Colonel Dragutin Dimitrijević. Boulder, CO: East European Monographs, 1989.

McDonald, David MacLaren. *United Government and Foreign Policy in Russia, 1900–1914*. Cambridge, MA: Harvard University Press, 1992.

McDonald, Patrick J. *The Invisible Hand of Peace: Capitalism, The War Machine, and International Relations Theory*. Cambridge University Press, 2009.

McMeekin, Sean. *July 1914: Countdown to War*. New York: Basic Books, 2013.

The Russian Origins of the First World War. Cambridge, MA: Belknap Press of Harvard University Press, 2011.

Mandelstam, Andrei N. "La politique russe d'accès à la Méditerranée au XXe siècle," *Recueil des Cours* 47 (1934): 603–802.

Mansbach, Richard W. and John A. Vasquez. *In Search of Theory: A New Paradigm for Global Politics*. New York: Columbia University Press, 1981.

Maoz, Zeev, Lesley C. Terris, Ranan D. Kuperman, and Ilan Talmud, "What is the Enemy of My Enemy? Causes and Consequences of Imbalanced International Relations," *Journal of Politics* 69(1) (2007): 100–115.

Marder, Arthur (ed.). *Fear God and Dread Nought: The Correspondence of the Admiral of the Fleet Lord Fisher of Kilverstone*, 3 vols. London: Jonathan Cape, 1952–1959.

Marks, Sally. "Smoke-filled Rooms and the Galerie des Glaces," in Manfred Boemeke, Gerald Feldman, and Elisabeth Glaser (eds.), *The Treaty of Versailles: A Reassessment after 75 Years*. Cambridge University Press, 1998, pp. 337–370.

Marshall, Alex. "Russian Military Intelligence, 1905–1917: The Untold Story behind Tsarist Russia in the First World War," *War in History* 11(4) (2004): 393–423.

Maurer, John. "Field Marshal Conrad von Hötzendorf and the Outbreak of the First World War," in T. G. Otte and Constantine A. Pagedas (eds.), *Personalities, War, and Diplomacy: Essays in International History*. London: Frank Cass, 1997, pp. 38–65.

The Outbreak of the First World War: Strategic Planning, Crisis Decision-Making and Deterrence Failure. Westport, CT: Praeger, 1995.

Mayeur, Jean Marie. *La vie politique sous la Troisième République*. Paris: Seuil, 1984.

Menning, Bruce W. "The Mobilization Crises of 1912 and 1914 in Russian Perspective: Neglected and Overlooked Linkages," forthcoming.

"War Planning and Initial Operations in the Russian Context," in Richard F. Hamilton and Holger H. Herwig (eds.), *War Planning 1914*. Cambridge University Press, 2010, pp. 80–142.

"Pieces of the Puzzle: The Role of Iu. N. Danilov and M. V. Alekseev in Russian War Planning before 1914," *International History Review* 25(4) (2003): 775–798.

Meyer-Arndt, Lüder. *Die Julikrise 1914: Wie Deutschland in den Ersten Weltkrieg stolperte*. Cologne: Böhlau, 2006.

Mezhdunarodnye Otnosheniia v Epokhu Imperializma, 3rd series. Moscow: Gos. sots., 1931–1940.

Midlarsky, Manus I. *The Onset of World War*. Boston, MA: Allen & Unwin, 1988.

Miquel, Pierre. *Poincaré*. Paris: Fayard, 1984.

Mombauer, Annika. "The Fischer Controversy, Documents, and the 'Truth' about the Origins of the First World War," *Journal of Contemporary History* 48(2) (2013): 290–314.

The Origins of the First World War: Diplomatic and Military Documents. Manchester University Press, 2013.

(ed.). "Special Issue: The Fischer Controversy after 50 Years," *Journal of Contemporary History* 48(2) (2013): 231–417.

"German War Plans," in Richard F. Hamilton and Holger H. Herwig (eds.), *War Planning 1914*. Cambridge University Press, 2010, pp. 48–79.

"The First World War, Avoidable, Improbable or Desirable? Recent Interpretations on War Guilt and the War's Origins," *Germany History* 25(1) (2007): 78–95.

"Of War Plans and War Guilt: The Debate Surrounding the Schlieffen Plan," *Journal of Strategic Studies* 28(5) (2005): 857–885.

The Origins of the First World War: Controversies and Consensus. New York: Longman, 2002.

Helmuth von Moltke and the Origins of the First World War. Cambridge University Press, 2001.

Mommsen, Wolfgang J. "Max Weber and the Peace Treaty of Versailles," in Manfred F. Boemeke, Gerald D. Feldman, and Elisabeth Glaser (eds.), *The Treaty of Versailles: A Reassessment after 75 Years.* Cambridge University Press, 1998, pp. 535–546.

"Domestic Factors in German Foreign Policy before 1914," in Wolfgang J. Mommsen (ed.), *Imperial Germany, 1867–1914.* London: Arnold, 1995.

"Domestic Factors in German Foreign Policy before 1914," *Central European History* 6(1) (1973): 3–43.

Montgelas, Max and Walter Schücking (eds.). *Outbreak of the World War: German Documents,* 4 vols., collected by Karl Kautsky. New York: Oxford University Press, 1919; trans. in one volume, Carnegie Endowment for International Peace, 1924.

Moran, Daniel. *Strategic Insights: Preventive War and the Crisis of July 1914.* Monterey, CA: Center of Contemporary Conflict, 2002.

Morgenthau, Hans J. *Politics among Nations: The Struggle for Power and Peace,* rev. 5th edn. New York: Alfred A. Knopf, 1978.

Moritz, Albrecht. *Das Problem des Präventivkrieges in der deutschen Politik während der erstern Marokkokrise.* Bern: Peter Lang, 1974.

Most, Benjamin and Harvey Starr. "International Relations Theory, Foreign Policy Substitutability and 'Nice' Laws," *World Politics* 36(3) (1984): 383–406.

Mulligan, William. *The Origins of the First World War.* Cambridge University Press, 2010.

Musulin, Alexander von. *Das Haus am Ballplatz: Erinnerungen eines österreich-ungarischen Diplomaten.* Munich: Verlag für Kulturpolitik, 1924.

Neiberg, Michael S. *Dance of the Furies: Europe and the Outbreak of World War I.* Cambridge, MA: Harvard University Press, 2011.

Neilson, Keith. *Britain and the Last Tsar: British Policy towards Russia, 1894–1917.* Oxford: Clarendon Press, 1995.

"'My Beloved Russians': Sir Arthur Nicolson and Russia, 1906–1914," *International History Review* 9(4) (1987): 521–554.

Neitzel, Sönke. *Kriegsausbruch: Deutschlands Weg in die Katastrophe.* Munich: Pendo, 2002.

Nichols, Thomas N. "Anarchy and World Order in the New Age of Prevention," *World Policy Journal* 22(3) (2005): 1–23.

Nicolson, Harold. *Lord Carnock: A Study in the Old Diplomacy.* London: Constable, 1937.

Offer, Avner. "Going to War in 1914: A Matter of Honor?" *Politics & Society* 23(2) (1995): 213–241.

Organski, A. F. K. and Jacek Kugler. *The War Ledger.* University of Chicago Press, 1980.

Otte, T. G. "Détente 1914: Sir William Tyrrell's Secret Mission to Germany," *Historical Journal* 56(4) (2013): 1–30.

The Foreign Office Mind: The Making of British Foreign Policy, 1865–1914. Cambridge University Press, 2011.

Paléologue, Maurice, *Au quai d'Orsay à la veille de la tourmente: Journal 1913–1914.* Paris: Plon, 1947.

Palmer, Robert R. *A History of the Modern World.* New York: Alfred A. Knopf, 1951.

Perrow, Charles. *Normal Accidents: Living with High Risk Technologies.* New York: Basic Books, 1984.

Poincaré, Raymond. *Au service de la France,* 7 vols. Paris: Plon, 1928.

Pokrovskii, Mikhail N. (ed.). *Die International Beziehungen im Zeitalter des Imperialismus,* 3rd series, 4 vols. Berlin: Reimar Hobbing, 1939–1943.

Vneshniaia politika Rossii v XX veke: populiarnyi ocherk. Moscow: Izd-vo Kommun. Un-ta im IA. M. Sverdlova, 1926.

Radziwill, Marie. *Briefe vom deutschen Kaiserhof, 1889–1915.* Berlin: Ullstein, 1936.

Ralston, David R. *The Army of the Republic: The Military and the Political Evolution of France, 1871–1914.* Cambridge, MA: MIT Press, 1967.

Rasler, Karen and William R. Thompson. *The Great Powers and Global Struggle, 1490–1990.* Lexington, KY: University Press of Kentucky, 1994.

"Global Wars, Public Debts and the Long Cycle," *World Politics* 35(4) (1983): 489–516.

Rauchensteiner, Manfred. *Der Tod des Doppeladlers: Österreich-Ungarn und der Erste Weltkrieg.* Graz: Styria Verlag, 1993.

Rauh, M. "Die britisch–russische Marinekonvention von 1914 und der Ausbruch des Ersten Weltkriegs," *Militärgeschichtliche Mitteilungen* 47(10) (1987): 37–62.

Reichsarchiv. *Der Weltkrieg, 1914–1918, vol. 1: Kriegsrüstung und Kriegswirtschaft.* Berlin: Mittler, 1930.

Reiter, Dan. "Exploding the Powder Keg Myth: Preemptive Wars Almost Never Happen," *International Security* 20(2) (1995): 5–34.

Renouvin, Pierre. *Les origines immédiates de la guerre, 28 juin–4 août 1914.* Paris: Costes, 1924.

Renshon, Jonathan B. *Why Leaders Choose War: The Psychology of Prevention.* Westport, CT: Praeger, 2006.

Reynolds, Michael A. *Shattering Empires: The Clash and Collapse of the Ottoman and Russian Empires 1908–1918.* Cambridge University Press, 2011.

Ribot, A. (ed.). *Journal d'Alexandre Ribot et correspondances inédites, 1914–22.* Paris: Plon, 1936.

Rich, David A. "Russia," in Richard F. Hamilton and Holger H. Herwig (eds.), *The Origins of World War I.* Cambridge University Press, 2003, pp. 188–226.

Richardson, James L. *Crisis Diplomacy: The Great Powers since the Mid-Nineteenth Century.* Cambridge University Press, 1994.

Rider, Toby J. "Understanding Arms Races Onset: Rivalry, Threat, and Territorial Competition," *Journal of Politics* 71(2) (2009): 693–703.

Rider, Toby J., Michael Findley, and Paul F. Diehl. "Just Part of the Game? Arms Races, Rivalry and War," *Journal of Peace Research* 48(1) (2011): 85–100.

Riezler, K. *Tagebücher, Aufsätze, Dokumente*, ed. Karl D. Erdmann. Göttingen: Vandenhoeck & Ruprecht, 1972.

Ripsman, Norrin M. and Jack S. Levy. "The Preventive War that Never Happened: Britain, France, and the Rise of Germany in the 1930s," *Security Studies* 16(1) (2007): 32–67.

Ritter, Gerhard. *The Sword and the Scepter*, 4 vols., trans. Heins Norden. Coral Gables, FL: University of Miami Press, 1970.

The Schlieffen Plan: Critique of a Myth. New York: Praeger, 1958.

Robbins, Keith. *Sir Edward Grey*. London: Cassell, 1971.

Röhl, John C. G. *Wilhelm II: Der Weg in den Abgrund 1900–1941*. Munich: C. H. Beck, 2008.

"The Curious Case of the Kaiser's Disappearing War Guilt: Wilhelm II in July 1914," in Holger Afflerbach and David Stevenson (eds.), *An Improbable War? The Outbreak of World War I and European Political Culture before 1914*. New York: Berghahn, 2007, pp. 75–95.

The Kaiser and His Court: Wilhelm II and the Government of Germany. Cambridge University Press, 1996.

"Germany," in Keith Wilson (ed.), *Decisions for War, 1914*. New York: St. Martin's Press, 1995.

"V. Admiral Müller and the Approach of War," *Historical Journal* 12(4) (1969): 651–673.

Ropponen, Risto. *Die Kraft Russlands*. Helsinki: Turku, 1968.

Rose, Andreas. *Zwischen Empire und Kontinent. Britische Außenpolitik vor dem Ersten Weltkrieg*. Munich: Oldenbourg, 2011.

Rossos, Andrew. *Russia and the Balkans: Inter-Balkan Rivalries and Russian Foreign Policy 1908–1914*. University of Toronto Press, 1981.

Rowe, David M. "The Tragedy of Liberalism: How Globalization Caused the First World War," *Security Studies* 14(3) (2005): 407–447.

Rüger, Jan. "Review Article: Revisiting the Anglo-German Antagonism," *Journal of Modern History* 83(3) (2011): 579–617.

Russett, Bruce. "Cause, Surprise and No Escape," *Journal of Politics* 24(1) (1962): 3–22.

Sagan, Scott D. "1914 Revisited: Allies, Offense, and Instability," *International Security* 11(2) (1986): 151–175.

Sample, Susan G. "Military Buildups: Arming and War," in John Vasquez (ed.), *What do We Know about War?* Lanham, MD: Rowman & Littlefield, 2000, pp. 165–195.

Sanborn, Joshua. "Russian Historiography on the Origins of the First World War since the Fischer Controversy," *Journal of Contemporary History* 48(2) (2013): 350–362.

Sazonov, Sergei D. *Fateful Years, 1906–1916*. New York: Stokes, 1928.

Schaepdrijver, Sophie de. *La Belgique et la Première Guerre mondiale*. Frankfurt: Peter Lang, 2004.

Schilling, M. F. *How the War Began in 1914*. London: Allen & Unwin, 1925.

Schlieffen, Alfred von. "War Today," in Robert Foley (ed.), *Alfred von Schlieffen's Military Writings*. London: Routledge, 2002.

Schmid, Michael. *Der "Eiserne Kanzler" und die Generäle: Deutsche Rüstungspolitik in der Ära Bismarck 1871–1890*. Paderborn: Schöningh, 2003.

Schmidt, Stefan. *Frankreichs Außenpolitik in der Julikrise 1914: Ein Beitrag zur Geschichte des Ausbruchs des Ersten Weltkrieges*. Munich: Oldenbourg, 2009.

Schmitt, Bernadotte E. *The Coming of the War 1914*, 2 vols. New York: Charles Scribner, 1930.

Schneider, Irmin. *Die deutsche Russlandpolitik, 1890–1900*. Paderborn: F. Schöningh, 2003.

Schoen, Wilhelm E. von. *Erlebtes: Beiträge zur politischen Geschichte der neuesten Zeit*. Stuttgart: Deutsche Verlags-Anstalt, 1921.

Schöllgen, Gregor. *Imperialismus und Gleichgewicht: Deutschland, England und die orientalische Frage*. Munich: Oldenbourg, 1992.

Schröder, Stephen. *Die englisch–russische Marinekonvention: Das deutsche Reich und die Flottenverhandlungen der Tripleentente am Vorabend des Ersten Weltkrieges*. Göttingen: Vandenhoeck & Ruprecht, 2006.

Schroeder, Paul W. "Preventive Wars to Restore and Stabilize the International System," *International Interactions* 37(1) (2011): 96–107.

"Necessary Conditions and World War I as an Unavoidable War," in Gary Goertz and Jack S. Levy (eds.), *Explaining War and Peace: Case Studies and Necessary Condition Counterfactuals*. London: Routledge, 2007, pp. 113–145.

"Stealing Horses to Great Applause: Austria-Hungary's Decision in 1914 in System Perspective," in Holger Afflerbach and David Stevenson (eds.), *An Improbable War? The Outbreak of World War I and European Political Culture*. New York: Berghahn, 2007, pp. 17–42.

"The Life and Death of a Long Peace, 1763–1914," in Raimo Vayrynen (ed.), *The Waning of Major War: Contrary Views*. London: Routledge, 2005.

Systems, Stability, and Statecraft: Essays on the International History of Modern Europe, eds. and Introduction David Wetzel, Robert Jervis, and Jack S. Levy. New York: Palgrave, 2004.

"A Pointless Enduring Rivalry: France and the Habsburg Monarchy, 1715–1918," in William R. Thompson (ed.), *Great Power Rivalries*. Columbia, SC: University of South Carolina Press, 1999, pp. 60–85.

"World War I as Galloping Gertie: A Reply to Joachim Remak," *Journal of Modern History* 44(3) (1972): 319–345.

Schulin, E. "Walther Rathenau Diotima: Lili Deutsch, ihre Familie und der Kreis um Gerhart Hauptmann," in H. Wilderotter (ed.), *Die Extreme berühren sich: Walther Rathenau, 1867–1922*. Berlin, Argon Verlag, 1994, pp. 55–66.

Schulte, B. F. "Neue Dokumente zu Kriegsausbruch und Kriegsverlauf," *Militärgeschichtliche Mitteilungen* 25 (1979): 123–186.

Seligmann, Matthew S. *The Royal Navy and the German Threat, 1901–1914: Admiralty Plans to Protect British Trade in a War Against Germany*. Oxford University Press, 2012.

Senese, Paul D. and John A. Vasquez. *The Steps to War: An Empirical Study*. Princeton University Press, 2008.

Serra, Enrico. "Lettres de Jules Cambon à Alberto Pansa," *Revue d'histoire diplomatique* 116(1) (2002): 88.

Shatsillo, Kornelii F. *Russkii imperializm i razvitie flota nakanune pervoi mirovoi voiny 1906–1914*. Moscow: Nauka, 1968.

Shea, Patrick. "Financing Victory: Sovereign Credit, Democracy, and War," *Journal of Conflict Resolution* (2013): DOI: 10.1177/0022002713478567.

Siegel, Jennifer. *Endgame: Britain, Russia, and the Final Struggle for Central Asia*. London: I. B. Tauris, 2002.

Silverstone, Scott A. *Preventive War and American Democracy*. New York: Routledge, 2007.

Smith, Woodruff D. *The Ideological Origins of Nazi Imperialism*. Oxford University Press, 1986.

Snyder, Jack *Myths of Empire*. Ithaca, NY: Cornell University Press, 1991.

   "Perceptions of the Security Dilemma in 1914," in Robert Jervis, Richard Ned Lebow, and Janice Gross (eds.), *Psychology and Deterrence*. Baltimore, MD: Johns Hopkins University Press, 1985, pp. 153–179.

   "Civil–Military Relations and the Cult of the Offensive, 1914 and 1984," *International Security* 9(1) (1984): 20–58.

   The Ideology of the Offensive: Military Decision Making and the Disasters of 1914. Ithaca, NY: Cornell University Press, 1984.

Snyder, Jack and Keir A. Lieber. "Correspondence: Defensive Realism and the 'New' History of World War I," *International Security* 33(1) (2008): 174–194.

Sondhaus, Lawrence. *Franz Conrad von Hötzendorf: Architect of the Apocalypse*. Boston, MA: Humanities Press, 2000.

Soroka, Marina E. *Britain, Russia and the Road to the First World War: The Fateful Embassy of Count Aleksandr Benckendorff 1903–1916*. Farnham: Ashgate, 2011.

Spaulding, Robert Mark. *Osthandel and Ostpolitik: German Foreign Trade Policies in Eastern Europe from Bismarck to Adenauer*. Providence, RI: Berghahn, 1997.

Steinberg, Jonathan. "The Copenhagen Complex," *Journal of Contemporary History* 1(3) (1966): 23–46.

Steiner, Zara S. *The Lights That Failed: European International History, 1919–1933*. Oxford University Press, 2005.

Steiner, Zara and Keith Neilson. *Britain and the Origins of the First World War*, 2nd edn. Basingstoke: Palgrave Macmillan, 2003.

Stengers, Jean. "1914: The Safety of Ciphers and the Outbreak of the First World War," in Christopher Andrew and Jeremy Noakes (eds.), *Intelligence and International Relations*. University of Exeter Press, 1987, pp. 29–48.

Stevenson, David. "From Balkan Conflict to Global Conflict: The Spread of the First World War," *Foreign Policy Analysis* 7(2) (2011): 169–182.

   "Was a Peaceful Outcome Thinkable? The European Land Armaments Race before 1914," in Holger Afflerbach and David Stevenson (eds.), *An Improbable War? The Outbreak of World War I and European Political Culture before 1914*. New York: Berghahn, 2007, pp. 130–148.

   Cataclysm: The First World War as Political Tragedy. New York: Basic Books, 2004.

   "Militarization and Diplomacy in Europe before 1914," *International Security* 22(1) (1997): 125–161.

   Armaments and the Coming of War: Europe, 1904–1914. Oxford University Press, 1996.

Stieve, F. (ed.). *Der diplomatische Schriftwechsel Iswolskis, 1911–1914,* 4 vols. Berlin: Deutsche Verlagsgsellschaft für Politik & Geschichte, 1925.

Stone, James. *The War Scare of 1875: Bismarck and Europe in the mid-1870s.* Stuttgart: Franz Steiner, 2010.

Stone, Norman. *The Eastern Front, 1914–1917.* New York: Scribner, 1975.

Strachan, Hew. "Preemption and Prevention in Historical Perspective," in Henry Shue and David Rodin (eds.), *Preemption: Military Action and Moral Justification.* Oxford University Press, 2007.

The Outbreak of the First World War. Oxford University Press, 2004.

The First World War, vol. 1: *To Arms.* New York: Oxford University Press, 2001.

Strandmann, Hartmut P. von. "Germany and the Coming of the War," in R. J. W. Evans and Hartmut P. von Strandmann (eds.), *The Coming of the First World War.* Oxford: Clarendon Press, 1988, pp. 140–159.

(ed.). *Walther Rathenau: Tagebuch, 1907–1922.* Düsseldorf: Droste, 1967.

Streich, Philip and Jack S. Levy. "Time Horizons, Discounting, and Intertemporal Choice," *Journal of Conflict Resolution* 51(2) (2007): 199–226.

Szilassy, Julius von. *Der Untergang der Donau-Monarchie: Diplomatische Erinnerungen.* Vienna: Neues Vaterland, 1921.

Tammen, Ronald L., Jacek Kugler, Douglas Lemke, Carole Asharabati, Brian Efird, and A. F. K. Organski, *Power Transitions: Strategies for the 21st Century.* New York: Chatham House, 2000.

Taylor, A. J. P. *The Struggle for Mastery in Europe, 1848–1918.* Oxford University Press, 1954.

Tetlock, Philip E. and Aaron Belkin (eds.). *Counterfactual Thought Experiments in International Relations: Logical, Methodological, and Psychological Perspectives.* Princeton University Press, 1996.

Thompson, William R. "Powder Kegs, Sparks and World War I," in Gary Goertz and Jack S. Levy (eds.), *Explaining War and Peace: Case Studies and Necessary Condition Counterfactuals.* London: Routledge, 2007, pp. 147–193.

"A Streetcar Named Sarajevo: Catalysts, Multiple Causation Chains, and Rivalry Structures," *International Studies Quarterly* 47(3) (2003): 453–469.

"Identifying Rivals and Rivalries in World Politics," *International Studies Quarterly* 45(4) (2001): 557–586.

(ed.). *Great Power Rivalries.* Columbia, SC: University of South Carolina Press, 1999.

On Global War: Historical-Structural Approaches to World Politics. Columbia, SC: University of South Carolina Press, 1988.

Thompson William R. and David R. Dreyer. *Handbook of International Rivalries, 1494–2010.* Washington, DC: Congressional Quarterly Press, 2011.

Trachtenberg, Marc. *History and Strategy.* Princeton University Press, 1991.

"The Meaning of Mobilization," in Steven E. Miller, Sean M. Lynn-Jones, and Stephen Van Evera (eds.), *Military Strategy and the Origins of the First World War.* Princeton University Press, 1991, pp. 195–225.

"The Meaning of Mobilization in 1914," *International Security* 15(3) (1990/1): 120–150.

Trumpener, Ulrich. "War Premeditated? German Intelligence Operations in July 1914," *Central European History* 9(1) (1976): 58–85.

Tuchman, Barbara. *The Guns of August*. New York: Macmillan, 1962.

Tunstall, Graydon A., Jr. "Austria-Hungary," in Richard F. Hamilton and Holger H. Herwig (eds.), *The Origins of World War I*. Cambridge University Press, 2003, pp. 112–149.

Turner, L. C. F. "The Russian Mobilisation in 1914," in Paul Kennedy (ed.), *The War Plans of the Great Powers, 1880–1914*. Boston, MA: Allen & Unwin, 1979, pp. 252–268.

"The Russian Mobilization in 1914," *Journal of Contemporary History* 3(1) (1968): 65–88.

Valeriano, Brandon and John A. Vasquez. "Identifying and Classifying Complex Wars," *International Studies Quarterly* 54(2) (2008): 561–582.

Van Evera, Stephen. *Causes of War: Power and the Roots of Conflict*. Ithaca, NY: Cornell University Press, 1999.

"The Cult of the Offensive and the Origins of the First World War," in Steven E. Miller, Sean M. Lynn-Jones, and Stephen Van Evera (eds.), *Military Strategy and the Origins of the First World War*. Princeton University Press, 1991, pp. 59–108.

"The Cult of the Offensive and the Origins of the First World War," *International Security* 9(1) (1984): 58–107.

Vasquez, John A. *The War Puzzle Revisited*. Cambridge University Press, 2009.

The War Puzzle. Cambridge University Press, 1993.

Vasquez, John A., Paul F. Diehl, Colin Flint, and Jürgen Scheffran. "Forum on the Spread of War, 1914–1917: A Dialogue between Political Scientists and Historians," *Foreign Policy Analysis* 7(2) (2011): 139–141.

Vasquez, John A., Paul F. Diehl, Colin Flint, Jürgen Scheffran, Sang-Hyun Chi, and Toby J. Rider. "The ConflictSpace of Cataclysm: The International System and the Spread of War 1914–1917," *Foreign Policy Analysis* 7(2) (2011): 143–168.

Verner, Andrew. *The Crisis of Russian Autocracy: Nicholas II and the 1905 Revolution*. Princeton University Press, 1990.

Vogel, Barbara. *Deutsche Rußlandpolitik: Das Scheitern der deutschen Weltpolitik unter Bülow, 1900–1906*. Düsseldorf: Bertelsmann Universitätsverlag, 1973.

Vietsch, Eberhard von. *Bethmann Hollweg: Staatsmann zwischen Macht und Ethos*. Boppard: Boldt, 1969.

Waltz, Kenneth N. *Theory of International Politics*. New York: McGraw-Hill, 1979.

Wayman, Frank W. "Bipolarity, Multipolarity, and the Threat of War," in Alan N. Sabrosky (ed.), *Polarity and War: The Changing Structure of International Conflict*. Boulder, CO: Westview Press, 1985, pp. 115–144.

Weinroth, H. S. "British Radicals and the Balance of Power, 1902–1914," *Historical Journal* 13(4) (1970): 653–682.

Weitsman, Patricia A. *Dangerous Alliances: Proponents of Peace, Weapons of War*. Stanford University Press, 2004.

Williamson, Samuel R., Jr. "General Henry Wilson, Ireland, and the Great War," in Wm. Roger Louis (ed.). *Resurgent Adventures with Britannia: Personalities, Politics and Culture in Britain*. London: I. B. Tauris, 2011, pp. 91–105.

"Austria-Hungary and the Coming of the First World War," in Ernest R. May, Richard Rosecrance, and Zara Steiner (eds.), *History and Neorealism*. Cambridge University Press, 2010, pp. 103–128.

"Leopold Count Berchtold: The Man Who Could Have Prevented the Great War," in Günter Bischof, Fritz Plasser, and Peter Berger (eds.), *From Empire to Republic: Post-World War I Austria*. University of New Orleans Press, 2010, pp. 24–51.

"Aggressive and Defensive Aims of Political Elites? Austro-Hungarian Policy in 1914," in Holger Afflerbach and David Stevenson (eds.), *An Improbable War? The Outbreak of World War I and European Political Culture before 1914*. New York: Berghahn, 2007, pp. 61–74.

"Confrontation with Serbia: The Consequences of Vienna's Failure to Achieve Surprise in July 1914," *Mitteilungen des Österreichischen Staatsarchivs* (1993): 167–177.

Austria-Hungary and the Origins of the First World War. New York: Macmillan, 1991.

"Military Dimensions of Habsburg–Romanov Relations during the Era of the Balkan Wars," in Béla K. Király and Dimitrije Djordjevic (eds.), *East Central European Society and the Balkan Wars*. New York: Columbia University Press, 1987, pp. 317–337.

"Theories of Organizational Process and Foreign Policy Outcomes," in Paul G. Lauren (ed.), *Diplomatic History: New Approaches*. New York: Free Press, 1979, pp. 137–161.

The Politics of Grand Strategy: Britain and France Prepare for War, 1904–1914. Cambridge, MA: Harvard University Press, 1969 (reprinted London: Ashfield, 1990).

Williamson, Samuel R., Jr. and Ernest R. May. "An Identity of Opinions: Historians and July 1914," *Journal of Modern History* 79(2) (2007): 335–387.

Williamson, Samuel R., Jr. and Russel Van Wyk (eds.). *July 1914: Soldiers, Statesmen and the Coming of the Great War: A Brief Documentary History*. Boston, MA: Bedford/St. Martin's, 2003.

Wilson, Keith M. (ed.). *Decisions for War, 1914*. New York: St. Martin's Press, 1995.

The Policy of the Ententes: Essays in the Determinants of British Foreign Policy. Cambridge University Press, 1985.

Wohlforth, William C. "The Perception of Power: Russia in the Pre-1914 Balance," *World Politics* 39(3) (1987): 353–381.

Wolff, Theodor. *Tagebücher 1914–1919*, ed. Bernd Sösemann. Boppard: Harald Boldt, 1984.

Würthle, Friedrich. "Dokumente zum Sarajevoprozess," *Mitteilungen des Österreichischen Staatsarchivs*, Erganzungsband 9. Vienna, 1978.

Die Spur führt nach Belgrad: Die Hintergründe des Dramas von Sarajevo 1914. Vienna: Fritz Molden, 1975.

Yamamoto, Yoshinobu and Stuart A. Bremer. "Wider Wars and Restless Nights: Major Power Intervention in Ongoing War," in J. David Singer (ed.), *The Correlates of War: vol. 2: Testing some Realpolitik Models*. New York: Free Press, 1980, pp. 199–229.

Zagare, Frank C. *The Games of July: Explaining the Great War*. Ann Arbor, MI: University of Michigan Press, 2011.

Zakher, Ia. "Konstantinopol' i prolivy," *Krasnyi arkhiv* 6 (1924): 48–76, 7 (1924): 32–54.

Zechlin, Egmont. *Krieg und Kriegsrisiko: zur deutschen Politik im Ersten Weltkrieg*. Düsseldorf: Droste, 1979.

Zeman, Zbyněk Anthony Bohuslav, "The Balkans and the Coming of War," in R. J. W. Evans and Hartmut P. von Strandmann (eds.), *The Coming of the First World War*. Oxford: Clarendon Press, 1988, pp. 19–32.

Zernack, K. "Das preußische Königstum, und die polnische Republik im europäischen Mächtesystem des 18. Jahrhundert," in Wolfram Fischer and Michael G. Müller (eds.), *Preußen–Deutschland–Polen: Aufsätze zur Geschichte der deutsch–polnischen Beziehungen*. Berlin: Duncker & Humblot, 1991.

Zuber, Terence. *Inventing the Schlieffen Plan: German War Planning 1871–1914*. Oxford University Press, 2002.

"The Schlieffen Plan Reconsidered," *War in History* 6(3) (1999): 262–305.

Index

Aehrenthal, Alois von, 134, 135, 136
Afflerbach, Holger, 6
Agadir crisis (1911). *See* Moroccan Crisis (1911)
agency
debate over role in outbreak of war, 18–21
Albania, 80, 178, 233
struggle for control of, 36
Albertini, Luigi, 31–32, 54, 56–57, 195, 214
Alexander II, Tsar, 122
Alexander III, Tsar, 126
alliances
influence on rivalry dynamics, 84
Allison, Graham, 271
Alsace-Lorraine annexation, 24, 76, 83, 120, 254
analytic perspectives, 5–6
Andrew, Christopher, 262
Anglo-Russian entente (1907), 21, 129
Anglo-Russian rivalry, 74
Apis. *See* Dimitrijević, Dragutin
archival evidence
approaches to research on, 11
arms races
influence on rivalry dynamics, 84
Artamonov, Victor, 41
Austria-Hungary
application of preventive war criteria, 217–222
"blank check" given by Germany, 147
consequences of fear of Serbia, 57–58
decision to go to war with Serbia, 42–45
decision-making interdependence with Berlin, 147–149
extent of Germany's influence, 218
German influence on actions in the Balkans, 177–180
German support for war with Serbia, 43–45
Halt in Belgrade proposal, 27
internal political crises in June 1914, 39
misjudgment of Russian response, 43–45

perceptions of Russia's revival, 104–108
pre-war rivalries and alliances, 80–81
response to assassination in 1914, 42–45
response to Russian mobilization before 1914, 36
response to the Second Balkan War, 180
rivalry with Russia, 221
road to the July 1914 ultimatum, 231–232
role in the outbreak of war, 17–18, 30, 217–223
signs of impending break-up, 102
threat from Serbian nationalism, 221
ultimatum to Serbia in July 1914, 245–246
See also Triple Alliance

Balkan League, 49, 178
Balkan Wars, 35, 36, 49, 96, 102, 103, 136, 150–151, 231, 238
avoiding inadvertent war, 177–180
closure of the Turkish Straits, 79
consequences of Turkey's defeat in 1911, 80
German position, 215–216
Balkans
French support for Russia, 18
influence of the Franco-Russian alliance, 47–53
Russian focus before 1914, 76–77
bargaining theory
application to the outbreak of war, 167
Bark, P. L., 236, 247, 248
Barnes, Harry Elmer, 31
Barrère, Camille, 259
Belgium
German demands on, 55
influence on Britain's involvement, 56
invasion by Germany, 30, 81, 82, 137, 193, 197
revised Schlieffen Plan for invasion, 156–157
Benckendorff, A. K., 242

Berchtold, Leopold von, 42–45, 46, 108,
    136, 178–179, 180, 190, 232
Berlin–Baghdad Railroad, 238
Bertie, Francis, 90
Bethmann-Hollweg, Theobald von, 22, 23,
    27, 38, 43, 46–47, 95, 98–99, 102, 103,
    104, 128, 136–137, 144, 148, 154,
    155–156, 158, 178–179, 180, 237
  consideration of British intentions,
    160–162
  conspiracy to blame Russia for the war,
    180–192
  domestic and political constraints on
    mobilization, 159–162
  expectation that France would restrain
    Russia, 267
  fear of Russian growth, 173
  manipulation of the German public,
    192–197
  policy preferences, 164–166
  question of preventive motivation, 212–217
  relative influence on decision-making, 164
  telegrams to the kaiser in July 1914,
    190–192
  timing of the declaration of war on Russia,
    192–197
  unwillingness to go to war over
    Morocco, 215
better-now-than-later thinking,
    201–202. *See also* preventive war
  among the Great Powers of Europe, 164
  logic of preventive war, 139
bias
  blame for the outbreak of war, 13–14
  issue in political science analysis, 15
Biliński, Leon, 41
bipolarization of the major powers, 65–67,
    68–74, 80–81
Bismarck, Herbert von, 127–128
Bismarck, Otto von, 116
  cauchemar des coalitions (nightmare of
    coalitions), 120
  logic of preventive war, 117
  use of preventive war as a diplomatic
    tactic, 120–123, 124–128
Black Hand terrorist organization
  Franz Ferdinand assassination plot, 40–41
  influence in Serbia, 39–41
blame for the outbreak of war
  assumptions and bias, 13–14
Bloch, Jean de, 265
Bobroff, Ronald P., 88
Bonar Law, Andrew, 55
Bosnia, 203
Bosnia-Herzegovina, 39, 48

Bosnian crisis (1908), 218, 230–231
Bosworth, R. J. B., 78–79
Boulanger, Georges, 125
Boulangism, 124
Bremer, Stuart A., 218
Britain
  challenge to global leadership, 81–83
  economic crisis in July 1914, 55–56
  economic warfare policy, 55–56
  entry into the war, 47
  factors influencing intervention and
    alliances, 77–78
  French need for Britain to enter the war, 53
  German consideration of Britain's
    intentions, 160–162
  inability to remain neutral, 174
  initial preparations for war, 262
  internal political crisis in June 1914, 39
  Ireland Home Rule question, 39
  Lloyd George war memoirs, 16
  perceptions of Russia's revivial, 89–94
  preoccupation with Ireland, 54
  pre-war rivalries and alliances, 80–81
  rivalry with Germany, 16–17, 81–83
  Russian uncertainty about, 241–243
  steps toward entry into the war, 54–56
  tensions with Germany, 38
  ultimatum before declartion of war, 197
  uncertainty of support for France,
    256–257
  See also Triple Entente
Buchanan, George, 92, 106, 194, 233,
    242, 243
Bülow, Bernhard von, 132–133, 237
Bulgaria, 36, 48, 151, 238
  defeat in the Second Balkan War, 80
  First Balkan War, 150–151, 235
  Second Balkan War, 180
bureaucratic politics
  use of preventive motivation, 205
Bush Doctrine, 119

Caillaux, Joseph, 254–255
Cambon, Jules, 96
Cambon, Paul, 256
Cardona, Luigi, 57
Castelnau, Édouard de, 95
cauchemar des coalitions (nightmare of
    coalitions), 120
Churchill, Winston, 27, 135
Ciganović, Milan, 40
Clark, Christopher, 14, 19, 39–41, 43, 50,
    53, 61, 140, 151, 165, 271
Clausewitz, Karl von, 253, 268
Clemenceau, Georges, 261, 269

Clerk, G. R., 89, 90–91
cognitive bias
  issue in political science analysis, 15
Cold War, 3, 12
Concert of Europe, 20
Conrad, Franz, von Hötzendorf, 21, 44–45,
    57, 58, 139, 155, 179
  arguments for a preventive war, 133–136
  hard-line advocate of war, 215
Constantinople, 79
constructivism
  application to the outbreak of war, 167
Conze, Eckart, 118
Copeland, Dale, 33, 130–131, 200, 203,
    205, 214, 217–218, 221, 222
Copenhagen complex, 130–132
Corbett, Julian, 131
counterfactual analysis, 26–28
  counterfactual arguments, 24–28
  minimal rewrite criterion, 26–27
  necessary condition counterfactuals, 25–26
crisis dynamics
  and rivalry interactions, 84
Crowe, Eyre, 89, 90, 91–92
cult of the offensive, 17
Cyrenaica, 134
Czernin, Otto, 105, 106

Danilov, Iu. N., 248
Dardanelles, 79
decision-making by political leaders
  considerations in the approach to war,
    252–253
  French considerations, 253
  influences on the process, 9
  mindset of the European leaders, 60–63
  processes leading to war, 4
  risk assessment, 252, 269–272
  theoretical perspective on France, 38,
    269–272
decline in strategic power
  motivation for preventive war, 199–201
defensive realism, 17, 145–146
  application to the outbreak of war, 167
Delcassé, Théophile, 97, 130
détente notion
  pre-war influence on Great Powers, 87
Deutsch, Felix, 100
diffusion of war
  mechanisms in the First World War,
    222–223
  research questions, 28–29
Dimitrijević, Dragutin, 39, 40–41, 58
diplomatic constraints on German
  mobilization, 159–162

diplomatic historians
  approach to research, 9–13
Disraeli, Benjamin, 122
Dobrorolskii, S. K., 250
documentary evidence
  approaches to research on, 11
  German White Book, 191–192
  initial release by governments, 13
  publication of, 31
  record of the First World War, 4–5
domestic constraints on German
  mobilization, 159–162
domestic pressures argument
  comparison with the preventive war
    perspective, 170–171
  problems with, 172
Doumergue, Gaston, 93, 98
Dual Alliance, 128, 152
Duroselle, Jean-Baptiste, 252, 269
dyads of participants in the First World War,
    219–220

economic crisis in July 1914, 55–56
economic imperialism, 16
economic warfare policy of Britain,
    55–56
Elman, Colin, 12
Elman, Miriam Fendius, 12
Entente Cordiale (1904), 256
Esher, Viscount Reginald, 131
European powers. See Great Powers of
  Europe

Falkenhayn, Erich von, 46, 137, 154, 158,
    195, 196
Fay, Sidney, 16, 31, 228
Ferguson, Niall, 25, 152–153, 264–265
First World War 168
  alternative explanation to preventive war,
    217–222
  application of preventive war criteria,
    217–223
  appraisal of preventive war criteria,
    208–217
  causal complexity, 4
  cost in lives, 62
  debate over the causes, 3–5
  diffusion mechanisms, 222–223
  dyads of participants, 219–220
  historical puzzles, 168–169
  immediate and long-term impacts, 3
  implications of explanations for
    outbreak, 65
  long-term reverberations, 62
  preventive war explanation, 197–198

why it broke out in 1914 and not sooner, 173–177
Fischer, Fritz, 7, 9, 12, 14, 32–33, 118, 145, 180–181, 195, 217, 228
Fisher, Sir John, 131–132
Flotow, Hans von, 49, 57
Foch, Ferdinand, 253
France
  advances in Morocco, 78
  alliances prior to 1914, 37–38
  commitment to Russia, 18
  decision-making in a theoretical context, 269–272
  decision-making in the approach to war, 253
  desire to maintain Italy's neutrality, 259
  domestic political debate on the war, 253–256
  financial support for Russian railroads, 257–259
  financial unreadiness for war, 263–265
  German declaration of war against, 193
  influence in the Balkans, 18
  internal political turmoil in June 1914, 38–39
  lack of readiness for war in 1914, 253–256
  military unreadiness for war, 259–263
  need for Britain to enter the war, 53
  perceptions of Russia's revival, 94–98
  political leadership unreadiness for war, 265–266
  precarious financial position by 1914, 263–265
  pre-war Anglo-French relations, 77–78
  pre-war rivalries and alliances, 80–81
  refusal to take preparatory military measures, 256–257
  rivalry with Germany, 81–83
  role in the Balkans, 18
  role in the outbreak of war, 24, 53
  slow mobilization of Russian ally, 257–259
  support for Russia, 244–245
  uncertainty of Britain's support in war, 256–257
  underestimation of German capabilities, 262–263
  unreadiness of the French people for war, 266–269
  unreliability of allies in 1914, 256–259
  vulnerability in a situation of war, 266–269
  See also Triple Entente
Franco-Prussian War (1870–1871), 7, 115, 123, 187, 265
Franco-Russian alliance, 83
  influence in the Balkans, 47–53

role in starting the war, 47–53
Franco-Russian rivalry, 74
Franz Ferdinand, Archduke, 36, 134, 178–179
  assassination in Sarajevo 1914, 18, 41, 138, 231, 232
  assassination plot, 40–41
Franz Joseph, Emperor, 36, 101, 133, 135–136, 137, 179
  conditions for going to war, 42
future research
  diffusion of war, 28–29
  observations on the slide to war, 57–62
  use of counterfactual arguments, 24–28

George V, King, 256, 257
German decision-making
  and perceptions of relative decline, 167–168
  and the Russian "Great Programme" of rearmament (1914), 151–152
  apparent change of policy on July 29–30, 1914, 168, 180–192
  belief in the inevitability of war, 163
  better-now-than-later thinking, 164
  "blank check" given to Austria-Hungary, 147
  consideration of Britain's intentions, 160–162
  constraints on rearmament in 1913, 151–156
  diplomatic constraints on mobilization, 159–162
  domestic constraints on mobilization, 159–162
  erosion of potential effectiveness of the Schlieffen Plan, 149–156
  expectations of a short war, 162–163
  fear of relative decline in power, 172–173
  fears of a declining military situation, 151–156
  impact of the Balkan Wars, 150–151
  inability to win the arms race, 151–156
  influence of hegemonic ambitions, 144–146
  influence of shifts in relative power, 162–163
  interdependence with decisions in Vienna, 147–149
  misperceptions of political leaders, 162–163
  people's war argument, 159–162
  plans for invasion of Belgium, 156–157
  policy preferences of the main decision-makers, 164–166
  preemptive pressures, 156–159

German decision-making (cont.)
  preventive war to maintain the status quo,
    144–146
  relative influence of leading
    decision-makers, 164
  revised Schlieffen Plan, 156–157
  revisionist preventive war strategies,
    144–146
  role of preventive logic, 139–140, 164
  sources of preventive logic, 149–156
  status quo versus revisionist preventive
    war strategies, 144–146
  threat from Russian pre-mobilization
    activities, 157–159
  timing of declarations of war, 168
German paradigm
  and the role of other states, 9
  challenges to, 7, 9, 15–18, 23–24
  erosion and new observations, 57–62
  new approaches to research on, 33–35
  origins and ongoing arguments, 30–35
  perspectives on preventive war, 21–23
  role of other powers, 30
  roles of Russia and France, 23–24
  summary of current thinking, 33–35
German–Russian rivalry, 74
German war planning, 173–177
  actions in the days leading up to war,
    180–192
  attempts to secure British neutrality, 174
  avoiding inadvertent war in the Balkans,
    177–180
  conspiracy to blame the war on Russia,
    180–192
  declaration of war against France, 193
  fear of Russian growth, 173
  generation of popular support for war,
    175–176
  German need for total war, 180–197
  growing sense of threat from Russia, 176
  influence on Austro-Hungarian actions in
    the Balkans, 177–180
  invasion of Belgium, 193
  making Russia appear to be the aggressor,
    176–177
  manipulation of the diplomatic
    environment, 176–177
  naval preparations, 174–175
  perceived need for a preventive war, 175
  preparations for a great war, 176
  preventive war explanation, 197–198
  recognition that Britain may
    intervene, 175
  secret conspiracy of civilian leaders,
    192–197

  timing of the declaration of war on Russia,
    192–197
  War Council (December 1912), 174–176
German White Book, 191–192
Germany
  alternatives to preventive war before
    1914, 132–133
  conditional support for Austrian war with
    Serbia, 43–45
  Copenhagen complex, 130–132
  dependence on Britain's neutrality, 47
  extent of influence on Austria-Hungary,
    37, 218
  historical rivalry with Russia, 227
  impression that France wanted to avoid
    war, 267–268
  internal political crisis in June 1914, 38
  international condemnation of preventive
    war, 137
  invasion of Belgium, 30
  Liman von Sanders crisis with Russia,
    79–80
  misjudgment of Austrian actions,
    45–47
  misjudgment of Russian response to
    Austrian action, 43–45
  motivations for preventive war, 7–8
  path to war, 45–47
  perceptions of Russia's revival, 38,
    98–104
  position during the Balkan Wars,
    215–216
  power transition hypothesis, 208
  pre-war Anglo-German relations, 77–78
  pre-war rivalries and alliances, 80–81
  proponents of preventive war
    (1886–1888), 124–128
  publication of diplomatic documents, 31
  question of preventive war, 208–217
  relations with Russia, 216, 220–221
  rivalry with Britain, 16–17, 81–83
  rivalry with France, 81–83
  Russian resistance to, 246–251
  Schlieffen Plan, 83, 149–152, 155–158, 195
  sinking of the RMS *Lusitania*, 30
  tensions with Russia in early 1914, 38
  See also Triple Alliance
Gibraltar, 78
Giolitti, Giovanni, 78–79
global leader decline
  structural transition, 68–74
global leadership
  rivalry between Britain and Germany,
    81–83
Goremykin, Ivan, 48, 90, 106, 230, 236, 248

governments
    initial release of documents, 13
    publication of diplomatic documents, 31
Great Powers of Europe
    better-now-than-later thinking, 164
    complexity of pre-war decision making, 87
    détente and anticipation of war, 108–110
    influence of the notion of détente, 87
    internal political crises in June 1914, 38–39
    role in the outbreak of war, 9
    unconditional commitments to one
        another, 18
"Great Programme" of rearmament
    (Russia 1914), 151–152, 240
Great War. See First World War
Greece, 80
    First Balkan War, 150–151
    Second Balkan War, 180
Grey, Sir Edward, 27, 32, 36, 38, 58, 89,
    92–94, 98, 104, 183, 188–189
    belated involvement in the European
        crisis, 54
    economic considerations in going
        to war, 56
    estimation of the cost of going to war, 55
Grigorovitch, I. K., 239
guilt over the outbreak of war
    assumptions and bias, 13–14

Habsburg monarchy
    perceptions of Russia's revivial, 104–108
    signs of impending break-up of the
        empire, 102
Haldane, Richard, 174
Halt in Belgrade proposal, 18, 25, 27, 46,
    162, 165, 212, 214, 221
Hart, Albert Bushnell, 30, 57
Hartwig, Nikolai, 40, 48–49
Heeringen, Josias von, 173, 175
Herrmann, David, 258
Herwig, Holger, 151
Hewitson, Mark, 33
Hildebrand, Klaus, 118
Hillgruber, Andreas, 118
historians
    approach to research, 9–13
    debate on the First World War origins,
        3–4, 8
Hitler, Adolf, 3, 31, 146
Hoffmann, Dieter, 33
Hohenlohe, Chlodwig von, 122
Holland
    avoidance in the revised Schlieffen Plan,
        156–157
Holstein, Friedrich von, 125

Holsti, Ole, 10
Hoyos, Alexander, 43, 107
Humbert, Charles, 261, 269

Ianushkevich, N. N., 249, 250
India, 89, 91, 107
intelligence operations
    information intercepts in the lead up to
        war, 49–52
interdisciplinary approach, 9–13
internal political crises
    June 1914, 38–39
international conflict theory
    influence of the First World War, 4–5
international relations scholars
    approach to research, 9–13
    debate on the First World War origins,
        4–5
international relations theory
    implications of explanations for the
        outbreak of the war, 65
    preventive war explanation for the First
        World War, 167–169
    range of explanations for the First World
        War, 167
international structural change
    debate over role in outbreak of war, 18–21
international system
    changes following crises in 1911–1914,
        35–39
Iran, 201
Iranian Revolution, 202
Iran–Iraq War (1980), 202
Iraq, 201, 203
Ireland
    Home Rule question, 39
Israel, 146, 201
Italo-Turkish War (1911–1912), 35, 150
Italy
    gains from the war, 62
    internal political strife in June 1914, 39
    invasion of North Africa, 134
    participation in the Triple Alliance, 56–57
    pre-war rivalries and alliances, 80–81
    results of the Balkan Wars, 36
    status in the Triple Alliance, 107–108
    uncertain position of neutrality, 259
    war with Turkey (1911), 78–79
    See also Triple Alliance
Izvolsky, Alexander, 96–97, 230, 267

Jagow, Gottlieb von, 100, 101, 102,
    103–104, 156, 177, 182, 195, 196, 260
Japan, 146
Jaurès, Jean, 266

Jervis, Robert, 60
Joffre, Joseph, 53, 133, 256–257, 262–263
Jonnart, Charles, 263
Jovanović, Jovan, 41
July Crisis (1914), 110, 138
    German consideration of British
        intentions, 161–162
    Kaiser's desire to solve, 216
    new approaches to research on, 33–35
    Russian decision to mobilize, 243–251
    study by Albertini, 31–32
    summary of current thinking on, 33–35

Kahneman, Daniel, 60
Kaiser, David, 213, 221
Kaunitz coalition, 120
Kennan, George, 3
Kennedy, Paul, 3
Kiderlen, Alfred von, 178, 215
Kingdom of Serbs, Croats, and Slovenes, 62
Knox, Alfred, 90
Kokovtsov, Vladimir, 90, 94, 99, 101, 230,
    235, 236, 237–238
Krivoshein, Alexander, 48, 232–233, 236,
    238, 247–248
Kugler, Jacek, 200

Lambert, Nicholas, 55–56
Lansdowne, Lord, 131
League of the Three Emperors, 121
Lebow, Richard N., 203
Lee, Arthur, 131
Levy, Jack S., 217
liberal theory
    application to the outbreak of war, 167
Libya, 36, 78
Lichnowsky, Max von, 174, 186, 188, 189
Lieber, Keir, 17, 82, 145
Lieven, Dominic, 228
Liman von Sanders crisis, 38, 79–80,
    90, 97, 103, 106, 231, 234–235,
    238, 242
Lindblom, Charles E., 210
Lloyd George, David, 16, 32
Loë, Walter von, 126
Louis, Georges, 94
Louis of Battenberg, Prince, 243
Lucius von Stoedten, Hellmuth, 101
Ludendorff, Erich, 154
Luneva, Iu. V., 229
Luxembourg, 193, 194
Luzzatti, Luigi, 132

Macedonia, 80
MacMahon, Patrice de, 120

Magyars, 39
Malobabić, Rade, 40
manpower mobilization
    increases before 1914, 36–37
Marxism–Leninism, 228
May, Ernest, 61
McDonald, Patrick, 152, 154
McMeekin, Sean, 88, 229, 239
Mendelssohn, Robert von, 100
Menning, Bruce, 51
Mérey, Kajetan von, 134, 135, 136
Messimy, Adolphe, 256–257, 261, 263
Metternich, Paul Wolff, 132
Michelet, General, 261
Middle East, 62
militarism, 16
military–industrial complex
    use of preventive motivation, 205
Miquel, Johannes von, 121
Molden, Berthold, 106–107
Moltke, Helmuth von, 22, 23, 37, 46–47,
    58, 59, 103, 121, 127–128, 144,
    145, 148, 149, 151, 152, 154–155,
    179, 185
    argument for preventive war, 174–175
    expectation of a long war, 162
    hard-line advocate of war, 215
    making Russia appear to be the aggressor,
        176–177
    need for public support for war, 159
    on France's military weakness in 1914,
        260–261
    policy preferences, 164–166
    preventive motivation, 209
    relative influence on decision-making,
        164
    revised Schlieffen Plan, 156–157
    role in the conspiracy to initiate war, 194,
        195–197
    threat from Russian pre-mobilization
        activities, 157–158
Mombauer, Annika, 12, 14, 58, 77–78, 118,
    145, 152, 155, 162
Montenegro
    First Balkan War, 150–151
Monts, Count, 130
Moran, Daniel, 119
Moroccan Crisis (1905), 21, 128, 131
Moroccan Crisis (1911), 35, 95, 98, 134,
    149, 150, 215, 254, 262
Morocco, 103
    French advances in, 78, 83
motivated reasoning, 15
Mulligan, William, 75–76, 213–214, 216
Mussolini, Benito, 31

nationalism, 16
Naumann, Friedrich, 130
naval power
  Anglo-German rivalry, 16–17
necessary condition counterfactuals, 25–26
Neilson, Keith, 88
Neitzel, Sönke, 118
newspaper press
  role in the outbreak of war, 16
Nicholas II, Tsar, 38, 107, 173, 235, 236,
    243, 244, 247
  exchange of letters with the kaiser,
    46–47, 52
  reluctance to approve Russian
    mobilization, 249, 251
  visit to the kaiser, 237
Nicolson, Arthur, 54, 89, 90–91, 104, 108
nonlinear rivalry ripeness (NRR) model,
    67–74
  bipolarization of the major powers, 68–74
  cascading effects in intersecting
    rivalries, 67
  complexity of rivalry fields up to 1914,
    68–74
  components, 65–67
  global leader decline, 68–74
  indicators of potential for conflict, 68–74
  pinball dynamics of the 1914 case, 68
  pinball dynamics of the pre-war rivalry
    field, 74–85
  regional leader ascent, 68–74
  rivalry intensity, 68–74
  significance of rivalry dynamics in the
    outbreak of war, role in onset of war,
    85–86
North, Robert, 9–10

offense–defense arguments, 85
offensive realism, 17, 145–146
Organski, A. F. K., 200
Ottoman Empire, 18, 49, 240, 242
  decline in the pre-war period, 78–80

Paléologue, Maurice, 50, 53, 94, 97–98, 245
Palmer, R. R., 32
Pansa, Alberto, 96
pan-Slavism, 48, 100, 101, 124, 125,
    126, 245
Pašić, Nikolai, 40–41, 49
peace research, 34
Persia, 91, 98, 106, 241
perspectives on First World War research,
    9–13
perspectives on the First World War
  outbreak, 5–6

Poincaré, Raymond, 24, 37, 44, 93, 94,
    96–97, 102, 254–255, 263, 268
  acknowledgment of France's military
    shortcomings, 268–269
  actions up to the outbreak of war, 53
  decision-making style, 272
  fears for the future of France, 268–269
  Franco-Russian alliance, 258
  French support for Russia, 244–245
  letter to King George V, 256
  reluctance to declare war on Germany, 267
  support for Serbia, 48
  uncertainty of Britain's support, 257
  visit to Russia in July 1914, 49–50, 53,
    256–257, 265–266
Pokrovskii, M. N., 228
political restraints on preventive war,
    137–138
political scientists
  approach to research, 9–13
  cognitive bias issue, 15
politics
  influences on decision-making, 9
Pollio, Alberto, 57
positivist research focus, 12
postmodernism
  influence on research approaches, 12
Pourtalès-Cronstern, Friedrich von, 99,
    100, 104, 187, 189, 194, 195
"powder-keg" models, 19–20
power
  and preventive war, 139
  multiple dimensions of, 146–147
  response to preceived shifts in, 7–8
power distribution
  motivation for preventive war, 202–203
power transition hypothesis
  German challenge to Britain, 208
power transition theory, 16
power transitions
  interaction with rivalry dynamics, 82–83
preemptive logic
  distinction from preventive logic, 141–142
preemptive wars, 201
preventive logic, 139
  distinction from preemptive logic,
    141–142
  role in decision-making, 142–144
  role in German decision-making,
    139–140
preventive motivation, 142–144, 203
  and definition of preventive war, 205–207
  use by the military–industrial
    complex, 205
  use in bureaucratic politics, 205

preventive war
  alternative explanation for the First World
    War, 217–222
  alternatives for Germany before 1914,
    132–133
  and hegemonic ambitions, 144–146
  arguments of Conrad von Hötzendorf,
    133–136
  as a European norm before 1914, 117–119
  as a legitimate instrument of state policy,
    116, 117
  as a state strategy, 142–144
  better-now-than-later logic, 139
  better-now-than-later thinking among the
    Great Powers, 164
  breadth of definition, 140–141
  Copenhagen complex as restraint on,
    130–132
  defining terminology, 142–144
  domestic and diplomatic constraints on
    Germany, 159–162
  explaining the absence of, 115
  explanation for the First World War,
    167–169, 197–198
  German need for total war, 180–198
  German perceptions of relative decline,
    167–168
  growing restraints on, 138
  international condemnation of
    Germany, 137
  logic of, 117, 139
  moral and ethical restraints, 119–120, 138
  motivations for, 7–8
  multiple dimensions of power, 146–147
  negative views within and outside
    Germany, 216
  people's war argument, 159–162
  perspectives on, 21–23, 116
  political function of the concept, 120
  political restraints on, 137–138
  possible aims of, 144–146
  preemptive pressures on Germany,
    156–159
  proponents among German general staff
    officers (1886–1888), 124–128
  question of legitimacy, 119–120
  reputational consequences as
    deterrent, 132
  response to relative decline, 146–147
  revisionist preventive war strategies,
    144–146
  risks associated with, 119–120
  Russian mobilization as justification for
    Germany, 136–137
  sources of restraint before 1914, 119–120

strategies for different types of threat,
    146–147
strategy to maintain the status quo,
    144–146
theoretical conditions for, before 1914,
    115–116
use by Bismarck as a diplomatic tactic,
    124–128
windows of opportunity before 1914,
    115–116
preventive war criteria
  applied to Austria-Hungary, 217–222
  applied to the First World War, 217–223
preventive war perspective
  comparison with other systemic
    explanations, 171
  comparison with the domestic pressures
    argument, 170–171
  comparison with the spiral model, 169–170
preventive war, theory of
  application of criteria to Germany,
    208–217
  better-now-than-later thinking, 201–202
  classical realist approach, 203–204
  criteria to define preventive war, 203–207
  criticisms, 203
  decline in strategic power as motivation,
    199–201
  evidence for occurrence of preventive
    wars, 203
  power distribution as motivation, 202–203
  presence of preventive motivation,
    205–207
  range of perspectives on, 199
  relative importance of preventive
    motivation, 203
  risks associated with preventive war,
    204–205
  timing of war initiation, 201–202
Princip, Gavrilo, 40–41, 43, 58
prospect theory, 272
Protić, Stojan, 41
Prussia, 80

Radowitz, Joseph Maria von, 121
rational actor theory, 271–272
realist approach to preventive war, 203–204
Redl, Alfred, 36
regional leader ascent
  structural transition, 68–74
regional leadership
  rivalry between France and Germany,
    81–83
Reininghaus, Gina von, 45, 58
Reinsurance treaty (1887), 127

relative decline
  as driver for preventive war, 167–168
responsibility for the outbreak of war
  assumptions and bias, 13–14
revisionist views on the origins of the war, 31
Reynolds, Michael, 88, 229
Ribot, Alexandre, 263, 264
Rich, David Alan, 229
Riezler, Kurt, 130, 181, 182, 190
risk assessment
  decision-making of French political
    leaders, 269–272
  risks associated with preventive war,
    204–205
rivalry dynamics 85
  between nations, 20
  Britain and Germany, 16–17
  complexity and unpredictability, 84–85
  in power transition situations, 82–83
  influence of alliances, 84
  influence of arms races, 84
  interactions with crisis dynamics, 84
  pinball dynamics of the pre-war rivalry
    field, 74–85
  role in the onset of war, 65–67
  significance in the outbreak of war,
    85–86
  streams of interacting rivalries, 74–84
  See also nonlinear rivalry ripeness (NRR)
    model
RMS Lusitania
  sinking by German submarine, 30
Rodd, Rennell, 54
Röhl, John, 33, 58, 162, 260
Romania, 36, 38, 48, 107, 151
Rößler, Konstantin, 120
Rothschild, Lord, 264–265
Royal Navy, 129
  threat to the German fleet, 130–132
Rupprecht of Bavaria, Crown Prince, 160
Russia
  attempts to create a treaty with Britain,
    38, 241–243
  Austro-Hungarian perceptions of
    Russia's revival, 104–108
  Bolshevik government, 4
  British perceptions of Russia's revivial,
    89–94
  consequences of defeat by Japan (1905),
    76–78
  decision to mobilize, 243–251
  desire to control the Turkish Straits, 49
  focus on the Balkans before 1914, 76–77
  French financial support for railways,
    257–259

French perceptions of Russia's revival,
    94–98
German conspiracy to blame Russia for
    the war, 180–192
German perceptions of Russia's revival,
    98–104
German response to pre-mobilization
    activities, 157–159
"Great Programme" of rearmament
    (1914), 89, 151–152, 163, 176, 240
hindrances to Russian mobilization,
    238–243
historical distrust of Germany, 227
historiography, 228–229
humiliation of the Bosnian crisis (1908),
    230–231
implications of the Russian revival,
    108–110
improvements in the railroad network, 89
inability to mobilize to support France,
    257–259
increasing willingness to risk war,
    229–238
interest in controlling the Turkish Straits,
    79–80, 228–229, 238–240
internal political crisis in June 1914, 39
July Crisis 1914, 243–251
Liman von Sanders crisis with Germany,
    79–80, 234–235
long-term radicalization, 229–238
mobilization, 18, 46–53
mobilization as German justification for
    preventive war, 136–137
mobilization before 1914, 36
mobilization in response to Austrian
    action, 43–45
mobilization intended as a deterrent, 227
pan-Slavists, 48
perceptions of Russia's revival, 88–89
pre-war rivalries and alliances, 80–81
pre-war significance in international
    politics, 87–88
problems with the partial mobilization
    tactic, 248–251
question of allegiance to Serbia, 245–246
readiness to resist Germany, 246–251
rearmament prior to 1914, 37–38
relations with Germany, 216, 220–221
responses to its growth in power, 20–21
role in the crisis of 1914, 33
role in the outbreak of war, 23–24
support from France, 244–245
tsarist regime, 4
uncertainty about Britain's intentions,
    241–243

Russia (cont.)
    unpreparedness for war, 238–243
    visit of Poincaré and Viviani in July 1914,
        44, 256–257
    See also Triple Entente
Russo-Japanese War (1904–1905), 8, 74,
    76, 89, 150, 237, 248

San Giuliano, Antonio, 49, 56–57, 134
Sazonov, Sergei, 38, 48–49, 50, 51–52, 53,
        101, 102, 106, 185–186, 187, 189, 196,
        231, 232, 239–240
    argument for Russia to take a hard line,
        247–248
    attempts to strengthen the Triple Entente,
        242–243
    French support for Russia, 245
    growing consideration of the military
        option, 233–235
    problems with Russian partial
        mobilization tactic, 248–251
    Russian allegiance to Serbia, 245–246
Schellendorff, Bronsart von, 126, 128
Schilling, M. F., 234, 247
Schlieffen, Alfred von, 116, 129–130
Schlieffen Plan, 17, 59, 77, 83
    activation in August 1914, 195
    erosion of potential effectiveness,
        149–156
    revised to avoid Holland, 156–157
Schmidt, Stefan, 50
Schmitt, Bernadotte E., 31, 32, 228
Schoen, Wilhelm von, 102, 268
Schroeder, Paul W., 20, 118
Schroeder, Stephen, 118
Second World War, 3, 12
secret alliances, 16
security dilemmas, 85
Serbia
    Austro-Hungarian decision to go to war,
        42–45
    consequences of Serbian terrorism, 57–58
    domestic turmoil up to 1914, 39–41
    expansion due to the Balkan Wars, 80
    financial support from France, 48
    First Balkan War, 150–151
    gains from the war, 62
    influence of the Black Hand organization,
        39–41
    knowledge of the assassination plot,
        40–41
    nationalist and territorial claims, 17–18
    results of the Balkan Wars, 36
    Second Balkan War, 180
    threat to Austria-Hungary, 221

ultimatum from Austria in July 1914,
    231–232, 245–246
Serret, Marcel, 95–96
Siegel, Jennifer, 88
Simon, Jules, 269
slide into war thesis, 4, 16
    future research, 57–62
    mindset of the European leaders, 60–30
    summary of observations, 57–62
Snyder, Jack, 17, 146, 208
Soroka, Marina E., 88
spiral model
    comparison with preventive war
        perspective, 169–170
    problems with, 171–172
spread of war. *See* diffusion of war
Stalin, Joseph, 228
state policy
    preventive war as legitimate instrument,
        116, 117
state system
    as a cause of war, 16
Steinberg, Jonathan, 130–131
Steiner, Zara, 54
Stevenson, David, 6, 52, 61, 230, 231, 232
Stolypin, P. A., 230, 233, 235–236, 238
Strachan, Hew, 52, 61
structural change
    debate over role in outbreak of war,
        18–21
structural neorealist theory
    application to the outbreak of war, 167
structural rivalries
    Britain–Germany, 81–83
    France–Germany, 81–83
structural transitions
    global leader decline, 68–74
    regional leader ascent, 68–74
structure and agency, 9
    causal complexity of processes leading to
        war, 4
    debate over influence, 18–21
    influences on decision-making, 9
Stumm, Wilhelm von, 182
substitutability of policies, 204, 205
Sukhomlinov, Vladimir, 233, 240
systemic explanations
    and the preventive war perspective, 171
    problems with, 172
Szápáry, Friedrich, 50, 105, 106,
        107–108, 179

Tankosić, Voja, 40
Taylor, A. J. P., 32, 118
temporary advantage as motive for war, 202

terrorism
  consequences of the 1914 Sarajevo
    assassinations, 62
Thiers, Adolphe, 120
Thurn, Duglas, 105, 106
timing of the war, 201–202
  why it occurred when it did, 8
Tirpitz, Alfred von, 129, 130, 131, 174–175,
    195–196
  lack of preventive motivation, 209–210
Trachtenberg, Marc, 229
Transylvania, 38, 39
Treaty of Versailles (1919)
  War Guilt clause, 3, 31, 255
Triple Alliance, 107–108, 134, 135, 230,
    235, 259
  role of Italy, 56–57
  status during 1911–1914, 37
Triple Entente, 117, 129, 136, 230, 242,
    259, 265
  Russian attempts to strengthen,
    242–243
  status during 1911–1914, 37–38
Tripolitania, 134
Tschirschky, Heinrich von, 183, 184, 186,
    187, 188, 189, 193
Tuchman, Barbara, 32
Turkey, 36
  attack by Italy (1911), 78–79
  First Balkan War, 150–151
  weakness and defeats in the pre-war
    period, 78–80
  See also Liman von Sanders crisis
Turkish Straits, 18
  Russian interest in controlling, 49, 79–80,
    228–229, 238–240
Turner, L. C. F., 228–229
Tyrrell, William, 89, 91–92, 93

United States, 55
  revisionist views on the origins
    of the war, 31
  views on the origins of the war, 30–31
unmotivated cognitive bias
  in political science analysis, 15

Van Evera, Stephen, 17
Viviani, René, 38–39, 44, 98, 257, 268
  visit to Russia in July 1914, 49–50, 53,
    256–257, 265–266

Waldersee, Alfred von, 125–128
Waldersee, Georg von, 37

Wandel, Franz von, 173
War Guilt clause
  Treaty of Versailles (1919), 3, 31, 255
War in Sight crisis, 120–123
Weines, Adolph von, 125
Wenninger, Karl von, 192
Wilhelm II, Kaiser, 23, 33, 45, 129, 131,
    132, 154, 156, 180, 260
  concerns about the prospects of general
    war, 210–212
  consideration of British intentions,
    160–162
  decision to support Austrian military
    action, 43
  dependence on Britain's neutrality, 47
  desire to solve the July 1914 crisis, 216
  enthusiasm for monarchical
    diplomacy, 102
  exchange of letters with the tsar,
    46–47, 52
  manipulation by Bethmann-Hollweg in
    July 1914, 190–192
  meeting with the tsar (1912), 98
  order for general mobilization, 195
  path to war, 46, 47
  policy preferences, 164–166
  relative influence on decision-making, 164
  Röhl's study of, 58
  telegram to the tsar on July 30,
    191–192, 249
  unawareness of impending declaration of
    war, 195
  unawareness of the plans for war, 198
  unwillingness to go to war over
    Morocco, 215
  visit from the tsar, 237
William I, German emperor, 123, 124,
    127–128
Williamson, Samuel, 218, 221, 231
Wilson, Henry, 54, 95
Wilson, Keith, 88
Witte, Sergei, 97, 237
Wolff, Theodor, 182, 260
world economy
  near-collapse in July 1914, 55–56

Young Turk revolt, 80
Yugoslavia, 62

Zabern incident, 38
Zimmerman, Alfred, 180
Zimmermann telegram, 31
Zuber, Terence, 17